THE HARWICH STRIKING FORCE

By the same author

British Naval Trawlers and Drifters in Two World Wars

The Power and the Glory:
Royal Navy Fleet Reviews from Earliest Times to 2005

Battle in the Baltic:
The Royal Navy and the Fight to Save Estonia and Latvia, 1918–1920

Southern Thunder:
The Royal Navy and the Scandinavian Trade in World War One

Bayly's War:
The Battle for the Western Approaches in World War One

Securing the Narrow Sea: The Dover Patrol 1914–1918

Blockade: Cruiser Warfare and the Starvation of Germany

Formidable:
A true story of disaster and courage

The Coward? The Rise and Fall of the Silver King

The Scapegoat:
The life and tragedy of a fighting admiral and Churchill's role in his death

www.steverdunn.com

The Harwich Striking Force

The Royal Navy's Front Line in the North Sea
1914–1918

STEVE R DUNN

Seaforth
PUBLISHING

Dedication

For Annabelle (Anna) Cuddihy, wife, mother, grandmother,
great grandmother.

Copyright © Steve R Dunn 2022

First published in Great Britain in 2022 by
Seaforth Publishing,
A division of Pen & Sword Books Ltd,
47 Church Street,
Barnsley S70 2AS
www.seaforthpublishing.com

British Library Cataloguing in Publication Data
A catalogue record for this book is available from the British Library

ISBN 978 1 3990 1596 7 (HARDBACK)
ISBN 978 1 3990 1597 4 (EPUB)
ISBN 978 1 3990 1598 1 (KINDLE)

Pen & Sword Books Limited incorporates the imprints of Atlas,
Archaeology, Aviation, Discovery, Family History, Fiction, History, Maritime, Military,
Military Classics, Politics, Select, Transport, True Crime, Air World, Frontline Publishing,
Leo Cooper, Remember When, Seaforth Publishing, The Praetorian Press, Wharncliffe Local
History, Wharncliffe Transport, Wharncliffe True Crime and White Owl

Typeset by Ian Hughes, www.mousematdesign.com

Printed and bound in Great Britain by CPI Group (UK) Ltd, Croydon, CR0 4YY

Contents

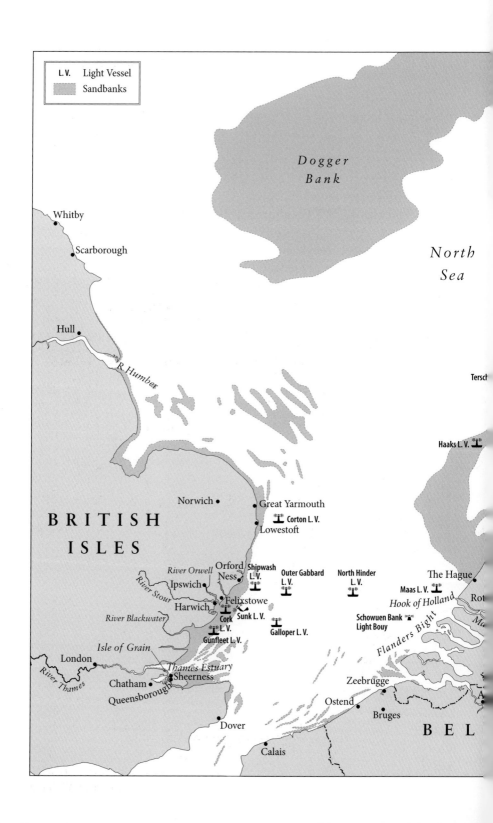

N

DENMARK

Vyl L. V.

Amrum Bank L. V.

Kiel

Kiel
Canal

Heligoland

Heligoland
Bight

Borkum Rift
L. V.

Schiermonnikoog

Rottumeroog
Rottumerplaat

Borkum

Juist

Norderney

Baltrum

Langeoog

Spiekeroog

Wangeroog

Cuxhaven

Brünsbuttel

Schillig
Roads

Ameland

Rif

Wilhelmshaven

Jade

Bremerhaven

Hamburg

River Elbe

hel
Griend

Emden

Jade
Bay

R. Jade

lam

NETHERLANDS

GERMANY

Bremen

River Ems

River Weser

River Rhine

0   80 miles

0   80 km

Map © Peter Wilkinson

Death on the wild North Sea! —
death from the shell that shatters
(death we will face with glee,
'tis the weary wait that matters): —
death from the guns that roar,
and the splinters weirdly shrieking.
'Tis a fight to the death; 'tis war;
and the North Sea is redly reeking
The North Sea, Miles Jefferey Game Day.
(On 27 February 1918, Flight Commander Day, an RNAS pilot flying a
Sopwith Camel F1 and based at Dunkirk, led an attack on six German
seaplanes but was shot down over the North Sea. He was observed clinging to
wreckage but drowned before rescue. Day served with the Harwich Force
during 1915–16.)

The strength of twice three thousand horse
 That seeks the single goal;
The line that holds the rending course,
 The hate that swings the whole;
The stripped hulls, slinking through the gloom,
 At gaze and gone again -
The Brides of Death that wait the groom -
 The Choosers of the Slain!
The Destroyers, Rudyard Kipling in *McClure's Magazine*, May 1898.

Farewell and adieu to you, Harwich Ladies,
Farewell and adieu to you, ladies ashore!
For we've received orders to work to the eastward
Where we hope in a short time to strafe 'em some more.
Harwich Ladies, Rudyard Kipling in *Fringes of the Fleet*, first published in the
Daily Telegraph November 1915.

Preface

The Royal Navy's Harwich Striking Force of light cruisers, destroyers and submarines was 'a unique command, charged with securing the approaches to the English Channel and preventing any German ships breaking out into the Atlantic and interfering with our shipping'[1] according to Lieutenant Brian Schofield RN, who served aboard HMS *Manly*, one of the destroyers based at the eponymous Essex town.

The Harwich Force was originally formed as the southern wing of the Grand Fleet. The stated intention was to provide light forces which could impede any movement by German surface vessels into the North Sea towards the east coast of England or the Strait of Dover. But in reality it was much more than that.

At the outbreak of the 1914–18 war, the Royal Navy faced five key strategic tests in home waters:

- To bring the German High Seas Fleet to battle and defeat it.
- The blockade of Germany, stopping up the exits from the North Sea via northern waters and the English Channel to deny Germany imports of raw materials, food and military supplies.
- Support for the British Expeditionary Force in France and Flanders.
- Prevention of a German invasion of eastern England.
- Trade protection such that Britain's food and war supplies could readily reach their destinations.

All of these missions would involve the Harwich Striking Force, to a greater or lesser extent. The Force stood in the front line of Britain's defence and attack, facing up to a foe whose shores and operating bases would come to be in an arc from northeast to southeast of Harwich. Led for the entirety of the war by the hard-driving Reginald Yorke Tyrwhitt, the Force pioneered naval carrier aviation and attack, developed the type of hydroplane vessel known as a coastal motor boat, mounted air-sea combined operations, hunted for submarines and protected minelayers in the North Sea. The Harwich Force fought German cruisers, destroyers and torpedo boats, took part in major naval battles alongside elements of the Grand Fleet and safeguarded merchant ships operating in the dangerous waters between Denmark, the Netherlands,

Germany and Britain. And yet, strangely, little has been written about their activities and less still at book length.

This volume attempts to right that wrong, telling the story of the Force's development, actions, men, ships and leaders. In a campaign now seldom mentioned (although of greater moment to the public during the war) sailors fought and died to ensure that Britain retained 'sovereignty of the seas', a phrase first coined by King Edward III, in the North Sea. Inevitably the narrative is also about Admiral Sir Reginald Tyrwhitt, given both the time he spent commanding the Force and his constant involvement in its actions. His 'voice' will be heard throughout; but it is not a biography.

To describe every detail of the activities of the Force throughout the war would require a multi-volume work of doorstop size. Rather this book tries to investigate the major and minor actions of the Harwich ships in an account which helps the reader to understand what it was like to be there, the challenges that had to be overcome and the stresses and strains of daily life that had to be endured. And as much as the story is about men and tactics, it is also about their ships, especially the destroyers and the light cruisers which were so hard worked during the campaign.

The operations at Harwich were not glamorous; it was a tough, grinding life of quotidian difficulty where any success was hard won and the slightest misjudgement might mean the loss of ships or lives. The history of the Force also reflects the limits of the technology of the time, as set against the aspirations of the combatants, together with the impact of weather on naval objectives, a problem as old as naval warfare itself.

Alongside the Striking Force, men fought and died in the Harwich auxiliary organisation of minesweepers and patrol craft, knocked up from fishing boats and passenger ships, and in the Royal Naval Air Service (RNAS, later the RAF) base at Felixstowe, just across the estuary formed by the rivers Stour and Orwell. Their tales are told here too.

The narrative is in chronological order, but a strict timeline is sacrificed when it is necessary to finish one aspect of the tale before commencing another. Naval ranks are given as at the time of the action described. The 24-hour clock is used throughout for clarity; where ante or post meridian was given in the original documents, the time has been converted. Finally, a date in brackets after the name of a ship is the year it was launched.

1

Harwich and an Emerging Threat

From ancient times, Britain's continental enemy had been France. When Edward III departed Portsmouth with his fleet on 28 June 1346, a voyage that would end with the crushing English victory of Crécy, it was merely the first of many occasions when an English (and later British) fleet would seek a French foe at sea. The Hundred Years War; the Seven Years War; the American War of Independence; the Napoleonic Wars; the invasion scares of the second half of the nineteenth century – the enemy at sea was always France (with a leavening of Spanish and Dutch from time to time).

Britain's naval dispositions reflected this. The major naval bases were Portsmouth and Plymouth, geographically placed to deny the Channel to vessels sailing into British waters on westerly winds from the French ports of the Mediterranean or coastal France (or Spain). Henry VII selected Portsmouth as a Royal Dockyard in June 1495 and the city has held a preeminent position in the Royal Navy ever since. Henry VIII was responsible for the creation of a permanent proto-navy, with the supporting anchorages and dockyards there.

With the acquisition by Britain of an empire based on trade, this westerly approach to Albion's shores gained an even greater strategic importance. The sea lanes of communication between Europe and America run mainly south of Ireland, through the area colloquially known as the 'Western Approaches'. As the historian Ben Wilson has noted, 'naval strategists, from Drake onwards, had seen the value of keeping a squadron in the Western Approaches. Ships placed far out to sea between Fastnet (at the southernmost tip of Ireland) and Finisterre could keep a watch for enemy fleets. They could convoy merchantmen. They could cover Ireland.'[1] Those squadrons could best be positioned at Plymouth or Portsmouth. Ships bound for the key ports of Liverpool, Bristol, London and Southampton had to transit through this area, as they navigated towards the St George's Channel or the Irish Sea. Its defence was vital.

As late as the 1860s, in response to heightened Anglo-French tensions, Britain invested enormous sums to protect the Portsmouth base with massive fortifications on both the land side and on artificial islands constructed in the sea approaches. But Germany's defeat of France in the Franco-Prussian War of 1870, and the subsequent unification of Germany under a Hohenzollern

Admiral Sir John (Jacky) Fisher, painted by Sir Hubert von Herkomer.
Fisher was First Sea Lord from 1904 to 1910 and from the end of
October 1914 to May 1915. He was a great admirer of Commodore
Tyrwhitt. (Author's collection)

Prussian king, caused France to seek new friends and Britain to worry about the rapidly industrialising state, with growing naval and expansionist ambitions, that lay across the waters of the North Sea. With a little assistance from King Edward VII, an *Entente Cordiale* was agreed between Britain and France that buried past differences and was signed on 8 April 1904. Two of the most powerful nations in Europe had reached a concord; but it posed a challenge to Germany's influence in Europe and the world.

At the same time, the Royal Navy gained a new executive head. First Sea Lord Admiral Sir John (Jacky) Fisher, a dynamo in human form and a man possessed of both reforming zeal and the energy to implement his plans, took office in October. Fisher recognised that the most likely enemy that Britain would have to face was not France but Germany. Admiral von Tirpitz,* with the enthusiastic backing of Kaiser Wilhelm II, was creating an Imperial German Navy designed to raise his country to first-class naval status. With other factors, including violent anti-British feeling during the Boer War and the German government's refusal to consider an alliance with Britain except on terms that guaranteed Germany a free hand and hegemony in Europe, Fisher was convinced that

* Secretary of State of the German Imperial Naval Office and arch-creator of the German fleet.

Germany was now the most probable foe. His political master, First Lord of the Admiralty Lord Selborne, certainly agreed with him. In a memo to the Cabinet, Selborne noted that 'the great new German navy is being built up from the point of view of war with us'.[2]

To ensure that Britain had the necessary concentration of forces, Fisher instigated a reorganisation of the fleets. He recalled ships from far-flung postings, concentrated the navy where he expected it to have to give battle (the Channel and the North Sea) and scrapped 150 ships deeming them 'too weak to fight and too slow to run away'. Five battleships were withdrawn from the China station in 1904 and the standing South American, North American and Pacific squadrons were abolished.

As Andrew Lambert has written, 'by early 1906 the centre of naval effort was shifting from the Mediterranean to the North Sea; Germany was not only the most likely but also the only realistic enemy. Russia was no longer a naval power and the French navy had collapsed.'[3] Fisher created a new entity – the Home Fleet – to be based at Sheerness, where easy access to the North Sea and the German coastline could be obtained and which was announced by the Admiralty on 24 October 1906. He stripped the Mediterranean, Atlantic and Channel Fleets of battleships and cruisers to make up this new force and backed it up with ships from the reserve.

Britain's east coast ports had historically been neglected; the focus had been Portsmouth and Plymouth. But now the most probable enemy lay across the North Sea, the 'German Ocean' (as it was widely known and called on maps of pre-1914), and that brought a fresh focus to the harbours and anchorages of the eastern littoral.

The North Sea

The North Sea is an arm of the Atlantic Ocean. It is a body of water some 600 miles long and just 360 miles wide which is bounded by the Orkney Islands and the east coast of Britain to its west and by the Scandinavian and German shorelines to its east. A large part of the European drainage basin empties into the North Sea, including water from the Baltic. The sea terminates in the north by becoming the Norwegian Sea and in the south where it narrows into the English Channel.

For the most part, the waters lie on the European continental shelf with a mean depth of around 300ft. But the North Sea is littered with shallow banks such as Dogger, a vast accumulation of glacial debris and moraine with a depth of just 50–100ft, or the Long Forties and Broad Fourteens, respectively some 240ft and 85ft in depth. Cleaver Bank, Fisher Bank and North Hinder (Noordhinder) Bank are other larger areas of raised seabed.

The weather pattern includes many rainy days, steady and powerful winds and a strong tidal changes between low and high tide every 12 hours. Mist and fog are common in all seasons and sudden storms can spring up with little warning. Equinoctial gales come in September. This combination of climatic and geographic conditions makes navigation difficult at all times. Writer and ex-mariner Joseph Conrad described the North Sea; 'a grey-green expanse of smudgy waters grinning angrily at one with foam-ridges and over all a cheerless unglowing canopy, apparently made of wet blotting paper.'[4] He nicely captures the lurking menace that the waters hold.

Of most interest for naval purposes was the 70-mile western portion of the German North Sea coast where four rivers make their outflow. The westernmost, the Ems, separating Germany and Holland, has Emden as its main port, which became an important U-boat base. The River Elbe is the easternmost, the gateway to Hamburg and the Kiel Canal. Between the Elbe and the Weser is a low-lying peninsula on which Cuxhaven sits. And finally, the Jade, which flows from the landlocked Jade Bight to converge with the Weser. The Bight and its estuary were a treacherous place to navigate with shifting sandbanks and required regular dredging and maintenance of channels and their markers. Wilhelmshaven lies to the northwest side of the Jade Bay. The passage out of the Jade is governed by the tides for deep draught ships, as they have to exit over the tidal river bar. But 10 miles out the waters widen into the Schillig Roads, where the German fleet often rode at anchor.

With regard to the German navy, the Kaiserliche Marine, the major German naval ports, or Reichskriegshäfen (Imperial War Harbours),* of Wilhelmshaven, on the Jade Bight, and Kiel, on the Baltic coast, had excellent access to the North Sea; from Wilhelmshaven directly and from Kiel via the Baltic or through the 60-mile long Kiel Canal. Opened in 1895, this connected the German Baltic coast to the North Sea at Brunsbüttel, at the mouth of the Elbe, saving a 250nm passage around the Jutland peninsula.

So, the new battleground was a confined piece of water, with problematic ambient conditions and ease of access for the potential enemy. It was not an easy sea for the Royal Navy to defend.

Strategy

Under international law, close blockade of an enemy's ports was legal but the closing off of large areas of the seas to them was not.† This close blockade had been the Royal Navy's traditional strategy. But Fisher foresaw that the

---

* So designated by Kaiser Wilhelm I in 1871.
† The Treaty of Paris (1856, and subsequently re-ratified at the Hague Conventions of 1899 and 1907) gave legal basis to the concept of blockade. The agreement, among other things, permitted 'close' but not 'distant' blockades. A belligerent was allowed to station ships near the three-mile limit to stop or inspect traffic with an enemy's ports; it could not simply declare areas of the high seas comprising the approaches to the enemy's coast to be off limits.

submarine, the torpedo and the light inexpensive craft which could deliver them made the shallow and confined North Sea unsuitable for the battleships and other large vessels of the navy's battlefleet. Nor, in any case, could warships stay close to the continental coastline, as in the days of the Nelsonian sailing fleet of old. They were too vulnerable to underwater attack and too dependent on regular refuelling. Instead, he strongly advocated a distant blockade in which the North Sea was sealed off at either end and patrolled only by light craft.

On 16 December 1912, Admiral George Callaghan, CinC Home Fleet, was instructed that in time of war he should base himself at the Firth of Forth and sweep the North Sea, without going more than halfway across. When in 1913 First Lord of the Admiralty Winston Churchill pressed a madcap scheme for the close blockade of the Heligoland Bight and the capture of the island of Borkum, Callaghan was dismissive, stating that such an approach was no longer a viable plan.

Accordingly, as the likelihood of conflict with Germany grew, Scapa Flow was designated the main battlefleet base. The Firth of Forth was developed for naval purposes at Granton, Invergordon and Rosyth. The Nore command, which included Chatham and Sheerness Royal Dockyards, gained in importance. It might be noted that Britain ignored international treaties in determining that its strategy against Germany would henceforth be based on a distant blockade.

But the long eastern coastline bordering the North Sea had one major problem. There was no deep-water harbour for a large naval force between the Thames and the Humber: except one.

Harwich

The town of Harwich lies on the estuarial confluence of the Rivers Stour and Orwell. The river flow created a large deep-water anchorage, the only significant safe haven between the Thames and the Humber, which meant that it was of maritime significance since earliest times. Harwich received its charter in 1238 but for many centuries the coast was a dangerous area of marsh and fen, often inundated by the North Sea and deemed unhealthy owing to the damp and misty climatic conditions.

Nonetheless, two famous seventeenth-century mariners hailed from Harwich. Christopher Newport was christened at St Nicholas' Church on 29 December 1561 and in 1607, he was the 'sole commander' of the Virginia Company's expedition which established Jamestown, the first permanent English settlement in America. And in 1620, the Pilgrim Fathers sailed to the New World in the *Mayflower*, a Harwich vessel, whose master was Christopher Jones, a Harwich resident living at 21 King's Head Street.

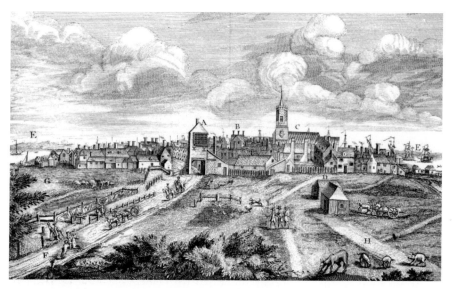

A view of the town of Harwich circa 1730, around the time of Daniel Defoe's visit.
(Author's collection)

The town's attractive harbour meant that in 1652 Harwich was established as a Royal Dockyard and continued as such for the next 60 years, closing in 1713 when it was leased to private operators. The last ship to be built there for the Royal Navy was HMS *Scarborough*, a Third Rate of 74 guns, launched in 1812. The town was fortified in 1657 with a redoubt and two batteries and in 1688 was the intended port of landing for William of Orange and his invited invasion until adverse winds forced him to Brixham instead. There was a further naval connection in the person of Samuel Pepys who was MP for Harwich twice in the seventeenth century and was appointed Secretary to the Admiralty in 1673, from which post he played a major role reforming the Royal Navy.

Daniel Defoe visited in 1722 and noted Harwich's formidable fort and harbour 'of a vast extent'. He also recorded the presence of an unusual chalybeate spring rising on Beacon Hill. Regarding the town itself, he thought that 'Harwich is a town of hurry and business, not much of gaiety and pleasure; yet the inhabitants seem warm in their nests and some of them are very wealthy'.[5]

By the 1750s Sir John Floyer and the Prince of Wales (later King George IV) had made the benefits of a seawater cure fashionable and Harwich was amongst the many coastal towns to establish baths and spas. Bathing machines came to its beaches and quack doctors to its streets.

In the nineteenth century, the town became the base for the Great Eastern

The Great Eastern Hotel, Harwich, pictured before the war.
(Photo; David Whittle/Harwich Society)

Railway Company's (GER) steamer services to Belgium and Holland. The GER opened the Great Eastern Hotel in 1865 to provide luxury accommodation for continental travellers, although the hotel was never commercially very successful. The GER also developed Parkeston Quay* between 1879 and 1883 on the southern side of the River Stour, upstream of the town itself, for use by its larger ships. Despite the gentrification, the town remained a sailors' port. One T West Carnie wrote in his book *In Quaint East Anglia*, published in 1899, 'it is such an out and out seaport and makes no attempt at being a watering place'.[6]

By the early 1900s Harwich was a busy fishing port with fishing smacks and other vessels trawling for shrimps and cod out in the North Sea. Fish was stored in large 'cod chests' and transferred to GER wagons for transport to Billingsgate market in London. Around the same time, about twenty 'bawleys' (a sailing vessel typified by a boomless cutter rig and probably named for mounting amidships a boiler for cooking shrimps) and small smacks fished all year round for whelks, which were used as bait for long-line fishing by large smacks at Harwich and elsewhere.

During the invasion scares of the first decade of the twentieth century, Harwich was considered to be a prime target for attack. The Eastern District Defence Scheme, as amended in 1904, envisaged that Harwich would be the most important fortress on the east coast due to its closeness to the continental

---

* Named after the then chairman of the GER, Charles H Parkes.

ports,* which rendered it liable to naval attacks or an assault with the object of seizing Parkeston Quay for use as a disembarkation place for an invading army. It was thought that the most likely form of incident would be a naval demonstration in support of landings elsewhere on the coast, with a view to capturing the fortress from the rear.

The Royal Navy had its eye on Harwich as a potential North Sea base by 1907. In that year, Commodore Lewis Bayly (in command of Destroyer Flotillas in Home Waters) was required by the Admiralty to take his destroyers to Harwich and to Dover and report on which was more suitable to use as the destroyers' headquarters. As Bayly later put it, 'at Dover we rolled and knocked about while at anchor; at Harwich we were in still water, and far away from the perilous attractions of a big town'.[7] In 1912, First Lord of the Admiralty Winston Churchill minuted the then Second Sea Lord, Prince Louis of Battenberg, that there should be shore facilities at Harwich, including leasing a 'football ground' and the provision of a 'good institute with a canteen, reading rooms, billiard tables and sleeping accommodation'.[8]

But the growing threat, and then the advent,† of war in 1914 changed the town permanently. There was a degree of fear and apprehension and some residents tried to bury their valuables, while many left for inland settlements. As in most of Britain, there was spy fever, with many innocent people suffering temporary arrest; every carrier pigeon was suspected of carrying messages to Germany and, of course, some were reported as having been sent up from Harwich.

In fact, a raid on Harwich would have met little armed resistance. Territorial gunners were manning the fort and a company of soldiers was sent from Colchester pending the arrival of the Essex Infantry Brigade (Territorials) who were in annual camp at Clacton and had suddenly to pack up and march to Harwich. There they were set to making trenches and redoubts. Additionally, the army began to commandeer houses, turning out the owners, and requisitioning barbed wire from stores and farms. Outposts were established and it is said in Harwich that some of the first shots of the war were fired by these Territorials who mistook some cows for Germans.

Harwich became a garrison town; after war was declared residents needed passes to travel in and out of the town, or to get to their work or homes. Called a 'Defence of the Realm Permit Book', this allowed access into the 'Harwich Special Military Area'. Out-of-town visitors needed passes and had to register at the police station. Thousands of sailors and soldiers thronged the streets and the locals were prohibited from visiting the seafront. Pubs (there were sixty) had to close at 2100 and street lighting was turned off; domestic lights had to

* Harwich is 126 miles by sea from the Hook of Holland and 296 miles from Wilhelmshaven.
† The declaration of war was announced to the town by the town crier.

be obscured by 1900. The Royal Navy took over the harbour and Parkeston Quay and the Great Eastern Hotel immediately became the garrison hospital.* A harbour boom† was put in place. Writing in 1916, Lieutenant Ronald Blacklock RN noted of Parkeston Quay that 'it looked very different to when I last saw it in 1914. There were now three depot ships alongside the quay and a very big flotilla of submarines. Many workshops, torpedo and mining stores, cinema and recreation rooms had been built on the quay.'[9] By December 1916, Parkeston Quay had become home to another Royal Navy section, the Admiralty Experimental Station working on anti-submarine measures.

Not only did the GER lose its hotel and quay, some of its ships were taken up by the navy too. The Admiralty requisitioned eight of the company's Harwich-based vessels. Among them were the cargo ships *Clacton* and *Newmarket*, which were turned into minesweepers while the passenger ships *Munich* (renamed the *St Denis*) and *St Petersburg* (renamed *Archangel*) became hospital ships and survived the war.

Of course, Britain still needed to import goods to keep both the Western and Home Fronts supplied and Harwich continued to operate as a commercial port as well as a naval one. Harwich's quays were used as an offloading point for large quantities of merchant shipping, bringing in supplies which had been sanctioned by officialdom as not aiding the enemy, and this was the case until the Admiralty declared the town a 'closed port' in May 1916. The residents of the town became used to the daily wail of ships' sirens that summoned officers and men back to their vessels and the next mission at sea. Every cruiser in harbour, following the flagship's lead, sounded off three times, each for three minutes.

Over the water from Harwich lies the Shotley peninsula, separating the rivers Stour and the Orwell, and home since 1905 to HMS *Ganges*, the Royal Navy boys' training establishment. Indeed, the whole riverine area became 'navalised'; north across the estuary at Felixstowe a major RNAS base had been created in 1913 where seaplanes were designed, constructed and operated. Originally and unimaginatively named 'Seaplanes, Felixstowe', it was retitled RNAS Felixstowe in July 1914 and the Seaplane Experimental Station, Felixstowe, on 1 April 1918.

All of this change came to pass by reason of the war and the realisation that it would, in naval terms, be decisive in the North Sea: and because of the coming of the Royal Navy's Harwich Force.

---

* Additionally, 'The Grange', a large house on Hall Lane was requisitioned as a hospital, as was 'The Cliff Hall' on Marine Parade. There was also an isolation hospital at Dovercourt.

† A boom defence was typically a series of 40ft-long timber baulks chained together and stretched across a harbour or river mouth to deny access to enemy surface craft. When any friendly vessel needed to pass through, the attending boom defence vessel (usually an old trawler or tug) had to draw the obstruction aside and, after passage, replace it in position.

2

The Harwich Force Forms, July and August 1914

Partly for reasons of cost saving, the ships of the Royal Navy of the immediate pre-war period were divided into three fleets – First, Second and Third – and three 'unified home commands' had been instituted on 31 July 1912. The Commanders-in-Chief of these organisations (Home, Channel, Atlantic) were under the control of the Commander-in-Chief, Home Fleets, Admiral Sir George Callaghan.

The First Fleet was effectively the ships comprising the main battlefleet, soon to be known as the Grand Fleet, the modern battle line and its consorts. The Second Fleet was ships manned by nucleus crews whose complements could be rapidly brought up to strength by drafts from naval barracks and reservists, and the Third Fleet comprised ships laid up under Care and Maintenance Parties, older vessels considered of limited worth but necessary to 'keep up the numbers' for public consumption and as a reserve.

The great battleships of the First Fleet were attended by many smaller ships, particularly destroyers. Such vessels had been designed to combat the growing threat posed by small, fast, cheap torpedo-carrying craft, known as torpedo boats. Large numbers of these might, it was thought, overwhelm a battleship's defences and sink it, or distract the battleship and make it vulnerable to the opposing fleet.

The original role of the torpedo boat destroyers, soon abbreviated to just 'destroyers', was to sally ahead of the battlefleet and deal with the torpedo-boat threat before they could attack the large, big-gun ships. They sprang from the ever-fertile brain of then Third Sea Lord, Jacky Fisher, who in 1892 ordered the development of a new type of ships equipped with novel water-tube boilers and quick-firing small-calibre guns. By 1913, they were recognised as an essential part of the fleet, with duties ranging from fighting off small enemy craft to reconnaissance and keeping the seas free of mines and submarines.

The destroyer flotillas of the First Fleet came under the command of a Captain (T)*, and on 1 December 1913 Captain Reginald Yorke Tyrwhitt was appointed to the role, additionally taking command of the third class protected cruiser *Amethyst*. In April the following year, a new entity was founded as a named command, originally referred to in the Navy List as 'Destroyer Flotillas

---

* 'T' for torpedo boat destroyer.

REPORTED TO HAVE " RUSHED " THE NARROWS AS FAR AS NAGARA : THE BRITISH LIGHT-CRUISER " AMETHYST " (MENTIONED IN DESPATCHES).
The " Amethyst," a light-cruiser which is credited at the moment of writing with having daringly | named in despatches as one of the light-cruiser squadron in the attack off Heligoland in August, and
" rushed " the Narrows of the Dardanelles, is a ten-year-old unarmoured ship of 3000 tons and 22 knots | at the battle off the Dogger in January. The " Amethyst " is stated to have traversed the length of
speed. mounting twelve 4-inch 25-pounder quick-firers and machine-guns, and manned by 296 officers | the Narrows as far as Nagara, regardless of the Turkish batteries and mine-field, and to have returned
and men. Her presence with the Dardanelles Fleet is something of a surprise. The " Amethyst " was | safely with casualties of 28 killed and about 30 wounded.—[Photograph by Russell, Southsea.]

HMS *Amethyst*, Tyrwhitt's first flagship in 1914, depicted in the *Illustrated War News* of
May 1915. It lauds her role at Heligoland Bight and, after leaving the Harwich Force,
subsequently in the Dardanelles. (US Naval History and Heritage Command NH 63007)

of the First Fleet'. That same month Tyrwhitt was appointed commodore
(second class)* and took responsibility for this new formation. In this change
lay the genesis of the Harwich Force.

Spring 1914 turned into summer and tensions in Europe simmered.
Instead of the annual manoeuvres usually conducted, it was planned to hold
a test mobilisation of the fleet in July. This was driven by a plangent need for
economy. In order to obtain Cabinet approval for the 1914–15 Naval
Estimates, First Lord of the Admiralty Winston Churchill had agreed to a
reduction of £1 million, which meant omitting three light cruisers, twelve
torpedo boats and cutting out the summer manoeuvres in favour of a test
mobilisation of the reserves. It transpired to be a serendipitous decision, given
the world situation that was developing.

Thus, from 15 July, as well as calling up the reserves for the usual two weeks
of training, the Admiralty conducted a full trial mobilisation of all three fleets
and combined this with a royal review of the fleet by the king, another

---

* A commodore (second class) is one who in addition to his flotilla responsibilities also commands his
  own ship with no captain under him.

advertisement for the navy and its power. It would have the added effect, perhaps, of demonstrating Britain's strength to Germany and others in such trying times.

The navy's ships had largely gathered by 17 July. The First Fleet was led by HMS *Iron Duke*, flying Admiral Callaghan's flag, the Second and Third Fleets by the pre-dreadnought *Lord Nelson*. *Iron Duke* (1912) carried ten 13.5in guns as main armament, supported by twelve 6in, and her Parsons turbines drove her at a top speed of 21.25 knots; she was the very latest thing in battleship design afloat at the time.

Reservists had been summoned from far and wide. They expected to spend a busy fortnight training and on manoeuvres before going home. Their presence allowed the navy to turn out the largest number of ships ever brought together in one place for review. Over 200 vessels participated, including twenty-four dreadnoughts and battlecruisers, twenty-five pre-dreadnoughts and eighteen large cruisers. The ships formed twelve lines stretching from the Isle of Wight to Portsmouth. Between 70,000 and 80,000 Royal Navy personnel were present at various times in the greatest fleet ever assembled in British waters. Tyrwhitt and his destroyers were there 'which were much admired, he wrote proudly to his wife, who had watched them . . . from HMS *Doris*'.[1]

The fleets then spent several days in exercises and on the 23rd were expected to disperse, and began to return to their home ports. Tyrwhitt's command sailed to Portsmouth for refit and leave and he, together with some thirty-two admirals and four other commodores, was due to attend a conference at the Admiralty. On the 25th Austria's peremptory ultimatum to Serbia expired; but still the reservists were leaving the fleet and any advantage Britain might have gained from the test mobilisation if and when war came was ebbing away. Meanwhile it was Goodwood race week. Tyrwhitt went home[*] and then attended a pre-Goodwood dance at a nearby country house, along with his friend Commodore Roger Keyes.

But as the global situation worsened, and with First Lord Winston Churchill away from his office and at the seaside building sandcastles with his wife and children, at 1600 on the 26th Admiral Prince Louis of Battenberg, First Sea Lord, issued the instruction that 'no ship to leave harbour until further orders' to the CinC Home Fleets. Tyrwhitt and other officers were interrupted at the dance with telegrams ordering them to their ships. The following day all leave was unexpectedly cancelled and officers and men were instructed to return to their duties.

Tyrwhitt was directed to Portland for instructions, where he was also given a sealed packet of orders to take to Keyes. On the 29th, the First Fleet, now the

---

[*] At this time, the Tyrwhitts lived at 'Ketellby', a house in Waterlooville, Hampshire.

Grand Fleet, sailed for Scapa Flow, taking the 2nd Destroyer Flotilla (2 DF) and 4 DF with it but dropping 1 DF and 3 DF off at Harwich. The Harwich Force was born. The 6th Destroyer Flotilla of twelve 'Tribal'-class destroyers sailed for Dover, to close off the southern end of the 'German Ocean'.* And on 4 August, the eight aging *Edgar*-class cruisers of the 10th Cruiser Squadron sailed for the Shetland Islands to shut off the northern end.†

The creation of a force at Harwich reflected the changed thinking about the role of the battlefleet in the North Sea. It was foreseen that there was a need to bring the German High Seas Fleet to action. Victory would free resources for other operations. Until this was achieved a very large fleet had to be maintained in readiness for battle. A smaller, more agile component of the Grand Fleet in the southern North Sea was required for observation duty – this was the Harwich Force, which formed the southern wing of the Grand Fleet. The overall intention was to provide light forces which could impede any movement by German surface forces into the North Sea towards the east coast of England or the Strait of Dover. According to Admiral Sir William Jameson, 'the Harwich Force was [initially] responsible for preventing enemy vessels passing unobserved and unattached through what is sometimes known as the Hoofden or Flanders Bight – an area bounded by the English, Netherlands and German coasts and by an arbitrary line drawn through the North Sea at the 54th parallel, say from Flamborough Head to the south of the River Elbe'.[2] This role expanded over the years of the war to encompass trade protection and freedom of surface movement, but that lay in the future.

Despite its detached location, Tyrwhitt's force came under the command of the CinC Grand Fleet, Admiral Sir John Jellicoe (who had dramatically replaced Callaghan on 4 August). Harwich also became the base for Keyes, who brought with him the 8th Submarine Flotilla of seventeen 'D'- and 'E'-class boats (after a false start that sent him to the Humber), together with their depot ships *Adamant* and *Maidstone*. The submarines were independent of the destroyers, with but not of the Harwich Force, and thus there were two separate commands at the base, with Keyes reporting directly to the Admiralty. Indeed, there was also a third command, given that HMS *Ganges*, the boys' training establishment at Shotley, was a separate responsibility under Captain (later Commodore) George Cuthbert Cayley RN, who had held the position since May 1913. Additionally, Cayley also became Senior Naval Officer, Harwich, on 3 September.

---

* See Steve R Dunn, *Securing the Narrow Sea* (Barnsley: Seaforth Publishing, 2017) for the story of the Dover Patrol.
† See Steve R Dunn, *Blockade* (Barnsley: Seaforth Publishing, 2016) for the history of the 10th Cruiser Squadron.

Admiral Sir John Jellicoe, who became CinC Grand Fleet on the outbreak of war.
(Author's collection)

Tyrwhitt and Keyes were long-term friends and lived near to each other; this would help the necessary cooperation in the early stages of the war. But what sort of men were they?

The Commanders

Reginald Yorke Tyrwhitt was born on 10 May 1870, the seventh child (and sixth by his second wife Caroline née Yorke) of the Reverend Richard St John Tyrwhitt, Vicar of St Mary Magdalen Church, Oxford. Like Nelson, he was the fifth son of a clergyman. The reverend's first wife, Eliza Anne, was the sister of the well-known Pre-Raphaelite artist John Roddam Spencer Stanhope; she died in giving birth to their first child in 1859.[*] Richard Tyrwhitt remarried in January 1861 and found time to write the book *A Handbook of Pictorial Art*, published in 1866.

Reginald's great-great-great grandfather had been a vicar and his brother Cecil took holy orders. His sister Kitty[†] became a nun. But the young Tyrwhitt was an unruly and adventurous child; the headmaster of his Oxford preparatory school[‡] wrote of him, Tyrwhitt later claimed, 'Dear Rev Tyrwhitt. Your son is no good and will come to a hard end.'[3]

So rather than the Church, he instead followed the path of his great-great grandfather, a Royal Navy captain. Aged 12 Tyrwhitt was sent to Burney's naval crammer to prepare him to take the entrance exam for *Britannia*, the Royal Navy's officer training ship. He succeeded at the third attempt, last but one of his term of thirty-one. After two years he passed out of *Britannia* twenty-first in the term, with his only first-class grade in 'seamanship'. But he had been a cadet captain and his conduct was rated as 'exemplary'.[4]

His career then followed the usual path of midshipman, sub lieutenant, courses at the Royal Naval College, Greenwich, gunnery at HMS *Excellent*, a brief spell on the royal yacht *Victoria and Albert* and finally, in January 1896, command of the torpedo boat destroyer HMS *Hart*. It was in destroyers that Tyrwhitt was to find his true metier. *Hart* was one of thirty-six so-called 27-knotters. She was brand new and Tyrwhitt commissioned her into the service. Flush-decked with a tumblehome, and 'turtleback' forward bridge, they were very wet ships, armed with a single 12pdr gun, five 6pdrs and two torpedo tubes.

From then until 1906 Tyrwhitt commanded eight different destroyers, rising in rank from lieutenant to commander. On 30 June 1908, he was advanced to captain and a year later (10 August 1909) placed in command of

---

[*] Who was Walter Spenser Stanhope Tyrwhitt RBA, a painter of landscapes and architectural subjects who exhibited at, *inter alia*, the Royal Academy and the Grosvenor Gallery and was a founder member of the Oxford Art Society.

[†] Christened Alice Catherine.

[‡] The Dragon School.

An imposing man; Reginald Tyrwhitt as a
rear admiral, taken from a press feature in
1918. (Author's collection)

Angela Tyrwhitt, née Corbally.
(Photo; private collection)

Topaze as Captain (D) of the Fourth Destroyer Flotilla. After a signal course
in 1910 he was appointed in command of *Bacchante* as Flag Captain, Fourth
Cruiser Squadron in the Mediterranean.

Directly from *Bacchante*, he became Flag Captain for the 6th Cruiser
Squadron in *Good Hope*, ending on 10 August 1912, when he took the position
of Captain (D) of the 2nd Destroyer Flotilla, flying his flag in *Bellona*. Finally,
as war loomed, in December 1913 this by now highly experienced destroyer
sailor became Captain (T) in command of the destroyer flotillas of the First
Fleet; and five months later became Commodore (T), known as 'Com T'.

During his rise in rank, his superior officers had commented fulsomely on
Tyrwhitt's abilities. Such encomiums included, *inter alia*, 'splendid technique,
pluck and nerve' in 1896; 'very zealous, excellent executive officer . . . handles
the men well' in 1904; 'Recommended for higher ranks' in 1909; and 'I have
every confidence in [Tyrwhitt]. He has carried out his duties with great ability'
in 1910.[5]

The naval historian Arthur Marder saw Tyrwhitt as holding 'all the aces'.
This referred to the (post-war) definition by Admiral William James of the
three aces that distinguished Nelson and any other 'perfect admiral'. Ace
number one was the gift of leadership; the second a fertile mind and creative
brain; and third, an eagerness to delegate and make full use of the brains of

junior officers.[6] Marder thought of Tyrwhitt as 'not terribly interested in strategy, he was wrapped up in ships, *materiel* generally and with tactics'.[7]

A keen fisherman in his leisure time, physically Tyrwhitt was robust, a broad-shouldered handsome man with a roman nose, pronounced cheekbones and a high domed forehead inherited from his father. 'He had played rugger for the navy and looked it.'[8] His resting face seemed to bear a determined set, with piercing eyes.

In 1902, whilst serving on the North American station in the second class protected cruiser HMS *Indefatigable* (1891), Tyrwhitt met, at the house of the Governor of Trinidad, an Irish-born dark-haired beauty, Miss Angela Corbally; before he left the island, Tyrwhitt had proposed to her and been accepted. They married in England in February 1903 and Tyrwhitt remained uxoriously devoted to his bride, writing to her every day that they were apart for the rest of his career. This then was the man who would command the Harwich Force for the duration of the war, a unique responsibility for no other sea-going flag officer remained in the same post for the duration.

Roger Keyes as a vice admiral in 1918. (Author's collection)

Forty-two-year-old Commodore Roger Brownlow Keyes was a small ship and submarine specialist who had served for much of his early career commanding destroyers and more latterly had been responsible for the submarine service, firstly as Inspecting Captain of Submarines from 1910 and then as Commodore of the Submarine Service in 1912. He had made his name during service in China where, commanding the destroyer *Fame*, he went to the rescue of a small British force which had been attacked and surrounded by irregular Chinese forces while attempting to demarcate the border of the Hong Kong New Territories. He went ashore, directing half the landing party, and, while *Fame* fired on the besiegers, Keyes personally led the charge which routed the Chinese and freed the troops.

Then in June 1900, during the Boxer Rebellion, Keyes commanded a mission to capture a flotilla of four Chinese destroyers moored to a wharf on the Peiho River. Together with another junior officer, he led boarding parties onto the Chinese destroyers, took them and secured the wharf; later he had to recapture one destroyer from the Russians. Shortly thereafter he took the heavily fortified fort at Hsi-cheng. Keyes loaded *Fame* with a landing party of thirty-two men, armed with rifles, pistols, cutlasses and explosives. His men quickly destroyed the Chinese gun mountings, blew up the powder magazine and returned to the ship.

He was a keen huntsman, an excellent shot, avid polo player and a prize-winning jockey. Keyes did everything at 100 miles per hour and had loved the cut and thrust of destroyer work. He was an ardent patriot and obsessed by the gentleman's code of chivalry. But he divided opinion. Jellicoe thought him unintelligent, whilst Arthur Marder described Keyes as one who 'may not have been the greatest intellect in the service'.[9] Another historian described him as 'not renowned for his outstanding intellect or technical facility'.[10] Marder, however, asserted that Keyes was 'one of the most attractive of men, warm hearted and full of boyish enthusiasm – a born leader with few brains',[11] and one of the submarine service officers at Harwich, Lieutenant Ronald Blacklock, said of him that 'he was extremely good and I think that he brought up the standard and morale of the submarines in a very big sense'.[12]

The Ships
Keyes commanded the 8th Submarine Flotilla at Harwich until February 1915, and led his forces personally from the flotilla leaders HMS *Lurcher* and *Firedrake*.

These ships were two from a sub-class of three, a development of the *Acheron*-class destroyers, known as 'Yarrow Specials'. They stemmed from the belief held by shipbuilder Sir Alfred Yarrow that it was possible to build strong, seaworthy destroyers with a speed of 32 knots. They were larger and faster than the *Acheron*s with a distinctively different appearance but carried the same armament, two 4in and two 12pdr guns together with twin torpedo tubes.

Tyrwhitt was still in *Amethyst*, much to his chagrin. She was a *Topaze*-class third class protected cruiser, launched in 1903, armed with twelve 4in guns and eight 3pdrs. She had a design speed of 22.5 knots but could only manage 18. He thought that *Amethyst* was far too slow for him and agitated with the Admiralty for a better ship.

Under his command he had two light cruiser (technically scout cruiser) flotilla leaders. Captain William Frederick Blunt in HMS *Fearless* (1912) led 1 DF, comprised of twenty destroyers and Captain Cecil Henry Fox, in HMS *Amphion* (1911), led 3 DF of nineteen. *Fearless* and *Amphion* had ten 4in guns and could make 25 knots. The destroyers were of the 'L'-class, modern (launched within the last 12 months), armed with three 4in and one 2pdr with two torpedo tubes and capable of 29 knots. Tyrwhitt's grumbles about his own ship were justified – every ship in his command could outstrip *Amethyst*.

HMS *Lurcher* (1912), Commodore Keyes's flagship in 1914.
(US Navy History and Heritage Command NH 59911)

First Blood

From 31 July, the Harwich Force* prepared for war. Brightworks and funnel bands were painted out, spare gear, woodwork and unnecessary items of clothing were sent ashore – the latter to be unceremoniously dumped in sheds or at Shotley Barracks – and each ship was issued with a hypodermic needle and a supply of morphine. Destroyers at this point did not carry a medically trained crewman, just a simple first aid kit. The paperwork which accompanied the needle instructed that they were 'to be used in action to quieten men who were so badly wounded that their suffering . . . would unnerve other members of the crew'.[13] Ammunition racks at the guns were filled and one gun per ship manned at night; and every ship exercised its gun crews daily.

Tyrwhitt was interested in the demeanour of his men as war approached; he wrote to his sister that 'they looked on it all as a joke at first, but when they saw the officers' private effects being landed, also armchairs and comforts and such like, they realised that something was up'.[14]

But he found the waiting onerous, not least because he worried about a pre-emptive German attack on the harbour. 'Harwich is likely to be attacked at any moment after war is declared', the commodore told his wife.[15] And to his brother Beauchamp he wrote, 'please look after Angey [sic] if she wants anything. She has money to the end of the month.'[16]

But finally, from 2300 on 4 August, Britain and Germany were at war.[†] The Admiralty signalled 'Commence hostilities with Germany' and immediately Tyrwhitt signalled his ships. 'The Commodore (T) wishes the officers and men of the First Fleet Flotilla the best of luck in defending their country', followed by 'raise steam for fifteen knots at 0630'.[17] As the ships slipped out of harbour on the 5th, they left behind them a detritus of floating gear, hats, chairs, etc which had still not made it to shore. Even at that early hour, many of Harwich's citizens had gathered at the harbour to see them off, while the boys from *Ganges* stood on the Shotley bank and cheered themselves hoarse. *Amethyst* and the *Acheron*-class destroyer *Ariel* towed out the submarines *E-6* and *E-8* respectively and when detached, these two set up the first submarine patrol of the Heligoland Bight. *E-9* soon joined them.

Tyrwhitt's plan was to reach the Outer Gabbard Lightship (20 miles east of Orford Ness) and then sweep for minelayers or other small enemy craft in the direction of Terschelling (an island off the northern Dutch coast, one of

---

* Technically, the force was still known as the First Fleet Flotillas; it was not until May 1915 that the Admiralty regularly referred to it as 'The Harwich Striking Force'. For simplicity, 'Harwich Force' will be used both before and after this date.

† 'His Majesty's Government have accordingly formally notified the German Government that a state of war exists between the two countries, as from 11 pm to-day' (*London Gazette* 28861, 4 August 1914).

the West Frisian Islands) and subsequently patrol southwestwards by day, coming back along the northern Dutch coast nearly up to Borkum by night.

The Admiralty had concerns that the Germans would immediately lay mines in the shipping lanes of the North Sea to disrupt British trade, despite the fact that the laying of 'automatic contact mines off the coast and ports of the enemy, with the sole object of intercepting commercial shipping' had been forbidden under Convention VIII relative to the Laying of Automatic Submarine Contact Mines of the Hague Treaty of 18 October 1907, article two.

Their concerns were justified. The converted passenger ferry *Königin Luise* had been requisitioned by the Kaiserliche Marine on 3 August 1914 to serve as an auxiliary minelayer. Immediately on the declaration of war she sailed from Emden carrying 200 mines to sow close to the major trade artery of the Thames Estuary. A perfunctory attempt at disguise had been made with a coat of paint, which was applied overnight, giving an impression of a Harwich–Hook of Holland ferry of the Great Eastern Railway Company.*

Whilst in the act of mining, the German was spotted by a trawler, and a radioed warning message reached Tyrwhitt about the same time that *Königin Luise* observed the patrolling British destroyers of 3 DF. At 1030 she sheered off to the north to try to escape them, desperately unloading her mines as she went. This took her away from a furious Tyrwhitt, who wanted to be the first to action, and nearer to HMS *Amphion* and her flotilla.

Captain Fox, having signalled 'good hunting' to his brood, took up the cause. Chased by *Lance* and *Landrail*, *Königin Luise* was brought to action around 1100 when *Lance* fired the opening shell from one of her 4in guns. It was the first British shot of the war. As *Linnet* and *Lark* came up, the German was steaming at a much-reduced speed. Shells were pumped into her, the disengaged gun crews crowding the engaged side and cheering every shot. At 1215, the enemy's crew began to abandon ship, although the engines continued to run and she slowly maintained her progress until turning on her side and sinking.

Out of the minelayer's complement of 140 men, forty-three were picked up, twenty of whom were taken into *Amphion*. The destroyers stayed out all night and on the following morning began to return to Harwich. Fox thought that he knew where the mines had been dropped and steered some seven miles away from the spot. But he miscalculated. At 0635, *Amphion* struck one of the eggs laid the previous day by *Königin Luise*. There was a violent explosion under the fore bridge and every man on the foredeck was killed, as were

---

* The usual paintwork of the company's steamers consisted of black hulls with a yellow band; white uppers with brown houses; and funnels of buff with black tops.

The 'L'-class destroyer HMS *Lark* (1913), in a painting by W J Sutton. She took part in both the Battles of Heligoland Bight and Dogger Bank. (Author's collection)

eighteen of the rescued German prisoners. Her keel was cracked and the fore part of the ship was on fire. HMS *Linnet* attempted to tow her to safety but a deep rent appeared across her deck and curved upwards. It was clear than *Amphion* was finished. Fox and his bridge team were badly burnt on the hands and face but managed to organise a calm abandonment. She settled by the head, her sides turning black from the raging internal fires, but within 15 minutes the accompanying destroyers had taken the survivors aboard.

As the fires reached the magazine, *Amphion* exploded; quantities of wreckage shot into the air and fell on the destroyers, injuring some sailors; a shell landed on *Lark* killing two ratings and one of the German survivors, and in *Linnet* a gunner was severely injured when struck by a flying hatch cover. In total 147 British sailors and one officer, Staff Paymaster Joseph Gedge[*] who had been in the coding room below the bridge, lost their lives. HMS *Amphion* became the first Royal Navy warship to be sunk in the war and the first ever to be sunk by a contact mine. Hubris and Nemesis had already struck and the war was only one day old.

---

[*] Gedge, a Freemason, was the first British officer in either service to be killed in the war.

Amphion's Engine Room Artificer 1st Class Henry Bennett, who had served in the Boer War and held the Long Service and Good Conduct Medals, was never to enthral his grandchildren with tales of South Africa. Nor would 37-year-old John Bond, the Master-at-Arms, another holder of Long Service and Good Conduct awards, return to his home. Eighteen-year-old Peter Lambell would not go back to his parents in Woolwich. And so the list of the dead went on; the army had yet to lose a man, but the navy was already in the thick of it. For Tyrwhitt, it meant that he now had to act as flotilla leader for 3 DF on top of his other responsibilities, and that he was already a ship down.

When the flotilla, having picked up *Amphion*'s survivors, neared Harwich they saw another steamer in the colours of a Great Eastern Railway's packet, flying the German Imperial Ensign. Fresh from seeing the end of *Amphion*, some of the destroyers opened fire on her until she ran up a Red Ensign. The boat was carrying the German ambassador, Prince Lichnowsky, who had arrived with his staff via a special train from London to Parkeston Quay for their return to Germany. On arrival at Harwich 'a guard of honour was drawn up for me. I was treated like a departing sovereign'[18] and he had departed on the GER steamer *St Petersburg* for Holland on passage to Germany.

As the impact of the first naval battle off the English coast settled in, the *Birmingham Mail* reported that

the British destroyers took the promptest measures to save those on board and the prisoners are now in Shotley Naval Barracks. Many are suffering from terrible wounds, and the Central News correspondent, on enquiring at Shotley this morning, found that four have had legs shot away, while two are armless. All were reported to be progressing well as could be expected. None of the crew of the *Lance* received any injuries. The German vessel was caught in the very act of laying mines about sixty miles from Harwich, off the Dutch coast . . . At Harwich Parish Church this morning special thanksgiving prayers were said, the *Te Deum* was read, and also a special prayer for the enemy's wounded.[19]

British opinion was outraged by the incident. Rather than send her fleet out to do battle, the German policy seemed to be to deploy minelayers and U-boats into the North Sea to wreak havoc in international waters. This was strictly against international law, as most recently expressed at the Declaration of London in 1909. As the navy's *Official History* later noted

such was the immediate success of the policy of mining in international waters which Germany had chosen to adopt. The indications were that the minefield had been laid between 3 degrees E long and the Suffolk coast – that is, right in the fairway – regardless of neutrals and of all the time-honoured customs of the sea. It was the first opening of our eyes to the kind of enemy we had to deal with, and yet so inhuman did the practice appear in the eyes of our seamen that as yet there was no thought of retaliation in kind.[20]

Eight days after the sinking, minesweeping trawlers from Harwich (another command based on the port, with but not of the Harwich Force) had swept and buoyed a clear channel inshore of this field. The channel was extended over the next months in the face of repeated mining of the east coast port,* into a fairway known as the 'War Channel'. This was a marked traffic lane, which eventually extended from Dover to the Firth of Forth, and was swept daily for mines, mainly by trawlers based at the Nore, Harwich, Lowestoft, the Humber, the Tyne and Granton. Soon the War Channel was being swept each day by up to eighty minesweeping trawlers and patrolled at night by drifters, often armed with nothing but the White Ensign, to deter minelayers. From now on, preventing the work of German minelayers would be an important part of the Harwich Force's work as well.

On Patrol

For the next few days, the destroyers settled into a routine of patrol; first 1 DF, then 3 DF, turn and turn about; Tyrwhitt remained at sea throughout. On the 8th, they were recalled as the British Expeditionary Force (BEF) was to begin its departure for France the following day and the Harwich Force was to deploy to protect it from any German naval interception (although in fact the Germans were quite happy for them to land as they thought it would be easier to deal with them there than at sea). Tyrwhitt then returned to the North Sea with 3 DF.

For the first weeks of the war, the Force patrolled enemy waters around Heligoland 24 out of 24 hours. Each flotilla spent a total of 66 hours in German waters and then returned to harbour for just 30 hours to refuel, take on provisions and grab a quick rest, if fortunate. However, for Tyrwhitt this routine was broken by a summons to the Admiralty. Jellicoe had decided that communication with Harwich from his northerly base was too difficult and asked the Admiralty to take responsibility for the issuance of orders to the Harwich Force instead. Tyrwhitt was briefed on this change in London and took the opportunity to once again press for a better flagship as 'he found himself . . . alone within a few miles of the German coast in a craft with a

---

* 180 mines off Southwold on 5 August; on 26 August off the Humber, 200 mines; and another 194 off the Tyne the same day, for example.

maximum speed of 18 knots'.[21] He was promised the first of the new oil-fired cruisers.

Returning to his ships, Tyrwhitt set up a regular patrol, one flotilla then the other, keeping a watch at night and in the early morning on an area formed by a line from Heligoland to the mouth of the Ems and then the Terschelling Light Vessel in order to report on any German vessels leaving port and/or likely to interfere with the crossing of the BEF. This patrol too involved 66 hours at sea followed by 30 in harbour in every four days and was kept up until mid-November. When the destroyers came in, they were moored at Parkeston Quay rather than a buoy, in order that officers and men might get a little respite on land or in the depot ship *Dido*, a converted *Eclipse*-class protected cruiser launched in 1896. The patrol nonetheless put a heavy demand on men and ships.

On the 13th, Tyrwhitt was once more summoned to the Admiralty, this time to meet Churchill and be told he should make a drive towards Heligoland. On the 15th he duly did as ordered but found nothing. He was 'rather bored at looking for nothing',[22] as he wrote to his wife.

That may have been so, but a good chance to come to grips with the enemy was missed three days later when, with the commodore in harbour and 1 DF on patrol, a four-funnelled German cruiser was spotted by *Lizard*. Blunt in *Fearless*, the only British vessel of the flotilla capable of dealing with such an enemy on an equal footing, mistook it for the *Yorck* (1904), an 8in-gunned opponent which outclassed his ship. He ordered a tactical withdrawal. But *Lizard* and *Goshawk*, now within range of the German, signalled that it was only a 4in-gunned vessels, the *Karlsruhe*. By then it was too late; a belated order to pursue was given but rescinded after an hour of fruitless steaming.

On the night of the 19th/20th, several destroyers of 1 DF were detailed to support bombardment craft which were firing at German troops approaching Ostend. The Belgian garrison had withdrawn to Antwerp, and uncertainty prevailed as to whether the city had already fallen to the enemy; so the *Acheron*-class destroyer HMS *Hind* (1911) was ordered to go and investigate.

Her captain, Lieutenant Commander Geoffrey Corlett, nosed quietly into Ostend harbour and tied up at the jetty. All seemed calm, but then a rumour spread like a bush fire that the Germans were expected any minute and suddenly there was a press of people seeking to get through customs and leave for Britain or elsewhere. There were two problems with this desire. The customs officers were tied up in red tape and overwhelmed and the two Belgian passenger ferries in harbour did not even have steam up.

Whilst Corlett was appraising the situation, an English woman with her small daughter approached him, revealed that she was the wife of a naval officer, and asked him for help. Corlett consigned them to his steward, then commandeered a car, armed himself and his signalman, and went into the town centre to try to find someone in authority to sort out the mess.

Failing in this regard, he returned and interviewed the two Belgian ferry captains; they refused to sail or take on any refugees, because they were afraid of mines and submarines. A Royal Navy officer is trained to take decisions; Corlett told them that they <u>would</u> put to sea, and that he would put an armed guard and his own stokers on board if they did not raise steam immediately. The Belgian masters saw the light. By 1130, the passenger ships had slipped and *Hind* escorted them to sea. Lieutenant Commander Corlett had helped save many civilian lives.[*] Then on the 21st, Tyrwhitt was instructed to 'make a demonstration'[23] off Ostend and was told not to fire on the town but to engage any enemy formations in the area. He saw nothing to shoot at.

The first two weeks of war had seen the Harwich Force sink one auxiliary minesweeper and lose a valuable light cruiser. Tyrwhitt and his men were frustrated and itching for a fight.

---

[*] The Germans finally entered Ostend after the Allied withdrawal of 11–13 October.

3

Into Battle, August–October 1914

The island of Heligoland sits some 29 miles off the German coast in the southeast North Sea, commanding the estuaries of the Rivers Elbe and Weser, and the waterways to Hamburg and Bremerhaven. Once owned by Britain, it was ceded to Germany in the 1890 Treaty of Heligoland–Zanzibar.

Imperial Germany turned the island into a major naval base. The island was fortified with concrete gun emplacements along its cliffs for 364 mounted guns, which included 142 'disappearing guns' (retractable into the rock), overlooking shipping channels defended with ten rows of naval mines. At the outbreak of war, the civilian population was evacuated to the mainland and the island became a key German base, additionally offering protection from vessels sailing to and from the southwest entrance to the Kiel Canal.

Reconnaissance by Keyes's submarines had identified that the waters around Heligoland were patrolled on a regular basis by relays of enemy destroyers. As Lieutenant Stephen King-Hall RN put it, 'little escaped their curious periscopes, and they soon discovered that the Germans were working

The Island of Heligoland depicted in a colour photolithograph around 1900.
(Library of Congress LC-DIG-ppmsca-00573)

a night patrol off the Bight with destroyers and light cruisers. It was the habit of these gentry to retire into the Bight at dawn each day.'[1] Keyes suggested to Tyrwhitt that a sweep down onto them might net some success amongst the returning vessels.

The two men agreed to the scheme and Keyes tried to obtain permission from the Plans Division at the Admiralty to implement it. They proved preoccupied but he managed to make a pitch direct to Churchill who approved the idea on the spot and on 24 August Tyrwhitt, who had gone to sea and was 100 miles from Harwich, was summoned to the Admiralty to thrash out the details.

The plan that emerged involved an inshore run from north to south along the German coast at 0400 followed by a sweep westward at 0800, when it was considered that the German patrols would be back in port and the day patrols out to seaward where they could be attacked. The Harwich Force would carry out the sweep and the 8th Submarine Flotilla would lie in wait close off the German harbours to intercept any vessels in transit either way. The 2nd Battle Cruiser Squadron of *New Zealand* and *Invincible*, based at the Humber, was to act in support if necessary.

Keyes and Tyrwhitt asked for Rear Admiral Sir David Beatty's battlecruiser force to be available in case heavy German units came out, but this was rejected by the Chief of the Naval Staff, Vice Admiral Frederick Doveton Sturdee. Accordingly, the commodores let the matter drop and the operation was decided upon for the early morning of 28 August. But when Jellicoe was informed of the plan, he was told that in fact the battlecruisers could support the sweep; then for good measure, Jellicoe added the 1st Light Cruiser Squadron (1 LCS) of Commodore William Goodenough, HMS *Southampton* (flag), *Birmingham*, *Nottingham*, *Falmouth*, *Liverpool* and *Lowestoft*, 'Town'-class vessels mounting eight 6in guns. Nor did anyone tell Keyes and Tyrwhitt who were now at sea; a radio message sent was not received and no check was made as to its receipt.[*]

Meanwhile, at last Tyrwhitt's heart's desire had been fulfilled, for he was allocated the brand-new light cruiser HMS *Arethusa*, lead ship of a class of eight, and named after a Greek Nereid. The type was conceived before the war to lead destroyer flotillas and defend the fleet against attacks by enemy destroyers. She was armed with two 6in and six 4in guns, with a 3pdr AA and four torpedo tubes. Fuelled by oil, cleaner and more efficient than coal, *Arethusa* was powered by eight boilers driving four steam turbines and four shafts with a design speed of 28.5 knots.

---

[*] A message was sent to Harwich where no attempt was made to forward it by W/T and it lay there until their return.

The light cruiser HMS *Aurora* (1913) at moorings off Harwich. She was a sister ship to Tyrwhitt's flagship, HMS *Arethusa*. (Author's collection)

She was just leaving the builder's hands when Tyrwhitt took her over in Harwich harbour at 0900 on 26 August. He was both delighted and concerned. 'She's a flyer and a ripper,' he confided to his brother Beauchamp, 'but it is rather a trial having a new ship's company and new guns. Everything new . . . I expect we shall soon get it in order but I would like to have a week to do it.'[2] The following day, *Arethusa* and *Fearless* led thirty-one destroyers out to sea while *Lurcher* and *Firedrake* took nine submarines; and they all headed for battle.

The Battle of Heligoland Bight

The time was 0330 on 28 August. It was a calm and foggy morning; indeed, the mist hung around all day and made conditions difficult for both sides. Visibility was restricted to three miles. Tyrwhitt had just sighted Goodenough's cruisers, which he had not been told were in the vicinity. He thought they were German and was about to open fire; but he challenged first and was somewhat relieved to find out who they were. Amazingly, he had to ask them if they were taking part in the action. Goodenough replied in the affirmative and further enlightened him that Beatty and the battlecruisers were somewhere to the northwest in support. A day of confusion had started as it was to continue.

At 0400, Tyrwhitt commenced his sweep from north to south with 3 DF in divisions in line ahead and with *Fearless* leading 1 DF two miles astern. For the next three hours they proceeded without incident. However, the Germans had got wind of what was coming and had made dispositions to turn the tables. Prisoner statements later revealed that wireless signals shortly before

The light cruiser *Fearless*, leader of 1 DF at Heligoland Bight.
(US Naval History and Heritage Command NH 61045)

midnight had indicated the approach of a strong force of destroyers and instead of the usual patrol being sent out, a counter plan was put in place. The idea was to send out some ships as bait to draw the British flotillas inside the Bight and to sail light cruisers to cut in behind them.

The stratagem worked. Tyrwhitt sighted an enemy destroyer, SMS *G-194*, around 0700 and hauled off after her, into the Bight. She and the rest of her flotilla turned to run for home and called for coastal artillery support, but the batteries could not tell friend from foe in the mist and withheld their fire. The two sides opened fire, inflicting no damage at long range. But now the German cruisers came up in support, *Stettin* (1905) and *Frauenlob* (1903), each sporting ten 4.1in guns, and *Arethusa* became heavily engaged with both.

Although the flotilla gave what aid it could, it soon became clear that *Arethusa* was badly handicapped. She had only had one target practice shoot and that had been discontinued because her brand-new semi-automatic 4in guns kept jamming; now they did the same in battle. Soon shells were hitting home, one setting fire to some cordite charges.

Fearless then arrived and engaged *Stettin*, which made off to the southeast with 1 DF following while *Arethusa* continued to battle *Frauenlob*, largely alone for her flotilla 'were attending to a tramp which, though flying Norwegian colours, seemed to be trying to cross ahead of the *Arethusa* in order to lay mines. Others were smashing up a small torpedo boat, which ran in from the westward, and though they thought they sank her she was eventually taken in in a pitiable state, lashed between two destroyers.'[3]

The drive to the west should have started at 0800 and at 0825 Tyrwhitt, noting that they were now too close to the coast, gave orders for it to commence. It was not a moment too soon for his flagship for she had only one gun, a 6in, in working order and both torpedo tubes were smashed.

Later Tyrwhitt wrote that 'we had twenty-five minutes hard at it and I can only wonder that everyone on the upper deck was not killed. The air seemed thick with bursting shells and the sea was alive with splashes from shell and splinters . . . both our torpedo tubes were shot to bits, fifteen hits on the side, eight of which penetrated and did great damage.'[4] Fortunately, with her parting shot, *Arethusa* landed a shell from her remaining gun on the enemy's fore bridge, killing thirty-seven men, including the captain, and causing her to sheer off. Tyrwhitt reformed his flotillas and headed westward.

Progress was slow for the feed tank had been holed and 'her engineer commander reported that he could only now get twelve knots . . . out of her'.[5] And breakfast would be late too; *Arethusa*'s cook, Robert Marner, preparing the morning repast in the galley, had one of his arms shot off. He saved himself from bleeding to death when 'seeing an empty cigarette tin, promptly clapped it on the stump and so saved his life'.[6] His mate, Fred Nunn, was killed.

Meanwhile, Goodenough's cruisers had heard the firing and steamed towards the sound of the guns. At around 0835, *Southampton* saw two black shapes, which revealed themselves to be German destroyers, travelling very quickly on her starboard bow. They had been patrolling seawards and hearing the firing in between themselves and the German coast, they were headed for home and safety. *Southampton* opened fire but the mist prevented any accuracy and the Germans replied with torpedoes which also missed their targets. The enemy disappeared into the fret.

At this point, Keyes in *Lurcher* observed 1 LCS through the mist; again, he had no knowledge that they were in the action and reported them as German cruisers. Goodenough picked up the message and the position given was a few miles to the southwest of where 1 LCS calculated they were. 'This sounded like business, so we abandoned our intention of trying to find the destroyer scrap and hastily shaped course to where we understood the two German cruisers had been seen. Sad to say, we were chasing ourselves; the discrepancy in our position and that calculated by the *Lurcher*, led us astray, and for about an hour we were on a wild-goose chase.'[7]

The six ships of 1 LCS continued to chase themselves for 50 minutes until

> suddenly everyone was electrified to see a periscope on the starboard
> bow, distant 500 yards. The helm was put over, the ship heeled and we
> prepared to ram her. The submarine made a steep dive and went down
> at such an angle that her tail nearly came out of the water ... About ten
> minutes later, the destroyer *Lurcher* appeared, flying the pennant of
> Roger Keyes who asked us why we were attacking his submarines.[8]

The cruisers hadn't been briefed to look out for British submarines. They had been trying to ram HMS *E-6*.

Meanwhile, as Tyrwhitt's forces swept westward, they ran into the German large torpedo boat *V-187*. Launched in 1911, she carried four torpedo tubes and two 8.8cm (about 3.5in) guns. She was a flotilla leader's boat and had been scouting beyond visual distance, but on getting a wireless signal from another destroyer that she was being chased, was steaming about east-southeast to her assistance. After making the challenge Captain Blunt in *Fearless* opened fire and ordered the 5th Division to chase. But now came a signal from Keyes, who had been searching for enemy submarines, according to the plan. He seemed to be coming in from seaward, and Captain Blunt, fearing it might be the *Lurcher* he was attacking, ceased fire and cancelled the signal to chase. He then lost sight of *V-187*, which appeared to have turned away.

In fact she was heading towards Heligoland in poor visibility when four British destroyers, *Goshawk*, *Lizard*, *Lapwing* and *Phoenix* of the 5th Division, again sighted her at about 0925. She turned and fled at her best speed (some 32 knots) towards the Jade estuary with the four destroyers in pursuit. But then the German torpedo boat saw part of 1 LCS to the west and reversed course away from them and back towards the pursuing destroyers. At top speed and in poor visibility, she manged to burst past them without damage but then ran into another division comprising *Ferret*, *Forester*, *Druid* and *Defender*, dead ahead. Trapped between two groups of destroyers, *V-187* came under heavy shelling at close range which set her afire and brought the torpedo boat to a standstill. Blunt, thinking her finished, took two of his divisions away to re-join Tyrwhitt and left two to deal with the German. Now followed one of those tragic misunderstandings of war. The British destroyers lowered boats to rescue *V-187*'s crew, but believing that the British were attempting to board the torpedo boat, she fired on *Goshawk*. The destroyers then opened fire on the German once more and she sank at 1010.

Once again, the Harwich Force vessels attempted a rescue, lowering their boats to facilitate it, but now *Stettin* arrived on the scene and opened fire, causing the destroyers to withdraw. Two of *Defender*'s boats had to be abandoned, carrying twenty-eight survivors of the enemy crew and ten British rescuers. 'Imagine their feelings; alone in an open boat without food, twenty-five miles from the nearest land, and that land the enemy's fortress, with nothing but fog and foes around them.'[9]

This tricky situation was resolved later in the day by one of Keyes's submarines, *E-4*, under the command of clergyman's son Lieutenant Commander Ernest William Leir. She surfaced by the two boats and took off the British sailors and three of the Germans. As the *Spectator* magazine described it, 'suddenly a swirl alongside and up, if you please, pops his Britannic Majesty's submarine *E-4*, opens his conning tower, takes them all on board, shuts up again, dives, and brings them home two hundred and fifty miles! Is not that magnificent? No novel would dare face the critics with an episode like that in it except, perhaps, Jules Verne.'[10]

Leir had no room for the remaining members of *V-187*'s crew, so gave them food and water and a course to sail for Heligoland. Such chivalrous behaviour would not survive many more years of war. In all twenty-four of the torpedo boat's crew were killed, fourteen wounded and thirty-three taken prisoner.

Keyes now knew that the 1st Light Cruiser Squadron was taking part; but his submarines did not. According to the plan, they would now be moving westwards; it was impossible to warn them of the situation so Goodenough considered it best to retire out of the danger area. And by now Beatty and his ships had arrived and they were marking time just outside the action area, turning circles and waiting for developments.

If the action so far can be considered in phases, this might be called the end of the second phase, and so far pickings had been slim. This was about to change as a sweep, which had become a series of short engagements, became a melee.

SMS *Strassburg*, German light cruiser of twelve 4in guns, launched in 1911 and pictured underway. She engaged *Arethusa* at the Battle of Heligoland Bight. (Author's collection)

Badly damaged, *Arethusa* could only make 10 knots, and Tyrwhitt ordered *Fearless* and 1 DF to keep the flagship in sight in case of trouble. Meanwhile, armourers and gun crews worked feverishly at getting the guns back in working order and by 1045 all except two 4in were back on line.

It was just as well for a third German light cruiser now appeared, SMS *Strassburg* (1911) coming up from the southeast. She carried twelve 4.1in guns with two torpedo tubes and represented a formidable opponent for the semi-crippled flagship. Shells fell alongside *Arethusa*, although none hit, as *Strassburg* opened fire; Tyrwhitt urgently called for a full flotilla attack from 1 DF and in the face of this *Strassburg* pulled away. Tyrwhitt thought this may be a ruse to lead his ships back towards Heligoland, so he called off the chase and resumed his western progress.

Now the destroyers sighted another German light cruiser, SMS *Mainz* (twelve 4.1in guns), off the port bow and headed in a northerly direction across Tyrwhitt's path. She had been lying at Borkum but had been ordered to come to the aid of her sister ships. But as the flotilla prepared to engage, she turned away through 16 points; for *Mainz* had just seen Goodenough's 1 LCS coming down from the north, following the sound of the guns.

Meanwhile, *Stettin* reappeared and was driven off and *Strassburg* returned to recommence her shelling of *Arethusa*. Tyrwhitt came under such sustained and heavy fire that he signalled to Beatty that he needed help and sent 1 DF to attack with torpedoes. No hits were made, but his assailant was driven away.

The 'L'-class destroyer HMS *Laurel*, badly damaged at the Battle of Heligoland Bight.
(© Imperial War Museum RP 2433)

The Harwich Force once more headed westwards; but now suddenly came upon the *Mainz*, fleeing from 1 LCS.

Arethusa and *Fearless* immediately engaged her and Tyrwhitt sent in his destroyers for a torpedo attack. It was repulsed by a torrent of gunfire; *Laurel* was hit in the engine room, blowing away a 4in gun, half a funnel and wounding her captain, Commander Frank Forester Rose, in both legs. He remained on the bridge until he collapsed from loss of blood, whereupon Lieutenant Charles Reid Peploe took command. The smoke and steam pouring from the damaged destroyer spoilt *Mainz*'s aim and *Laurel* slipped away. On board *Liberty* her commanding officer, Lieutenant Commander Nigel Kenneth Walter Barttelot, was killed. First a shell took one leg off and then another decapitated him. Like *Laurel*, *Liberty* could take no further part in the action.

Laertes was rocked by a salvo of four shells; her boiler room was damaged, temporarily cutting off all steam to the engines, leaving the ship motionless. Another shot destroyed the middle funnel, while a gun was also hit. The ship would probably have been lost were it not for the prompt action of two men; Stoker Petty Officer Frederick Pierce was in the engine room when a shell exploded in number two boiler. Blinded by smoke, in danger of death by scalding from escaping steam and breathing in the fumes of spent explosive, he 'behaved with conspicuous coolness and resource' in acting to prevent further damage. Pierce later died from burns received. And Stoker Petty Officer Stephen Pritchard 'gallantly dived into a cabin flat immediately after a shell exploded there and worked a fire hose'.[11] In a red-hot inferno of smoke, flames and terrific heat Pritchard finally got the blaze under control. Both men were later awarded the DSM. Two crewmen were killed outright and nine severely wounded. While *Laertes* was seriously damaged and stopped in the water, *Lapwing*, under the command of Lieutenant Commander Alexander Hugh Gye, went to her aid despite heavy fire and manoeuvred to pass a tow. However, it parted in getting underway.

Fearless became engaged with *Stettin* once again and then found herself the target of attack from two new opponents, *Cöln* (1909, twelve 4.1in) and *Ariadne* (1900, ten 4.1in). There could be no doubt that Tyrwhitt and his ships were up against it. Men were dying, falling at their posts, still trying to keep the guns firing and the engines running. In the mist and fog crews and ships were taking a terrible battering.

But so now was the *Mainz*; turning away from another destroyer attack she blundered into 1 LCS. 'As soon as the *Mainz* saw us, she ceased fire on the sorely tried *Arethusa* and very wisely fled like a stag. At 10,000 yards the squadron opened fire, and the German replied with a straggling fire from her after 4.1in guns. Most of her shots fell short but a few hummed over us.'[12]

The German light cruiser SMS *Mainz* (1909), destroyed at the Battle of Heligoland Bight in 1914. (US Naval History and Heritage Command NH 46822)

SMS *Mainz* was now under the fire of about fifteen 6in guns and suddenly two yellow flashes amidships were seen as she was hit twice. But it was nigh impossible to spot the fall of shot properly in the mist at the range of 10,000 yards. In the gloom, 1 LCS lost track of her prey. But when she reappeared, she was stopped. The torpedo attacks had taken their toll[*] and gunnery salvos poured into *Mainz*. After ten minutes of this punishment her crew began to abandon ship. *Southampton* signalled in International Code 'Do you surrender?' A boatswain lowered her ensign in response; and her main mast slowly toppled to the deck. Admiral von Tirpitz's son Wolfgang calmly stepped out of the control top, now lying on the deck, and walked away into captivity. 'She . . . lay a smoking battered wreck, her anchor flush with the water. Ant-like figures could be seen jumping into the water as we approached.'[13] Keyes took *Lurcher* right alongside the sinking German and at considerable risk to his ship lifted 200 crewmen off.

Arethusa was still in difficulties and *Fearless* was engaged in an unequal battle with *Stettin* and *Cöln*; but then the cavalry arrived. Beatty had to consider that the Bight might be mined and that its confined waters were dangerous for his big ships (the action was still only 28 miles from Heligoland due to the constant fighting). But he also had a duty to rescue the flotilla and had received Tyrwhitt's signal. He hesitated; to his Flag Captain, Ernle Chatfield, Beatty said that 'I ought to go forward and support Tyrwhitt, but if

---

[*] Later analysis showed that twenty-four torpedoes were fired at her by seventeen ships with eleven claimed hits.

The 'Town'-class light cruiser HMS *Southampton* in a painting by Oscar Parkes. Launched in 1912, she mounted eight 6in guns with a design speed of 25.5 knots. (Author's collection)

I lose one of these valuable ships the country will not forgive me'. Chatfield replied that 'surely we must go',[14] which convinced Beatty to order all five battlecruisers* to head for the action at full speed.

He later convincingly justified his decision:

> The situation appeared to me critical. The flotillas had advanced only ten miles since 0800, and were only about twenty-five miles from two enemy bases on their flank and rear respectively. Commodore Goodenough had detached two of his light cruisers to assist some destroyers earlier in the day, and these had not yet rejoined. As the reports indicated the presence of many enemy ships – one a large cruiser – I considered that his force might not be strong enough to deal with the situation sufficiently rapidly, so at 1130 the battlecruisers turned to E S E, and worked up to full speed. It was evident that to be of any value the support must be overwhelming and carried out at the highest speed possible.[15]

---

* HMS *Lion*, *Queen Mary*, *Princess Royal*, *New Zealand* and *Invincible*.

Beatty's flagship at Heligoland Bight, Dogger Bank and Jutland, HMS *Lion* (1910) as pictured in 1919. She mounted eight 13.5in guns with a top speed of 28 knots.
(US Naval History and Heritage Command NH 77291)

His magnificent ships ploughed on towards the last position Tyrwhitt had given and burst out of the mist and into the battle at 1237. Lieutenant King-Hall later wrote:

> It is difficult to describe the impression produced by these monsters as, following in each other's wakes, they emerged one by one from the mist and flashed past like express trains . . . volumes of smoke poured from their funnels, their turrets trained expectantly . . . a succession of salvos rolled out from *Lion* and her squadron. One German disappeared in a cloud of steam and smoke; the other drifted away in the mist, burning furiously and sinking.[16]

Beatty arrived just in time to rescue *Fearless*. His ships destroyed *Cöln*; fired on by *New Zealand*, she was hit several times, but managed to slip away to the north. About 15 minutes later, she turned back southeast to return to port and ran into Beatty's ships again. After two of *Lion*'s 13.5in shells had hit home she was abandoned and sank at 1425.

Ariadne was struck several times by the British guns and one shell penetrated the forward boiler room. Coal bunkers caught fire and five boilers were disabled. Two of the battlecruisers closed to just over 3,000 yards range and poured in salvos. With fires raging fore and aft, *Ariadne* flooded her forward magazine to prevent the flames reaching the her ammunition. Beatty allowed her to limp away and she was abandoned and sank.

Stettin, coming to aid *Ariadne*, was set ablaze but manged to escape, ten salvos all missing her. The battlecruisers held the field; they had fought in exactly the way that their creator, Admiral Sir John Fisher, had conceived, overpowering light forces with speed and firepower. Tyrwhitt signalled to his ships 'Retire' at 1300.

It still remained for Tyrwhitt to get his battered cruiser home. She struggled on until 1900 when her engines stopped altogether and the commodore had to wireless for assistance. Two hours later, the bulk of a ship loomed out of the darkness and a voice shouted 'Is that you Reggie'? It was HMS *Hogue* and his old friend Captain Wilmot Nicholson. 'I was never so glad to see him before,' Tyrwhitt wrote later.[17] *Hogue* 'took my ship in tow in a most seamanlike manner, and, observing that the night was pitch dark and the only lights showing were two small hand lanterns'[18] and brought her back to Sheerness, where Churchill was awaiting them.

There the First Lord came aboard and came with them up to Chatham. He 'fairly slobbered' over Tyrwhitt, promising him any ship he liked as his replacement flagship.[19] To his wife Tyrwhitt wrote 'it was really awfully fine and not quite half so unpleasant as I expected . . . we lost eleven killed including poor Westmacott [his signals officer of 48 hours standing] who was killed at my side . . . we had fifteen direct hits . . . besides shrapnel holes'.[20]

SMS *Ariadne* (1900), sunk by the battlecruisers at Heligoland Bight in 1914.
(Author's collection)

Lieutenant Eric Walter Poyntz Westmacott was an outstanding hockey player, a left wing who had represented the Royal Navy in 1912 and 1914. He was struck down by a random piece of shrapnel; a foot or so the other way, it would have killed Tyrwhitt.

Heligoland Bight was a clear British victory: three German light cruisers and a torpedo boat were sunk and three light cruisers damaged with 1,242 Germans killed, captured or wounded. The Royal Navy had one light cruiser and three destroyers damaged but lost no ships. Forty British sailors were killed and fifty-six wounded. As for the damaged destroyers, *Laurel* was able to sail back to Harwich at just 10 knots. After transferring her wounded, *Liberty* was able to return to port without assistance. *Laertes* recovered only a little power and had to be towed back to harbour.

The battle could so easily have gone the other way; neither Keyes nor Tyrwhitt knew that Beatty or 1 LCS were in support and had they not decisively intervened, the result could have been very different. The German battlecruisers SMS *Moltke* and *Von der Tann* were ordered out but could not pass the Jade Bar until 1200, owing to low tide. They did not in fact cross it until 1400 as the German staff had expected the British to advance to the river mouths and attack their heavy ships as they emerged; U-boats were positioned for that eventuality. The German battlecruisers were further delayed as Hipper ordered them to wait until he joined them with his flagship, *Seydlitz*, which had been hampered by condenser problems. If they had come out in a timely manner, they might have done to the Harwich Force what Beatty was able to do to the German light cruisers.

Moreover, Tyrwhitt was probably wrong to take out an untried and untrained cruiser and in having it severely damaged, cost the navy a valuable resource and scarce dockyard time at a moment of considerable threat. He later justified himself in a letter to his sister; 'everything about her new and untried. I could not refuse to take her or I might have never seen her again, but I did have misgivings.'[21]

The planning of the raid was poor. As Lieutenant King-Hall later noted, 'as may be deduced from these extracts, the staff work was almost criminally negligent and it was a near miracle that we did not sink one of our submarines or that one of them did not sink us'.[22] As historian Richard Hough has highlighted, 'the irony was that in the Battle of Heligoland Bight all these staff failings were manifested but a minor victory had been achieved and a disaster avoided by old-time individualism and blind courage, assisted by more than a fair share of luck.'[23]

There was little co-ordination between the different squadrons and flotillas and communications were poor. As well as the failure to tell Keyes and Tyrwhitt that they were being supported by Beatty and Goodenough, Keyes and Tyrwhitt did not give the speeds and courses of their ships when requesting assistance. As for the Germans, they mistakenly assumed that British light forces would not be backed up by heavy ships. They also committed their light cruisers piecemeal.

For the British public, however, it was a major success; 'Navy's Smashing Blow at the German Fleet: Great Victory in the North Sea' screamed the *Daily News and Leader*.[24] Captain Blunt was awarded the DSO 'in recognition of his repeated vigorous and dashing attacks on the enemy'.[25] As for Tyrwhitt, he became a hero overnight. He was made a Companion of the Order of the Bath (CB) and became a household name. Angey was proud; but also worried. 'It's so glorious to think that Reggie did such splendid work but I shall be terrified when I know he is out for blood again.'[26]

However, Beatty, who relished praise, was disappointed that he did not get the recognition he felt he deserved. Writing to his wife Ethel he commented that he was 'not so much disappointed as disgusted . . . my real opinion has been confirmed that they would have hung me if there had been a disaster'.[27] He did eventually receive a letter of appreciation from the Admiralty, via Jellicoe.

Meanwhile, the Germans decided to replace their patrol system with mines. By September, they had laid minefields to the west of Heligoland and placed greater reliance on trawlers and other small craft for routine patrols. Kaiser Wilhelm became even more determined not to risk his nice shiny battlefleet.* He ordered that it was not to fight any action outside the Bight or the Skagerrak and even inside the Bight it was to avoid action with superior forces. Occasional sorties by the battlecruisers were permitted and U-boats, destroyers and minelayers were encouraged to act energetically.

*   *   *

As a replacement for *Arethusa*, Tyrwhitt was given the 'Town'-class *Lowestoft* (1913), loaned from 1 LCS. He disliked her; 'slower and rather too big for my job. I shall be glad to get back to A [*sic*] as it is very unsatisfactory always hunting one's hounds with new horses and new hunt servants.'[28]

Keyes and Tyrwhitt put together another plan for a joint sweep towards the Bight, where the German patrols were still operating (for the moment), setting out on 8 September for an operation on the 10th. The Grand Fleet

---

* Kaiser Wilhelm II saw the fleet as his personal property; 'Willie's toys', as King Edward VII once called them. 'The Kaiser ignored [von Tirpitz's] urgent request that he be granted a free hand in directing the operations of the fleet and retained in command Admiral von Ingenohl, an officer of mediocre ability, who owed his advancement to the personal friendship of the Supreme Warlord and to prolonged service on the Imperial Yacht' (Bywater, *Strange Intelligence*, p 43).

A builder's model of the 'M'-class destroyer HMS *Mastiff*, which served at Harwich in the 1st and 3rd Destroyer Flotillas. She was one of the Thornycroft-built variants of the standard design and all six of the company's 'M'-class destroyers were faster than the Admiralty's boats. In addition to the higher freeboard, their distinguishing characteristic was the flat-sided middle funnel. Developing 6,800 horsepower more than the standard vessel's designed output, *Mastiff* reached 37.5 knots on her trials and in 1915 was reputed to be the fastest warship afloat. (© National Maritime Museum SLR0110)

came down from Scapa to within 100 miles of the Bight in case any heavy units could be tempted out. But the flotillas ran into a thunderstorm and sighted not a single German ship of any description.

Among the vessels which took part in this abortive operation was a new addition to the Harwich Force, the 'M'-class destroyer *Miranda* which had been delivered from Yarrow's River Clyde yard on 29 August. She was the first of a new class, fast (34–35 knots), three 4in and four torpedo tubes. These 'Ms' arrived in dribs and drabs throughout the next few months and became part of 3 DF but were eventually formed into an additional unit of the Harwich Force, the 10th Destroyer Flotilla, in mid-1915.[*]

But success attended the Harwich submarines. At dawn on 13 September 1914 HMS *E-9*, under the command of Lieutenant Commander Max Kennedy Horton, torpedoed the old German flotilla leader SMS *Hela* (1895) six miles southwest of Heligoland. *Hela* was of an obsolete type, armed with four 8.8cm (3.5in) and six 5cm (2in) guns plus three torpedo tubes, and had been used as a tender for the fleet from October 1910 through to the outbreak of war. She was then deployed in the patrols in and around the Bight and had been present at, although not engaged in, the Battle of Heligoland Bight. When she was sunk, the vessel had been conducting a training cruise. Hit amidships by two torpedoes, at a range of 600 yards, she sank within 30 minutes. But, in a

---

[*] The Admiralty-designed 'M' class were the standard destroyers of the First World War. More than eighty were built to the Admiralty's standard specification and a further twenty-nine were constructed according to individual builders' plans. The 'M' design was repeated in 1916, with only slight modifications, and known as the Admiralty 'R' class.

A lithograph by Hugo Graf of the German flotilla leader *Hela* (1895) torpedoed by HMS *E-9* on 13 September 1914. (Author's collection)

testament to the ship's discipline, all but two of her crew were rescued by *U-18* and another German vessel.

Horton was chased by anti-submarine forces throughout the day but made in back to Harwich safely. As he entered harbour, he flew the Jolly Roger, instituting the tradition for submarines returning from successful combat patrols. And *E-9* chalked up another Harwich success three weeks later, when Horton sank the destroyer *S-116* (1902) on 6 October off the mouth of the Ems. He was awarded the DSO for these two achievements.[29]

A Player's Navy Cut tobacco and cigarettes advert citing the success of *E-9* in the sinking of the *Hela* and *S-116*, as published in the *Illustrated London News* of 19 December 1914. (Author's collection)

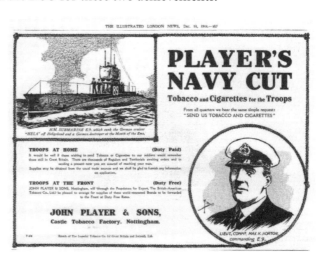

Foolhardiness

On 14 September, both Tyrwhitt and Keyes were ordered to a conference in Scotland with Churchill, Jellicoe and other senior officers. Here Churchill pressed his plans for a major assault on, and capture of, Heligoland together with his idea (more likely Fisher's acting as éminence grise) for an attack on Kiel from the Baltic by destroyers and light cruisers – i.e. by Tyrwhitt.

Both of these schemes were rejected. Jellicoe wrote that 'the reduction of Heligoland would involve far more serious losses in capital ships than would compensate for any advantage gained'.[30] As for the Baltic idea, Tyrwhitt was even more forthright.

> I threw cold water on the proposals of two very distinguished admirals whose proposals were the equivalent of a death warrant of a very large number of officers and men, besides being impossible and displaying considerable ignorance of the defences of Germany. It was not pleasant . . . as it is not easy to disagree with the proposals of people who are old enough to be my father but at the same time I was not going to agree to murdering half of my command and what is more I carried my point.[31]

Churchill, of whom Tyrwhitt nonetheless wrote 'I like him and admire him intensely apart from his politics',[32] retreated with his tail between his legs.

Horton's success aside, September was a poor month for the Royal Navy. On the 5th, the scout cruiser *Pathfinder* was torpedoed off St Abbs Head with the loss of most of its 270 crew. Then on the 22nd three old cruisers – known officially as Cruiser Force C but unofficially as the 'live bait squadron' – were patrolling off the Dutch coast in the Broad Fourteens. Tyrwhitt had argued for their withdrawal, as had Keyes and other senior officers; their opinions had been dismissed by Sturdee as showing a lack of knowledge of naval history. A Broad Fourteens patrol, he averred, was necessary to keep the Scheldt open. Force C had originally been stationed there to provide cover for the crossing of the BEF and because of a concern that the Germans might try to block the Scheldt estuary, and then left in position. But now the cruisers were performing no useful duty and were extremely exposed. At 0625, first HMS *Aboukir*, then *Hogue* (at 0655), then finally *Cressy* (at 0735) were all torpedoed by *U-9*.

In foul weather, Tyrwhitt was out at sea in *Lowestoft* when he picked up the news. As the weather abated, he set course for the scene and on arrival found the waters full of men and boats awaiting rescue. 'We went first up to a small English trawler which was loaded with men. They looked just like rows and rows of swallows on a telegraph line, all huddled together to keep themselves warm, they were all naked or nearly so.'[33]

At this point, the commodore received no less than three U-boat warnings; he threw a protective screen of destroyers in a circle around the scene and got his ships' boats out in heavy seas to save who could be saved. His friend Nicholson had been the last to leave his ship, as tradition enjoined, walking from the bridge and onto her bottom as *Hogue* turned over. He survived. Sixty-two officers and 1,397 men were lost. A public, which had eagerly anticipated some major new Trafalgar and the sweeping from the seas of the German fleet, was feeling disappointed.

Nor did the advent of October bring any relief. Whilst the Harwich Force continued patrolling in the North Sea, much further north the 10th Cruiser Squadron was attempting to operate the distant blockade of Germany. On the 15th, the squadron was on patrol off Aberdeen, deployed in line abreast at intervals of about 10 miles. The old (1891) *Edgar*-class cruiser HMS *Hawke* stopped at 0930 to pick up mail from her sister ship *Endymion*. After recovering her boat with the mail, *Hawke* proceeded at 13 knots, without zig-zagging, to regain her station. She was out of sight of the rest of the squadron when at 1030 a torpedo from the same German U-boat as had accounted for the three cruisers in the Broad Fourteens, *U-9*, torpedoed her; *Hawke* quickly capsized and sank. A search for the missing ship found a raft carrying one officer and twenty-one men, while a boat with a further forty-nine survivors was rescued by a Norwegian steamer. Five hundred and twenty-four officers and men died, including the ship's captain, Hugh Williams.

A ray of light shone on Harwich, however, for *Arethusa* returned from repairs and her sister ship *Aurora* joined the squadron; she was soon to be under the command of Tyrwhitt's friend Wilmot Nicholson. Another *Arethusa*-class vessel arrived at Harwich at the same time, HMS *Undaunted*, commanded by another returnee, Captain Cecil Fox, now recovered from his wounds. This meant that 1 DF could revert to his leadership. Two days after the loss of *Hawke*, Fox was able to bring some much-needed lustre to the navy's name and that of the Harwich Force.

Fox Bags Some Hounds

At the beginning of October, the army decided to move the BEF to a position on the sea flank and this meant opening up new lines of communication to Dunkirk and shortly afterwards Ostend. The navy would have to guard the transports. On 5 October, for example, both Keyes and Tyrwhitt were ordered to protect the crossing of the 7th Division during its transit from Dover to Zeebrugge.[34]

Additionally, a minefield was to be laid in the southern North Sea to provide a barrier against interference in these movements by U-boats and the minelayers needed destroyer protection too. This threw fresh patrolling responsibility on the Harwich Force's shoulders and put paid to any further plans for incursions into the Bight. On top of that, the weather was still very rough and this meant days of 'rolling, rolling, rolling, watchkeeping, sleeping and at intervals eating something which did not need cooking'.[35]

But Antwerp fell to the Germans on 13 October. Tyrwhitt took his forces to the coast to try to prevent U-boats getting in and basing themselves there. Two of his ships were attacked by submarines without success and the Germans continued to press the Belgian army so the bulk of the Dover Patrol had to be committed to coastal operations in support of them and the French. There was little or nothing left to guard the entrance to the Channel except the Harwich flotillas. To cover continued army transfers they were maintaining a watch in the Broad Fourteens.

Information had been coming in of activity by the German flotillas in the Bight. In the evening of the 16th it became more definite. German destroyers had been seen in the Bight once more and Fox took *Undaunted* and the First Division of his flotilla (*Lance, Lennox, Legion* and *Loyal*) to investigate. At 1400 the following day they were steaming about 50 miles southwest of Texel Island, like Terschelling one of the Friesian Islands and best known for its breed of wool-producing sheep.

Suddenly, they saw a squadron of four German torpedo boats, comprising the vessels from the 7th Half Flotilla SMS *S-115, S-117, S-118* and the leader *S-119*, about eight miles ahead, steaming in line abreast about half a mile from each other, heading east. These vessels were of an old type, designed in 1898 and completed in 1904. Although nearly equal in speed to the British at 28 knots, they were inferior in armament, with three 5cm (2in) guns. The biggest danger to the British squadron was the five 17.7in torpedoes carried by each German boat. All of Fox's ships outranged the Germans; the destroyers had three 4in guns and his cruiser seven 4in and two 6in weapons.

The enemy flotilla was part of the Emden Patrol and had been sent out of the Ems River to assess what British ships there were in the area; hounds looking for a scent. Possibly they hoped to interfere with the Dover Patrol's coastal operations. But one of their number developed a faulty condenser and they were shepherding her back to their base. At first, mistaking the RN ships for their own, the Germans made no attempt to flee. But as realisation dawned, they scattered fan-wise whereupon Fox signalled 'General Chase'. *Lennox* and *Lance* shot off to intercept the easternmost boats and *Legion* and *Loyal* made after the others. *Undaunted* opened fire at the vessel nearest to it.

Fire from *Legion, Loyal* and *Undaunted* damaged *S-118* so badly that her bridge was blown off the deck, sinking her at 1517. *Lance* and *Lennox* engaged *S-115*, disabling her steering gear and causing the German vessel to go round in circles. *Lennox*'s fire also destroyed the bridge of *S-115*.

The 'L'-class destroyer HMS *Legion*, in a picture postcard listing her 'battle honours' obtained while serving with the 3rd Destroyer Flotilla at Harwich. (Author's collection)

The two central boats in the German flotilla, *S-117* and the flotilla leader *S-119*, essayed a torpedo attack on *Undaunted*, which she was able to manoeuvre away from, while *Legion* and *Loyal* finished off *S-118* and then came to aid their flotilla leader. *Legion* attacked *S-117*, which bravely continued to discharge her torpedoes and engage with her guns, but she too lost her steering mechanism and was sunk at 1530.

Lance now joined *Loyal* in firing at *S-119*; the German managed to fire a torpedo which hit *Lance* amidships but failed to explode. But her defiance was short lived and the torpedo boat was sunk in a hail of gunfire at 1535. *S-115* somehow remained afloat despite further shelling by *Lennox*, which in the end sent over a boarding party. They found the ship a complete wreck with only one crew member on board; he was very pleased to surrender. Finally, the little ship went down under fire from *Undaunted* at 1630.

None of the torpedo boats had struck their flags and all fought bravely to the end. One officer and twenty-nine men were pulled from the water, as was the flotilla commander and captain of *S-119*, although he died of his wounds shortly afterwards, while 218 German sailors lost their lives in the action. British casualties were one officer and four men wounded. *Legion* was hit by a shell and *Lance* had some machine-gun damage but otherwise the British ships were unscathed.

Sinking four German vessels was a considerable fillip to the Royal Navy and the nation, coming as it did only two days after the loss of the *Hawke*. Newspapers made the most of it and Captain Cyril Fox had his photo splashed all over the front pages. The *Daily Mirror* was typical. Two days after the action its banner headline screamed 'Brilliant Naval Feat off the Dutch Coast; Victory for the hero of the *Amphion*.'[36] Fox and Commander Wion de Malpas Egerton of *Lance* were pictured.

Moreover, there was an additional and unexpected benefit; on 30 November, a British trawler pulled up the sealed chest thrown overboard from *S-119* by her captain. The chest contained a codebook used by the German light forces stationed on the coast, which helped the British to read German wireless communication for some time afterwards.*

Tyrwhitt, however, was bitterly disappointed that he had again missed out on an action; 'just my luck . . . the very day [Fox] takes on he gets a delightful show' he wrote.[37] But he had a small consolation prize. The following day, Tyrwhitt in *Arethusa* and accompanied by *Meteor* and three other destroyers was on patrol in the Broad Fourteens when they sighted the German hospital ship *Ophelia*, which claimed to have been sent out to rescue survivors from the sunken boats. She had been observed ten days earlier by one of the 8th Flotilla submarines and subsequently kept under investigation. From her movements it was deemed that she was breaking the Geneva Convention by acting as a scout. *Meteor* was sent to board and investigate the vessel and as she approached the German ship observed *Ophelia*'s captain throw overboard a number of documents and secret codes. Tyrwhitt seized the vessel as a spy ship,† and telegraphed the Admiralty to inform them that she had been 'making wireless reports and acting as a scout' while supposedly a hospital ship.[38]

The German navy was forced to change tactics in the English Channel and along the coast of Flanders. There were fewer sorties into the Channel and the torpedo boat force was relegated to coastal patrol and rescuing aircrew.

---

* This was the VB, or Verkehrsbuch, code, which translates as 'traffic' or 'transport' book. It was used by small patrol craft, submarines and attachés. The other two German naval codes were SKM, used for the bulk of daily messages, and HVB. The Admiralty could read them all, through its Room 40 code-breaking section, by December.

† She was subsequently put into British service as SS *Huntly* and sunk by *UB-10* on 20 December 1915.

4

Yarmouth, Scarborough and Cuxhaven, October–December 1914

The German battlefleet had been built on the principle, first adumbrated by Admiral Alfred von Tirpitz, of 'Risikoflotte', the risk fleet. In essence this posited that, if the Kaiserliche Marine (German Imperial Navy) reached a certain level of strength relative to the Royal Navy, the British would try to avoid confrontation with Germany. The belief was that if the two navies fought in opposition, the German Navy would inflict sufficient damage on the Royal Navy such that Britain would lose its naval dominance and sovereignty of the sea, crucial to maintaining control over the British Empire.

But as the German fleet grew, financed by successive German Naval Laws and championed by Kaiser Wilhelm II personally, Britain responded in kind. The irony of Tirpitz's strategy was that it forced Britain to focus its attention on the North Sea, build better and more technologically advanced ships and come to an accommodation with its traditional enemy, France.

The German battlefleet was named the High Sea Fleet (Hochseeflotte) in 1907 (it had previously been known as the Home Fleet). But unlike the original theory, it now faced the entire might of the Grand Fleet. Japan had destroyed the Russian Navy in 1904–05 (up until then Russia had been seen as a probable naval enemy for Britain). The concentration of ships in home waters, rendered possible by reducing the presence in the Mediterranean Sea and allowing the French to shoulder more of the burden there, made even more ships available for the North Sea. The final nail in the coffin of the 'risk fleet' was that Britain adopted distant blockade, rather than the close blockade anticipated, and therefore the fleet was not regularly exposed in the confined waters of the North Sea.

Thus German naval strategy from the start of the war quickly evolved to one in which the Admiralstab (the German Imperial Admiralty Staff) would try to engineer a situation whereby a portion of the Royal Navy's capital ships could be isolated and overwhelmed by a larger German force, or drawn over minefields and U-boat concentrations, thus whittling away at Britain's naval strength. Provocations intended to draw out the British ships included coastal raids, Zeppelin attacks and assaults on trade.

*   *   *

Near the end of October 1914, the Royal Navy went through an upheaval at the very top. First Sea Lord Prince Louis of Battenberg had been under attack for his German heritage before war broke out and on the advent of conflict things grew worse. He felt it deeply and also thought it unfair. In Parliament and in the press he was reviled, particularly after the naval reverses of September and October. Battenberg was suffering from gout and the naval staff he had created failed to function properly, throwing more onus on him. Additionally, Churchill's meddling was driving him to a nervous breakdown. He asked to resign and after some difficulty with his Cabinet colleagues and the king, Churchill replaced him on the 30th with the septuagenarian Admiral Lord Fisher, the man who largely created the battlefleet which was now at war and who had previously left the office in January 1910.

The quotidian patrolling in the North Sea by the Harwich Force continued through the autumn and into winter. On 29 October, Commander Charles Freemantle in *Badger* rammed *U-19* near Terschelling, bending the bows of his ship, and claimed to have sunk it. In fact the submarine got home, although it lost some crewmen in the attack.

But overall, they hardly saw an enemy. The divisional commanders of the flotillas began to lay down 'bait' to try to entice the Germans out. One enterprising captain towed a float filled with flammable material out to the mouth of the Ems and set it alight, hoping to convince the enemy that it was a mined destroyer; still there was no response. In early November a light cruiser and two destroyers poked their bows out, but withdrew when they saw the Harwich Force off their coast.

Cruisers and destroyers at Harwich by W L Wylie. The drawing shows *Arethusa*-class light cruisers and 'L- and 'M'-class destroyers at Harwich in the early years of the war. The destroyer on the right is an 'L' class. (© National Maritime Museum PW0924)

However, German mining of the North Sea had continued apace since the *Königin Luise* on 5 August. Their activities off the east coast, coupled with British defensive counter-mining, had created the War Channel. In all this came to stretch for about 540 miles. British and German minefields intermingled on the east side of this channel and it was decided not to sweep them as they formed an almost impenetrable barrier protecting the ports themselves.

Then on 2 November 1914, the British government declared the North Sea a prohibited area. All neutrals were warned that unless their ships complied with the regular routes laid down by the Admiralty (and also generally submitted to being searched for goods intended to aid the enemy – contraband – as part of this process) they sailed at their own risk. Only in the designated swept channels would they be safe, and these were only known to the navy.

As the *Spectator* magazine put it;

All merchant ships are warned of the danger they will run if they enter the North Sea – now a mined area – except under Admiralty directions. This 'closed' area is not, of course, closed in the literal sense. Neutral ships have a right to enter it. But they are advised not to do so without accepting the highest degree of safety that the British Navy can guarantee them. For this purpose, the military area is defined as being bounded on the north by a line drawn from the northern point of the Hebrides, through the Faroe Islands, to Iceland. Ships entering the North Sea, should come by the Strait of Dover. Then they will be given sailing directions so that they can avoid the minefields.[1]

Mines were a pervasive problem in the North Sea for the rest of the war.

A watercolour sketch, again by W L Wylie, showing light cruisers and destroyers moored up at Harwich. (Author's collection)

Raids on Great Yarmouth, Lowestoft and Scarborough

On 3 November, the Germans made a raid in force on Great Yarmouth, bombarding the town. Shortly after 0700, Tyrwhitt was surprised by a signal from HMS *Halcyon*, a minesweeping gunboat stationed at Lowestoft, which was then working near Smith's Knoll, stating that she was engaged with a superior force. At the same time big shells began to fall close to the beach at Yarmouth and Gorleston. Three battlecruisers, *Seydlitz*, *Moltke* and *Von der Tann*, the heavy cruiser *Blücher*, and three light cruisers, *Kolberg*, *Graudenz* and *Strassburg*, had left the Bight the previous evening with orders to make a raid against the English coast. It was misty and the first inkling that *Halcyon* had that something was wrong was when, in response to her challenge, 11in shells began to fall around her.

Local Royal Navy forces put up what resistance they could and reported at 0745 that the enemy was headed off to the southeast. Tyrwhitt, who had already ordered *Aurora* and *Undaunted* to make for Smith's Knoll with all speed, and was himself rushing to get to sea, decided to set out for Terschelling with his flagship and another division of destroyers to try to cut off the enemy's retreat. He ordered *Aurora* and *Undaunted*, with her destroyers, to head there.

At 1100, a fisherman coming in to Lowestoft reported having seen the Germans laying mines as they retired.* Before noon a general warning had

---

* Submarine HMS *D-5* of the 8th Flotilla was sunk by one of them, while responding to the attack.

gone out from the Admiralty in this regard. In the meantime, Tyrwhitt, with *Arethusa* and six destroyers, swept along the Suffolk coast on his way north. *Aurora* had not received the commodore's orders and thus *Undaunted*, with her destroyers, was making for Terschelling alone. When she had reached a position near the mid-sea rendezvous, she sighted to the southward four German cruisers. These now gave chase and Blunt took his forces northward, but then began to turn to the west to try to lead the enemy vessels south towards Tyrwhitt. Sensing a trap, the Germans gave up the chase of *Undaunted* and made off easterly towards Terschelling Light. Blunt then resumed his course and followed them, doing his best to keep in touch. Tyrwhitt decided that he must come to *Undaunted*'s assistance and steered to join with Blunt's flotilla. But the Admiralty, having realised that Tyrwhitt's forces were considerably overmatched recommended by wireless that he concentrate. *Undaunted* was accordingly recalled and by 1500 the Harwich Force had assembled three light cruisers and thirteen destroyers in the middle of the North Sea and began to sweep past Terschelling to the Bight. It proved fruitless. The enemy had slipped away. There was, however, an accidental success, for the German cruiser *Yorck* (four 21cm/8.3in, ten 15cm/5.9in guns) ran into one of her own side's mines in the field which defended Jade Bay and was lost with half of her crew.

SMS *Yorck*, sunk by mines in the Jade with the loss of half her crew, seen here in 1910.
She is passing under the Levensau Bridge over the Kiel Canal.
(US Naval History and Heritage Command NH 45198)

With Antwerp, Ostend and Zeebrugge now firmly in German hands, and U-boats shipped overland in kit form to those ports, the German underwater presence in the North Sea was growing. On 12 November, a signal told that a submarine had been sighted in the Blackwater River, a shallow estuary between Harwich and the Thames. Seven destroyers were despatched to find it, led by HMS *Ferret* (1911), an *Acheron*-class vessel under Commander Geoffrey Mackworth. In the dark they carefully navigated the sandbanks of the Wallet, off Walton-on-the-Naze, to reach the Blackwater, where they became dimly aware of a small grey object in the water and a flashing light. Mackworth called for full speed and ramming stations before his searchlight revealed a small lifeboat with Keyes in it. He had been ordered to sink boats across the estuary to entrap the U-boat but, being dubious as to the veracity of the report, had contented himself with impounding some quantity of anti-submarine netting and was trying to set it out. It all turned out to have been a flight of ducks on the water anyway.

There now followed a period of comparative rest for the Harwich Force, although continued fear of an invasion (baseless, it was never a German plan) led to ships having to get steam up every morning at 0530 to be ready to intercept mythical enemy transports. But then a squall blew up on land which disturbed the equilibrium. On 4 December, Tyrwhitt was promoted to commodore first class.[2] This brought about two consequences. Firstly, it meant that he no longer 'drove his own ship' but had a ship's captain under him. This was not altogether to Tyrwhitt's liking for he enjoyed ship command. He promoted 38-year-old Ernest K Arbuthnot[*] RNR, his number one, to acting commander and gave the captaincy of *Arethusa* to him. To Lieutenant Commander Bertram Ramsay, who had sent him congratulations on his elevation, he wrote that 'I am pleased at any higher rating and was quite content before but as you say one may as well take what one can get, as one never knows when one will be found out'.[3] Secondly, it made Tyrwhitt senior to Keyes. So far Keyes had been ahead in seniority on the Navy List. He took the change badly, not least because he believed that the newly-appointed First Sea Lord, Jacky Fisher, disliked him (which was true; Fisher confused him with an officer called John Keys[†] who had supported Admiral Lord Charles Beresford in his feud with Fisher). The two quick-tempered (and in Keyes's case vain) commodores had a row about it and became estranged. Eventually both realised that this was bad for the service they were engaged on and made up after a few days; but the relationship was never as strong again.

---

[*] Arbuthnot had retired as a lieutenant RN (rank achieved in 1898) but rejoined the navy as a reservist in 1914.

[†] Keys was Beresford's naval secretary.

The German battlecruiser SMS *Seydlitz* (1912), mounting ten 11in guns. She was Hipper's flagship for the coastal raids of 1914. (US Naval History and Heritage Command NH 46838)

Meanwhile further disasters continued to haunt the navy; HMS *Hermes*, a seaplane carrier converted from a cruiser, was sunk on 31 October by *U-27* in the English Channel with the loss of twenty-one men, and the following day, Rear Admiral Christopher 'Kit' Cradock and his two obsolescent cruisers, *Good Hope* and *Monmouth*, were sunk off Coronel by a much superior German squadron under Vizeadmiral Graf von Spee, with the loss of 1,600 sailors. There were no survivors. Poor staff work and Churchill's interference were to blame. Better news came on 8 December, for Cradock was avenged by a force under Vice Admiral Doveton Sturdee, removed from his position as chief of staff by Fisher, commanding two battlecruisers sent from the Grand Fleet.

As the absence of two capital ships from the Grand Fleet became public through this success, and because the Yarmouth raid had led to adverse comment regarding the navy's ability to protect the civilian coastline, the Admiralty was concerned that another attempt at coastal raiding might be attempted. Intelligence gained suggested this might be on 14 December and as a result the 2nd Battle Squadron from Jellicoe's forces and Goodenough's 1 LCS were sent south, as were Beatty's battlecruisers.

The Harwich Force was ordered out too and Jellicoe suggested that they rendezvous with the heavy ships headed down the coast. But Tyrwhitt had already been instructed to try to get in touch with the enemy off the east coast and shadow them if he could. Accordingly, he made towards Yarmouth, arriving at 0630 on the 16th. The weather was filthy and he sheltered his force behind the shoal banks,* awaiting developments. Keyes meantime was ordered to place his submarines at Terschelling.

The Germans did assault the English coast; but at Scarborough.

---

* There are extensive shoals off the Norfolk coast running from Caister south to Great Yarmouth, including Caister Shoals, Cockle Shoals, Cross Sands, Corton, Holm Sands and Scroby Sands.

Vice Admiral Franz von Hipper who commanded the German battlecruiser force (1st Scouting Group) from 1914 until August 1918. His bombardment of English coastal towns in 1914 earned him in Britain the soubriquet of 'the baby killer'. (Author's collection)

Konteradmiral Franz Hipper with the battlecruisers SMS *Seydlitz*, *Von der Tann*, *Moltke* and *Derfflinger*, the armoured cruiser SMS *Blücher*, the light cruisers SMS *Strassburg*, *Graudenz*, *Kolberg* and *Stralsund* and eighteen destroyers shelled the town and also bombarded Whitby and Hartlepool. At the same time, the cruiser *Kolberg* laid 100 mines off Filey. When he received a signal with news of the attack, Tyrwhitt took four light cruisers and all his destroyers and tried to get out of the sheltering shoals through the Haisborough Gap. But the seas were too steep. He sent the destroyers back to Yarmouth and proceeded with the cruisers; and found nothing. In bad weather he was too far away to making contact and in any case the German force evaded all British ships, although sightings were made several times, and returned home safely.*

Across the three towns bombarded there were 122 civilian deaths with 443

---

* The Admiralty ordered Tyrwhitt to place himself under the order of Vice Admiral Warrender, 2nd Battle Squadron, for the interception of the Germans after the raid (CHAR 13/37/34, CAC).

The German battlecruiser SMS *Von der Tann* (1909), eight 11in guns, pictured in 1911.
In 1914 she participated in the Battle of Heligoland Bight and coastal raids but
was damaged in the Cuxhaven air attack and thus missed Dogger Bank.
(US Library of Congress LC-DIG-ggbain-16927)

wounded.[4] In Scarborough, one shell went through three houses. It went straight through a house on the Esplanade, made a hole in the garden wall then struck No 1 Belvedere Road across the road, killing a servant girl, and then hit No 2, finally embedding itself in the garden – all of this without exploding. The architect of the renovated Royal Hotel Whitby, Louis Norman Sanderson, was living on the Esplanade at the time. Possibly as a result, he joined the RNVR as a sub lieutenant on 28 December.

The raid had an enormous effect upon British public opinion and became a rallying cry against Germany; Churchill wrote to the mayor of Scarborough of 'the stigma of the baby killers of Scarborough'.[5] Lieutenant King-Hall noted in his diary that 'as an exhibition of Teutonic frightfulness, it may be held to have succeeded. Its most permanent result was the stimulus it gave to recruiting',[6] and locally-born artist James Clark painted *The Bombardment of the Hartlepools, 16 December 1914* for the Royal Academy's Summer Exhibition.

But the raid was also a source of much criticism of the Royal Navy for failing to prevent it.* This was resented by the men of Harwich. As Tyrwhitt put it 'frightful weather and no fortune. We saw nothing, much to Their Lordships' disgust . . . I never had a chance as we started 600 miles behind them.'[7]

'Their Lordships' disgust' had been forcibly expressed to Tyrwhitt by Fisher himself and the commodore had robustly defended himself; but he feared the consequences. 'I believe I am hanging by a thread as I deeply offended Lord F[isher] the other day. I need hardly say that it was an unfortunate affair in which I was the scapegoat and was really as innocent as a lamb . . . I don't expect more rope.'[8] Tyrwhitt was perhaps guilty of exaggeration here, for Fisher was basically an admirer of the commodore.

Stopping the Zeppelins; the Raids on Cuxhaven

In order to examine the role of the Harwich Force in the development of naval aviation it is necessary to return the beginning of the conflict. At the outbreak of war, the Kaiserliche Marine had established a naval airship and seaplane base at Nordholz, close to Cuxhaven, a town on the shore of the North Sea and at the mouth of the River Elbe. From here Zeppelin dirigibles could patrol over the North Sea, far above the height attainable by existing British warplanes, and attack shipping, especially minelayers and sweepers. Moreover, in Parliament and amongst the citizenry, there was considerable concern, and more than a little fear, that they would perpetrate bombing raids on coastal towns and ports and on London and major inland cities.[†]

On 3 September 1914, Secretary of State for War Lord Kitchener had asked Churchill if the navy, via the RNAS, could take over responsibility for Britain's aerial defence as the RFC was fully committed in France. Churchill consented; 'it was no use sitting down and waiting for a year while [defensive] preparations were completing . . . I decided immediately to strike . . . at the Zeppelin sheds'.[9] Thus Churchill, and hence the navy, became interested in attacking Zeppelins at their bases.

But Cuxhaven was beyond the range of the land-based aircraft available at the time and difficult, if not impossible, to assault from the sea. Churchill

---

* Admiral Sir Henry Oliver, who became Chief of the Admiralty War Staff at the end of 1914, placed the blame for the raid on the Admiral of Patrols, George Ballard, whose responsibilities included coastal defence. 'We had a useless R A on the East Coast of England and I could not get him shifted. When the Germans bombarded Scarborough and Hartlepool, we knew from Room 40 the afternoon before that something was intended but not enough to know what. He had definite orders to send out two submarines from Hartlepool to be at gun range, according to visibility, off the harbour at dawn. He failed to send them out the night before and they did not start out till after the bombardment began; one was crossing the bar while the shells were falling. We lost a fine chance of laming a battlecruiser and perhaps bringing on an engagement if her consorts delayed retiring to help her' (Oliver, *Memoirs* II, pp 117–18, NMM).
† Fears that were realised in 1915.

nonetheless agitated that something needed to be done to discourage and disrupt operations there and Tyrwhitt and Keyes developed a plan to use RNAS seaplanes to attack the base.

On 24 October, Tyrwhitt left harbour at 0500 and once again headed for the Ems estuary; half of his forces would attempt a sweep looking for enemy vessels. The other half were taking naval seaplanes to a suitable point in the Bight where they could take off and launch a raid against Cuxhaven. The aircraft were carried on the light cruisers' decks. This dual operation was supported by the battlecruisers *Invincible* and *Inflexible* and a division of destroyers from the Grand Fleet. It was, as Tyrwhitt wrote to his wife, 'a novel form of attack' which found him 'bursting with excitement and hoping for great things'.[10] But it was a washout. *Fearless* led her destroyers along the German coast and sighted not a thing. And the seaplanes, overloaded with armaments and fuel, were unable to take off in a heavy rainstorm which enveloped the little armada. What was more, two torpedoes were fired at *Arethusa* during the operation, both of which fortunately missed. Tyrwhitt was bitterly disappointed, raging to Angey that 'I am sick to death of everything connected with aviation'.[11] At the Admiralty, Churchill was more forgiving, offering the opinion that the aeroplanes should be launched from long barges or lighters, with some form of accelerating windlass. A further operation was scheduled but the continued bad weather put paid to it. For seaplanes to be hoisted out onto the water a smooth sea was required and this was sadly lacking through the autumn. So there matters rested for the moment.

But Tyrwhitt continued to refine his proposals for an air assault and shortly after Fisher's accession he secured an interview with the new First Sea Lord. Fisher was enthusiastic and promised more ships. At this time, he also took a shine to this fighting sailor, a man who reflated his own aggressive temperament. 'Lord Fisher considered him the personification of pugnacity', noted Arthur Marder.[12]

Encouraged by Fisher's comments, Tyrwhitt finalised a new strategy for an air attack on Cuxhaven. Thus far, the seaplanes had been towed out to position or carried on the decks of the cruisers and craned out into the sea. Churchill's idea of barges had not been taken up (although it would be later) but ships specially adapted as seaplane carriers had been added to the navy and Fisher assigned these to the Harwich Force.

HMS *Engadine*, *Riviera* and *Empress* were converted cross-Channel passenger steamers built for the South East and Chatham Railway's Dover/Folkestone to France services. The first two ships were completed in 1911, turbine driven and capable of 21 knots; *Empress* was older and slower, built in 1907 and with a speed of 18 knots. All three were taken up at the start of the war and had been fitted with, *inter alia*, three canvas hangers – two aft and one forward – each housing a seaplane.*

Observing increased activity in German naval ports, the plan to attack Cuxhaven was now supplemented to include the entire Grand Fleet, which would make a full sweep down the North Sea, while Tyrwhitt would trail his coat close to Heligoland to try to draw out elements of the German High Seas Fleet and at the same time mount an air attack from the seaplane carriers against Cuxhaven.

The force sailed on 23 November but the Admiralty ordered the three carriers back to port with an escort of all the destroyers. The three *Arethusa*-class cruisers, *Aurora*, *Arethusa* and *Undaunted*, carried on and, joined by one destroyer which had become detached from the main force, made a high-speed run towards Heligoland Island. But again, the enemy refused to come out and take the bait. Some shots were fired from the fortress guns, they sighted two submarines, which dived away, and a single seaplane which dropped five bombs on them, all of which missed. In the commodore's view 'the whole show was not exactly a failure but it was stopped in the middle of the night by the Admiralty. I was perfectly furious.'[13]

Still Tyrwhitt continued to push the idea, taking the opportunity of dinner with the Churchills to advance his point of view. Permission for another attempt was granted, with the operation planned for a few days before Christmas. But it was felt that the assembling of the seaplanes and their embarkment onto the carriers might be observed by patrolling German U-boats if carried out in daylight and finally the raid was confirmed for Christmas Day itself. On 23 December, nine seaplanes flew from their base at Felixstowe and landed in the harbour after sunset, the first time they had ever flown at night.

Plan 'Y', as it became known, required all three carriers to be escorted by the Harwich force to within 12 miles north of Heligoland, whereupon the aircraft would be hoisted out and take off. The Grand Fleet would again sally into the North Sea; and Keyes's submarines were stationed in a line south of Heligoland, to both attack any vessel coming out and to rescue downed airmen. The intention was for the seaplanes to attack Cuxhaven, reconnoitre the anchorages and report on any ships present, fly westwards along the coast to Norderney Gat[†] and hence then to seaward to meet up with their mother ships. They were of a mixed bag; four Short Improved Type 74, three Short Type 81 folders[‡] and two Short Type 135 folders. The navigational plan and briefing were conducted by the well-known author Erskine Childers, now a

---

* In 1915, one large aft mounted steel hanger would replace the canvas 'tents'.
† Norderley is one of the East Frisian Islands. The Gat is the passage between Norderley and Juist.
‡ 'Folder' for the wings which folded back parallel to the body, a mechanism patented by Short's in 1913.

lieutenant RNVR, who had sailed extensively in the area before the war and written the book *Riddle of the Sands*, the plot of which is placed on the coast near Cuxhaven.

The submarines sailed on the 23rd; then, on Christmas Eve, Tyrwhitt led the three *Arethusa*s out of harbour at 0500 with the carriers and most of the destroyers. They departed in such a hurry that several mess stewards were left stranded on the pier, forlornly waving the Christmas delicacies they had been sent out to acquire. *Fearless* and eight destroyers followed at 1000 to make for the rendezvous point where the seaplanes were to be picked up and where a heavy attack might be expected in the raid's aftermath. In total thirty-four vessels were deployed from Harwich and the Grand Fleet concentrated in the middle of the North Sea in the hope that the Germans would respond by sending out their major warships. Such was the uncertainty about the potential German response, destroyer captains Geoffrey Mackworth of *Ferret* and Charles Fremantle of *Badger* shook hands and 'agreed they would be lucky if they ever saw Harwich again'.[14]

All three seaplane carriers and their flying operations were under the

Side-on view of the Short Type 74 seaplane # 818 on the water at Harwich with Flight Lieutenant J M Levy in the cockpit. Type 74s took part in the Cuxhaven raid of Christmas Day 1914. This seaplane was known to be on board the light cruiser HMS *Aurora* on 6 March, 20 March and 23 March 1916, when this photograph was taken.
(© National Maritime Museum N 22825)

overall command of Squadron Commander Cecil John L'Estrange Malone, who was also captain of *Engadine*. He had been the second man in history to fly an aeroplane off the deck of a moving ship. Just before departure, Chief Petty Officer Mechanic James William Bell of HMS *Empress* had been given sixteen bombs, each weighing 20lbs, and told to drill holes in them so that they could be slung under the seaplanes. The rest of the crew were told to move aft in case Bell blew them all to bits. Luckily, the 21-year-old didn't. These were Hales bombs, manufactured by the Cotton Powder Company of Faversham, Kent. The bombs were actuated by a small propeller behind the fins which began to revolve when the missile was dropped. Apart from three bombs per plane, the only weapons on the two-seater aircraft were the pilot's revolvers, with six packets of ammunition. Only three planes would carry observers in the second seat and just one of them carried a rifle.

At 0445 on the 25th, an incident occurred which nearly put paid to the whole operation. The squadron sighted four German fishing trawlers, from whom a low-power radio burst was heard, followed by Heligoland's 'urgent' call and then by seventeen other messages picked up in Tyrwhitt's flagship, all of which seemed to be prefaced by the term 'urgent'.

It seemed certain that the Harwich Force had been spotted by the enemy, with at least another 90 minutes steaming to go. Tyrwhitt was conflicted, but in the light of the disappointments earlier in the year, and with sea conditions as near perfect as they could be, he decided to press on. Later he confessed

An artist's enthusiastic impression of the Cuxhaven raid of 25 December 1914, as depicted on a French-produced postcard.
(Author's collection)

that 'I very nearly turned tail'.[15] As the commodore debated what to do, a bright star suddenly shone forth from the murk and mist. 'It was the biggest star I have ever seen,' Tyrwhitt wrote to his sister Polly, 'but it put heart into me and I had no more misgivings.'[16] It was just Venus, magnified in the fog, but for the vicar's son Tyrwhitt, it was a reassuring omen on this holy day.

By 0600 on Christmas morning the force was finally in position and by 0630 all nine planes were in the water, although the engines of two planes – a Short Type 81 and a Short Type 74 – refused to start and they had to be hoisted back on board. The remaining seven planes flew off into a misty sky, reaching the German coast an hour later. On their way they drew gunfire from enemy ships, and over land the fog became thicker, forcing the pilots to fly low as each tried to spot landmarks along the way. Only one aircraft, a Type 74 from *Riviera*, intentionally bombed anything. Flight Lieutenant Charles Edmonds dropped three missiles aimed at the light cruisers *Stralsund* and *Graudenz*. They missed.

Withdrawing towards the pickup point, the Harwich ships had been sailing

The light cruiser SMS *Stralsund*, bombed by Lieutenant Edmonds on Christmas Day 1914.
(US Naval History and Heritage Command NH 92631)

in formation at a speed of 20 knots but due to condenser problems, *Empress* began to fall astern. *Undaunted* was detailed to stand by her, while the rest of the Force sailed on. Two Friedrichshafen seaplanes attacked the carrier with six bombs, one exploding only 20ft off the bow but without damaging ship or crew. Zeppelin *L-6* followed up, attacking with both bombs and machine-gun fire. The crew of the *Empress* attempted to drive the Zeppelin away, initially with rifle fire as their 12pdr in the stern was blanked by the superstructure. From a distance, the cruisers opened fire with their main armament directed upwards and eventually first one and then another Zeppelin were driven off. But it was Leading Seaman Mills, the aft 6in gun layer of *Undaunted*, who made the first hit on a Zeppelin in action with surface ships. While firing shrapnel, he put sixteen holes into *L-6* with a near miss.[17]

The attacks beaten off, Tyrwhitt's force headed for the rendezvous point, met *Fearless* and her brood and sighted a Zeppelin some five miles distant. First one, then two more planes appeared and landed next to the carriers. As they were being hoisted in, a submarine was spotted and Tyrwhitt immediately ordered the destroyers to circle around the carriers as a shield. Zeppelin *L-5* appeared and the cruisers fired at it with rifles and the recently fitted 6pdr anti-aircraft gun. Tyrwhitt himself took a turn at driving off the enemy owning 'I confess to emptying eight rifle magazines into [the] seaplanes myself'.[18] Finally deciding that no more aircraft would return (four had run out of fuel and ditched), Tyrwhitt decided to withdraw, having made a sort of history – the first attack on land targets by aircraft launched from the sea, and the first air-sea combined operation for the Royal Navy.[*] Further attempts on the retiring force were made by U-boats *U-20*, *U-22* and *U-30* but zig-zag manoeuvring prevented any success. As the Harwich Force returned home without loss or damage, Tyrwhitt made a signal; 'I wish all ships a Merry Christmas.'[19]

The missing air crews all survived. One pilot was rescued by a Dutch tug, one landed next to Keyes in *Lurcher* and the remaining two were picked up by the submarine *E-11* under Lieutenant Commander Martin Naismith. But the raid was not a success. Fog, low cloud and anti-aircraft fire were problematic and Cuxhaven was not molested. Nevertheless, the raid demonstrated the feasibility of attack by ship-borne aircraft and showed the strategic importance of this new weapon. *Flight* magazine wrote that 'the Cuxhaven raid marks the first employment of the seaplanes of the Naval Air Service in an attack on the enemy's harbours from the sea, and, apart from the results achieved, is an occasion of historical moment. Not only so, but for the first time in history a

---

[*] But not the first for any navy. On 27 November 1914, Japanese naval seaplanes had attacked German and Austro-Hungarian warships in Kiachow Bay, Tsingtao.

naval attack has been delivered simultaneously above, on, and from below the surface of the water',[20] and an anonymous American 'New York military expert' was quoted as describing the raid as 'the best strategic move of the war'.[21]

The appearance of aircraft over the Schillig Roads alarmed the heavy ships lying there, so much so that in a scramble to weigh anchor and leave, *Von der Tann* fouled a cruiser, both sustaining damage. And on 7 January 1915, a Danish informant named Hartvig Kjobenhavn had his message to the *Daily Mail* intercepted by the Admiralty censor. It reported that 'the British aerial raid on Cuxhaven had forced the German Admiralty to remove the greater part of the High Seas Fleet from Cuxhaven to various places on the Kiel Canal'.[22] As for the commodore, he wrote 'for the life of me I can't make out why they did not come out and bludgeon us as we sat on their doorstep'.[23]

*   *   *

The much-anticipated and feared Zeppelin attack on Britain came on 13 January 1915. Great Yarmouth was bombed and so were a number of Norfolk coastal villages; four civilians were killed and fourteen wounded. A scheduled sweep of the Bight on 15 January was cancelled the day before and instead Tyrwhitt was summoned to the Admiralty to discuss another attempt to bomb Cuxhaven in retaliation. This was scheduled for the 23rd, and indeed Keyes's submarines had left harbour as planned; but they were recalled and the Harwich Force ordered to join Beatty for what became the Battle of Dogger Bank (for which, see the next chapter). No sooner was Tyrwhitt back at Harwich from that encounter on the 27th, and his ships refuelled, than at 0800 on 29 January he again sallied out with the seaplane carriers. But the weather supervened once more. Northwesterly winds and high seas threatened to damage the planes in their canvas tents and take-off from the rough seas would have been impossible in the conditions. At 1330, the commodore called the operation off. Thus ended another attempt to destroy the Cuxhaven naval base from the air. *Engadine* and *Riviera* were detached for refits. *Empress* stayed but was then loaned out to the Dover Patrol. Tyrwhitt got on with the sea war. But he and the Harwich Force had initiated an entirely new tactic in naval warfare.

Tyrwhitt may or may not have considered this 'first'. He was more concerned regarding the condition of his destroyers. 'We have an appalling number [of destroyers] on the sick list, shamed I am to say it, there have been an endless number of collisions. I can't make it out, as they are such good fellows but damnably careless.' As an experienced destroyer captain, such lapses annoyed him. 'Certainly, the weather is very trying in this narrow harbour but my complaint is that by the exercise of ordinary seamanship most of these accidents could have been avoided. I have slung out two COs [commanding officers] to encourage the remainder.'[24]

The weather remained a constant threat; 'I didn't know Harwich harbour could produce such a sea,' he wrote to Angela at the end of 1914, 'barges and small craft were wrecked galore and we could do nothing to help them. No boat could look at it.'[25]

The first Zeppelin raids also produced commercial opportunities. The *Daily Chronicle* offered insurance against them. Here is *The Vow of Vengeance*, drawn for the paper by Frank Brangwyn ARA. (Library of Congress LC-USZC4-11189)

5

The Battle of Dogger Bank and Beyond, January–July 1915

The German raids on the east coast of England in 1914 were intended to cause a portion of the Grand Fleet, or the battlecruisers, to come out and be isolated and defeated in detail by the High Sea Fleet. But each had occasioned the British fleet coming out, in one strength or another, and nearly catching the German battlecruisers, the reverse of what was intended. Hipper convinced himself that this must be because British or neutral fishing vessels in the Dogger Bank area were reporting his movements to the British and he was determined to put an end to it.

The plan was to send the battlecruisers of the 1st Scouting Group to clear the area of fishing vessels and dubious neutrals and to attack any small Royal Navy warships that they came across, with the High Seas Fleet covering the withdrawal. This limited operation conformed to the ban by the Kaiser on aggressive moves by the High Seas Fleet, which had been reiterated on 10 January. What Hipper did not realise was that the Royal Navy was able to read German signals[*] and that it was Room 40, the signals intelligence group at the Admiralty, that was giving warning of his operations. As Hipper prepared for this new mission, Room 40 was once again able to issue an alert. It was this alert which had led to the cancellation of the planned 24 January attack on Cuxhaven.

The 1st Scouting Group and their support sailed on 23 January and comprised three battlecruisers, *Seydlitz*, *Moltke* and *Derfflinger*; *Von der Tann* was still under repair from the effects of the Cuxhaven air raid and was replaced by the slower and less well-armed heavy cruiser *Blücher*. There were also four light cruisers and a strong destroyer flotilla.

Beatty, with his battlecruisers and Goodenough's 1 LCS, together with Tyrwhitt and the Harwich Flotilla were ordered to a rendezvous on the northeast part of the Dogger Bank and the Grand Fleet was directed to a holding position further north. With the commodore were his three *Arethusa*-class light cruisers and thirty-five destroyers. Despite some fog, Tyrwhitt met Beatty at 0700 on the 24th with *Arethusa* and seven fast 'M'-class destroyers led by Captain the Honourable Herbert Meade[†] in

---

[*] The German navy started the war with three principal codes, and 'within four months the Admiralty had acquired copies of all of them' (Boyd, *British Naval Intelligence*, p 106).

[†] Son of Admiral of the Fleet Richard James Meade, Fourth Earl of Clanwilliam.

Meteor. Aurora and *Undaunted* were 13 miles astern with the rest of the destroyers.

Here the trailing cruisers sighted SMS *Kolberg* (1908), twelve 10.5cm (4.1in) guns, with four destroyers in company. Nicholson, in *Aurora* and wanting to be certain, ordered a challenge by searchlight which brought the response of a single letter flashed from the German light cruiser and a burst of gunfire, which was immediately returned. The German fire was accurate but fell off as *Kolberg* sustained hits. Nonetheless, *Aurora* was struck three times. The German received a hit below the waterline and after a shell exploded under her forebridge, *Kolberg* turned away and headed east. *Aurora* and *Undaunted* then resumed their course.

However, they next observed enemy forces far off their starboard quarter and turned to keep them in sight. This brought them in touch with *Southampton* and 1 LCS to whom they reported the presence of the German ships they had seen. A few minutes later, Goodenough spotted the German main body, which, having spread out for a sweep of the area, had hastily concentrated on receiving the alarm from *Kolberg*.

Meanwhile, having seen the gun flashes, Beatty worked up speed to give chase, with Tyrwhitt and his 'M'-class vessels in company, and by 0750 he could see the smoke of the German battlecruisers. Hipper had turned away and was making all steam to escape to the southeast. Tyrwhitt was ordered to take his destroyers and get ahead of Beatty's force to scout the ships he was opposing. To his chagrin Tyrwhitt, on Beatty's disengaged side, could not get enough speed out of *Arethusa* to overtake the barrelling *Lion* and her kindred. But the 'M' class were the fastest destroyers in the fleet and were unleashed to go ahead, as they worked up to their full speed of 35 knots. They closed the range to 9,000 yards before the rearmost enemy ship, *Blücher*, altered course to open fire and forced them to turn away. But as soon as *Blücher* resumed her progress, Meade carried on and was able to close and report course and strength.

The destroyers were recalled and Tyrwhitt dropped back so as not to foul the battlecruisers' range with his smoke. But then at 0920 Beatty ordered him ahead again to counter what appeared to be a developing German torpedo attack; once more, his ship could not pass the battlecruisers and he had to send Meade and his brood on alone. But no such action came.

The running fight which now developed has been described many times, and did not really involve the Harwich Force. It therefore seems redundant to cover it in detail here. Sufficient to say that in a stern chase lasting several hours, *Lion* received a hit which crippled her, causing Beatty to lose control of the tactical situation. Moreover, an emergency turn-away from a non-existent submarine and imprecise signalling by Beatty's flag lieutenant caused

The *Lion*-class battlecruiser *Princess Royal* (1911), to which Beatty transferred his flag at the Battle of Dogger Bank. (Author's collection)

the British force to focus on *Blücher*, which was set ablaze and wrecked, whilst allowing the remainder of Hipper's ships to escape. Before they did so, *Meteor* had led three other destroyers in a torpedo attack against *Blücher** and was hit by a shell in the forward boiler room, which put her out of action, killing three stokers outright and wounding two men, one of whom (another stoker) died the following day. Probationer Surgeon James Alexander Stirling RNVR courageously descended into the stokehold after *Meteor* had been hit and by candlelight amputated the leg of a stoker which was badly fractured and jammed amongst a mess of twisted iron and steel caused by the shell. Stirling received the DSC for his actions.[1] *Meteor* was eventually towed back to the Humber by the destroyer *Liberty*.

The 1 DF Harwich destroyer *Attack* had the privilege of going alongside the injured *Lion* at 1134, no small feat of seamanship by Lieutenant Commander Cyril Callaghan,† for which he was Mentioned in Despatches,[2] to take off Beatty for transfer to the battlecruiser *Princess Royal*. Until 1220, when the admiral gained the battlecruiser, his flag proudly flew from the little 770-ton *Acheron*-class destroyer.

---

* *Mentor* claimed a hit.
† Son of Admiral Sir George Callaghan, who had been replaced by Jellicoe at the start of the war. In June 1915, Captain (D) of 1 DF (Blunt) wrote a scathing evaluation of Callaghan, marking him below average ability and that he was 'unfit for independent command. Wine bills high . . .'. Tyrwhitt, however, noted his own high estimation of Callaghan and Beatty's special appreciation in his despatches from the battle (ADM 196/46/130 & ADM 196/142/524, NA).

Arethusa had finally been able to join the action, putting two torpedoes into *Blücher* as the enemy lay dying. At 1145 Tyrwhitt signalled that the cruiser had stuck her flag and closed to rescue survivors. Shortly afterwards the German ship capsized and sank. All of *Arethusa*'s boats were deployed to rescue survivors, but were strafed by a German Taube aircraft, and when a Zeppelin came up seemingly bent on attack too, Tyrwhitt withdrew. 'I was within 50 yards of her and picked up 130 men. We were bombed by a seaplane while picking up the survivors. What a delightful nation they are,'[3] the commodore wrote the following day.

When one lucky German was being hauled out of the sea by a particularly stout stoker called Clark, he said 'Hello Nobby, fancy seeing you here'. It turned out they had been next-door neighbours in Hull.[4] Amongst those rescued by the flagship were seven German officers. A practising Christian, with a solid faith, Tyrwhitt was 'kind to them, so much so that they could not understand it and said so . . . one of [them] was a particularly decent fellow and the senior officer, so I gave him my cabin, which I was not using. When he left, I gave him a box of cigarettes on which he wept and said many things which sounded strange coming from a German.'[5]

An iconic picture of SMS *Blücher* sinking. Until the Second World War, the original hung in the Naval Secretary's office at the Admiralty. (Photo; private collection)

Most of the POWs were transferred to *Undaunted* and, after first instructing the commodore to make a sweep towards Heligoland, Jellicoe instead ordered the Harwich Force to screen *Lion* which was being slowly towed to Rosyth by the older battlecruiser *Indomitable*. Fifty-five destroyers and seven cruisers were deployed in the task and, in a state of anxiety about the presence of submarines, Tyrwhitt told his destroyers to fire or ram anything that even vaguely looked like one, without regard to the consequences. They arrived safely at the Forth of Firth early on the 26th.

With *Blücher* sunk, 'technically, the Dogger Bank was a British victory. The enemy had fled the field, *Seydlitz* had been damaged, over 1,000 German seamen had been lost (killed or taken prisoner). British casualties were less than fifty . . . the *Lion*'s injuries were not vital.'[6] But despite press adulation, the Royal Navy had lost the chance for an annihilating battle, and for Beatty, 'the disappointment is more than I can bear to think of. Everybody thinks it was a great success when in reality it was a terrible failure.'[7] As for Tyrwhitt and the Harwich Force, the commodore thought 'it was not our day and all we did was watch the battlecruisers slogging one and other'.[8]

Nonetheless, Spink and Co of London, medallists and philatelists, produced a medal commemorating Dogger Bank and Heligoland Bight. The obverse represented two oval medallions one above the other, joined by a knot. The upper shows a sinking cruiser and the date '28 AUG 1914'. In the exergue is written 'MAINZ SINKING'. The lower medallion depicts a ship on her side, above '24 JAN 1915' and in the exergue 'BLÜCHER SINKING'. Two smaller cartouches at the sides depict (left) *Lion* shown steaming to the right. Over a flagstaff with an Admiral's flag and scroll is the inscription 'BEATTY'. On the right, *Arethusa* is pictured steaming to the left with her flagstaff wearing a commodore's broad pennant and the inscription 'TYRWHITT'. The reverse gives details of the major ships involved in both actions. The medal was manufactured in bronze, silver and gold and sold in aid of naval orphanages.

A silver medallion struck by Spink of London in 1916 celebrating the successes at Heligoland Bight in 1914 and Dogger Bank in 1915. It depicts *Mainz* and *Blücher* sinking, HMS *Lion* and HMS *Arethusa*. Beatty and Tyrwhitt are 'name checked'. On the reverse are listed the names of some of the participating ships. (Author's collection)

Frustration

On return to Harwich another row broke out between Keyes and Tyrwhitt. This time it was pure jealousy on Keyes's part, for he felt that Tyrwhitt was Fisher's blue-eyed boy whilst he was at best a whipping post. What Keyes really wanted was a light cruiser to go to sea in – which Fisher persistently denied him and to which idea Tyrwhitt failed to lend support (in Keyes's mind, anyway).

Meeting Churchill, Keyes told him that it might be best if he were posted elsewhere and on 8 February he was appointed Chief of Staff to Rear Admiral Carden for the action to force the Dardanelles. His departure, regretted by Tyrwhitt, did however pave the way for a rationalisation of command at Harwich. Captain Arthur Kipling Waistell, captain of the depot ship *Maidstone*, took overall command of the 8th Submarine Flotilla and was ordered by Fisher to work under Tyrwhitt. Although technically Waistell took his orders from the Admiralty, the commodore now had a measure of overall control of the principal fighting groups in the port, destroyers, light cruisers and submarines. 'The SMs are not exactly under my command,' he wrote to Angela, 'but they work under me which comes to the same thing.'[9]

Arethusa went to Chatham on 1 February for a much-needed refit and received a grand reception from the batteries at Sheerness, which cheered her

Admiral Gustav Heinrich Ernst Friedrich von Ingenohl, in command of the German High Sea Fleet from the beginning of the war until 2 February 1915. (Author's collection)

as she sailed up the river. The uplifting nature of the welcome was spoiled when Arbuthnot ran the vessel heavily into the side of the dock at Chatham, provoking Tyrwhitt to remark that he would rather drive his own ship and break it himself. He transferred his flag to *Penelope* (1914), another *Arethusa*-class vessel, on his return to Harwich although most of his command had been ordered away to look for U-boats in the North and Irish Seas and escort troopships crossing the English Channel.

On 2 February 'the Dogger Bank action cost [High Seas Fleet commander] von Ingenohl his command'.[10]

> The *Admiralstab* reviewed the whole conduct of the war since the High Sea Fleet had been in Admiral von Ingenohl's hands, and came to the conclusion that he had not realised the truth that dissipation of forces is always disastrous, particularly for the weaker side. The only possibility of guarding against further disasters appeared to be a change of command. Moreover, the confidence of officers in their leader had been shaken, and this mistrust might spread to the nation, with serious results. In view of these opinions, it was decided to relieve both Admiral von Ingenohl and also his Chief of Staff.[11]

He was replaced by Admiral Hugo von Pohl, who cautiously followed the Kaiser's orders not to risk his big ships.

Then two days after this change of command, Germany declared unrestricted submarine warfare. This meant that any ship, naval or civilian, would be torpedoed and sunk on sight and without warning; the announcement stated that 'Germany now declares all waters surrounding Great Britain and Ireland . . . as an area of war . . . beginning 18 February 1915 it will endeavour to destroy every merchant ship found in this area without it always being possible to avert the peril that threatens persons and cargos'.[12] This was a direct attempt to disrupt the Allied supply chain and in part retaliation for the increasingly successful Allied blockade of Germany.

Room 40 again provided intelligence that U-boats were concentrating in the southwest approaches, the vital trade corridor for Britain, and *Undaunted* and a division of 3 DF were sent to Pembroke to help counter them. Harwich was sadly denuded should a threat come.

Although he had become an enthusiast for air attack, Tyrwhitt soon lost this capability. Early in February, *Engadine* and *Riviera* were withdrawn from service for refits, which would see them gain proper hangers and better lifting equipment. This left only *Empress* with three planes and that same month she was detached from the Harwich Force to assist in the bombing of German submarine bases in Belgium.

February was thus a month of frustration for Tyrwhitt; 'we have hardly been out,' he wrote to Keyes.[13] But for his scattered destroyers it was a hard slog. 1 DF spent the month beating up and down the English Channel on escort duty. And then between the 9th and the 15th it was ordered to protect minelayers laying a new field to defend the eastern entrance to the Dover Straits.1 DF finally arrived back at Harwich on the 16th but then *Fearless* and eight destroyers were sent out to search for submarines reported to be off the North Hinder Light Vessel. The effort proved fruitless.

On the 22nd, 1 DF was engaged in patrolling to give warnings to merchant ships that there were U-boats at large and then at the end of the month, Mackworth in *Ferret* was ordered to take one division and make the 450-mile trip to Avonmouth in order to escort transports on the first leg of their journey to the Dardanelles. Meanwhile, *Fearless* and the remainder of 1 DF, together with their depot ship *Woolwich*, were transferred to Beatty's battlecruiser command at Rosyth.

Commander Barry Domvile* in *Miranda* expressed the frustration of many; 'I was here there and everywhere. In the early spring working with minelayers in Sheerness . . . later escorting six knot monitors down the channel to Ushant with my 35 knot destroyer – a particularly brilliant brainwave of someone's at the Admiralty . . . then getting a dicky propeller shaft put right on the Clyde.'[14]

Tired of inactivity, Tyrwhitt devised a plan to attack the German naval wireless station at Norddeich,† near the Frisian coast. After much badgering and a meeting with Churchill he was given the go-ahead. With no carriers, seaplanes were to be carried on the decks of the cruisers, two to a ship. The raid was first postponed due to the late arrival of the aircraft; and then on 19 March it snowed and the raid was again called off. Finally, they got away in the morning of the 20th with *Arethusa*, *Penelope*, *Undaunted* (returned to the fold) and the newly available *Empress*, together with twelve destroyers. But the weather intervened once more, the wind becoming too strong and the attempt was scratched at 0500.

In the evening of the 23rd, the conditions seemed propitious, so Tyrwhitt hared off, leaving Harwich – and King George V, who was due to visit on the 24th and invest the commodore with the CB he had been awarded for his actions at Heligoland. Apparently, the king (a former Royal Navy officer himself) took it in good part. However, this sally was also blighted by the weather. A few miles short of the take-off point, they ran into a dense fog bank.

---

* The son of Admiral Sir Compton Edward Domvile, CinC Mediterranean Fleet 1902–05.
† Norddeich handled communications to and from some 1,500 German warships and merchant vessels at sea in the eastern North Atlantic, Norwegian Sea, Baltic Sea, North Sea, the Channel and as far south as the Cape Verde Islands.

A view of the destroyer HMS *Landrail* (1914) hove to with her bow missing. On 24 March 1915 she lost it in a collision with the light cruiser *Undaunted*. (The stern is out of focus.) (© National Maritime Museum N22786)

Tyrwhitt hoisted a flag, only just visible in the fog, white with five small black crosses,* the signal to abandon the operation. The force reversed course and, finding clearer conditions, turned back again. Ten miles from the coast they came into fog once more and reversed direction for the second time. Tyrwhitt tried to coordinate the movements of the ships by blasts on the siren, prearranged signals for course and speed.

But in turning in the fog, the flotillas became disorganised. In *Murray*, Lieutenant Commander Taprell Dorling suddenly heard three loud blasts of the siren from an unseen ship ahead; it was the signal 'I am going astern'. He stopped engines, went slow astern, sounded his own siren three times; and prayed. Almost immediately he heard a huge crashing noise from behind his ship. In the confusion, the destroyer *Landrail* (1914) collided with *Undaunted* sheering off 20–30ft of her bow. The cruiser had a huge V-shaped gash in her port side through which water was pouring into her hull. And *Landrail* was 'a horrible sight – her forecastle half its original length . . . through the torn, jagged holes [in her bow] we could even see the mess stools and tables. The forepart of her forecastle deck had collapsed until the stem head was touching the water.'[15]

---

* In the RN 1913 signal book, a white flag with five black crosses meant 'negative'.

Both ships had their radios knocked out and it was over 90 minutes later that Tyrwhitt was informed that *Mentor* had taken *Landrail* in tow and *Undaunted* was heading home with 3ft of water in her engine room, escorted by *Murray* and another destroyer. *Undaunted* had lost three men, all drowned. One of them, Master at Arms George McLean, had brought his wife, Barbara, to Harwich where she lived at 29A King's Head Street. Stoker Arthur Robinson's wife in Halling, Kent, would never see her husband again. Death in war is a known risk; but to die in an accident in war is tragic. That afternoon, as the cruiser steamed homeward, Dorling heard '*Undaunted*'s bugles sounding the last post and the crackle of the three volleys of rifle fire as the remains . . . were committed to the deep'.[16]

The remaining ships spread out to find the crippled destroyer. But it was not until 0200 on the 25th that the fog lifted and 1500 before they found them. *Mentor*'s tow had parted twice and the seas were now quite rough. Nicholson in *Aurora* was ordered to take *Landrail* in tow but at 1600 the 3½in wire gave way. A 5½in wire was attached; but at 1845 this also parted. The situation was critical, for *Landrail* was drifting onto a lee shore off Terschelling.[17]

Now the flagship tried; three times they got a hawser secured and twice it broke. But the commodore was not going to leave one of his crippled children at sea. He lowered a boat and used it to pass another hawser onto *Landrail*. This third attempt worked and they set off for home at 2300 having spent over 40 hours just off the German coast. At 5 knots *Arethusa* slowly dragged her charge to safety through what was now a howling gale; they reached Yarmouth at 2100 on the 26th and Harwich the following morning, where two tugs took over. Tyrwhitt went to bed – the first time he had slept in 96 hours.

Undaunted meanwhile had got back without further incident; her captain (and Captain 'D' 3rd Destroyer Flotilla), Francis Gerald St John, received 'Their Lordship's Appreciation' for how St John was able to bring *Undaunted* safely into harbour 'under very trying circumstances'.[18]

A May Day Victory

After the 7th Torpedo Boat Half Flotilla was lost in the action off Texel (see above, Chapter 3), the German naval authorities were reluctant to commit any further forces for offensive operations off the coast of Flanders. This was in line with their general withdrawal of patrols seen around Heligoland.

But 60-year-old Admiral Ludwig von Schröder, recalled from retirement and appointed as the local Flanders area naval commander, felt that there were many opportunities for interference with British shipping if he had sufficient naval resources. Eventually the authorities in Berlin relented and he was sent a force of small torpedo boats and submarines. He formed these into the Flanders Torpedo Boat Flotilla made up of fifteen 'A'-class torpedo boats under

The German regional commander of naval forces and marines in Flanders,
Admiral von Schröder, in front of the City Hall in Bruges.
(US National Archives and Administration NAID 17391048)

the command of Korvettenkapitän Hermann Schoemann. The 'A' class were
designed as coastal torpedo boats, displacing 107 tons, 134ft long, lightly
armed with a single 5cm/2in* deck gun and two torpedo tubes; they could also
carry four mines. Built in 1914, their top speed was 20 knots.

On 1 May 1915, two German seaplanes reported a formation of four British
armed trawlers off North Hinder Bank. One of the seaplanes was forced to
make an emergency landing with mechanical problems and Schoemann was
ordered out with SMS *A-2* and *A-6* to rescue the seaplane's crew and find and
destroy the trawlers.

The trawlers were part of the Auxiliary Patrol, civilian vessels taken up by
the Admiralty together with their peacetime crews and turned into patrol or
minesweeping units. At this time in the war, they operated in groups of three
or four, commanded by a 'dug-out', a retired naval officer recalled to the flag.
Great Yarmouth-based HMT *Columbia*, *Barbados*, *Chirsin*† and *Miura* were
under the command of Lieutenant Sir James Domville, 5th Baronet, RNR who
had originally left the navy in 1912.‡

---

* Later versions carried two 3.5in guns.
† Actually a German trawler taken as a prize.
‡ He was the son of Rear Admiral Cecil Henry Domville, from whom he inherited the baronetcy in 1904.

At the same time as the trawlers were spotted, the old destroyers HMS *Recruit* and *Brazen*, both launched in 1896 and part of the Nore Local Defence Flotilla, were out on patrol near the Galloper Light Vessel. Thirty miles southwest of the lightship *Recruit* was torpedoed by *U-6*. She broke in two and sank quickly with the loss of thirty-nine men (nearly all of them from the boiler room) and four officers; twenty-two crewmen were rescued.

Now *Brazen* and, separately, the trawlers, were enjoined to search for the U-boat. But off Thornton Ridge, Foreness, Schoemann saw the fishing boats first. The trawlers were overmatched, being capable of only 9–10 knots and armed with a single 3pdr gun. For reasons of speed, Domville could not flee so he determined to fight it out. Both torpedo boats made attacking runs against the British vessels and of four torpedoes fired one hit *Columbia* (1887), sinking her. The Germans pulled a lieutenant commander and two deckhands from the waters and locked them below as prisoners.

On first becoming engaged Domville, in *Barbados* (1907), came under heavy fire. 'At the outset the skipper of the *Barbados* was wounded, so that Sir James Domville had to carry on in the wheel-house by himself. This part of the ship was the enemy's target, and inside this structure Lieutenant Domville was being hit by splinters.' But his ship kept plugging away with its little 3pdr gun. 'On several occasions he was knocked down. But the trawlers put up such a stiff fight that after twenty minutes the nearer of the torpedo-boats was compelled to increase the range to 1,200 yards.'[19] Now *Barbados* saw clouds of steam from *A-6* and obvious shellfire damage brought the ship to a halt,

A German 'A'-class torpedo boat, similar to *A-2* and *A-6* which were sunk by Harwich Force destroyers on 1 May 1915. The photograph is of *A-68*. (Author's collection)

although as *Barbados* closed on her the German managed to get under way once more. This caused Schoemann to decide to withdraw.

Half an hour later, by firing his gun and blowing the siren, Lieutenant Domville was able to attract the attention of the Harwich Force destroyer *Leonidas*, which was on patrol off to the southwest. The 3 DF consisting of the 'L'-class HMS *Laforey*, *Lawford*, *Leonidas* and *Lark*, all equipped with three 4in guns and capable of 29 knots, responded to the call at full speed. Now it was the German ships that were overmatched and they fled for the Flanders coast with the British giving chase. Once caught, a running fight developed which lasted for an hour; but the result was not in doubt. Both German torpedo boats were sunk and Schoemann died with his command. It was a much wished-for victory in action, even if accounting for only two small enemy ships. The commander of one of the destroyers signalled to division leader Commander Graham Richard Leicester Edwards in *Laforey* 'it is the custom in our fishing association to put back all fish under six inches in length'.[20]

Columbia had sixteen crew lost with only one deckhand, Arthur Ames,[21] saved. The Germans lost two vessels and thirteen killed, with forty-three taken prisoner. There was some rancour after it was revealed by the captured Germans that the three men taken from the sinking *Columbia* had been left to die when the German vessel went under. These included 47-year-old Lieutenant Commander Walter Hawthorn RNR (acting in the rank of lieutenant), who had emigrated from England to Canada in 1910. 'The death of Lieutenant Commander Hawthorn was a great loss to the Auxiliary Patrol Service. At the beginning of the war he had come to England from Canada at his own expense as a volunteer, and he had been constantly employed in most dangerous work ever since.'[22] The sailors' excuse was that 'their prisoners were below and time was short; so whilst they took the first opportunity to save themselves, they left three British sailors to their fate'.[23]

The Admiralty expressed their appreciation of the way in which the trawlers had fought a superior force, and sent a letter on vellum* to Lieutenant Sir James Domville. Petty Officer Arthur Frederick Hallett, who had fired *Barbados*'s 3pdr gun throughout the action, was awarded the DSM.[24] Commander Edwards received 'Their Lordships' Appreciation'.[25]

The Admiralty also sent a telegram to the Senior Naval Officers, Lowestoft and Harwich, the CinC Nore and the Rear Admiral Dover, stating that there were more of these torpedo boats in Belgian ports whose intentions were the destruction of British Auxiliary Patrol vessels. Such vessels were ordered to cruise in company and not to approach the Belgian coast unless supported by destroyers.[26]

---

* At that time, the equivalent of a Mention in Despatches.

A stern view of the seaplane carrier HMS *Ben-my-Chree*, displaying the aft aircraft hangars. Note the two rear-mounted anti-aircraft guns. (Author's collection)

But in fact the action demonstrated to Admiral Schröder that the 'A' class were simply not good enough ships to use for raiding; and the defeat enhanced Schröder's pleas for reinforcements and heavier vessels, a request which was eventually satisfied.

Return to the Air

On 20 April *Empress* too departed to undergo the same reconstruction as had benefited her sisters. But at the end of the month the Harwich Force gained a replacement, HMS *Ben-my-Chree*,* a former Isle of Man packet ship converted to a seaplane carrier and with the same type of aft hangar shed as was being fitted to *Riviera* and *Engadine*, both of which rejoined Tyrwhitt on 3 May.

The commodore immediately decided on another attack against the Norddeich radio station, which met with the same fate as before, frustrated by high seas. On the 6th he tried again, this time to be foiled by fog. In the confusion, the destroyer *Lennox* was rammed by *Ben-my-Chree*, but with little damage to either. For both these attempts, in addition to its seaplanes *Ben-my-Chree* carried a Sopwith Schneider† on a forward platform from which it was supposed to take off via dollies under its floats.

Showing commendable tenacity of purpose, Tyrwhitt went out once more on the 11th. This essay met with ill-fortune. The Schneider would not start; but *Engadine* manged to launch three aircraft. They were all engulfed in fog

---

* 'Woman of My Heart' in Manx.
† Basically a 'navalised' Sopwith Tabloid.

HMS *Caroline*, the first 'C'-class cruiser. *Conquest* and *Cleopatra*, which joined the Harwich Force in May 1915, were effectively identical. *Caroline* survived two World Wars to become a museum ship in Belfast. (© National Maritime Museum N01582)

before accomplishing anything; one returned safely; another plummeted from the sky, killing the pilot; and the third crashed on landing but the aviator and the wrecked machine were rescued by a destroyer.

After these failures, Tyrwhitt rather gave up on aviation for a while, although he had little choice. *Engadine* was sent to join Beatty's forces, *Ben-my-Chree* was despatched to the Dardanelles and *Riviera* went to his near neighbour, the Dover Patrol.

A Double Reorganisation

In May, the Harwich Force acquired two 'C'-class light cruisers, *Conquest* and *Cleopatra*. These were brand-new ships, launched in January 1915, with two 6in and eight 4in guns and a top speed of 28.5 knots. Together with *Arethusa* and *Penelope*, the four ships were designated as a new entity, the 5th Light Cruiser Squadron (5 LCS). *Undaunted* and *Aurora* continued as the leaders of 3 DF and 10 DF* respectively but were generally away on escort duty or in the South Western Approaches at this time.

With little destroyer cover available, Tyrwhitt was reduced to patrolling in two relays, primarily looking for Zeppelins to shoot down. Indeed, by the end of May, 10 DF had been removed entirely and sent to the western coast to counter U-boat activity in the trade routes. It was a pretty thin time for the Harwich Force.

---

* The 10th Destroyer Flotilla was at this time comprised entirely of 'M'-class vessels and had replaced 1 DF in the Harwich command.

Meanwhile, relations between the two mercurial men at the top of the Admiralty, Churchill and Fisher, came to a head over the Dardanelles campaign. The failure of the attempt to force the Dardanelles by naval power alone had meant the landing of a large force of soldiery, which immediately incurred heavy losses. It seemed to many people that Britain was engaged in a war in Anatolia which it could not win.

But Churchill kept on pushing, sending more and more ships and equipment there. Additionally, Churchill's arrogation to himself of the powers which had traditionally belonged to the First Sea Lord and the Board of Admiralty had become a matter of great contention between the Sea Lords, Churchill and Jacky Fisher himself. Churchill increasingly issued orders for ships and equipment to be sent without Fisher's prior consent. At 0500 in the morning of 15 May, Fisher received four minutes from Churchill calling for yet more reinforcements to the Dardanelles. It was the straw that broke the camel's back. Before he ate his breakfast, Fisher sent his resignation to both Churchill and Prime Minister Herbert Asquith.

Fisher's resignation set in train events that Churchill and Asquith found themselves powerless to resist. His departure, coupled with the breaking news concerning a shortage of high explosive shell on the Western Front, threatened to topple the Liberal government. To stave off opposition attacks on his ministry and the progress of the war, Asquith was forced to agree to a coalition. And the Conservative Party's price for coalition included the sacking of Churchill. On the 20th Asquith wrote to Churchill asking him to leave the Admiralty, a departure which Churchill reluctantly accepted the following day.

The coalition government was formed on the 25th, with Conservative ex-prime minister A J Balfour as First Lord of the Admiralty. As his First Sea Lord he had a compromise candidate, Admiral Sir Henry Jackson – a good administrator and a fine technician but lacking much verve. Tyrwhitt did not want Fisher to go; 'he is my friend as far as I can see,' he told his wife.[27] But on meeting Balfour, the commodore remarked that '[he] is a delightful person to talk to . . . he could not have been nicer and I left prepared to die for him'.[28] In fact the double appointment ushered in a period of calm, much needed at the Admiralty after the tumult of Churchill; but it also heralded a period of placidity and lack of drive.

S-1 Captures a Trawler

HMS *S-1* joined the 8th Submarine Flotilla at Harwich in January 1915. The 'S' class was a little-known type of submarine whose origins lay in a visit by the Admiralty to FIAT-San Giorgio La Spezia yard in Italy back in the summer of 1911. Here they saw the Italian-designed *Medusa* class in construction and were apparently impressed. Back in the UK, Scott Shipyard, owner of FIAT's

Laurenti double hull licence since 1909, offered to build copies of the type for £50,000 apiece.

The Admiralty accepted the quotation and *S-1* was the lead ship of the class, launched on 28 February 1914. She boasted a partial double hull for a size comparable to the 'C' class, excellent buoyancy and good cruising trim, in part due to a refined hull design with a 'ducktail' stern. Although the same size as the 'C'-class, their diving speed and top speed were inferior.

But the Harwich submariners disliked them. 'They were everything a submarine should not be,' thought Lieutenant William Guy Carr RNR, and 'were most unreliable.'[29] This was proven on 21 June 1915. *S-1* was on the first day of a patrol under Lieutenant Commander Gilbert Hilton Kellett, who had commissioned the vessel. Kellett was nine miles north of Heligoland, where he remained submerged all day owing to the presence from time to time of a Zeppelin, a seaplane, nineteen armed trawlers and a destroyer, the latter of which he fired a torpedo at but missed.

That night *S-1* surfaced to charge batteries, whereupon the port engine broke down. Next day, the crew worked to repair the engine whilst submerged at the same time as another Zeppelin and a Parseval airship cruised overhead. But the engine could not be ministered to and the advent of the 24th found Kellett and his men with the batteries run down and no means of recharging them. They were in enemy waters, surrounded by patrol vessels and enemy air cover; they might as well surrender.

But salvation presented itself in the form of a solitary German trawler, the *Ost*; using what little battery power was left, Kellett steered for it, came to the surface, manned the 12pdr gun and captured the trawler. He put his first lieutenant and five men aboard, fixed a towline and pointed the trawler at Great Yarmouth, all the while keeping the submarine's gun trained on the German fishermen.

On the 25th, the trawler's engine broke down. Lieutenant Commander Kellett was not to be defeated. He sent his engineers over and they worked on the old machinery until it spluttered back into life; but only just, for they could now only coax 4 knots out of the German. On the 26th, the engine failed again; and once more, the Royal Navy's technical expertise was equal to it. *S-1* and her prize finally reached Yarmouth the following day.

The captured trawler was fitted with a 6pdr, renamed *Cromsin* and sent to the Mediterranean as a minesweeper. Kellett received 'an expression of Their Lordships' appreciation for resource displayed in capturing German trawler'.[30] After this, the only three boats of the 'S' class built, having been derived from a design intended for Mediterranean waters and seemingly unfitted for the North Sea, were given to Italy in October 1915.

Absent Friends

The 10th Destroyer Flotilla, although notionally part of the Harwich Force, was spending much more time in the southwest than in Harwich. On 13 June they were again ordered to Avonmouth, once more to escort transports carrying the 13th Division on the first leg of their journey to the Middle East. From there they moved to Devonport, to provide an escort for troopships of the 12th Division on their way to the Dardanelles. On 2 July *Mentor*, *Manly* and *Miranda* escorted the liner *Empress of Britain* with 4,500 soldiers aboard, on passage from Liverpool to the Dardanelles campaign. *Mentor* and *Miranda* left her at about 1700 to return and collect *Aquitania*, another Dardanelles-bound liner, now a troopship, with nearly 6,000 men on board and which had set out from Liverpool on 3 July.

The destroyers left *Aquitania* on the morning of 4 July, west of the Scilly Isles, and set course back to Plymouth; 30 minutes after they departed the liner, *U-39* fired a torpedo at the troopship, which fortunately missed. But the U-boat soon found another potential victim.

The *Anglo-Californian* was owned by the Nitrate Producers Steam Ship Co Ltd. (The Anglo Line) and was normally engaged in the South American nitrate trade. In 1915 she was chartered by the Admiralty to carry 927 horses – for military use – from Montreal to Avonmouth. On American Independence Day, she was some 90 miles SW of Queenstown when, at 0800, she was intercepted by *U-39* whose commander, Kapitänleutnant Walter Forstmann, ordered 59-year-old Captain Frederick Daniel Parslow to stop. Parslow's ship was unarmed but she was fast and he decided to run for it. By manoeuvring to keep his stern to the enemy, Parslow held the German off, despite the U-boat opening fire from her deck gun. Parslow's son, also Frederick, was the vessel's second officer and he steered the ship while his father ordered course changes based on the German's fall of shot. Some shots went home, nonetheless. All the while, the *Anglo-Californian* was transmitting SOS signals. Eventually, after some 90 minutes and tiring of the game, Forstmann hoisted the abandon ship signal and Parslow, conscious of his responsibility to his 130-man crew, decided to obey.

But his SOS calls had been picked up by *Mentor* and *Miranda* who were now haring back towards the scene. They urged him to delay abandonment as they were on their way and requested that he continue to transmit as a sort of homing beacon. Parslow complied with the request but it soon became clear to the U-boat that he had no intention of stopping. She opened a withering fire on the bridge and when out of ammunition, closed and fired on anything that moved with rifles. By now, Captain Parslow was dead, literally blown apart by a shell, which removed his head and arm; but his son remained at his post, steering the ship by lying prone on the deck and moving the spokes of the wheel from its bottom. The destroyers arrived too late to save Parslow, but were able to drive off the submarine. They escorted the limping, but still floating, transport into Queenstown. Captain Parslow was posthumously awarded the Victoria Cross in 1919.

On Patrol (Again)

At Harwich, June continued in a quotidian way. On the 2nd *Arethusa* and *Undaunted* sighted a Zeppelin. *Arethusa* managed to get her seaplane off the deck and into the water but it had only just taken off when the aircraft was forced to turn back with mechanical problems. The cruiser opened fire at the airship which made off. A few hours later, a seaplane appeared and dropped three bombs, all of which fell harmlessly in the sea.

A burst of German wireless activity convinced Tyrwhitt to stay out at sea overnight; but nothing resulted from it and he returned back to Harwich on the 4th through the seemingly ever-present North Sea fog. This three-day patrol followed one on 29 and 30 May, which meant that the cruisers had only one intervening night in harbour. Everyone was tired.

Zeppelins were now reported nightly near Harwich and the Force mounted night patrols across their likely routes without ever intercepting one. Bored with inactivity and lack of success, Tyrwhitt proposed a plan to Jackson whereby he would carry out another aerial raid on Cuxhaven. On 3 July he left harbour; but again it was a farce. Although shadowed most of the way by German airships, when they reached the launch area the aircraft had been too badly knocked about on the deck to function. The force returned to port. The sad fact was that the technology behind heavier than air flight had not yet matured sufficiently to be fit for purpose at sea, at least at sea on the deck of a cruiser. Tyrwhitt's ideas were ahead of his *matériel*. The same day that Tyrwhitt departed, Harwich was bombed for the first time, a seaplane attacking the Landguard Fort, and Felixstowe was attacked by Zeppelins on the night of the 7th/8th, causing some damage.

On 18 July, the force was ordered out to hunt for an injured U-boat reported to be 100 miles off Peterhead, in the far north. But as they steamed into the teeth of a gale with five cruisers and sixteen destroyers, the Admiralty recalled them. Nearly everyone on the flagship had been seasick and they all got wet and bashed about for nothing.

So it was that, at the end of July, the Harwich Force was frustrated, a little bored, widely scattered; and keenly awaiting developments.

6

Raiders, Prizes and Mines, August–December 1915

On 4 August, First Sea Lord Admiral Sir Henry Jackson paid a visit to Harwich. He was, thought Tyrwhitt, 'exceedingly nice and complementary' whilst 'not possessed of much small talk'.[1] Nonetheless, he had at least taken the trouble. Jackson's visit marked the start of a busy August for the Harwich Force; four days later, they were called out to hunt a raider.

SMS *Meteor* was an opportunistic conversion of a captured British vessel, the SS *Vienna*, seized at Hamburg on the outbreak of war. Of typical English appearance, the Kaiserliche Marine decided that she would make an excellent covert auxiliary cruiser and minelayer. She was armed with two 8cm guns (3.5in), two machine guns and approximately 350 mines, entered service in May 1915 and placed under the command of Korvettenkapitän Arthur Friedrich Wolfram von Knorr.

On 29 May 1915 *Meteor* set out on her first mission, to lay mines in the White Sea and attack Allied merchant ships transporting coal and other

The German auxiliary cruiser (hilfskreuzer) SMS *Meteor*,
once the British freighter *Vienna*. (Author's collection)

The 1,500grt Isle of Man Steam Packet Company SS *Ramsey* which, as HMS *Ramsey,* was sunk in 1915 by SMS *Meteor*. She is seen here in happier times, circa 1912, when she could carry over 1,000 passengers. (Author's collection)

materiel to Russia. She sank three freighters and her mines accounted for five ships, all British. *Meteor* returned unharmed in June 1915.

Her second mission was to lay mines in the Moray Firth. She sank a small Danish sailing ship but, attempting to pass through the 10th Cruiser Squadron's Northern Blockade, just after dawn on 8 August she was challenged and ordered to stop for inspection by the Armed Boarding Vessel *Ramsey*, an ex-Isle of Man Steam Packet Company vessel, built in 1895 and fitted with two 12pdr guns. Whilst pretending to conform, *Meteor* was able to manoeuvre into a firing position and suddenly opened a devastating gunfire and torpedo attack, quickly overwhelming *Ramsey* which sank with the loss of fifty-three men, including the ship's captain, Lieutenant Charles Raby RNR. Von Knorr rescued four officers and thirty-nine seamen and took them on board his ship as prisoners of war. However, the sinking proved a Pyrrhic victory, for *Ramsey* had managed to radio a report of her attacker before she went down. That night Tyrwhitt was ordered to sea and to take his light cruisers towards Horns Reef in an attempt to intercept the German raider.

It was only 48 hours since the commodore had come in from a sweep of the Bight, but at 2230, *Arethusa*, *Conquest*, *Cleopatra*, *Aurora* and *Undaunted* set out to sea once more in line ahead and at top speed. From the north 1 LCS and Commodore Le Mesurier's 4 LCS were also directed to find the *Meteor*.

At daybreak the Harwich ships transitioned to line abreast and spread out over five miles to extend the range of search. Later, at 0800, Tyrwhitt's force was overflown by a German seaplane, which his anti-aircraft fire failed to discomfort. It sped away to give von Knorr a warning. A Zeppelin also found *Meteor* and passed on the information that there were British cruisers across her line of retreat to the Jade and led her north on roughly the same course as Tyrwhitt was making, some 40 miles astern. Two Zeppelins began to shadow the squadron, keeping out of gunnery range, and passing reports of progress back to the cruisers' intended prey.

At about 0930, Tyrwhitt received a message from the Admiralty telling him that they placed *Meteor* 90 miles west of Horns Reef at 0400. This seemed erroneous to the commodore and he decided to ignore it and hold on to the rendezvous point he had originally been given and which still seemed to him and to Lieutenant Watson, the navigator, more likely to succeed. Once in position, the cruisers turned west and spread out at 10-mile intervals. His persistence was rewarded, for at 1230, *Cleopatra* sighted *Meteor*; and *Meteor* sighted *Cleopatra*.

Von Knorr knew that he could not escape; his ship was slower, less well armed and outnumbered. He gave orders to scuttle. Before so doing, he placed the survivors from *Ramsey* in a passing Swedish lugger, to which he also transferred himself and his crew. *Arethusa* closed the Swede, and being informed by signal that the survivors of *Ramsey* wished to be picked up, ordered them to steer southwest. Tyrwhitt had no present desire to heave-to and effect a transfer as his squadron was threatened not only by the two persistent airships but also by U-boats reported to be in the area.

The British prisoners persuaded their captors to steer in the required direction and, when they came upon a Norwegian vessel, they transferred to it, leaving von Knorr and his crew behind. They were eventually collected from the Norwegian by Tyrwhitt's forces. *Meteor*'s brief career, in which she had sunk ten ships of which four had been neutral Scandinavians, for a total of 17,000grt, was at an end.[*] First Lord Balfour was effusive in praise for Tyrwhitt's work but the commodore was modest; 'I got full marks for it but it was more by luck that by anything else.'[2]

---

[*] Interestingly, all of the Harwich Force light cruisers present received prize money for the sinking of the *Meteor*, even though she committed *felo de se* (*London Gazette* 29853, 8 December 1916).

Zeppelins over the East Coast

As noted in Chapter 4, the first Zeppelin bombing attack on Britain was 13 January 1915 when Great Yarmouth and some Norfolk coastal towns were hit. The raid had actually been intended for the Humber, but poor navigation coupled with winds affecting steering brought the enemy to the Norfolk coast instead.

Everyone expected London to be a target. On 1 January 1915, Churchill warned the Cabinet of an attack on London 'by airships on a great scale at an early opportunity'.[3] Indeed, on 10 January, the London Hospital received a warning from the War Office to expect air raid casualties. Some people sent their children away to the country.

But no such raid took place; the scare faded. Then came May; on the nights of 10, 17 and 26 May Zeppelins bombed Southend and other Thames Estuary locations, and on the last day of the month, a single Zeppelin loitered over the inner northeast suburbs of London for 45 minutes and dropped eighty-nine incendiary bombs and thirty grenades. Seven civilians were killed.

Harwich Force resources were deployed to protect London.[*] At this time, only the cruisers had anti-aircraft guns, the destroyers just having Maxim machine guns on improvised mountings. The former were sent to patrol the coast from Lowestoft to Orford Ness and report to Tyrwhitt and the Admiralty of any Zeppelins sighted; given the opportunity, they were encouraged to attempt to engage them. But in fact, few Zeppelins were observed in this way and no successes against them recorded.

Harwich, as a port town and situated not far from the direct route to London, was clearly in danger of a Zeppelin raid. If one was sighted overhead, the usual procedure was to ignore it unless actually attacked, for fear of attracting the airship's attention and bomb load. Harwich remained untouched until 12 August, when just before midnight a Zeppelin appeared out of the clouds at 10,000ft and passed over Shotley, Parkeston Quay and the ships in harbour, dropping its bomb load as it did so. Four bombs hit Parkeston village; others missed the quay and the moored submarines by just a few feet. Several destroyers had near misses. One bomb exploded so close to a destroyer that everyone on deck was knocked down. On another, the captain's servant was so excited that he forgot that the gangway guardrails had been taken down and fell into the water.

All ships that could bring a weapon to bear blazed away into the night sky, without seemingly causing any inconvenience to the attackers. When it was all over, nineteen civilians had been injured by a bomb which fell on Tyler Street, and were taken to Parkeston School for first aid treatment; some were subsequently transferred to hospital. Harwich had been blooded.

---

[*] Other naval craft were situated in the Thames Estuary and armed with anti-aircraft weapons.

HMS *Mentor*, Minelaying and Controversy

The 10th Destroyer Flotilla had returned to Harwich at the end of July. They were pleased to be back; Commander Barry Domvile noted that 'the Harwich Force was never happy far from its home; there was always the fear of missing a good thing'.[4]

The war in the North Sea was increasingly becoming one of mines and submarines. In order to hinder the latter by use of the former, the Admiralty proposed laying another minefield in the Heligoland Bight. Known as Operation 'AZ', the initiative called for four fast minelayers to create a field on the western edge of Borkum Riff. Eight Harwich destroyers would form their direct escort, while Tyrwhitt and 5 LCS together with the destroyers still at Harwich covered their retirement (two light cruiser squadrons from Rosyth, each with a destroyer division, were to cooperate from the northward). Submarines were to wait across the line of the enemy's probable advance.

Harwich sent the eight destroyers to Sheerness on 13 August to serve as the minelayers' direct escort. But they had no sooner started out than the operation was cancelled; intercepted German signals demonstrated that a minelayer was engaged in lengthening the mine barrier off the Ems, the very area targeted by the British plans, and a few days later, more German signals to incoming U-boats showed that they had themselves mined the position very close to that intended by Operation 'AZ'.

HMS *Princess Margaret*, a Dumbarton-built 5,934grt ex-Canadian Pacific Railway passenger liner taken up for service as a minelayer in December 1914. (Photo: Alamy)

However, this was not the end of the plans for mining in German waters. Although the concept of mining near Borkum Riff had come to grief, the project of laying another offensive minefield in the Bight was not abandoned. But now it was to be sited not at the Nordeney exit from the Jade but by that of the Amrum Bank. The necessary orders were issued on 15 August.

Only one minelayer was to be used, the converted passenger liner HMS *Princess Margaret*, and her close escort was again to be provided from the Harwich Force destroyers, while 5 LCS were to cruise to the westward providing distant cover. The orders specified the minefield was to be laid in an irregular curve, passing 10 miles west of the Amrum Bank Light Vessel. The orders also detailed the tactics to be employed by the destroyer escort. If the enemy attacked, the destroyers were enjoined not to leave the minelayer but were to keep contact with her, maintaining a running fight.

On the 16th, *Arethusa* was due to depart for a refit and Tyrwhitt was going home for a few days leave. But he had no desire to be left out of any action and invented the excuse that *Arethusa* was complete with oil and could not go to Chatham until it was used up. He told the Admiralty that he would go out in her with 5 LCS.

The operation commenced at 1645 on 16 August, when the *Princess Margaret* departed Sheerness under the command of Captain Shirley Litchfield,* Captain-in-Charge of Minelayers. He was met by two divisions of 10 DF, *Mentor, Minos, Moorsom, Miranda, Morris, Manly, Matchless* and *Medusa*. Meanwhile, Tyrwhitt took 5 LCS in *Arethusa* with *Penelope, Cleopatra, Conquest* and the destroyer leaders *Undaunted* and *Aurora*, and sailed from Harwich at 0900 on the 17th, accompanied by four destroyers of 3 DF, *Laurel, Lysander, Lookout* and *Llewellyn*.

All went well until 1600 when a number of trawlers were spotted, some neutral, some presumed German. Then, between 1800 and 1900, Litchfield picked up wireless signals in code which seemed to come from the trawlers. He instructed *Miranda* to board one of them. The crew abandoned their fishing boat and Litchfield later ordered it sunk.

At 1850, *Minos* heard more wireless signals in the near neighbourhood. Though the signals could not be decoded, they seemed to have some reference to the *Princess Margaret* and her eight destroyers; *Medusa* was directed to board the trawler from which the signalling appeared to come. She was German, had no radio, and was on this occasion released.

Litchfield was concerned that the minelayer, which had a maximum speed of 19 knots and was thus slower than any of the destroyers, had been reported;

---

* Who was actually Frederick Shirley Litchfield-Speer. He used the shortened version of his name in the navy.

furthermore, the Admiralty had advised him the German 2nd Torpedo Boat Flotilla had been ordered out.

At 2045, Litchfield sighted four German destroyers a mile or so off to the southeast; and worse, some searchlights, apparently of two cruisers, shone out to the northward of the enemy destroyers. He turned onto an opposite course and called for best speed, assuming that the escorting destroyers had also seen the enemy and would engage them. As the minelayer turned, a loud sound astern was heard. Litchfield thought it was the escort opening fire.

In fact, five German vessels out on patrol, *B-98*, *B-109* and *B-110* (all armed with four 8.8cm/3.5in guns, six torpedo tubes and with a top speed of 36 knots), together with *G-103* and *G-104* (similarly armed but a little slower) had sighted *Princess Margaret* in the gloom and made to attack with torpedoes. *B-98* fired two at 2,000 yards range with the large ship clearly in its sights and then all made off at high speed.

Commander Inman in *Mentor* fleetingly saw some lights flash, identified incoming attackers and turned to place his vessel between the minelayer and the enemy, shouting 'starboard ten, full speed, guns stand by'.[5] Immediately afterwards, his vessel was struck in the bows. A column of water knocked down everyone on the bridge, a dense cloud of black smoke hid everything, and the ship began to settle by the head. Her bows had been blown off. But no other British ship saw the hit; and the rest of the destroyers made off with *Princess Margaret* as their orders told them to.

Tyrwhitt learned that the operation was abandoned at 2141 and steered to meet *Princess Margaret*, but failing to find her and learning from the Admiralty that a superior German squadron had left the Jade, he made for Harwich and

A *G-101*-class destroyer, the same as the 'G' class which encountered *Mentor* on in August 1915. They had been ordered for the Argentine Navy from the German shipyard Germaniawerft in 1912. Still under construction at the outbreak of war, they were seized by the Kaiserliche Marine. (US Naval History and Heritage Command NH 92717)

The 'M'-class destroyer HMS *Mentor* (1914). In August 1915 she was torpedoed by a German destroyer and had her bows blown off, as shown in the photograph. She managed to get back to Harwich unaided. (© National Maritime Museum N03109)

home. But for *Mentor* and her crew, it was a solitary battle for existence. 'The lower portion of her bows had been completely blown away, until the deck of the forecastle from about the foremost gun hung vertically down towards the water with the stem-head submerged.'[6] Fortunately, the ship was under the command of Edward Tyrell Inman, another clergyman's son, who was '[the] best trainer of officers and men', possessed a 'high sense of duty' and was a 'strict disciplinarian but popular for his sense of justice'.[7]

The explosion had destroyed her wireless so calling for help was not an option. It had also smashed all the signalling and oil lamps. Inman disposed of her confidential books and armed his guns and torpedoes for instant action, while his engineering team shored up her bulkheads, placed collision mats and generally tried to save the ship.

Not only did Inman have no radio, his navigational facilities were gone too. He set course westwards, the direction he had last seen the minelayer depart, and began the 360-mile journey home, his bow-less ship nosing into a rising sea 'pushing the whole ocean in front of her' as he later put it.[8] At 1530, off the entrance to G Channel through the east coast minefield, Inman sighted two British submarines and through the agency of their wireless was able to tell of their survival. In a remarkable piece of ship handling, Inman got *Mentor* safely back to Harwich at 1700 with only three men injured and his ship saved.

Tyrwhitt was furious that 'a few German torpedo craft had been able to approach the squadron within a mile, torpedo one of the seven British destroyers present, and cause the abandonment of a carefully planned operation without a single shot being fired at them'.[9] To the Admiralty he criticised both the orders that his destroyers had been placed under and

Litchfield's disposition of them. Their Lordships rejected his opinion, leading to another exchange of letters in which he stated the obvious; 'minelaying must be accepted as a dangerous operation, and should only be undertaken on the darkest nights of the months or during foggy or misty weather'.[10]

Such strictures did not deter the Admiralty and a new plan, Operation 'CY', was developed for mining the Bight. Three minelayers were to be used, *Princess Margaret*, *Angora* and *Orvieto*, each to have a close escort of two destroyers. With *Arethusa* in refit at Chatham, Tyrwhitt did not go on leave but instead transferred his pennant to *Cleopatra*. Early on 10 September he set out in her to support the minelayers which were protected at a distance by battlecruisers, light cruisers and destroyers, all from Rosyth, together with a screen of six Harwich submarines, to cover the minelayers withdrawal. 5 LCS plus the newly-arrived flotilla leader *Nimrod*, with five destroyers, were the Harwich Force's contribution and this time the mission was successful, three fields being laid west and northwest of Amrum Bank.

*   *   *

The Harwich Force now comprised 5 LCS, 9 DF (previously 3 DF and renamed on 7 September*), 10 DF plus *Undaunted*, *Aurora*, *Nimrod* and another new arrival, *Lightfoot*. The latter two ships were members of the *Marksman* class, specifically designed as flotilla leaders, fitted with additional communications equipment and designed to be able to keep up with the latest fast destroyers. Launched in 1915 and equipped with four 4in guns and two twin 21in torpedo mounts, they were capable of 34 knots.

Notionally there were around thirty-five destroyers in the flotillas at this time. But in reality, the Harwich Force was still being pulled from pillar to post owing to the endless calls for escorts to cross-Channel troop movements and anti-submarine activity away from home. Additionally, in the 8th Submarine Flotilla Tyrwhitt could be supported by two depot ships, two destroyer leaders and nineteen submarines, of which ten were 'E' class, all under Captain Waistell.

The Commodore Takes Some Prizes

Like Hipper in 1914, the Admiralty was concerned that trawlers fishing the abundant grounds of the North Sea hid either German spy vessels or German fishermen catching food for Teutonic tables. Both were anathema. So in addition to the quotidian patrolling of the enemy's coasts, the Harwich Force was now tasked with making sweeps towards the Skagerrak in search of such ships.

---

* The 3rd DF designation was assigned to a force attached to the Grand Fleet.

Between 29 September and 1 October, Tyrwhitt swept up to Jutland Bank and hoovered in five trawlers sunk, nine captured and eight set free as innocent neutrals. Prize crews were put aboard the captured trawlers which were sent back to England.

The exercise was repeated the following week. On 6 October, the Harwich vessels captured fifteen trawlers and sank one (which was short of coal). The vessels seized were a particular boon, for trawlers were in great demand as auxiliary warships around British coasts and in the North Sea, as well as for duties such as boom defence, despatch vessels and even as fishing boats. Prize trawlers put into use as minesweepers or auxiliary patrol vessels were given names ending in '-sin'. Twenty-nine German prizes were so used during the war, of which twenty-seven were captured by North Sea patrols. They were deployed mainly in the Mediterranean. For the British sailors, rounding up fishing boats was 'quite a popular jaunt for it always meant fresh fish for supper for the whole ship's company'.[11]

Such sweeps also increased the pressure of the blockade of Germany, for all the sunk or detained boats had been found to be operating on the German government's account. The Harwich Force patrols, which now extended up to the Danish as well as German coasts, effectively shut down this source of food.

Occasionally, the Harwich ships were able to seize bigger prey. At 0600 on All Hallows' Eve, and about 58 miles north of the Borkum Riff Light Vessel, the sweep picked up the Swedish steamer *Osterland* with a cargo of Swedish iron ore consigned to Rotterdam; from there it would undoubtedly find its way to Germany. Tyrwhitt put a prize crew aboard and sent the ship to the Humber for investigation. And another Swedish cargo vessel carrying iron ore for Germany was captured by the Harwich Force on 20 December, the SS *Porjus*.

Changing the Steersman

By October 1915, the strained relationship between Tyrwhitt and his flag captain, Ernest Arbuthnot, came to a head. Arbuthnot, not without reason, felt he was the captain of the ship and should be able to run it day-to-day without interference from Tyrwhitt. The commodore, a hands-on, hard-driving destroyer captain of old, found it difficult to let go. Arbuthnot asked to be reassigned.* Tyrwhitt was not sorry; 'I could not have stood Arbuthnot much longer,' he wrote to Angela, 'and I am intensely relieved to think he is really going. I hope whoever takes his place will be a gentleman.'[12] The latter comment is intriguing but, at this distance in time, Delphic. Arbuthnot's Admiralty record gives Tyrwhitt as stating 'I consider him perfectly competent

---

* He was appointed to the minesweeping sloop HMS *Iris* (1915) in the 1st Minesweeping Flotilla, at Granton.

to command HM ships but lacking the experience necessary in his present position.[13]

As his replacement, Tyrwhitt asked his old friend, 37-year-old Commander Barry Domvile, to accept the position. Domvile was less than keen. He had just taken command of *Lightfoot*, which he enjoyed, had been very happy on his previous ships and was a clever* and opinionated man who valued his independence in command.

In the end, he relented. Domvile became flag captain to Com (T). 'Barry has joined,' the commodore told his wife, 'I feel so happy and I am sure I shall love him and I know I shall get on with him'.[14] Domvile was, of course, a gentleman. And Tyrwhitt did the right thing by him, getting Domvile made up in rank to Acting Captain at the end of 1915.

Mined! The Travails of HMS *Matchless*

There was a war of mines in the North Sea. The War Channel up the east coast of Britain was fully isolated by a bank of mines, both British and German, with defined swept channels through it. These were kept clear by constant sweeping and made dangerous by German counter-mining, increasingly from their Belgian based UC-type submarines. Likewise, the coastal regions of Germany, Holland, Denmark and Belgium all featured minefields, both British and German, laid to impede trade or the egress and entry of U-boats and warships.

On the night of 8/9 November, the Harwich Force was once again out escorting *Princess Margaret* together with *Angora*, another minelayer converted from a passenger vessel and built in 1911 for the British India Steam Navigation Company. Their mission was to lay a field off the Amrum Bank. But, not unusually, the weather was vile, and Tyrwhitt ordered the destroyers back to Harwich. It was raining, dark and there was a nasty toppling sea running. The 'M'-class destroyer *Murray* with *Matchless* to her stern (both launched in 1914) were trying to find the Orford Ness Lighthouse, looking to pick a course for the coast. Both ships had been at sea for 48 hours, during which time they had not seen the sun, stars or land and their knowledge of where they were was now fairly inaccurate.

At 1751 precisely, Lieutenant Commander Henry Taprell Dorling, captain of *Murray*, heard a loud explosion from behind him. It was *Matchless*; she had struck a mine and her stern had been blown off, taking her rudder and screws with it. Her captain reported to Dorling that he thought his ship would float but that it couldn't move. That much was evident, for she could be seen even

---
* On qualifying as a lieutenant, in 1898 he had won the Beaufort Testimonial (for pilotage and navigation), Ryder Memorial Prize (for French) and the Goodenough Medal (seamanship).

in the dark to be lying over to starboard by about 30 degrees, was badly down by the stern and water was washing across half of her deck.

Dorling determined to tow the stricken destroyer to safety. But every attempt to get a line to her by hand failed. Eventually, *Murray* sent a whaler and seven men to carry a line across, a perilous task in high seas. This proved successful and a towing cable was secured. Both ships were broadside on to the wind, pointing southeast. Dorling adjudged that they needed to head southwest to find Harwich, which meant dragging *Matchless*' head around. At 1915, he gently eased up the power to his shafts and began to pull. At 2030, as it started to rain, they had not moved an inch. More power could break the tow wire, but it had to be risked. Slowly, *Murray* increased her revolutions until she was producing the equivalent power for 16 knots – but still not moving.

Then imperceptibly, *Matchless* moved; only to swing back again. And then move a little more. It was finally at 2215 that she came around to the southwest and they were able to head for where they thought Harwich might be. With *Murray* showing revolutions for 8 knots, and making about 3.5, the two ships edged forwards until at dawn they spotted the much-desired Orford Ness Light.

A light cruiser came out from Harwich to meet them and ordered Dorling to go faster. By semaphore, she asked for 10 knots. That caused the towing wire to part 'like a piece of pack thread'.[15] But they were in calmer waters; the cruiser took *Matchless* in tow and to safety. Remarkably, no-one had been killed, or even injured, although *Matchless*' aft 4in gun had been blown in the air and landed barrel first, piercing the roof of a sub lieutenant's cabin – in which he was asleep at the time. Eventually she was taken to Chatham and patched up. It was only when back in harbour that Dorling was informed that they had been manoeuvring to secure the tow in a new minefield laid by *UC-6* two days beforehand.

Another Airborne Raid

Tyrwhitt's enthusiasm for striking from the air had not been satiated and novel ways of getting aircraft nearer the target were examined.

On 5 November, a Deperdussin monoplane from the RNAS base at Felixstowe, with wheels rather than floats, took off from a three-track framework mounted over *Aurora*'s forecastle. Surprisingly, it was a success; but the set-up masked the cruiser's forward 6in gun and it took an appreciable time to dismantle; the idea was not progressed at Harwich.*

---

* Although later experiments resulted in such platforms being fitted to large numbers of cruisers before the war's end.

Deck-launched planes were experimented with in 1915. Here is the Harwich Force's
Arethusa-class light cruiser *Aurora* in November 1915 with a French-built Deperdussin on
the forecastle runway. The aircraft bears the red circle with a white centre identification
roundel which was used by the RNAS up to the end of 1915, when the familiar blue, white
and red one was substituted. (© National Maritime Museum N22556)

The steam packet SS *Viking* in peacetime before her conversion to a seaplane carrier.
(Author's collection)

Furthermore, to the commodore's joy, Harwich gained a new seaplane carrier when HMS *Vindex* joined at the end of November. She had been converted from the fast passenger ship SS *Viking*, built in 1905 and operated by the Isle of Man Steam Packet Company.

Vindex was the first of the 'mixed carriers'; she was configured such that a forward launching platform for land planes was fitted for aircraft with undercarriages. The first to take off from her was a Bristol C single-seater scout on 3 November. Facilities for handling seaplanes were mounted aft, with hoists and a hangar, and in total she could carry seven aircraft, although two were disassembled for passage. On 4 December *Vindex* was escorted out to attack a new German airship base at Hage* and another thought to be at Hoyer (Schleswig). But fog doomed the mission to abandonment (as it did to two later attempts on 18 and 29 January 1916) and two seaplanes were lost in the confusion.

On the 13th Tyrwhitt took the cruisers and destroyers out for a sweep but was forced to send the destroyers back because of bad weather. Then, as it worsened further, Domvile and Watson persuaded him to return with the cruisers too.

On the 20th, he made another sweep through the Bight as a piece of coat-trailing for the battlecruisers, which were at short notice for steam. But he

---

* A small East Frisian town in Lower Saxony.

Side view of the seaplane carrier HMS *Vindex*, converted from the fast passenger ship SS *Viking* in 1915 and showing her prominent seaplane hangar aft. She joined the Harwich Force in November 1915. (Author's collection)

found no trade and the weather was terrible. Then on the 30th, the Admiralty prohibited him from going out in bad weather for fear that a ship would be damaged and fall prey to the enemy. The instruction made Tyrwhitt very angry; 'Today I wrote to Their Lordships . . . I was furious at not being able to go out for any customary prowl around.'[16] And he fumed some more when a German minelayer was reported to be out.

A Short seaplane taking off near Harwich. The picture was taken from the quarterdeck of aircraft carrier HMS *Vindex*. Note the two 12pdr deck guns. (© Imperial War Museum Q 73674)

The Life and Loss of *E-6*

The short but eventful career of HMS *E-6* gives an example of the workload of the Harwich Force's submarines. She was a Group 1 'E'-class submarine, launched in November 1912 and commissioned the following year. Armed with four 18in torpedo tubes and capable of 15 knots surfaced and 9.5 knots submerged, she and her sisters formed the core of the Harwich-based submarines in the early part of the war.

According to submariner Lieutenant Ronald Blacklock; 'the job of the Harwich submarines was to act as scouts for the Grand Fleet; we patrolled enemy waters with the object of reporting by wireless if any capital ships came out'.[17] *E-6*'s short career saw her doing just that.

Under her captain, Lieutenant Commander Cecil Ponsonby Talbot, she participated in the Harwich Force's first action of the war, when *Amethyst* towed her out to Terschelling for her first patrol. During the Battle of Heligoland Bight, she was nearly rammed by HMS *Southampton*. On patrol in the Bight, she fouled her hydroplane guard on a mine cable on 25 September 1914 but Talbot manged to extricate his vessel from a potentially fatal problem.

Then in April 1915, now commanded by 31-year-old Lieutenant Commander William James Foster, she fired torpedoes at German targets, a submarine on the 13th and a torpedo boat (*S-168*) the following day; both missed. And on 30 May she fired on the battlecruiser *Moltke*, again without success.

By September, *E-6* became part of the frenzied anti-Zeppelin activities. Fitted with four 6pdr anti-aircraft guns, she and *E-8* were sent into the Bight to look for German airships and attack them. They did not succeed in shooting any down. And on 24 October, Foster made two attacks on German light cruisers; neither target was hit.

On Boxing Day, *E-6* was once more assigned to patrol duty in the North Sea, on this occasion to hunt for U-boats. The Admiralty had reached the conclusion that German submarines were likely to come out into the North Sea by Horns Reef, and Foster was ordered to intercept them; after six days out, they would be relieved.

An early 'E'-class submarine, *E-1*, identical to *E-6* which was sunk by mine at the end of 1915. (Author's collection)

The 12pdr gun of an 'E'-class submarine, the most common type of sub in the Harwich
Force in 1915. It was mounted to the rear of the conning tower. This is a group 2 or 3 vessel,
E-9 upwards, as *E-1* to *8* did not originally mount guns.
(National Museum of US Navy 9608-4)

Just outside Harwich, near the Sunk Light Vessel, *E-6* was unwittingly
approaching the position where the armed trawler *Resono* had been mined
just a short while beforehand, with the loss of thirteen lives. A destroyer on
the spot frantically signalled to Foster that he was standing into danger.
Although it seemed that the signal had been read and understood, for some
reason the submarine continued on its course. She hit a mine and blew up,
sinking with all hands, thirty-one men in total.

E-6 was victim to a new field laid by the German minelaying submarine
UC-5. 'Her loss was perhaps the biggest naval disaster yet attributable to the
UC minefields.'[18] In West Byfleet, Gertrude Foster would never celebrate
another festive season with her husband. John and Sarah Coyles would not
see their 26-year-old stoker son George in Doctor Street, New Seaham Colliery,
again. Nor would Edward and Cecilia Tuck see their son Francis, another
stoker, in Milford Street, Cambridge. It was not a good end to the year.

*   *   *

The war which 'would be all over by Christmas' had dragged on for another full year. 1915 had not been a triumph for either the navy or Britain in general; a total of 855,721 gross tons of British merchant shipping had been sunk by German action, 87 per cent of it by the U-boats.[19] Only 650,000 tons of replacement capacity had been built.

For the navy, 1915 had started badly with the sinking of the battleship HMS *Formidable* on 1 January, torpedoed with the loss of 583 men. The battleships *Irresistible*, *Ocean*, *Goliath*, *Triumph* and *Majestic* had all been sunk in the disastrous and costly Dardanelles campaign, from which on 28 December it was decided to withdraw. The armoured cruisers *Argyll* (wrecked) and *Natal* (internal explosion) were lost, with severe cost to life. And no great Trafalgar had been fought, sweeping the German navy from the seas, despite the expectations of most of the public and, indeed, the Royal Navy too. As historian David Morgan-Evan put it,

> the Fleet proved unable to prevent the German navy from bombarding seaside towns – killing civilians and bringing the destruction of war to familiar British holiday destinations in the process – cries of 'where was the Navy?' were quick to emerge from incredulous elements within British society. Victories at Heligoland Bight, the Falklands, and Dogger Bank did little to assuage growing demands for the fleet to do more.[20]

At Harwich it had been mostly a year of frustration. The weather and the primitive technology had prevented any success from the air. The German ships had largely refused to come out. And countless sweeps across the North Sea produced little in the way of results.

As for the Army, the Western Front had turned into a war of attrition. In 1914 the British had suffered 90,000 casualties of which 50,000 were killed. That effectively wiped out the pre-war British regular army. Then 1915 brought a litany of failure. In March, Neuve Chapelle cost 11,200 British casualties; April and the Second Battle of Ypres 59,275; May saw 11,619 casualties at Aubers Ridge and 16,648 at Festubert, where the CinC of the British Expeditionary Force Sir John French withdrew on the 25th, citing shortage of ammunition, and with no gains to set against his not-inconsiderable losses. Coupled with the later Battle of Loos (59,247), these encounters caused the loss of most of the pre-war Reservists and Territorials. Secretary of State for War Lord Kitchener's recruitment drive had produced millions of men, but many were not yet ready for combat. And the scale of losses, and dissatisfaction with the prosecution of the war, caused the government to ask for the resignation of French on 6 December. Everyone wondered what 1916 would bring.

7

The Loss of the *Arethusa*, January and February 1916

1916 began with the Harwich Force undertaking a blockade operation. The Admiralty received information that a suspicious iron ore carrier, the Swedish SS *Nordland*, was on passage for Rotterdam. Commodore Tyrwhitt was ordered to intercept and went out with his cruisers on 2 January to try to meet her off Terschelling. Disregarding the instructions that he should not risk his ships in poor weather (noted in Chapter 6), he put out into a gale with seas so dreadful that some vessels recorded rolling through 45 degrees each way. The Force boarded several ships, none of which proved to be the *Nordland*. The weather, bad when he left Harwich, now became appalling so they returned to harbour on the 5th. The return was not without incident, for the seas were so rough that 29-year-old Lieutenant Commander Edward Ogle Disney of the *Arethusa* was washed overboard without anyone noticing. He died alone, amid crashing waves, watching his ship recede into the distance; it was not realised that he was gone until he failed to turn up for his watch. On the 6th it was reported that *Nordland* had never sailed.

The weather during the first two years of the war had not been Tyrwhitt's friend. The winter of 1914/15 had been the wettest on record with 16.6in of rain falling in December, January and February,* with nearly 20in in Coulsdon, Surrey. 1915/16 came close to beating this record with 14.7in between December and February.[1] The constant fog the Harwich Force experienced was probably a function of this, and November 1915 to March 1916 inclusive was remarkable for the extreme variation of the weather from ice and snowstorms in November to mild temperatures in January. It was difficult to know what to expect day-by-day and the adverse conditions kept Tyrwhitt confined to harbour, given the strictures from the Admiralty concerning the risk of venturing out in poor climatic circumstances.

On the 10th the Force stood by for a seaplane raid, but it was cancelled due to the weather. And the next day the submarine patrol was sent out but then recalled for the same reason. By the 16th, Tyrwhitt was moved to grumble that they would 'develop into the limpet fleet if we don't get a move on soon. We have not been outside for ten days.'[2]

---

* A record not broken until 2013/14.

Back to the Air

Tyrwhitt was a man of considerable tenacity. The consistent failure of his attempts to make airstrikes against Zeppelin bases did not deter him and he went to the Admiralty to badger First Sea Lord Jackson for permission to conduct more such operations.

By the end of 1915, experiments with flying seaplanes off *Vindex*'s forecastle, and successfully picking them up, had been completed and Tyrwhitt's pleas to the Admiralty gained him permission to carry out two operations. The first, codenamed 'ARH', was an attack on the Hage airship sheds near Norddeich on the western side of the Bight; the other, imaginatively called 'HRA', targeted the sheds at Hoyer on the Schleswig coast. For the latter, as the picking-up rendezvous for the seaplanes would have to be in the neighbourhood of Horns Reef and hence the German High Seas Fleet, battlecruiser support would be provided at a distance and the Admiralty would be responsible for planning and timing. But for 'ARH' at the Borkum end of the Bight such support seemed unnecessary and since the whole force used would come from Harwich the selection of the date was left to Tyrwhitt, who would take charge of the operation and provide the resources.

On 5 January, Tyrwhitt received approval of the plan for 'ARH' that he had submitted. But continuing bad weather and gales delayed the operation until the 18th, when there was a break in the conditions. That morning, six submarines left Harwich to form a patrol line in case of the emergence of enemy ships, provoked by the attack; they were *E-23*, *D-3*, and four of the new 'H' class, *H-1*, *H-6*, *H-8* and *H-10*. Captain Waistell was also with them in *Firedrake*.

A model of the submarine HMS *D-1*, which served with the Harwich Force until August 1916. The 'D' class were the Royal Navy's first submarines capable of operating significantly beyond coastal waters. They were also the first boats to be fitted with wireless transmitters. Ten were laid down between 1907 and 1910, though only eight were completed. They were armed with three 18in torpedo tubes and a 12pdr gun.
(Photo; Creative Commons GFDL CC-BY-SA)

The H class had been ordered in November 1914 when, desperate for materials for shipbuilding, the Admiralty contracted Bethlehem Steels in the USA to supply ten American 'H'-class submarines in kit form. They were assembled, to avoid contravening US neutrality, in the Canadian Vickers works at Montreal. A second batch was also ordered on Bethlehem, again to be shipped to Vickers Canada for fitting out. The first block arrived in the UK in May and June 1915, and four joined the Harwich force in October, but the later orders were delayed by the US government until America entered the war in 1917.

Tyrwhitt sailed in *Arethusa* in the afternoon of the 18th with his light cruisers and destroyers, together with *Vindex*. For once it seemed that the weather gods were smiling on him and the barometer was steady; but soon after passing the position where the force turned to approach the Bight they ran into fog.

The time set for the release of the aircraft was 0700; by 1000 there was still fog near the shore and a strong wind had arisen from the southwest. As Tyrwhitt considered his options, further problems were heaped around him by the news that *H-6* had gone aground off Ameland* in neutral Holland. If the submarine could not be freed, the Dutch would intern it and the crew. This and the weather persuaded the commodore to call off the operation and he despatched the carrier back to harbour, escorted by two destroyers, whilst taking the rest of his force to find the missing sub.

He failed, but Waistell discovered her in neutral territorial waters in the Friesche Gat, so firmly aground that he considered that no attempt could be made to get her off. Unwilling to lose valuable and experienced submariners to internment, Waistell sent a motor boat to take off some of the crew. Two officers, the coxswain, chief engine room artificer (ERA) and eight ratings had been picked up when Tyrwhitt countermanded any further such rescue because of the risk of loitering in an exposed position when he could hear considerable German radio activity.

Condemning *H-6* and her remaining twenty-two crew to their fate, the Force took off at 20 knots, which rapidly became eight as a southwesterly gale strengthened, and eventually reached home without further mishap. Yet another air attack attempt had been ended by the weather.

The submarine was indeed interned by the Dutch and on 4 May 1917, she was sold to the Netherlands navy, becoming HNLMS *O-8*. Nor was this the end of her multi-navy life. In 1940, the Dutch scuttled her after the German invasion but the Germans recovered the boat and put her into service.

*   *   *

---

* One of the West Frisian Islands off the north coast of the Netherlands.

The Royal Navy entered the war with no effective underwater anti-submarine weapon. Improvisation produced a number of stopgap measures. These included primitive depth charges made from aircraft bombs attached to lanyards which would trigger their charges. A similar idea was a 16lb guncotton charge in a lanyard-rigged can; two of these lashed together became known as the 'depth charge Type A'. These were followed by the Egerton depth charge, which comprised equal pairs of 75lb charges of TNT, separated by 120ft of electrical triggering wire. This had an estimated danger radius of 25ft. They were in general use by destroyers and other vessels in early October 1915.

On 11 January 1916 the scout cruiser HMS *Blonde* (1910), operating from Scapa Flow with the Grand Fleet, was damaged by an unprompted explosion of an Egerton charge which killed two able seamen. Jellicoe immediately ordered that the Egertons be withdrawn from all ships under his command, which for these purposes included the Harwich Force. They were not replaced by any other anti-submarine weapon.[*] This would serve to annoy Commodore Tyrwhitt before the month was out.

Tyrwhitt was determined to try Operation 'ARH' again but once more the climatic conditions were unfavourable until the 28th. Again he proceeded to sea with *Vindex* in company and arriving at the designated position, the carrier was ordered to begin hoisting out her aircraft. Before she could obey the order, a torpedo was seen to pass so close ahead of *Arethusa* that it seemed actually to graze her stem.

Captain Domvile had recently become engaged to Alexandrina von der Heydt (they would marry on 9 February). As he saw the torpedo racing towards them, he thought that 'another marriage which had been arranged would not take place'.[3] He turned into the track, seeing no submarine but spotting another torpedo, which also missed his ship.

Tyrwhitt ordered *Vindex* away and withdrew with the rest of his force at full speed, cancelling the operation as he went. As they did so, the ships were enveloped in thick fog which would in any case have aborted the plan. Back in Harwich, he wrote a furious note to the Admiralty; 'had the *Arethusa* and eight destroyers in company been fitted with Egerton's depth charge,' he wrote, 'the submarine could hardly have escaped. The position from *Arethusa*'s point of view was an ideal one, and I strongly urge that we may be permitted to rearm with the only offensive weapon for dealing with submarines that is at present available, as we have no means of retaliation.'[4] As a result of his representation the Harwich Force was allowed to refit the Egerton charge on the understanding that it was all done strictly by the manual. But the birth of naval carrier aviation was proving difficult!

---

[*] The Type-D and Type D-star charges, the first true depth charges to be designed from scratch, came into use during 1916 as the rate of manufacture allowed.

The Death of a Nereid

For much of the latter part of 1915, the German High Seas Fleet had been confined to port or the immediate area around its bases. But the unenterprising von Pohl was dying of cancer and had been succeeded at the turn of the year by Vizeadmiral Reinhard Scheer, who was of an altogether more aggressive frame of mind.

Tyrwhitt had taken the Harwich Force out for a practice cruise on 9 February. When the Admiralty picked up signals indicating that some sort of German fleet activity was brewing, he was ordered to send the destroyers home to refuel and to take 5 LCS and set up a patrol line northwest of Texel to look for any approaching enemy formation. The Harwich submarines not at sea and the destroyers were put on 30 minutes notice for sailing and the Grand Fleet was readied for steam at an hour's warning.

In the later afternoon of the 10th, Tyrwhitt was instructed to refuel the cruisers. The Admiralty had developed an appreciation that an attack on the

Admiral Carl Friedrich Heinrich Reinhard Scheer, commander of the High Seas Fleet from January 1916 to August 1918. (Author's collection)

coast was planned and the Harwich Force was ordered to sea, with the submarines, to guard against that eventuality.

Meanwhile, that same day Scheer indicated his new more forward policy by sending a destroyer sweep into an area east of the Dogger Bank where the 10th Sloop Flotilla was minesweeping. They were found in the darkness by the German destroyers who engaged with gunfire and fired torpedoes, sinking HMS *Arabis* at around 2300.

At 0030 on the 11th the news of the attack reached the Admiralty and was also sent directly to Tyrwhitt. It was thought the destroyers might be the advance guard of the anticipated High Sea Fleet coastal raid and Tyrwhitt sailed with all of 5 LCS, *Lightfoot* and eighteen destroyers at 0200 to try to guard the main channel through the east coast mine barrier. But signals intelligence then revealed

Arethusa was a nymph and daughter of Nereus and hence a Nereid. The river god Alpheus fell in love with her but as she wanted to remain a chaste attendant of Artemis, Arethusa fled from her home in Arcadia beneath the sea and eventually emerged as a fresh water fountain on the island of Ortygia in Syracuse, Sicily. She and her would-be lover are shown here as *Aréthuse et Alphée* by Léopold Burthe. (Author's collection)

that any planned coastal raid had been aborted owing to fog off the Jade and the Grand Fleet and Harwich Force were ordered to return to harbour at 1950.

The route home took the Harwich Force through mine-infested waters. Travelling at 20 knots they had passed by the North Cutler Buoy, just outside the northern entrance to Harwich, when *Arethusa* struck a mine, killing nine men outright, all of them in the aft boiler room. The engines stopped at once and she began to settle by the stern. Captain Colin Maclean in *Lightfoot* tried to effect a tow, but the hawser snapped; Commander Fischer Burges Watson in *Loyal* then tried with the same result. The flagship drifted, grounded on Cutler Shoal and broke in two.

Only then did Tyrwhitt give the order 'abandon ship'; in the process two more men were killed when a Carley float overturned and entangled them in the webbing at its floor. The commodore was the last man to leave the ship; and even after that, he went briefly back on board, for reasons discussed in Chapter 17.

He had believed himself to be the last man to depart the ship, but a stoker who had slept through the whole thing then appeared on deck waving and shouting. Another stoker 'escaped by climbing up the inside of the funnel. He was seen appearing over the top . . . his clothes had all been burnt off and his injuries were terrible.'[5] The man's name was Joe Honey and a fellow sailor from *Arethusa* named Weaver met him again after the war and noted that 'he looked awful – his face and hands seemed to be just skin stretched over the bones. But he seemed quite happy about everything.'[6]

The following day Tyrwhitt returned to his cabin to salvage his papers and the ship continued to lie where she had grounded, slowly disintegrating in the waves. *Arethusa* had packed a lot of action into her 18-month career; but now she was just scrap.

The Admiralty telegraphed to Tyrwhitt 'the loss of your flagship which has so well upheld her historical reputation under her present officers and men is much regretted, but we are relieved to hear that the loss of life is not greater. A new ship to replace *Arethusa* is not available at the present moment.'[7] The lack of a replacement ship rather irked Tyrwhitt, who had been promised *Centaur*, then on the stocks, by Admiral Jackson in August the previous year. But she would not be ready until at least May. He was ordered to choose another from his existing ships in which to fly his broad pennant and picked *Cleopatra* again.

Captain Domvile was spared the ordeal of a court martial for the loss of his ship as he had been absent on honeymoon at the time; in any case the Admiralty eventually waived the formality, although not before first informing Tyrwhitt that he would face a court martial for the loss of his flagship. His furious response led to swift backtracking.

8

Zeppelins and Tragedy, March 1916

The Germans had declared a war zone around the Britain Isles within which merchant ships would be sunk without warning on 1 February 1915. But the sinkings of the passenger liners *Lusitania* (May 1915), *Arabic* (August 1915) and *Hesperian* (September 1915) by U-boats and the loss of America life had caused outrage in the neutral United States. The US government protested at the deliberate attack on non-combatant vessels and the deaths of its citizens. A sharp exchange of diplomatic notes ensued and the temper of the country at large was inflamed. These caused concern in Berlin, for the Kaiser and many of his ministers wished to keep America neutral and out of the war.

The American government's diplomatic protests had been so sharp that the Kaiser and his chancellor, von Bethmann-Hollweg, felt constrained to act. German ambassador to the USA, Johann Heinrich von Bernstorff, was told to inform the American government that, until further notice, all passenger ships would only be sunk after a warning and the saving of passengers and crews, a message he passed to US Secretary of State Robert Lansing at the end of August. German naval opinion was not in favour of such concessions and Admiral Alfred von Tirpitz, State Secretary of the Imperial Navy Office, offered his resignation in protest.[*] It was declined by the Kaiser.

Instructions to U-boat commanders were reinforced. They were prohibited from attacking liners of any nationality without giving due warning and ensuring the safety of passengers. As this was considered to expose the U-boats to unacceptable risks of attack and loss, in September 1915 Germany took the decision to withdraw them from western waters altogether. They were concentrated instead on the Mediterranean, where the chances of meeting liners with Americans aboard were considered small.

This had provided a blessed relief in the Western Approaches and in the North Sea. Harwich Force destroyers 'on loan' to the western commands returned home and passenger vessels were left unmolested. But Germany changed this policy on 10 February 1916. Objecting to the arming of merchant ships, which exposed the U-boats to gunfire when they surfaced, neutral

---

[*] Tirpitz did eventually resign. He had strongly advocated unrestricted submarine warfare, which was resisted by Chancellor Bethmann-Hollweg who, tiring of Tirpitz's constant criticism of his policies, engineered a situation whereby the Kaiser asked Tirpitz for his resignation, which was given on 19 March 1916.

nations were informed that 'in view of the aforesaid circumstances, enemy merchantmen carrying guns are not entitled to be regarded as peaceful merchantmen. The German naval forces, therefore, after a short interval in the interest of neutrals, will receive an order to treat such vessels as belligerents.'[1] Further communications made it clear that the new policy, which meant that defensively-armed merchantmen were liable to be torpedoed without warning, would come into force on 1 March. In reality, the policy meant that all merchant ships were once more under threat of torpedo attack.

This was in line with Scheer's policy of increasing the naval pressure on Britain. On 5 March he demonstrated the new approach by taking the bulk of the High Seas Fleet to a position off Texel, the furthest south they came in the whole war, to try to attack British light forces sent out to chase away Zeppelins on bombing raids over England. Tyrwhitt, hearing reports of an enemy near Texel, left port on the 6th at 0900. He thought that this time he may be able to intercept and fight a like foe. But when he sought Admiralty permission to do so he was refused; the intelligence that the German fleet was out had been

The Harwich Force's elusive enemy; a Zeppelin in flight. This is *L-64*, built in 1918 with her first flight on 11 March and commissioned two days later. The ship was quickly in service and was involved in a raid on the North of England on the evening of 12 April. At the end of the war she was taken over by Britain. (US Naval History and Heritage Command NH 60773)

received in Room 40 and Tyrwhitt would have sailed into their arms. It was a lucky escape but his disappointment in being unable to come to grips with the enemy on a level playing field showed when he wrote to Roger Keyes that 'the Harwich Force is not nearly so much in evidence now, as our opposite numbers . . . are just double our weight in guns and tons. I have very direct orders about not taking them on.'[2]

However, increasing Zeppelin bombing raids on London and other cities were straining the political debate. London's theatreland was attacked in October 1915, the Midlands in January 1916, and Hull at the beginning of March. Parliament was riled. On 7 March, First Lord of the Admiralty Arthur Balfour presented the Naval Estimates to the House of Commons. He painted a picture which some found rather too optimistic. In the subsequent debate Winston Churchill, now out of office and a backbencher, lambasted the Admiralty; 'a strategic policy . . . purely negative in character, by no means necessarily implies that the path of greatest prudence is being followed. I wish to place on record that the late Board [i.e. Churchill's administration] would certainly not have been content with an attitude of pure passivity during the whole of the year.'[3] He went on to address the Zeppelin issue. 'We hear a great deal about air raids. A great remedy against Zeppelin raids is to destroy the Zeppelins in their sheds. I cannot understand myself why all these many months, with resources far greater than those which Lord Fisher and I ever possessed, it has not been found possible to carry on the policy of raiding.'[4] Churchill even called for the return of Fisher. There was, of course, much of the self-serving in his speech. But it had the effect of raising the Admiralty from its quotidian torpor. Raids from the sea shot up everyone's agenda.

The Attack on Hoyer

Therefore Operation 'HRA' was reconstituted. Hoyer, on the Schleswig coast, opposite the island of Sylt, was again the target. By mid-March weather conditions seemed appropriate. Tyrwhitt finalised the orders on the 22nd and on 24 March he sailed. With Tyrwhitt in *Cleopatra* were the 5th Light Cruiser Squadron, *Aurora*, *Nimrod*, and two divisions of 10 DF, plus *Undaunted*, *Lightfoot*, and two divisions of 9 DF, twelve destroyers in total, with *Vindex* carrying seaplanes.

The carrier was to be escorted to a position eight miles southeast of the Vyl Light Vessel where she would release her seaplanes, cruise in that area to recover her brood and then be escorted back to Harwich. The battlecruiser force from Rosyth would be in distant attendance. It seemed simple.

The following day, at 0530 and despite the bitter cold and snow squalls, *Vindex* got her seaplanes away successfully, two Sopwith Baby aircraft and three Short 184s. Shortly after take-off a torpedo was seen approaching

Cleopatra; fortunately, it was observed in time and was avoided by a speedy helm order. Tyrwhitt left some destroyers to keep the submarine underwater, notwithstanding that 'he suspected it to be one of our own',[5] and the Force proceeded to the Vyl lightship to wait for the returning seaplanes.

But success did not attend them. Only two aircraft were picked up. One seaplane crashed in Germany; a Sopwith Baby suffered engine failure on its way back and had to land near the coast; and a Short 184 landed to help but then found it could not take off again. All three pilots were made prisoners of war and although the Baby was sunk by its pilot, the Germans recovered it and subsequently flew it with German markings. Of the two pilots who returned to the carrier, one bombed a factory and the other made the not insignificant discovery that the airship base was actually not at Hoyer but at Tondern, further inland. He had also found that his bomb release had jammed and he was forced to return with his 'cargo'.

Meanwhile, in the course of looking for the submarine which had fired at the flagship, *Lightfoot*, with two divisions of destroyers, sighted at 0840 two German armed trawler patrol boats (Vorpostenboot) about six miles off the northern end of Sylt Island, steaming towards the shore. Three 'M'-class

A Sopwith Baby floatplane, such as flew from HMS *Vindex* on 25 March 1916 in the attack on Hoyer. The Baby (also known as the Admiralty 8200 Type) was a development of the two-seat Sopwith Schneider which won the eponymous trophy in 1914. It had a wooden structure with fabric covering. A Lewis gun was mounted either above the fuselage firing through the propeller arc, without the aid of synchronisation, or over the top wing. (Author's collection)

destroyers, *Morris*, *Mansfield* and *Murray*, were within range of them. Outgunned, it took only minutes for the first trawler, *Braunschweig*, to be sunk. The other, the *Otto Rudolf*, was frequently smothered in smoke which impeded the destroyer's aim and it was after 0900 before she was despatched and her crew rescued by HMS *Murray*. It was 'chicken butchery',[6] according to Commander Dorling.

The guns of the trawlers had done no damage to the British ships; but now the caprices of fate would. Seeing *Mansfield* open fire on the trawlers, *Laverock* left her place in the line and surged past *Lassoo*, opening fire and altering to port to bring all guns to bear. The flotilla leader *Nimrod* signalled to her to return to her position, a signal which was also seen in *Medusa*, where it was taken to apply to them. In turning to obey she was run into by *Laverock*, which emerged from the smoke of battle intending to take up the position for which *Medusa* was also steering. *Medusa*'s engine room began to fill with seawater and though at first the flow of water was checked by a collision mat, it was soon obvious that she could not steam.

After 30 minutes or so, *Lightfoot* took *Medusa* in tow, keeping two destroyers with her and sending the rest to join Tyrwhitt. The difficulty of towing a crippled ship, no more than seven or so miles from the enemy's coast, was compounded by the presence of German seaplanes overhead, who maintained a steady bombing attack. They kept this up for some four hours, operating in relays, while the escorting destroyers fired their 2pdr pom-poms at them to keep them at a height which reduced their bombing accuracy. There were a number of near misses, but no hits. And by 1100 the tow had only moved a mile from the collision site, at which point Tyrwhitt arrived with 5 LCS. He had detached *Vindex*, increased to 25 knots and come hurtling to the scene as soon as he had been informed of the problem. The commodore ordered *Aurora* to stand by *Medusa* to assist, and the whole squadron moved off westward. Seaplanes continued to fly over them, dropping bombs without effect, though *Conquest* was once nearly hit.

By trial and error, it was found that the speed of towing could be 12 knots and at this pace the squadron proceeded for home, enemy aircraft appearing at intervals and being engaged by the guns of the cruisers. But at 1238, a message was received from the Admiralty ordering Tyrwhitt to return to base at once. Although they didn't say as much, it was believed that the High Sea Fleet might be coming out; the Grand Fleet was ordered to readiness. But Tyrwhitt still harboured hopes of saving the damaged destroyer. He instructed the escort with *Vindex* to re-join him and stayed at sea in deteriorating weather with high winds and snow. Then, at 1940 the tow parted. In the conditions, affixing a new one was impossible and at 2015, Tyrwhitt signalled '*Lightfoot* take off *Medusa*'s crew and sink *Medusa*. *Nimrod* and destroyers proceed north

15 knots. *Aurora* close *Lightfoot* and assist.' Thirty minutes later he asked whether it had been possible to take off the crew; MacLean in *Lightfoot* replied that so far he had been unable to do so, and the commodore signalled at 2105 to *Aurora*, 'cancel orders. Tell *Medusa* to put out all lights and that we will come back to her in the morning.'[7] The captain of *Medusa*, Lieutenant Commander Cecil Rupert Hemans, reported that she was sinking anyway.

Meanwhile Beatty and the battlecruisers had arrived and stood by; with this protection available, the ever-belligerent Tyrwhitt proposed to the Admiralty that he should make a sweep with the battlecruisers to catch any German scouting forces returning at daylight. This was rejected out of hand.

It was pitch black; the Admiralty had warned that German light forces may be out, despite the by now gale-force weather. At 2215, Captain Frederick Parland Loder-Symonds in *Cleopatra* observed close on his port bow a sudden shower of sparks, as if from a coal-burning vessel at high speed. He immediately ordered a turn towards the apparition and at high speed rammed amidships the torpedo boat *G-194*, which had been returning from patrol with her sister ship *G-193*. *Cleopatra* cut the German vessel in half, sinking her with all ninety-three men aboard killed.

But this success was short lived; his change of course brought *Cleopatra* perilously close to *Undaunted*, the next astern and in endeavouring to avoid each other the two ships collided, the *Undaunted* striking the flagship a

SMS *G-194* (1911) was sunk when rammed by HMS *Cleopatra* on 26 March during the return from the raid on Hoyer. She was a *S-138*-class torpedo boat, armed with one 88mm/3.5in and two 50mm/2in guns and three torpedo tubes. The photograph shows a slightly earlier version of the class, *V-150*.
(US Naval History and Heritage Command NH 45405)

glancing blow on the port quarter and causing slight damage to the stern.

The squadron sailed on in the dark and once more *Undaunted* and Captain St John were abandoned and damaged. Her bows were stoven in and the collision bulkheads would not tolerate a speed of more than 6 knots. Moreover, Tyrwhitt in *Cleopatra* had lost contact with the rest of his ships during the manoeuvres and was unaware that *Undaunted* was damaged (having mistaken the noise of the impact for an exploding boiler in *G-194*) until he received a signal from St John asking for a ship to stand by him.

While this was going on, a superb piece of seamanship by Lieutenant Commander Vernon Butler in *Lassoo* was responsible for saving *Medusa's* ship's company. Heeding Heman's call, he first went alongside the sinking destroyer, despite the filthy weather, to take men off. But the waves knocked the two ships together and to avoid damage to his own vessel he pulled off and instead put his bow against the side of *Medusa* and the remaining crew were able to jump onto his forecastle. As Commander Dorling noted 'with two little ships rolling, pitching and grinding together in heavy seas and in pitch darkness it required a cool head and consummate nerve'.[8]

Tyrwhitt ordered *Undaunted* to head for the Tyne; St John replied that he could make 6 knots but would like an escort for help in case the bulkheads gave way, and a submarine screen. This request was seemingly ignored, for Tyrwhitt took his cruisers to join Beatty, who was sweeping back to the vicinity in which the *Medusa* had been abandoned. He had some hope of meeting the German battlecruisers alone, intending if they were closely supported by battleships to withdraw towards the Grand Fleet, which was now also at sea. *Aurora* and *Conquest* linked up with Beatty, while *Cleopatra* left at noon for Harwich. However, the Admiralty informed Beatty that Scheer had cancelled any sailings due to the conditions and so he sent four destroyers to escort *Undaunted* and set his own course for Rosyth and home.

Another operation to attack the Zeppelin sheds had failed in its objective, lost a destroyer,* damaged a cruiser and sunk a German torpedo boat. And the weather had again been terrible. To cap it all, the submarine *E-24*, which had sailed from Harwich on 21 March to conduct a minelaying operation in the Bight, had disappeared. She was never seen or heard from again. Lieutenant Commander George Napier and his thirty-four crew were missing presumed dead.[†]

---

* *Medusa* did not sink after abandonment and was subsequently reported to be still afloat. Accordingly, three Harwich submarines – *E-4*, *D-6* and *E-29* – were despatched on 30 March with orders to locate and sink the wreck and to deal with any German vessels which might also be looking for the derelict. They were unsuccessful on both counts.

† Her wreck was discovered in 1973 with damage consistent with hitting a mine.

Anti-Zeppelin Futility

Politicians and citizenry remained nervous and concerned by the increasingly frequent bombing attacks by Zeppelin airships. And having been volunteered to defend the nation against such raids, the navy was finding it difficult to redeem this promise. At 11,000ft, Zeppelins could turn off their engines and drift in silence to carry out surprise attacks. Successive damaging Zeppelin attacks in 1915 and 1916 caused public outcry and government embarrassment. In response, street lights were dimmed and guns, searchlights, and observers were mobilised. Some RNAS and RFC squadrons were recalled from the Western Front and anti-aircraft guns installed around London.

But like the Harwich Force's travails with aircraft carriers, the problem was once more one of technology. The Zeppelins flew at altitudes above the effective range of most defensive weapons. Interception in the air was difficult; the airships operated at night and, although the fighter aircraft then available could eventually reach the altitude of the Zeppelins, they took too long to do so. Their weapons were machine guns firing rifle bullets which usually made only small holes in the Zeppelin's fabric gas envelope. The minimal pressure differential between the inside of the gasbag and the atmosphere was too small to cause rapid loss of the hydrogen and the tiny quantities which did leak from the bullet holes did not produce a sufficiently rich gas mixture to be flammable. Damage, even if inflicted, was rarely enough to cause a loss of altitude or control.

As has been noted, the navy sometimes tasked its ships with Zeppelin interception duties. One of the more curious of these operations was when, in December 1915 and January 1916, the Dover Patrol was ordered to send all its monitors* to the Thames Estuary to shoot at Zeppelins. The smaller vessels used their searchlights to illuminate the airborne intruders and the larger ships fired shrapnel from their big guns at maximum elevation, hoping that the falling fragments might puncture the dirigibles' skin. The tactic was not a success as when the anticipated attack came on 31 January, 'the attacking airships were too far to the north'.[9]

At the same time, the Harwich Force was ordered out to intercept them, taking with them two trawlers, *Kingfisher* and *Cantatrice*, both specifically equipped with seaplanes for anti-Zeppelin operations. However, the Force was unable to locate the approaching Zeppelin formation due to thick fog. *Kingfisher* and *Cantatrice* were two of four trawlers purchased by the Admiralty in May 1915; they were equipped for carrying a seaplane by fitting a platform aft. (The other ships were *Jericho* and *Sir John French*. The *Christopher* was added slightly later.) Based at Great Yarmouth, they carried

---

* Shallow-draft but heavy-gunned vessels designed for close inshore bombardment of land targets.

either a Sopwith Schneider or a Sopwith Baby and generally launched in the evening, from around the Haaks Light Vessel. But although seaplanes were flown off on many calm nights in 1915 and 1916 no German airships were ever spotted.

The beginning of April 1916 was a dark moon phase, ideal for night bombing operations and the German naval command organised a continuous series of airship raids to cover the British Isles from the Firth of Forth to London. The moon would be new on the night of 2/3 April and the first raid was planned for 31 March. Seven Zeppelins were to be utilised in an attack on the south of England. Fortunately, Scheer sent a wireless message to his fleet giving out the information which was intercepted by the Admiralty.

The raiders were first sighted at 1850, passing over a minesweeper which reported them, and at 1900 and again at 2000 two divisions of the Harwich Force destroyers were ordered to ready for sea to intercept the overhead course of the airships. *Mentor*'s division sailed at 2300 for Cromer and *Murray*'s at 0100 on 1 April for Lowestoft. Bombs were already falling on Essex and Suffolk towns. Just before midnight an airship was sighted at Knock Deep going slowly with her tail down and low in the air. A signal from her calling for help eliciting the reply that destroyers would come out from Zeebrugge to assist her. Both were intercepted by Room 40.

The Admiralty immediately ordered Tyrwhitt, together with the admirals at the Nore and Dover, to send out destroyers to attack the wounded Zeppelin and any forces assisting her. Com T sent *Nimrod* and *Lightfoot*, each with a destroyer division, to sweep as far as the North Hinder Light Vessel. But their services were not required for the airship, *L-15*, came down in the Thames Estuary around 1215 and was 'arrested' by the armed minesweeping trawler *Olivine*, once of Hull and armed with a single 12pdr gun, which took off her crew.

The Harwich destroyers patrolling at the North Hinder and off Norfolk had seen nothing and were recalled, for another Zeppelin raid was expected that night. Tyrwhitt again sent a division to Cromer and another to Lowestoft, returning in the afternoon. They observed no airships, the raid having taken place to the northward.

On the night of 2 April, German military, as opposed to naval, airships staged another raid, attacking Ipswich, villages to the north of Felixstowe and, curiously, Epping Forest. Once more, the Harwich Force destroyers were turned out. Four sailed to the North Hinder to intercept these raiders on their return trip to Belgium, departing harbour at 0430. But the result was the same; they saw nothing of the airships, which in any case were probably home before the destroyers started out, nor did they observe any hostile surface craft. They were recalled about noon.

A Montague whaler, the standard five-oar sea boat of the navy in the First World War. They were clinker built from wych or sand elm, with a drop keel and were double ended. This was the type of boat in which forty-two men lost their lives in two incidents during the great storm of 28 March 1916. (Photo; Clem Rutter via Creative Commons)

The final raid in this week of bombing was planned for the night of 4 April. Two Zeppelins took part;* once more their signals were intercepted and the Admiralty ordered Tyrwhitt to intercept them on their return, 'should the risk of mines permit'.[10] Mines would not deter the commodore and at 2300 he sent out *Laforey*'s division to the Wash. But nothing was seen in the dark, despite the fact that *L-11* passed over them near Corton Light Vessel. No ship's log makes any mention of seeing a Zeppelin.

Thus ended a week of entirely futile ship-based anti-Zeppelin activity. The scourge was only mastered by the development during the course of the year of faster-climbing aircraft and special bullets. Technical advances led to gun magazines for anti-Zeppelin missions which were loaded with a mix of

---

* Another five airships were to have raided the north of England that same night but a strong adverse wind ended the plan. However, three Zeppelins did make the attack on the 5th.

Pomeroy explosive bullets – standard .303 British cartridges packed with a 155-grain cupronickel-jacketed lead bullet inside which was a hollow copper tube filled with 15 grains of seventy-three per cent dynamite – Brock explosive bullets containing potassium chlorate, and Buckingham incendiary bullets enclosing pyrophoric yellow phosphorus.

Tragedy at Harwich

When the Harwich Force ships were in harbour, shore leave was usually granted by watches. Three days before the commencement of Scheer's aerial offensive, on 28 March, HMS *Conquest* had liberty men ashore, as did a number of other vessels. They would be ferried there and back by the ships' boats, of which *Conquest* had four, a motor boat, the captain's barge, a twelve-oar cutter and a five-oared whaler.

By early evening, all except the latter had been to the pier, picked up their complement of returning sailors and safely regained their ship. But the delights of Cobbold's beer, cinema, cafes or fleshpots detained more than a few and the whaler had to wait for stragglers. Eventually, she was loaded up with thirty-nine *Conquest* crewmen, plus the yeoman of signals from *Cleopatra* and a black and white dog belonging to one of the engine room artificers. For a smallish 27ft boat, generally rated to carry twenty-seven including the oarsmen, it was overloaded. But regardless, the whaler set off to be rowed the three-quarters of a mile distance to where her parent cruiser was anchored.

The weather had been poor all day. A widespread and severe northerly gale with an associated blizzard had been blowing across much of East Anglia, the east and south Midlands, parts of southeast England and the West Country during both the 27th and 28th. Snow set in after nightfall of the 27th and in some places lasted over 24 hours with depths of 0.8 inches over the east Midlands.[11]

As the whaler reached the half-way point in its journey, a violent gale and snowstorm suddenly sprang up. At Dover the wind was recorded at 46mph (Beaufort Force Nine).[12] Even the sheltered harbour was lashed by huge waves and visibility fell to nil. In *Conquest*, men waited anxiously for a sight of their shipmates and the last leave boat. But there was no sign of it. Eventually, the whaler was judged overdue, and when the storm had abated a little a search was launched by all the Harwich ships' motor boats; but no trace was found.

Dawn and calmer weather revealed the extent of the disaster. The boat had been washed out to sea and then back to the shore a few miles down the coast. 'There was not one survivor but marks in the sands showed that some of them had tried to crawl away before succumbing. The little dog was found at the side of his master.'[13]

Amongst the dead were Sidney Gillingham, a stoker who served, for reasons best known to himself, as John Cash; Petty Officer Stoker Thomas

The bodies of those who died in the storm of 28 March 1916 are buried in the churchyard of St Mary's, Shotley, as are many others of the Harwich Force. (Author's collection)

Chitty, aged 46, once an auctioneer's assistant, holder of the Africa General Service Medal and who had seen action in Somaliland; Leading Seaman William Ernest Owen Smith, granted the Messina Medal in 1908;* Petty Officer Edwin Hughes who had charge of the forty or so boy seamen on board *Conquest*; and 20-year-old Ship's Steward Assistant Edgar Hodges. Seven bodies recovered were buried in the churchyard of St Mary's, Shotley. Another seventeen sailors and a Royal Marine were interred in the churchyard extension of All Saints, Walton-on-the-Naze.†

The loss suffered by *Conquest* overshadowed two other deaths and a remarkable individual act of heroism. Another whaler liberty boat from the destroyer *Melpomene* was also caught in the storm, swirled around the harbour and eventually driven a mile up the river from Parkstone jetty where it stuck in deep mud. Twenty-two-year-old Robert Arthur Startin had been advanced in rank to lieutenant RN that very day. He was the son of Admiral James Startin, famous in the navy as a fearless horseman, a gymnast and an athlete.

---

* The Messina Medal was issued by the Italian Government as a commemorative medal to people involved in the relief effort after a massive earthquake which had devastated Messina leaving almost 100,000 dead.
† Now maintained by the Commonwealth War Graves Commission.

On hearing of the missing craft, Lieutenant Startin set out alone to search for it. When he found the whaler, it was half full of water and six sailors were lying in the bottom, helpless and exhausted.

Despite the conditions, Startin walked into the river and waded through deep mud, often up to his armpits, for some 300 yards. He roused the sailors from insensibility roughly shaking them and hitting them with his stick. Then he set about getting them to shore. He began with a crewman who seemed incapable of being awakened. This man had to be forcibly dragged through the mud all the way to the shore by Startin and the coxswain of the boat. After an hour, only 40 or 50 yards had been gained; but luckily, a light was seen moving inshore. Startin ordered the crew to remain in their craft whilst he went to the light, which proved to be carried by a search party, helpfully equipped with a rope. This rope was taken backwards and forwards personally by the lieutenant, going from the shore to the boat until each sailor had been rescued. All the while, 'this exhausting and dangerous task in the deep mud was being performed under the most trying weather conditions'.[14] In spite of Startin's heroism, two of the men later died of exposure. But four were saved and for his bravery and determination, Lieutenant Robert Startin was awarded the Albert Medal, Gazetted 9 May 1916.*

Forty-two sailors had died on one day in tragic incidents that had nothing to do with the war and everything to do with the elemental forces that have confronted mariners since man first put to sea.

---

* Startin Senior would also win the award in 1918, making the only father and son combination to be awarded the medal. Admiral Startin had previously been given the Royal Humane Society Bronze Medal in 1883.

9

Eastertide Raids and the Battle of Jutland,
April and May 1916

The Harwich Force was often called upon to 'lend' destroyers to its near neighbour the Dover Patrol or to support it in its operations against the Belgian coast.

Following their declaration of 1 March 1916, the Germans had ended their self-imposed exile from the waters around Britain. U-boats again sailed from Zeebrugge and Ostend and increasingly found that they could readily pass through the Dover Barrage, with many coasting along the surface of the Channel under cover of darkness.

In an attempt to curtail the submarine menace, an operation was conceived by the commander of the Dover Patrol, Vice Admiral Reginald Bacon, to lay a coastal mine and net barrage off the Belgian coast, between Nieuwpoort and the entrance to the River Scheldt, aimed at restricting the movements of the Flanders U-boats and minelayers. A significant force was put together, including six divisions of net drifters (to lay the nets), four large minesweepers (to clear the passage in and out) and escorting destroyers, six minelaying trawlers, two monitors (to provide a diversionary bombardment) with the addition of a division of Harwich Force 'M'-class destroyers, *Milne*, *Melpomene*, *Medea* and *Murray* together with eight Harwich 'L' class and the Flanders coast patrol from Dunkirk. The ships were in place by 0400 on Easter Monday, 24 April, and by 0730 had laid a 15-mile double line of mines and 13 miles of mined nets, 5,077 mines in total, 12 miles off the coastline. It was no small achievement.

The minesweepers and most of the other vessels returned to port but the drifters were still at work putting the finishing touches to the newly laid nets and the four 'M' class and two monitors remained with them. As the drifters went about their work, the force was attacked by German aircraft without result. But at about 1445, three German destroyers came out of Zeebrugge to offer battle.

Milne had been detached to look for a U-boat, but the remaining Harwich Force 'M'-class destroyers went to full speed and raced towards the enemy as both sides opened fire. The German ships made back towards the shore and when the British vessels were about 10,000 yards from the coast, heavy enemy guns hidden in the sand dunes commenced firing at them and 'within a few seconds we received the full attention of a fair proportion of the fifty-four pieces of ordnance, varying in size from 12in downwards'.[1] Plumes of water rose around the destroyers. *Murray* was struck on the forecastle by a 6in shell which passed through the ship's side, luckily without exploding, and she was able to clear danger with the help of a smokescreen by about 1550.

Melpomene (built originally for the Greek navy and, ironically, named for the Muse of Tragedy) was hit at about 1540 by one of the shells fired by the German destroyers. The shell ricocheted into her without exploding but flooded the engine room, and she lost way. Now returned, *Milne* took her in tow, but then tangled the towing cable in one of her own propellers. So far they had been inshore of the new minefield but now *Murray* went ahead and called for a drifter to show them the way through the mined nets, followed by the limping *Melpomene* with *Milne* lashed to her port side and *Medea* to starboard, offering both protection and motive power to their stricken sister. Seeing an easy prize the German destroyers once more ventured out from under the shelter of their shore batteries and closed to 8,000 yards at which point *Murray* dropped back to lay smoke as cover for the retreat of her brethren.

At this critical point the brave and risky (given her slow speed and lack of manoeuvrability) intervention of the monitor *Prince Eugene* settled the case. Her commander, Captain Ernest Wigram DSO, a veteran of the Falklands and Gallipoli campaigns, opened fire on the German destroyers with her twin 12in guns, massive artillery which would utterly destroy the enemy vessels, if it hit. The Germans turned and ran for home.

Once more the shore batteries opened fire and *Medea* was struck by a shell on the quarterdeck, a second close to her funnels, and then by a third, but continued at full speed and all the ships were clear after about six minutes under fire. *Medea* lost two men and a third died of wounds the following day. *Milne* went into the floating dock in Dover to have the cable unwound from her port propeller, *Murray* received a temporary patch on her bow until her next refit, *Medea* went to Chatham for repairs, and *Melpomene* was dry-docked in Dunkirk to be patched up before sailing for a full English dockyard repair job. The Harwich Force could ill afford to lose so many ships from service at the same time.

The Easter Rising

While the four Harwich 'M'-class ships were battling it out off the Belgian coast, groups of armed men began to seize strategic positions in Dublin. The Easter Monday Irish Rising had begun.

The Easter Rising was intended to take place across all Ireland; however, a variety of mishaps resulted in it being effective primarily only in Dublin. On

24 April 1916 the rebel leaders and their followers, many of whom were members of the rump of a nationalist organisation, the Irish Volunteers, or of small radical militia groups, such as the Irish Citizen's Army and the Irish Revolutionary Brotherhood (IRB), seized the city's General Post Office and other key locations. Early that afternoon, from the steps of the post office, Patrick Pearse, one of the uprising's leaders, read a proclamation declaring Ireland an independent republic and stating that a provisional government (comprised of IRB members) had been appointed. It was war.

That same day, Scheer arranged for six airships to attack Norwich, Lincoln, Harwich and Ipswich while a battlecruiser squadron shelled Great Yarmouth and Lowestoft. *The Times* headlined this as 'all apparently part of a concerted German plan'[2] and many believed at the time that the raids were designed to disrupt the British response to the rising. According to the British official naval history of the war, the German Naval Staff had agreed to support the rising with a demonstration of the German fleet towards the Flanders bight, 'but it was to be extended further so as to force the enemy out of port.' Scheer himself stated that 'I expected to achieve this by bombarding coastal towns and carrying out air raids on England the night the fleet was out'.[3] Whatever the reason, the Harwich Force were again in the thick of the action.

The Lowestoft and Great Yarmouth Raids

On 24 April, Admiral Scheer took his ships out. On the basis of faulty intelligence, he believed that the British had two strong forces at sea, to the north off Norway and off the southeast coast of England.[*] He intended to sail between them, bombard the coast and then engage whichever portion of the British ships were attracted to him.

His bombardment targets were Lowestoft and Great Yarmouth. Lowestoft was a base of operations for minelaying and sweeping, while Yarmouth was a harbour for some of the Harwich Force submarines. The German ships involved included the 1st Scouting Group, comprising of the battlecruisers SMS *Seydlitz*, *Lützow*, *Derfflinger*, *Moltke* and *Von der Tann* commanded by Konteradmiral Friedrich Boedicker, 'baby killer' Hipper being indisposed through illness. They were supported by the four light cruisers of the 2nd Scouting Group and the fast torpedo boat flotillas, VI and IX, with their two command vessels. The main fleet, consisting of Squadrons I, II and III, Scouting Division IV and the remainder of the torpedo flotillas was to stand off in reserve, ready to come into action if the bombardment group ran into superior forces

---

[*] Scheer may have been misled by historical intelligence; it had been a feature of British war planning in 1908 (Plans W1 and W2) that there should be a northern and southern fleet. This was also the case in the War Game Manoeuvres of 1912.

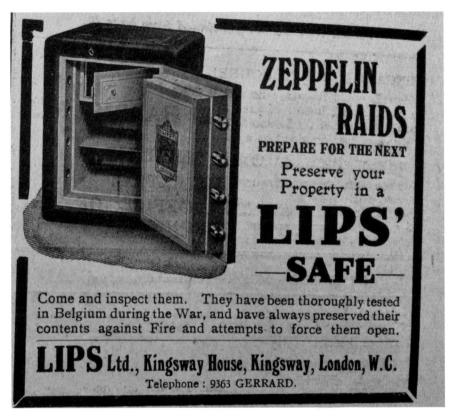

Every cloud has a silver lining. The Zeppelin scare and menace was put to use as an advertising 'hook' by some. Here Lips' Safes, founded in 1870 in the Netherlands, take advantage of such fears. (Author's collection)

They were accompanied by eight Zeppelins which, after dropping their bombs, were to provide reconnaissance for the battlecruisers. Two U-boats were sent ahead to Lowestoft, while others were stationed off, or laid mines in, the Firth of Forth. Additionally, seven U-boats had been despatched to lay mines off Harwich in the hope of catching the Force as it came out.

By noon, all the German assets were in place and they began to pick a route through the British minefields. But at 1600, *Seydlitz* struck a mine and was forced to turn back, escorted by two destroyers and a Zeppelin; Boedicker transferred his flag to *Lützow*.

The Admiralty knew that the German ships were at sea at midday. At 2015 an intercepted wireless message gave the information that the enemy was aiming for Great Yarmouth. At 1550, the Grand Fleet was placed at two hours readiness and at 1905 was ordered to sail south from Scapa Flow while the

The bombardment of Lowestoft on 25 April 1916 as imagined in a painting by Hans Bohrdt.
He was art tutor to Kaiser Wilhelm II, who funded many of the painter's projects.
(Author's collection)

battlecruisers were likewise instructed to depart from Rosyth. Nobody gave Tyrwhitt any orders at all.

That night the Zeppelins bombed Norwich, Lincoln, Harwich and Ipswich. The Harwich Force was finally called out at 2300. But it was a much reduced group due to other commitments, including the support of the Dover Patrol off Belgium. Flying his pennant in *Conquest*, Tyrwhitt led out *Cleopatra*, *Penelope* and *Lightfoot* with the seven destroyers that were immediately ready to sail. *Nimrod* followed later with another eight destroyers.

His instructions from London had been to make for a point between Southwold and the Hook of Holland but as the commodore left port, he received another message saying that the German battlecruisers would pass this position within two hours; if he followed orders then at best he would only be able to intercept them on their return. On his own initiative and following Fisher's dictum that 'any fool can obey orders',[4] he decided to sail straight up the coast to the point of the German attack.

It was a bright moonlit night and the odds were clearly not in Tyrwhitt's favour. But he thought that if he could attract the Germans' attention, he would be able to draw them away from Lowestoft and Yarmouth and save the towns from much damage. At about 0350 on the 25th, the light cruiser SMS

Rostock, one of Boedicker's screening ships, sighted British ships in a west-southwesterly direction. Simultaneously, Tyrwhitt reported the sighting of four battlecruisers and six cruisers to Jellicoe and Beatty. He stood on towards Lowestoft to give Boedicker a good sight of him but the German admiral was not to be drawn, merely detaching light forces to chase Tyrwhitt away. The battlecruisers opened fire on the town at 0410 for ten minutes, destroying 200 houses and two defensive gun batteries, injuring twelve people and killing three. The ships then moved off to Great Yarmouth where fog made it difficult to see the target.

Realising that the Germans were now headed for Yarmouth, Tyrwhitt turned his force back to the north, sighted Boedicker's light forces and opened fire on them. Hearing the sound of the engagement, the battlecruisers broke off from bombardment of the town and headed for the sound of the guns. They opened a heavy fire from a range of 16,000–18,000 yards, at which it was impossible for the British ships to reply. Tyrwhitt immediately turned his ships through 16 points together, reversing his course, a manoeuvre which put his flagship at the rear of the line. For 13 minutes, *Conquest* was subjected to heavy gunfire and was struck by five heavy shells.

It was a dangerous period. Boy Seaman William Spencer, acting as captain's messenger, recalled 'we soon found out what we were up against when we started getting the stuff thrown at us that the town had been getting. Battlecruisers of the *Derrflinger* and *Lützow* class turned their 12in guns on

The German light cruiser *Rostock* (1912), ten 4.1in guns, which took part in the Lowestoft raid. She was the first German ship to sight the Harwich Force destroyers' approach. Here she is pictured in the *Illustrated London News* of 10 June 1916 after she had been sunk at Jutland. (US Naval History and Heritage Command NH 43041)

our little fleet and as soon as our 6in guns came into range we let then have something back.'[5] One shell passed through the funnel; then 'a salvo hit her [*Conquest*] on the aft deck and knocked the after-superstructure gun over the side . . . I was appalled at the damage.'[6] The explosion also set ablaze some cordite, stored next to the gun. Without thought for his own safety, Ordinary Seaman William David Williams, known to his mates as Taffy, barehandedly threw the burning charges overboard and saved *Conquest* from a possible disaster. Aged just 18, Swansea-born Williams had joined the navy as a boy in January 1915. After less than a year in *Conquest*, he would be awarded the DSM for his actions.[7] But it came at a price. His hands were severely injured and just eight months later, on 23 August, he was invalided out of the navy, owing to 'burns both hands in action'.[8]

Conquest took a severe battering; twenty-three men were killed, including Tyrwhitt's personal servant. The destroyers too took a pounding; the captain of HMS *Manly* was Lieutenant Commander Ernest Kirkby, a former rugby player for the Royal Navy XV before the war and a 'big jolly man'.[9] While great plumes of water thrown up by the German shells rose all about them Kirkby strolled unconcernedly around his bridge, smoking a cigarette and showing the required degree of sangfroid under fire. The coxswain was a white-haired chief petty officer from Ireland and as a salvo roared over their heads, he instinctively ducked. 'Now coxswain . . . I believe I saw you ducking,' solemnly intoned Kirby. 'Sure you did not sir . . . it must have been the pitching of the ship that you were observing', was the reply.[10]

HMS *Laertes* was hit by a shell which penetrated the boiler room, putting one boiler out of action and wounding five men. She would most likely have blown up and sunk except for the swift response of Stoker 1st Class Ernest John William Clarke. He unhesitatingly went to release the steam pressure valves and in so doing was very badly scalded, which left him with 'extensive burns to the face, arms and hands'.[11] Thirty-eight-year-old Clarke, who had been in the navy since 1898, received the DSM[12] for saving his ship; but he did not live to enjoy it, dying from his injuries on 10 May.

The Harwich Force had at least spared Great Yarmouth from much damage and possibly ameliorated the attack on Lowestoft. Boedicker turned away and started to withdraw, perhaps fearful that Tyrwhitt was drawing him onto a larger British force. Lieutenant Brian Schofield in *Manly* noted that 'for a difficult half an hour the Germans gave us everything they had got but Com (T) withdrew in a leisurely manner until, suspecting that they were being lured into a trap, the German ships turned and ran for home'.[13] Tyrwhitt was having none of that. As soon as he realised that his opponent was no longer pursuing him, he reversed course again and in the damaged *Conquest*, still capable of 20 knots, he led his forces back towards the enemy. He regained visual contact at 0830, about the same time as the Admiralty ordered him to return to base.

As Tyrwhitt headed for Harwich, *Penelope* was torpedoed by *UB-29*. 'The explosion carried away her stern post and rudder; the whole after part of her had practically been blown off. But she managed to steam back to Harwich at 22 knots steering with her engines.'[14] *Conquest* made it to Chatham, carrying in her an unexploded 8in German shell.

During the engagement, the Germans had attacked two armed fishing boats. *King Stephen* had been converted to the Q-ship *Ledger* but in a previous life as a fishing vessel had gained German opprobrium when the skipper refused to rescue the crew of the Zeppelin *L-19*, which had crashed into the sea near Dogger Bank. Ledger/King Stephen was sunk by a destroyer, *G-41*, and the crew taken prisoner. The second was the drifter *Moss*, once of Yarmouth, armed with a solitary 3pdr gun, which was damaged in the shelling of Lowestoft with six men killed including Skipper Percy Shreeve.*

Meanwhile Beatty, and far behind him Jellicoe, had been struggling through heavy seas in the hope of cutting off the German retreat. But by noon it was clear that such pursuit was hopeless. As this realisation dawned, the Harwich submarine HMS *E-22* was torpedoed just before 1200 by *UB-18*. She had been part of a patrol line established to intercept the German raiders. Commissioned only on 8 November the previous year, she had played the lead role in a curious experiment which was yet another essay at trying to intercept raiding Zeppelins.

In a trial run, *E-22* had carried two Sopwith Schneider seaplane scouts mounted aft on her casing. The idea was that the submarine transported the aircraft out to sea, saving their fuel usage. When an airship was sighted, *E-22* would submerge, hopefully in calm waters, so the planes would float on the surface. They would take off, attempt an interception, and then return to the east coast of England at Felixstowe. The experiment was tried once and not repeated.

Thirty-one of her thirty-three crew died when *E-22* was sunk, including her captain, on his first mission in her, 30-year-old Lieutenant Reginald Thomas Dimsdale. He was the younger son of Charles Robert Southwell Dimsdale, 7th Baron Dimsdale, a title awarded in the Russian peerage to his ancestor Thomas by Catherine the Great in 1762. His older boy had already been killed at Ypres; now he had lost both his sons. The two survivors had been on the bridge and got clear; they were picked up by the attacker and made prisoners of war.

---

* The drifter lived to fight another day, serving in the Second World War as the anti-submarine vessel *Guiding Light*.

The Germans claimed a victory.

At daybreak on April 25 a section of our high sea forces bombarded with good success the fortifications and important military buildings at Great Yarmouth and Lowestoft, and afterwards opened fire on a detachment of enemy airmen, small cruisers, and torpedo boat destroyers. A big fire was observed on one cruiser. One destroyer and two enemy patrol boats were sunk. One of the latter was the trawler *King Stephen* which refused some time ago to save the crew of the German Airship *L-19* when in distress. The crew* of the trawler were taken prisoner.'[15]

Aftermath

As the German ships headed for home, they avoided the patrol lines of submarine sent to intercept them, encountering only two neutral steamers and some fishing vessels.

Arthur Marder thought that 'the raid was hardly a brilliant exploit, whether from the point of view of strategy, tactics or results'.[16] The Germans had sunk one patrol vessel and damaged another, and badly damaged two light cruisers and a destroyer; they had also sunk a submarine. In exchange they had a major unit, the battlecruiser *Seydlitz*, laid up after mining. The damage done to the naval establishments at Yarmouth and Lowestoft was light. Moreover, the German battlecruiser squadron had failed to take advantage of its superior numbers to engage the Harwich Force and inflict greater damage. The German U-boats sent out to intercept British ships leaving harbour had not found any targets. Nor had six British submarines stationed off Yarmouth and six more off Harwich.

However, Germany did suffer U-boat losses; *UB-13* was lost on a mine net with no survivors and on the 27th one of the German patrol submarines, *UC-5*, was captured when it grounded on the Shipwash Shoal off Harwich. The crew attempted to sink her but the scuttling charges failed to explode. She was later salvaged and used to raise war bonds in the UK and USA. *Firedrake* claimed prize money for her capture, which was not in fact paid until 1920.[17]

At least the town of Lowestoft was grateful for the intervention of the Harwich Force. On 3 May, the mayor wrote to Their Lordships at the Admiralty from his town hall;

My Lords
I am desired by the Town Council to express to the Lords of the Admiralty the high appreciation of the inhabitants of this borough of

---

* It was a different crew to that of the airship incident, although the Germans took some convincing of the fact.

London Road in Lowestoft at the junction with Freemantle Road,
damaged in the 25 April 1916 raid. (Author's collection)

the splendid way in which, during the bombardment of the town on the morning of April 25th, the enemy ships, though greatly superior force, were engaged by the British squadron. The council is convinced that, but for this plucky intervention at a critical moment, the town would have suffered much greater destruction of property and loss of life. It is also desired, if it meets with Their Lordships' approval that an expression of appreciation may be conveyed to the gallant officer in command and the officers and men under him

I have the honour to be, your Lordships Obedient Servant

J W Brooke,* Mayor.[18]

---

* John Walter Brooke (d 1924) was the owner of J W Brooke and Co, an engineering company in Lowestoft which latterly specialised in the application of the internal combustion engine to marine propulsion. He was mayor from 1914 to 1917.

The Admiralty copied the letter to Tyrwhitt and he circulated it to all commanders and ships who took part.

But Beatty and Tyrwhitt were both enraged by the missed opportunity to catch the High Seas Fleet and by what they saw as a lack of coordination at the Admiralty. On 18 May Beatty wrote to Jellicoe on their joint behalf attacking the Admiralty War Staff for its lack 'of cohesion and combination between the various units . . . the system of water tight compartments [in Whitehall] has reached its climax'. He accused the Chief of the War Staff, Vice Admiral Henry Oliver, of having 'priceless information given to him [from Room 40] which he sits on until it is too late for the sea forces to take action'.[19]

Beatty continued in the same vein, the anger steaming off the page.

> There was absolutely no reason why every unit should not have been on the move three and a half hours before it actually was. Commodore (T) did not actually leave Harwich until 2300. He received many contradictory orders . . . he had no idea where I was or where I was going. I had no idea of anything appertaining to the Harwich Force . . . [there was] no plan, no combination and no decision.[20]

It was a damning indictment.

Beatty and Tyrwhitt met and the former tried to put together a more constructive memorandum based on their discussions that nonetheless made telling points. On 26 May, he wrote to 'The Commander in Chief' (Jellicoe) but meant for Admiralty consumption;

> I have the honour to report that my conference with Commodore (T) was of the utmost value in so much that we were enlightened considerably on points which effected our respective commands in the event of having to cooperate.
>
> I would submit . . . that it would be most advantageous and in the best interests of the Service if a further conference could take place, at which those who construct and devise plans and operations and those who have to carry them out should meet and gain that communion of thought without which successful accomplishment is doubtful. To this end I submit the following points on which it is desirable the commanders of such as the Harwich Force and the Battle Cruiser Fleet should be enlightened and receive guidance as to how the Admiralty intends them to act under certain circumstances.[21]

He went on to suggest that the Harwich Force should be kept at a certain minima of ships, such that he knew they could support his battlecruisers if

The pre-dreadnought battleship *King Edward VII* (1903), part of the 3rd Battle Squadron
sent to Sheerness in April 1916. Her mixed battery of 12in, 9.2in and 6in guns made spotting
the fall of shot and gunnery control difficult and the type was made obsolescent by the
launch of the all-big-gun HMS *Dreadnought* in 1906.
(US Library of Congress LC-DIG-ggbain-17323)

necessary; that neither of them knew if the Force would be used to attack an
enemy fleet; what positions should the Harwich Force and the Battlecruiser
Fleet take up if the enemy came out; that they should be informed of any
orders given to the Dover Patrol in the light of the enemy coming out; they
should be told if any new minefields had been laid which were not in the Secret
Fleet Orders; that they were unaware of any Admiralty plans for dealing with
all enemy offensive operations, other than invasion; and that positions should
be defined which they could take up without waiting for further instruction
when an alarm is given.

Moreover, the raid had demonstrated how open the eastern coast of
England was to attack, especially now that Tyrwhitt had lost two more light
cruisers while *Conquest* and *Penelope* were repaired. Tactically, the Admiralty
felt obliged to find a way to get heavy units into the North Sea more quickly
for future raids. As a result, the 3rd Battle Squadron, under Vice Admiral
Edward Eden Bradford and consisting of seven *King Edward VII*-class pre-

HMS *Carysfort* (1914) which became Tyrwhitt's flagship in May 1916.
(US Naval History and Heritage Command NH 61308)

dreadnought battleships, was moved from Rosyth to Sheerness on 29 April, together with HMS *Dreadnought* herself.

The *King Edwards*, dating from 1903 and armed with four 12in, four 9.2in and ten 6in guns, were known as the 'Wobbly Eight'. In a fight with the German all-big-gun battleships or battlecruisers they were likely to come off worst, not least because 'these ships were quite useless owing to their roll and the proximity of their guns to the waterline. They were useful only in reasonably calm weather or against shore targets.'[22] The squadron probably provided scant comfort to the men of Harwich, who in any case had to detach eight destroyers to keep watch over them.

Jellicoe, who never felt that he had enough destroyers for the Grand Fleet, believed he had insufficient to provide a full screen for the battlefleet and so two divisions (eight ships) of 9 DF and 10 DF were sent from Harwich to join him at Scapa,* further denuding the forces available to Tyrwhitt.

A(nother) New Flagship

So far in the war, Tyrwhitt had flown his broad pennant in four ships, losing or damaging three of them. The idea of giving him HMS *Centaur* had been dropped as she was not yet finished, as had the proposal that he should have the 'improved *Arethusa*', *Canterbury*. Now he was offered *Carysfort*, of the same class as *Centaur*.

---

* They were *Lydiard, Moorsom, Turbulent, Liberty, Morris, Termagant, Landrail* and *Laurel*.

HMS *Carysfort* was a 'C'-class light cruiser of the *Caroline* sub-class, launched in November 1914 and completed in June the following year. The *Caroline*s were enlarged and enhanced versions of the preceding *Arethusa*-class cruisers, capable of 28.5 knots and mounting two 6in and eight 4in guns, two torpedo tubes and a single 6pdr Hotchkiss anti-aircraft gun.

Since commissioning she had been operating with the Grand Fleet but now Captain Domvile was sent to the Clyde to take her over and bring the cruiser down to Harwich, where she arrived on 30 April. Tyrwhitt moved his flag to her and Domvile was once again flag captain. Shipless since the loss of *Arethusa*, Domville had been gainfully employed organising the coastal motor boat (CMB) base at Queenborough.

The *Sussex* Pledge

On 24 March *UB-29* torpedoed and sank without warning the French-flagged passenger steamer *Sussex*, crossing between Dieppe and Folkestone. She was carrying 53 crew and 325 passengers, including American citizens. The ship was severely damaged, with the entire bow forward of the bridge blown off. Some of the lifeboats were launched, but at least two of them capsized and many passengers were drowned. In total at least fifty lost their lives. Several Americans were injured. *Sussex* remained afloat and was eventually towed stern-first into Boulogne Harbour.

Following on from the promises extracted by the US government from the Imperial German Court in 1915, this further breaking of their undertaking with regard to passenger vessels enraged public opinion in the United States, and caused another heated exchange between the US and German governments. Panicked by the strength of the American diplomatic notes,[*] which implied that they would break off diplomatic relations if Germany did not immediately comply with International Law, on 4 May 1916 Germany issued a declaration, the 'Sussex Pledge'.

The key elements of this undertaking were that passenger ships would not be targeted; merchant ships would not be sunk until the presence of weapons had been established, if necessary by a search of the ship; and ships would not be sunk without provision for the safety of passengers and crew. It effectively represented the suspension, once again, of the unrestricted U-boat campaign and was therefore one less thing for the Harwich Force and the Harwich-based anti-submarine auxiliaries to worry about. In April, 141,193 gross tons of British merchant shipping had been lost to enemy action; in June it fell to 36,976 tons.[23]

---

[*] On 18 April US President Wilson threatened a diplomatic break if attacks on passenger liners were not stopped.

The Dog that Didn't Bark – Jutland

Many, many books have been written about the Battle of Jutland, which took place on 31 May 1916; this volume will not add to that number, for the simple reason that the Harwich Force did not take part in it, except for the 9 and 10 DF ships on detachment to the Grand Fleet. The best destroyer commander and the most experienced destroyer skippers were kept chained to port, attack dogs curbed on a leash by the Admiralty.

The course of the battle was characterised by misleading Admiralty communications to Jellicoe, poor signalling by Beatty, and missed opportunities due in part to overcaution. As a result, the contest was inconclusive, although with heavy British loses, but remained a tactical victory for the Royal Navy. What a difference an aggressive light forces leader like Tyrwhitt might have made.

Signals intercepted by Room 40 on 30 May indicated that the High Seas Fleet was coming out. Jellicoe and Beatty were alerted and were at sea by 2230. Tyrwhitt was told to stand by for action with all available ships and be ready to sail at daylight. If he had been released at that point, Tyrwhitt's force would have reached Jellicoe by nightfall and could have participated in the night actions of the 31st which, without him, allowed Scheer and his fleet to escape. Instead, the Admiralty held him back, possibly fearful of a detached German squadron, under cover of the main fleet action, falling on Dover or Dunkirk and shipping in the Downs.

Tyrwhitt fretted all through 31 May as the battle unwound far to his north. As early as 0450 he sent a telegram to the Admiralty pointing out that he had received no orders. He was told that he was to remain at one hour's notice. To ease his tension, he went to his nearby home to do some gardening but returned when his flagship picked up Beatty's transmission that he was in action with the enemy battlecruisers.

At 1715, he could take no more and gave the command to put out to sea, telling the Admiralty what he was doing at the same time. As he did so he received a message from Whitehall telling him to complete with fuel and be ready to relieve the light cruisers and destroyers with the battlecruiser squadrons. He ignored it and held on to his course northwards. The Force had got as far as the Cork Light Vessel when Tyrwhitt received a peremptory signal instructing him to return to Harwich immediately and await orders. Turning to Domvile, the commodore remarked 'I might as well have gone on mowing the lawn'.[24] Eventually, at 0330 on 1 June, the Harwich Force was ordered to sea to escort the damaged battleship *Marlborough* to the Humber. A little later Com (T) was told there was no need of him and he could return to base.

The failure to utilise the Harwich Force and the question of coordinating its movements with the Grand Fleet were discussed at a meeting at the

A German *König*-class battleship at Jutland as imagined by the Stuttgart-born illustrator Claus Bergen. (US Library of Congress)

Admiralty on 25 June but no clear-cut solution was arrived at. The Admiralty staff held to the position that, as they could not know Scheer's intentions whenever he put to sea, they could not order the Harwich Force north until the enemy's intentions became clear.

But retaining Tyrwhitt and his ships at Harwich made little sense. 'The precise reasons for retaining the Harwich Force remain obscure',[25] noted the authors of the Naval Staff Appreciation of 1921. They hypothesised three potential reasons. Firstly, that the High Seas Fleet might come south. But if it did how could Tyrwhitt with five light cruisers and twenty destroyers oppose it? Secondly, the Admiralty might have been expecting a repeat of Lowestoft. However, what could the Harwich Force do which was over and above what it had done on 25 April, namely retire? In both these instances, the Force was not a fit instrument for the tune the Admiralty wanted to play. The only other conjecture was defence against invasion but this was not likely and, given the warnings the Room 40 could provide, would not be a secret. As the Naval Staff

Appreciation notes 'one of the previously recognised duties of the Harwich Flotillas was to assist the Commander in Chief [Jellicoe] in a fleet action, and this important function seems to have been to a large extent forgotten or overlooked'.[26] It will be recalled that Jellicoe had delegated direction of the Harwich Force to the Admiralty back in 1914. 'His [Tyrwhitt's] retention there [at Harwich] must be regarded as a grave mistake' was the overall view of the Naval Staff Appreciation. Reginald Tyrwhitt and his captains would have agreed.

As for the commodore himself, his bitterness showed through in a letter to his wife. 'There is no doubt that we got a kicking.'[27] And five weeks later, he was still fuming, writing to Keyes that 'I'll never forgive that old figurehead Oliver, who was at the bottom of it all . . . I got snubbed for going to sea on my own account . . . I know I was right and anyone in my place would have done the same.'[28]

10

The Beef Trip, June–August 1916

By June 1916, the Harwich Force had been at war for nearly two years. They were continuously in action, running patrols day and night, and enduring the capricious and often difficult climatic conditions of the North Sea as well as enemy action. It was not a glamorous job, and often there was little to show for their efforts. A meritorious contribution to the Battle of Heligoland Bight for sure, minor action at Dogger Bank, some German trawlers and merchants taken, a serious attempt to drive forward naval aviation and air/sea combined operations, and Lowestoft and Great Yarmouth saved from greater destruction. But a limited amount of evident success does not indicate a lack of effort nor does it show the 'nil return' – enemy warships reluctant to come out of harbour, U-boats forced to remain underwater where they could do less damage, minelayers confined to port and British mining facilitated.

In all of this activity, Tyrwhitt led from the front, usually at sea with his command and enduring the same risks and privations that they did. Thus, it was welcome recognition for Tyrwhitt (and by association the Harwich Striking Force) when, on 2 June, he was one of three naval officers awarded the DSO* in the King's birthday honours 'in recognition of the services rendered by them in the prosecution of the war'.[1] Keyes and Litchfield-Speer were the other two.

At this halfway point of the year, Tyrwhitt had a force, on paper, of 5 LCS which comprised five light cruisers, plus *Undaunted* and *Lightfoot* leading 9 DF of twenty-one 'L'-class destroyers and *Aurora* and *Nimrod* with 10 DF, comprising fifteen 'M' class. There were also eight ships which, though based at Harwich, were permanently attached to the 3rd Battle Squadron at Sheerness.

There were many demands on these resources and Scheer exacerbated the situation when he decided to use Zeebrugge as a major destroyer base for training and operations and thus vastly strengthened German surface forces in the area. On 8 June, for example, twelve German destroyers appeared east of Dunkirk where they were engaged by vessels of the Dover Patrol. The

---

* Technically, the commodore was made a Companion of the Distinguished Service Order, an award given for 'specific acts of gallantry or more generally for distinguished service over a period' (Duckers, *British Gallantry Awards*, p 23).

Harwich Force was called out but the Germans had left before they arrived; it was another fruitless sortie.

In addition, frequent calls for assistance from the Dover Patrol or from the naval base at Dunkirk were a considerable handicap to the commodore, the more so when the Admiralty ordered him to detach two cruisers and eight destroyers to Dover in July. One of these was *Cleopatra*, which promptly struck a mine on 4 August. She had left Dunkirk to patrol off Thornton Ridge on a hazy morning and around 0400 was making 15 knots when she sighted a floating mine. Suddenly another mine was seen right ahead and, before Captain Loder-Symonds could avoid it, the mine exploded on the port side, dismounting the after 6in gun. She was taken in tow by *Attentive* of the Dover Patrol for Dunkirk and then on to Chatham where she was in dock for two months. Gallingly, 'it was almost certainly a British mine as she was within four miles of a British field laid from Dover on May 26 1916'.[2] The need for refits and the occasional accident also reduced the numbers available to Harwich.

In August Tyrwhitt complained to First Sea Lord Jackson that he had only three destroyers available at Harwich because the rest were absent on all sorts of odd jobs, from hunting U-boats at Portsmouth and Dogger Bank or looking after minesweepers. This gained him the return of two light cruisers and four destroyers from Dover. 'I expect the Vice Admiral Dover will have some remarks to make,' Tyrwhitt harrumphed, 'but I don't think I shall worry about them.'[3] The return of his ships was particularly useful because in July the Admiralty imposed a new task on the Harwich Force.

Feeding Britain

One of the objectives of Britain's distant blockade of Germany was to prevent goods entering the North Sea and reaching German ports. As historian Richard Hough put it, the North Sea became 'a marine no man's land, with the British Fleet bottling up the exits'.[4]

But trade destined for the neutral countries of Norway, Sweden, Denmark and the Netherlands was initially unaffected. All of these nations had long-established trading relations with Germany and vice-versa and Germany was dependent on such countries for key supplies including iron ore, copper, fats, and dairy and meat products.

Shortly after the British blockade began, it became obvious that the Scandinavians and Dutch were massively increasing their import of all types of industrial raw materials and food. It was clearly too much for domestic consumption and was in fact being re-exported to Germany at good profit. Britain responded with two pieces of legislation. On 29 October 1914, an Order in Council decreed that once it become apparent that a neutral port was being used as a transhipment point for goods destined for Germany, all ships sailing for that port could be at risk of seizure by the British authorities. Additionally, it legislated that raw materials were henceforth transferred from the conditional to the absolute list and thus to be taken as contraband in any and all circumstances.

In November, given that the Germans were freely mining the North Sea, the British decided to do likewise. On the 2nd, it was announced that the whole of the North Sea was declared a military area. Any ship entering the North Sea would be subject to an examination. The Royal Navy would lay minefields to channel ships into specific safe routes, which could only be ascertained by putting into Lerwick, Kirkwall, or the Downs to obtain guidance or escort. All ships wishing to sail within the North Sea should either use the safe route via Dover and the Downs and then travel up the east coast of Britain, or put into Kirkwall for examination.

Britain was dependent on imports for many key items. Nearly two-thirds of the calorific intake of the British people came from abroad. Supplies of industrial materials such as cotton, oil or rubber were completely dependent on imports, which also provided a large share of the ore or metals worked by British factories. Three-quarters of the wool woven in British mills was shipped in from overseas. It was essential that these goods could still be sourced and thus a political as well as a military solution was required to ensure that Germany was denied such vital goods whilst Britain was able to obtain them for her own use.

In the case of the Netherlands, the country was a key supplier to Britain of dairy, meat and fresh food products. But the Dutch domestic position was complicated by two factors – its geographical proximity to Germany and its obligations under the 1868 Rhine Navigation Convention, which expressly forbade the contracting parties, which included both Germany and the Netherlands, to put any legal obstacles in the way of the free flow of goods on the river connecting the Ruhr via Rotterdam with the North Sea.

Clearly, the neutral governments would be reluctant to compromise their position in German eyes, even if they wished to, by signing unilateral deals with Britain. To avoid such embarrassment, British politicians sought to negotiate trade agreements with industry bodies. In Holland this idea originated with the Minister for Agriculture, Industry and Trade Marie Willem Frederik Treub, who in August 1914 created the 'Grain Bureau', a government monopoly which purchased grain and distributed it to bakeries and millers. Treub gave Britain guarantees that any grain purchases would be for Dutch consumption only. Germany accepted this only because the Dutch government stressed that famine threatened if it did not act, but warned that any further infringement of the Rhine Navigation Convention would be unacceptable.

Treub now developed an alternative plan; a new company would be founded to act as a clearing house for Dutch goods, offering Britain guarantees that goods imported under this scheme would not be sold to Germany. When Francis Oppenheimer, the British Commercial Attaché in The Hague, heard of the plan he pushed for its acceptance. On 26 December 1914, a convention was agreed and the two countries signed a (secret) covenant whereby the Dutch Government assured its British counterpart of the 'standing and good faith' of the directors of the new Nederlandsche Overzee Trustmaatschappij (Netherlands Overseas Trust Company, NOT). This organisation, separate and distinct from the government, announced that importers could use its offices to import contraband goods, provided they signed a contract promising not to re-export to Germany.* The reciprocal of this agreement was that Britain gained access to Dutch dairy and meat products, and this meant that the goods taken by Britain could not go to Germany. The first shipments under this new protocol were received in January 1915.

Oppenheimer was rewarded for his perspicacity by being traduced in Parliament. On 16 July 1916, Major Rowland Hunt (MP for Ludlow) asked the Under Secretary for Foreign Affairs (Lord Robert Cecil),

> whether, in view of the fact Sir Francis Oppenheimer, our Commercial Attaché at The Hague, is the son of a German, and was born and educated at Frankfort [sic], in Germany, and that his mother lives in Germany, and that the British Minister at The Hague refers everything connected with British trade in Holland to him, he can see his way to appointing a British-born and British-bred subject in his place during the War?[5]

Cecil brushed the question off.

This agreement was modified from time to time, such as when on 1 March 1915 Allied reprisals against unrestricted submarine warfare forbade all trade destined for Germany, not just that of contraband articles.

By 1916, three issues made ensuring the smooth continuation of the Anglo-Dutch trade one of pressing importance. Firstly, the available Dutch and British tonnage for shipments was being steadily depleted by German mines or submarines. Secondly, both Germany and Britain began to suffer from the impact of a bad summer for farmers (the winter would be worse). Thirdly, the

---

* The key paragraph read; 'His Majesty's Government is ready to accept the consignment of cargos to the Netherlands Oversea Trust as a guarantee that these cargoes are destined for home consumption in the Netherlands ... [send] information concerning each individual consignment addressed to the Netherlands Government to His Majesty's Legation at the Hague so that unmolested passage of such consignment may be secured' (ADM 137/2805, ADM 137/2837, NA).

British government formed a Ministry of Blockade in February 1916, which took a much firmer line in the interdiction, management and control of goods into and from the neutral countries. A new trade deal with the Netherlands was agreed in June by which a large amount of food which had previously been sent to Germany was now directed to Britain.

The result of all these issues and machinations was that Tyrwhitt and the Harwich Force now had a new duty to perform – assuring the safety of the Anglo-Dutch shipping trade. This quickly became known as the 'Beef Trip' and the first convoy was run in July 1916, from the Hook of Holland to Harwich.

Convoy was not new. Parliament had addressed this issue at least five times during the Dutch, French Revolutionary and Napoleonic Wars of the seventeenth, eighteenth and nineteenth centuries. The Compulsory Convoy Act of 1798, for example, compelled all British merchant ships sailing between British ports in time of war to sail in convoy protected by the Royal Navy, for which service a fee was charged for the oversight provided. This Act was repealed in 1872, after pressure from ship owners. This repeal represented a major change in emphasis for the Royal Navy, although this was little recognised at the time. The navy's role was now defined by phrases such as 'securing the sea communications', 'protecting the ocean highways' and 'preserving the sea routes'; all phrases that hid the fact that merchant ships would no longer receive direct protection.

At the start of the war, convoy was resisted by the Royal Navy for both psychological and operational reasons. The navy saw itself as an offensive force; nursemaiding slow cargo ships was both defensive and demeaning. Additionally, the Admiralty vastly overestimated the number of ship movements that had to be escorted in any convoy situation, and so rejected the concept as unworkable with the resources to hand. So it can be imagined that the Harwich Force's hard-driving destroyer captains were less than happy to be given the assignment. 'Frankly, we detested it,' recalled Commander Taprell Dorling. 'It would have been easier if all the ships of the convoy had steamed at the same speed ... when the leader arrived at the Maas, the convoy was spread over fifty miles of sea ... with no more than four destroyers to guard it.'[6]

The issue for Tyrwhitt was how to organise the protection of the merchant ships to be effective but not occupy too much of his limited resources. This was especially difficult as the fastest route lay only 50 or so miles from the concentration of German destroyers and U-boats at Zeebrugge and was but a quick dash from the Heligoland Bight. He devoted two light cruisers and five to ten destroyers to the task, often under his personal command. The Force did not at this stage convoy the merchant ships as such but rather kept a permanent patrol route running across from just off Harwich to the Schouwen Bank and thence to Maas.

The Germans soon showed their intentions. On 22 July, Tyrwhitt led out *Carysfort, Canterbury* and eight 'M'-class destroyers. *Canterbury* and one division were sent to watch the route near the North Hinder Light and he himself took *Carysfort* to the Maas area. Meanwhile, a six-ship German torpedo boat section left Zeebrugge looking for the merchantmen. At around 0015, *Carysfort* and her division sighted three of them dead ahead, three miles off. The enemy turned east and made off, pursued by the flagship which had just got them in firing range when a squall of rain hid them from sight and they fled under a heavy smokescreen, disappearing from view. A frustrated commodore ordered *Canterbury* to see if she could acquire them and cut off their retreat. Captain Percy Molyneux Rawson Royds in *Canterbury* found them and opened fire at 0210 in a stern chase. The destroyer *Matchless*, just returned from dockyard repair, could not keep up and the captain of *Milne*, Lieutenant in Command Hugh Troup, felt that he must stand by his division leader. *Canterbury* too was struggling with the speed necessary and this left just two destroyers pursuing the Germans and approaching a large minefield. Royds called off the chase. The incident clearly showed that if they wanted to, the Kaiserliche Marine could readily attack the crossing route.

Given the demonstrable risk, by the end of July a system of convoy proper had been implemented. Each group of four to nine cargo vessels was spaced at intervals of two to three days and were given a direct escort of a light cruiser and four destroyers. A similar group of warships patrolled the area off the Dutch coast near Schouwen Bank to deal with any destroyers coming out of Zeebrugge. Westbound convoys left Holland at the same time as the eastbound ships passed the North Hinder Light. Much to the disgust of the destroyer officers, convoy escort 'became the principal – and blasphemously execrated – activity of the Harwich Force'.[7]

Crossings were firstly made at night to make interception more difficult; but this led to navigational issues and straggling. On 21 September, a merchant ship in the eastbound convoy was picked off. It was the Great Eastern Railway steamer *Colchester*. She had been one of four ships which had orders to pass seven miles to the northward of the North Hinder at 2200. There the escorting destroyers would wait to pick them up and accompany the merchantmen to Dutch territorial waters. On a dark and clear night, the waiting destroyers saw only two steamers eastbound. They held back from making signals in order not to attract the enemy's attention; and since *Colchester* had not arrived, two of the destroyers remained at the rendezvous to wait for her and the other ship. Neither appeared; in fact, the fourth had not sailed. Nothing was known of the GER ship until the 23rd, when Berlin announced that she had been taken into Zeebrugge during the night of 21/22 September.

Given this loss, Tyrwhitt again changed the plan. Under orders he issued on 5 October, there was a reversion to daylight sailing and the route was divided into eight sections, each of which contained a destroyer zig-zagging at 15 knots; in other words, convoy was abandoned and area patrolling instituted.

Finally, in November, Tyrwhitt ordered a return to convoy with a direct escort whereby the eastbound ships sailed first and were escorted to the Hook of Holland, from where the westbound ships were chaperoned back to England by the same escort group. An eyewitness described the convoy thus;

> in the dark hours of the chosen morning fifteen or sixteen cargo boats would gather in XI channel near the Shipwash and would be picked up there by destroyers and light cruisers from Harwich. The merchant ships would get into formation and start across the North Sea. The keen destroyers, sharp as needles, would zigzag and throw circles around them, like a group of rat-terriers chasing a cat around a knot of old ladies. They did this in order to intimidate any submarine commander out pot-hunting . . . the swift light cruisers, stately and imperturbable, would boil along well out on the dangerous flank, apparently ignoring the fuss and fury of the show going on near them, but keeping a good look-out in case a striking force of Hun destroyers made a snatch at the convoy.[8]

'It was a dangerous duty,' wrote journalist Edward Knight, 'enemy minefields had to be traversed, and the convoys were liable to be attacked by submarines, light craft and seaplanes, for the Germans were ever on the lookout to intercept them.'[9] But the security resulting from this routine convoy system allowed for increasing the size of the groups escorted twice a week. The convoys of 27 November, for example, consisted of eight eastbound and eleven westbound ships. From the inauguration of convoys to Holland in July 1916 to February 1917, the only loss recorded was that of *Colchester*.

The Sinking of HMS *Lassoo*

On 13 August 1916, four destroyers, HMS *Lance*, *Lassoo*, *Lennox* and *Laverock*, were taking a convoy of some seven ships across to Holland. The convoy was straggling when it passed the North Hinder, and *Lassoo* was ahead, zig-zagging at 20 knots, to screen two cargo ships and steering for the Maas Light Vessel. The sun had not yet risen, the sea was smooth and visibility for once was good. Suddenly, at 0537 and about 10 miles west of the Maas Light Vessel, she was struck on the starboard side towards the stern. The pom-pom was blown into the air, and the aft torpedo tubes tumbled into the sea and she broke in two. *Lance* stood by her and both ships lowered their boats to transfer the crew of *Lassoo* to her sister ship. Her captain, Lieutenant Commander Vernon Saumarez Butler, and twelve men remained on board on the chance that she might be towable.

Butler and ERA Arthur Chipchase went down into the pitch-black engine room to investigate whether the bulkheads were holding. On returning, but before they could make any decision, the aft engine room bulkhead collapsed and she turned on her side. Butler ordered the remaining men on the forecastle to dive into the sea. The unfortunate ERA slipped as he tried to go over the side of the ship and went down with her, entangled in the berthing-rails. Butler walked off his ship along the now-horizontal funnel and grabbed hold of a floating fender until he was picked up. Six men died, including 21-year-old Surgeon-Probationer Gerald Stewart Freeman RNVR. The medical student son, for whom James and Katherine Hamilton Freeman, of Austral House, Huntly, in Aberdeenshire, held such high hopes was never coming back to them, or to the University of Edinburgh to complete his degree.

Tyrwhitt believed that *Lassoo* was sunk by a mine, despite there being no known minefield nearby. On 15 August he wrote to Sir John de Robeck, 'I don't think it was a submarine'.[10] The authors of Naval Monographs XVII in 1927 and Professor Temple Patterson in 1973 also ascribe the sinking to a mine.[11] But German records clearly show that *Lassoo* was torpedoed by Gustav Bach in *UB-10*.

The month of August had been cruel to the Harwich force, losing both *Cleopatra* and *Lassoo*. These losses could be ill afforded, for Tyrwhitt's team was spread far and wide. Apart from the destroyers with the 3rd Battle Squadron, and the dispositions mentioned earlier in this chapter, there was still a division at Dover. In addition, the Admiralty ordered him to send a division to Immingham, to assist Rear Admiral Stuart Nicholson commanding the east coast flotillas, and which was away from 2 to 18 August. On the 22nd Tyrwhitt complained that he had 'one division at Devonport, one at Dunkirk, one at the Humber and only three at Harwich'.[12] And four weeks on he was still able to protest that 'I have generally had five to six divisions away'.[13] 'Commodore (T) may sometimes have wondered why his famous flotillas were called the Harwich Force,'[14] mused the anonymous author of the Naval Staff Monographs.

Deadly Collision

The losses of August were not confined to surface operations. On the 15th, the 8th Submarine Flotilla was exercising off Harwich. HMS *E-41* was playing the role of target and *E-31* and *E-4* that of the hunters. At 1030 *E-41*, running on the surface at 12 knots, suddenly saw the periscope of *E-4* on the starboard bow, about 50 yards away and passing across *E-41*'s bows. Lieutenant Alfred Winser ordered the helm hard-a-starboard and her engines stopped but a collision was inevitable. *E-4* crashed into the forepart of *E-41* and sank, taking all thirty-two crew with her.

In *E-41* an attempt was made to close the foremost bulkhead door but the water was rising rapidly, Winser ordered everyone on deck. While the men were still going up, the boat sank by the bows and went down in 90 seconds. The rising air pressure blew open the upper conning tower hatch and carried two sublieutenants and four ratings to the surface. *Firedrake* was quickly on the spot and found three officers, one of whom was Winser, and eleven men.

The most remarkable survivor, however, came to the surface an hour and a half later. Stoker Petty Officer William Brown had gone aft as the boat sank and found himself alone in the unlighted engine room. His only means of escape from there was via the torpedo hatch. With water rising round him, he started to disconnect its gearing and unship the strongback. Three times he dived under water to work the wheel of the gearing and several times he received a nasty electrical shock from the switchboard. Still the water rose steadily compressing the air pressure; and still the hatch proved recalcitrant. His most strenuous efforts only succeeded in opening the hatch half-way but air pressure always slammed it shut again, crushing his hand on the last occasion.

In an atmosphere polluted with poisonous chlorine gas and now with only one usable hand Brown, as a forlorn hope, decided to flood the boat as quickly as possible. Opening a deadlight in the bulkhead he allowed the engine room to flood completely. With the water right up to the coaming of the hatch he knocked out its pin, raised the hatch and escaped. He rose 40ft to the surface and was plucked out of the water by *Firedrake*.

Tyrwhitt was distressed. Writing to Rear Admiral Sir John de Robeck, newly commanding the 3rd Battle Squadron at Sheerness, Tyrwhitt noted that 'sadder still *E-41* and *E-4*, they both sank from collision only thirteen men saved. They were exercising just outside the Cork Lightship.'[15]

The CO of *E-4* was 31-year-old Queensland-born Lieutenant Commander Julian Tenison RN, who had joined *Britannia* in 1900 aged 15. He was the son of a successful barrister living in Hobart, Tasmania, who traced his familial lineage to Thomas Tenison, Archbishop of Canterbury for 21 years from 1694. In January 1920, Julian's sister published a memoir, *A Character-sketch of Lieutenant-Commander Julian Tenison RN, Born June 22, 1885. Died for his King and Country, August 15, 1916*. And in Canterbury Cathedral, Tenison is the dedicatee of a carved and decorated alabaster wall tablet. Both vessels were later raised and salvaged by lifting craft and returned to service around May 1917.

The High Seas Fleet Comes Out

At 2100 on 18 August, Scheer led the High Sea Fleet out to sea once more. He had two objectives in mind. Firstly, an attack on Sunderland, in a continuance of his tactic of trying to draw out a portion of the Grand Fleet which he could then overwhelm. His second aim was to bolster the morale of his fleet after Jutland and to show the world that the Kaiserliche Marine was still a potent force.

Following the damage to his battlecruisers at Jutland, there were only two available to him, *Moltke* and *Von der Tann*, so the intended bombardment group was strengthened by the addition of three battleships, *Bayern*, *Markgraf* and *Grosser Kurfürst*. Scheer's total force of heavy ships comprised eighteen dreadnought battleships and two battlecruisers; Zeppelins scouted ahead of him and U-boats formed patrol lines to both observe and intercept the British fleet.

Once again, Room 40 alerted the Admiralty that the German fleet was preparing to leave harbour and the Grand Fleet put to sea, temporarily under the command of Admiral Burney, as Jellicoe was having a break (he joined his flagship by light cruiser from Dundee). They were at sea before their enemy.

Tyrwhitt was ordered to sail for Brown Ridge and to be on the lookout for the German fleet by early dawn on the 19th; with his pennant in *Carysfort* he took all of 5 LCS, *Lightfoot* and his remaining eighteen L- and 'M'-class destroyers. By 0300 Tyrwhitt was in position and patrolling at 20 knots. Around 1000 a message from a submarine indicated that the High Seas Fleet was to his north and, having relayed the message to Jellicoe, the commodore

HMS *Iron Duke* (1912), Jellicoe's flagship during his command of the Grand Fleet. She was armed with ten 13.5in and twelve 6in guns and could sail at 21.25 knots.
(US Library of Congress LC-B2- 4991-8)

The German battlecruiser *Moltke* (1910), armed with ten 11in and twelve 5.9in guns.
She took part in all the coastal bombardments, including the aborted Sunderland one of
19 August 1916. (US Library of Congress LC-DIG-hec-01140)

steamed northwards, hoping to get in touch with the enemy or get behind
their line of retreat.

Jellicoe was heading southeast until the light cruiser HMS *Nottingham* was
torpedoed at 0600 and again at 0710, sinking her. Unable to tell if it was a
torpedo or a new minefield, Jellicoe assumed the latter and turned north, away
from the German ships.

Meanwhile Scheer had received a Zeppelin sighting report which indicated
that a number of battleships and light cruisers were to his south. Believing
this to be the detached portion of the British fleet which he had so set his heart
on finding, he turned towards it and abandoned the bombardment planned
for Sunderland. But he had been misled – it was the Harwich Force that the
airship had spotted.

At 1254, Tyrwhitt had not seen the enemy, or received any fresh orders,
and so decided to return to his assigned station, setting course away from the
High Seas Fleet as he did so. Scheer then learned from a U-boat that Jellicoe
and the Grand Fleet were coming down on him some 65 miles distant and at
1435 gave up his chase of the Harwich ships and headed for home.

Despite receiving, later than intended, a confusing series of signals from
Jellicoe, Tyrwhitt divined what Scheer was doing and turned again on a course
which would give him a chance of intercepting the enemy. And at 1730,
Lightfoot reported that she had sighted a large number of vessels steering east;
the commodore first turned south to give himself some sea room and then
settled onto a course to shadow the German Fleet.

Realising that he was being tailed, Scheer made dispositions for a night
attack by stationing a powerful force of destroyers to his rear. Tyrwhitt would

surely have made such an attack under cover of darkness but two things now deterred him. Firstly, at 1832, Jellicoe signalled that he was too far away to support him (in fact he was already retiring); and secondly, the Harwich Force would not be able to make contact with the German ships until after the moon had risen. At 1932 the commodore signalled that he had called off the chase. To have taken the offensive, unsupported and in bright moonlight, would surely have resulted in failure and ill-affordable losses to his ships. 'I retired gracefully as I did not feel inclined to take them on alone,' he wrote later.[16]

There was, however, one success for the Harwich Force to enjoy. The 8th Flotilla submarine HMS *E-23*, under Lieutenant Commander Robert Ross Turner, had managed to torpedo the battleship SMS *Westfalen* north of Terschelling at 0505 on 19 August; but the German ship was able to return to port, with an escort of destroyers.

Tyrwhitt's turning away drew criticism in some quarters, even from the Germans. Their official history of the naval war remarked that 'the reasons which caused him and Admiral Jellicoe not to attack the heavy German forces . . . and leave them entirely unmolested stand in basic opposition to the German conception of the use and independent attack of torpedo boat forces'.[17]

But there was never any official criticism of Tyrwhitt's actions, at the time or later. Tyrwhitt berated himself for not standing on longer when he had turned back at 1254, writing to Jellicoe, 'I am afraid we failed you . . . and I am kicking myself'. With regard to the night attack, he added 'I could have made one but I don't think I would have succeeded in doing any harm and should most certainly been cut up as the night was not very dark'.[18]

The battleship SMS *Westfalen* (1908), torpedoed by *E-23* during the action of 19 August 1916. She mounted twelve 11in and twelve 5.9in guns. The torpedo put her out of action for two months. (US Library of Congress LC-DIG-ggbain-25466)

New Orders

August also brought the issuance of new instructions for the Harwich Force. After Jutland, both Jellicoe and the Admiralty set up various working groups to distil what learning could be gained from the battle and make any necessary changes to orders and to tactics or *matériel*.

Among the outputs from this process were new Grand Fleet Battle Orders. As part of these Jellicoe, who was convinced the object of Scheer's sorties was to lure the fleet over submarines, specified that the fleet would not go further south than a line drawn roughly from the Farne Islands to Horns Reef, except if there was a good possibility of bringing the High Seas Fleet to action in daylight. Effectively this meant that the whole of the east coast south of the Tyne was to be defended by the local port flotillas, the Harwich Force and the 3rd Battle Squadron.

New orders were also created for the flotillas at Harwich (see Appendix 1). It will be recalled that Jellicoe had delegated direction of Tyrwhitt's forces to the Admiralty and that they gave the commodore no directive to support the Grand Fleet before or during the Jutland action.

These new instructions, issued from the Grand Fleet flagship HMS *Iron Duke* on 24 August, specifically enjoined the Admiralty to send the Harwich Force out to one of five named rendezvous points in the southern North Sea 'until sufficient information is available'. This positive intent no doubt pleased Tyrwhitt. But the fear and caution within the Admiralty regarding any potential secondary attack on Dover/Dunkirk placed a caveat on this, one insisted upon by the Admiralty in a letter of 19 August; paragraph five of the battle orders states that 'in the event of the enemy having stronger flotillas than the Dover Patrol can account for, based on the Belgian Ports, it may be necessary to retain some part of the Commodore (T)'s force in southern waters'. This didn't please Tyrwhitt.

A Grudge Match

The Harwich Force's nearest 'neighbour' was the Dover Patrol, based in the eponymous port just over 100 nautical miles by sea to the south and at Dunkirk. It was commanded by Vice Admiral Reginald Hugh Spencer Bacon.*

Bacon had left the navy in 1909 to become managing director of the Coventry Ordnance Works but rejoined for the war and on 13 April 1915 he was appointed to command of the Dover Patrol. He had been a favourite of Fisher and a member of the 'Fishpond' as a young officer and his association with him had no doubt played a role in his appointment, as did his familiarity with things technical, an attribute that would be increasingly important in the

---

* Known to the navy, or at least the lower deck, as 'Porky'.

development of the mine and barrage defences of the Channel. As Churchill wrote of him 'in everything that concerned machinery, invention, organisation, precision, he had few professional superiors'.[19]

However, Bacon was a divisive character, being a poor delegator and giving the arrogant impression that he could manage without help from anyone. Additionally, he had an adamantine belief in the veracity of his own ideas and the error of all who disagreed with him. According to Arthur Marder, he 'had not the gift of drawing loyal service from his officers and men . . . and was not a popular figure'.[20] He was a polarising character. People either liked him or hated him and he was certainly not a friend to all and sundry.

In 1916, the relationship between Bacon and Tyrwhitt came under great strain, owing to Bacon's constant demands to be 'loaned' Harwich Force destroyers, and his special pleadings based on his friendships with Jackson and Jellicoe (whose biography he would write after the war). Moreover, Bacon was often eager to disparage Tyrwhitt's plans for offensive action and instead advance his own, more narrowly defensive ones.

Neither was Dover a popular billet for the Harwich Force crews. Access to the harbour was through two gaps in the Southern Breakwater, called the eastern and western entrances, but captains were explicitly warned that the tides were very strong and ingress and egress could be difficult. Many sailors thought it a harbour only in name. The tidal streams were extremely variable, the winds strong and coaling and oiling difficult. A future First Sea Lord, Andrew Cunningham, felt that 'in any sort of weather Dover harbour is one of the worst in the world'.[21]

Tyrwhitt regularly complained that when his ships were assigned to Dover, the vice admiral worked them too hard. The emotionally committed destroyer-man was appalled at the way ships and crews were exploited by the more technocratic Bacon. On one occasion he complained that Bacon kept one of his destroyers at sea for 19 days, held his vessels at 30 minutes' notice for steam, and when they were returned to him the crews were worn out and slept for 48 hours. 'Did you ever hear of such a way of treating TBDs [destroyers],' he asked de Robeck.[22] In September he penned that 'I have not heard much of the VA Dover except that he runs four of my TBDs to death every eight days with unfailing regularity'.[23]

The relationship between the two Reginalds was to be further disturbed by Tyrwhitt's aggressive plans for the deployment of a new kind of boat.

11

Frustrated Plans, September–December 1916

In the summer of 1915, three officers of the Harwich Force, Lieutenants Geoffrey Hampden,* William Bremner and John Anson,[1] approached Commodore Tyrwhitt with an idea for a new kind of offensive vessel, specifically intended to attack the German fleet in the Schillig Roads. This was the genesis of the coastal motor boat (CMB) or sea skimmer.

The proposed boats operated on the hydroplane principle; the concept developed by the three officers was that a very fast, shallow draught vessel would be ideal for attacking German ships in their harbours. It would be able to pass over the defensive minefields without triggering mines and its high speed would allow rapid strike and escape.

Tyrwhitt 'supported the scheme very strongly'[2] as he had long wanted to take the attack directly to the German fleet. But the Admiralty was unimpressed; it was 'was sceptical as to the design, raising doubts as to stability, trim, etc'.[3] Nonetheless, the concept was strongly backed by the navy's torpedo and mining school, HMS *Vernon*. They endorsed the original request for thirty-two such craft to be ordered 'sufficient to make a thorough job of the attack'.[4] But in January 1916, the Admiralty grudgingly gave its consent to the acquisition of just twelve.

The Thornycroft company were approached to build them as '[they] are the exponents of that particular type of hull, and so the CMBs were ordered from that firm and were constructed on their patent *Miranda*† principle'.[5] For

Lieutenant William Bremner, one of the three 'inventors' of the CMB. Bremner later took part in the Baltic Campaign of 1918–20 and won the DSO for his part in the CMB attack on Kronstadt, where he was taken prisoner.
(Photo by permission of David Bremner)

---

* Hampden, who had been wounded in both legs during the pursuit of the SMS *Emden*, and had only a quarter vision in his right eye, was probably the leader of the trio. In 1918, his commanding officer stated that 'the development of the CMBs in His Majesty's service was largely due to him' (ADM 196/152/4, NA).
† *Miranda IV* (1910) was the culmination of a series of experimental boats built by Thornycroft to explore hydrofoil or stepped-hull designs. She was a 29ft-long single-step hydroplane, capable of 35.5 knots.

the planned attack on the Schillig Roads they were to be carried across the North Sea in the light cruisers' davits, which put a limit on their size and weight, and they were designed accordingly. They were 40ft in length, and weighed about 4 tons fully loaded. The boats made use of the lightweight and powerful petrol engines becoming available and a variety of armament was carried, including torpedoes (and later depth charges or mines), together with light machine guns, such as the Lewis gun. The CMBs were of monocoque construction with a 'skin' of Honduran mahogany backed by oil-soaked calico which 'fed' oil to the wood over time to prevent it drying out. Power came initially from 250 brake horsepower V-12 aircraft engines made by Sunbeam and Napier and later used engines from Green's and of Thornycroft's own manufacture. This made them very fast (they could hit 40 knots and average 35) and able to skim over the top of minefields by aquaplaning. They were beautiful to look at. One naval officer wrote, 'I do not know who invented the CMB but this little vessel was a masterpiece of ingenuity, so much so that I wept with envy when I saw the first one go over from Dover to Dunkirk'.[6] However, CMBs were not good sea boats and could only really cope with Sea State Two. They were armed with the 18in Mark VIII torpedo, chosen on account of its heavy warhead and also because of its good depth-taking qualities. These were fired over the stern of the craft, tail first. The CMB skipper then had to make a sharp turn away to avoid his own torpedo. Three or four men was the usual crew.

A restored CMB on the River Thames. Note the torpedo launching trough.
(Photo; Dr V A Michell)

Sir Charles Madden as an admiral, painted in 1922 by Reginald Grenville Eves. As Jellicoe's chief of staff, Madden rejected Tyrwhitt's plan to capture Zeebrugge. He was CinC of the Atlantic Fleet after the war and served as First Sea Lord in the late 1920s.
(Author's collection)

It was decided to base the CMBs away from Harwich and so the South Eastern and Chatham Railway Company's Queenborough pier was commandeered as their headquarters, where the boats could be hoisted out of the water by electric cranes and placed on trucks. It was here that Captain Barry Domvile had briefly commanded after the loss of the *Arethusa*.

By autumn 1916, all twelve boats had been delivered and training completed. But there was a problem. Tyrwhitt could not get the Admiralty to consent to the operation; neither would Bacon support him, although de Robeck provided as much backing as he could muster. Tyrwhitt thought Bacon wanted the CMBs for Dover, writing that 'the streaky one* is doing his best to get the skimmers for his own purposes'.[7]

---

* Tyrwhitt's disparaging nickname for Bacon.

The Admiralty raised objection after objection. On 17 August, Tyrwhitt wrote to de Robeck 'icy cold water was poured on the general scheme by . . . . Madden'.* Moreover, he got rapped on the knuckles for telling Jellicoe about his plan; 'TLS [Their Lordships] were annoyed with me because I said anything to the CinC but that of course is the result of the semi-jurisdiction they both hold over me.'[8]

The Admiralty insisted on a widespread reconnaissance by air, believing rumours of a boom across the anchorage, so during the rest of the month Tyrwhitt prepared a revised plan. 'The revised orders for the skimmers have been sent to the CinC,' he informed de Robeck, 'and I am ordered to visit him to discuss them as soon as the reconnaissance has been carried out . . . I am sure it will be winter before everyone is satisfied'.[9] But this proved problematic. In September, the lack of destroyers at Harwich meant that 'we have been so short of TBDs that I have not been able to carry out the reconnaissance'.[10]

The next attempt at a reconnaissance by air took place on 28 September. A Curtiss flying boat[†] took off from Harwich with a four-man crew (which included Erskine Childers as an observer). The plan was for it to land next to Tyrwhitt's cruisers at sea, refuel from them and then fly a three to four hour mission to survey the Roads. Soon after take-off, however, the weather began to deteriorate and the commodore decided to call the event off. He ordered some of the destroyers to retrace their course in the hope of spotting the flying boat and signalling that it should return to base, while he himself remained at the agreed refuelling position in case the 'turnaround' signal was missed. It was, and Flight Lieutenant A Q Cooper arrived overhead at 1015. He was ordered by lamp signal to return but could not without more fuel and so landed next to Tyrwhitt's ships. Once down, the sea was too rough for him to take off again. *Landrail* took the flying boat in tow but while this operation was proceeding, the aircraft hit the destroyer's hull and was damaged beyond its ability to fly again. Lieutenant Commander Francis Edward Henry Graham Hobart took off the airmen and his ship continued to tow the damaged craft almost all the way to Harwich before the flying boat became too waterlogged and sank.

In October, more misery ensued. On the 22nd *Vindex*, returned to the fold, took two Short floatplanes out towards the coast. They took off successfully and the carrier headed for home, leaving the aircraft to be recovered by the cruisers. But 'our reconnaissance failed on Sunday. Everything went splendidly until the two seaplanes arrived near the Schilling Roads which were covered by dense fog'. Then in recovering the aircraft onto the ships in a strong wind,

---

* Vice Admiral Charles Edward Madden was Jellicoe's chief of staff (and his wife's brother-in-law).
† Probably an H-4 'Small America'.

they were damaged. To make matters worse, the commodore was 'enjoying the worst cold I ever had'.[11]

Eventually, according to Lieutenant William Bremner, the plan was dropped; 'nothing happened and it eventually transpired that owing to the heavy mining in the Bight, the Admiralty would not allow the Harwich Force to go sufficiently close to Schillig Roads to drop the CMBs with any chance of success'.[12] Furthermore, Bacon did succeed in getting the CMBs for his own command; in January 1917, four boats were sent to Dunkirk and the main base was moved from Queenborough to Dover where large maintenance workshops were erected.

The second major clash between Tyrwhitt, Bacon and the Admiralty was over 'Zeebrugge, which has been allowed to grow until it is a thorn in our side'.[13] Since Scheer had concentrated his destroyers there it had become a wasp's nest of activity for U-boats and light forces and this was deeply troubling to Tyrwhitt and his Beef Trip escort duties. In 1914 and again in early 1916 Vice Admiral Lewis Bayly, in charge of the Coast of Ireland Command and hence the Western Approaches and thus in the thick of the anti-submarine effort, produced a detailed proposal for landing troops in occupied Belgium to seize Ostend and Zeebrugge. Ambitious in scope and objective, it called for men and equipment that were both in short supply and was quietly shelved.

Then in the autumn, Tyrwhitt also produced a plan. This called for the destruction of the lock gates by an explosive-packed blockship protected by smoke and poison gas. The possibility that the poison gas would impact on the local populace was something he had overlooked but the Admiralty didn't and they rejected the idea. Undismayed, on 23 November, Tyrwhitt recast his thinking and now proposed an attack on Zeebrugge harbour mole and the capture of the town itself to effect operations against the German flank. However, at a conference with Jellicoe, Bacon and Oliver, his thoughts were not favourably received. Bacon strongly criticised Tyrwhitt's ideas. He preferred his own idea of an attack on the gates using long-range bombardment (see Chapter 13).

The commodore was a great deal less than impressed. Livid, Tyrwhitt expostulated that 'all my pet schemes were turned down, including the CMBs, and what is more the streaky one has got them under his wing'.[14] And to Keyes he wrote that Bacon had become a worse enemy than the Germans, unwilling to take risks and 'our bugbear . . . the streaky one has obsessed everyone at the Admiralty and does exactly what he pleases with them'.[15]

A New Flagship

On 20 July, Captain Domvile was appointed to a brand-new light cruiser, HMS *Centaur*. In the course of the war thus far, Commodore Tyrwhitt had flown his broad pennant in *Amethyst* (rejected), *Arethusa* (sunk), *Cleopatra* (damaged), *Conquest* (damaged) and *Carysfort*. Having commissioned her, Domvile brought *Centaur* to Harwich on 11 September and Tyrwhitt transferred his pennant to her.

Before the war, Turkey had ordered a pair of scout cruisers. When the war started, construction was halted. But a considerable amount of material had already been prepared and much of this was used in the construction of *Centaur* (and her sister *Concord*). Built by Vickers Limited, she had been laid down in January 1915 and was launched on 1 January 1916.

Centaur mounted five 6in and two 3in guns, with a couple of 2pdrs for anti-aircraft work, and could steam at 28.5 knots. However, her introduction to Harwich was not auspicious. She arrived with a 15-degree list which refused to right itself. Her steering gear broke down when she was at sea (Tyrwhitt briefly transferred to *Conquest* again while this was rectified). Domvile also disliked the fact that she had all her 6in guns on the centre line, which meant that it gave him only one gun at the front. He foresaw that his ship would often be chasing the enemy. However, once her teething problems were dealt with, she provided good service.

In the same month as *Centaur* came to Harwich, the 9th Submarine Flotilla arrived and strengthened Tyrwhitt's underwater armoury. They were all 'E'-class vessels, the class which provided the backbone of the Harwich submarines for much of the war.

As well as a new flagship, Tyrwhitt was informed that on 15 September he had been made a Commandeur (the third tier of five) of the French Légion d'honneur (Legion of Honour). He was baffled and asked de Robeck 'what should I do about the Legion of Honour? Should I write to thank somebody, and if so who? Nobody here knows!'[16]

A Submarine Success

On 6 October, the Germans ordered the resumption of overt submarine warfare (under cruiser warfare terms) and thus Scheer no longer had submarines available for fleet work. Jellicoe's fear of being lured over a U-boat line was therefore largely groundless for the moment. As a result of this sudden dearth of U-boats, Scheer was uninterested in a bombardment of a coastal town; instead, he turned his attention to trade. 'Lacking submarines,' he later stated, 'I was forced to adopt a different scheme, and instead of making for the English coast and luring the enemy on to our line of submarines before the actual battle took place, I had to make a wide sweeping advance with torpedo craft to take stock of merchant traffic, and to capture prizes, with the fleet following up to support the light craft.'[17]

He had collected information regarding the sailing of British merchant ships and issued them to the fleet. In particular, he was interested in the Wilson Lines ship SS *Harrogate*, which was leaving Bergen for Hull on 18 October with a cargo of zinc, and the Swedish steamer *Anund*, which was reported to be departing Gothenburg for England the same day with a cargo of iron ore.

On 18 October, Scheer once more put to sea with the High Seas Fleet. Again, at around 1730, Room 40 was able to provide intelligence of his intentions and departure. But this time, in line with Jellicoe's new instructions, the Grand Fleet was only put at short notice for steam. Tyrwhitt was ordered out, as per his revised Battle Orders, to North Hinder. He left at 0100 on the 19th with *Centaur* and six light cruisers, together with *Nimrod* and fourteen destroyers.

But this time it was a Harwich Force submarine which caused Scheer to abandon his mission. *E-38*, under Lieutenant Commander John de Burgh Jessop, was part of a patrol line of four Harwich boats off the Dutch coast. He had been there since 13 October and was now some 50 miles north of Terschelling, when at 0632 he sighted the funnels and masts of heavy ships to

The *Bremen*-class light cruiser SMS *München* (1904), torpedoed by the submarine *E-38* on 19 October 1916. She managed to get back to harbour but was decommissioned in November, as not being worth repairing the damage sustained. *München* mounted ten 105mm/4.1in guns, two torpedo tubes and could carry fifty mines.
(US Naval History and Heritage Command NH 46826)

the eastward and altered course to the north to attack. He saw the battlecruisers of Scouting Group 1 but their course took them away from him. Then at 0650 he spotted light cruisers and fired at one of them. The torpedo didn't run true and missed. Now a swarm of destroyers came to defend their bigger brethren and for two hours Jessop dodged their attempts to sink him before, at 0843, he was able to fire both fore tubes at 1,300 yards range. As the submarine dived again, the roar of an explosion could be heard throughout his boat. *E-38*'s batteries were now exhausted and the air inside his vessel very stale, both of which meant he could not follow up. Jessop had hit the light cruiser SMS *München*. This convinced Scheer that the British knew his location and he cancelled the planned sweep and returned to port. When Tyrwhitt arrived at his designated position, he was informed that the Germans had turned back.

The damaged *München* took on around 500 tons of water and salt water got into her boilers, contaminating the freshwater feed to her boilers. She was taken under tow, first by the torpedo boat *V-73*, and then by her sister ship *Berlin*. The following day, the crew got her engines back in operation and she steamed into the Jade at 7 knots, headed straight for the Wilhelmshaven dockyard.

Lieutenant Commander Jessop was awarded the DSO 'in recognition of the skill and determination which he showed in making a successful submarine attack on an enemy light cruiser on the 19th October, 1916'.[18]

Experiments

One of the characteristics which stands out about the Harwich Force and its commander was Tyrwhitt's encouragement of innovation, be it CMBs or naval aviation, of which he was a strong proponent as has already been demonstrated.

This willingness to think outside the box was evident in an experiment whereby an RNAS airship was towed out to sea behind a light cruiser, travelling at 26 knots, to allow the airship to extend its range and time over enemy waters/coastline. The experiment involved the 'Coastal' airship *C-1*, towed behind *Carysfort* on 12 May 1916.[19] The force also developed an early form of aerial refuelling by passing petrol cans on the end of a line up to the receiving craft; in another version a pressurised hose was taken aloft in a bosun's chair to replenish fuel at a height of 100ft. However, in the end the Admiralty decided that towed balloons/airships would mark the position of the fleet too conspicuously.

The Force also examined the use of kite balloons flown from a destroyer as an aid to spotting U-boats. This was not, however, considered a success. Tyrwhitt expressed the view that 'we are rather done in here owing to shallow water. The submarines promptly sit on the floor when they see a kite balloon which rather spoils our style.'[20]

In this they were in disagreement with a later view taken by the US Navy after they had entered the war. In 1918, a USN report noted that 'neither dirigibles nor heavier-than-air machines should be designated for this duty [convoy escort], although they may be employed as escorts on special occasions'. However, they came down heavily in favour of kite balloons. Their advantages included the facts that 'the distance patrolled equals the distance advanced by the convoy during daylight hours – fog neglected' and 'a surface vessel can be directed with precision towards any object sighted'. Analysis demonstrated that 'vessels in a convoy escorted by two kite balloon vessels were three times as safe from attack as when they are not so escorted'. As a consequence, it was recommended 'to use kite balloons for escort and patrol duty where practicable'.[21] Once again, the Harwich Force was thinking ahead of the game, although at this point coming to the wrong conclusion.

November and December; the Cost of War

During the latter two months of the year, the Harwich Force was constantly out on sweeps, hunting Zeppelins or escorting the Beef Trip. Additionally, there were minor panics and call-outs to deal with. Two typical instances occurred at the end of November which indicate the often fruitless and dangerous quotidian work, tiring on both men and ships.

On the night of Sunday, 26 November, a flotilla of German destroyers came to within 30 miles of Harwich without let or hindrance. In the course of their sweep, they stopped the Dutch steamer SS *Beijerland* at 2230, about 10 miles north of Shipwash, inspected her for contraband cargo and took her pilot prisoner.

Fifteen minutes later, the Dutch ship's master heard firing to his south; it was some German destroyers sinking the armed trawler *Narval*, which was on passage from Grimsby to Harwich; her crew were taken prisoner by the flotilla and a Berlin press communique reported the ship sunk. *Narval* had previously been a Belgian Ostend-registered fishing vessel, brought to Britain by her crew after the Germans invaded their country. She was taken up by the navy, armed with a 12pdr gun and became an auxiliary minesweeper.

None of this action was known to the Harwich Force, although the enemy approached to within five miles of the coast near Aldeburgh. Eventually, at 2345, a directional sound receiving station reported gunfire from a mysterious ship. Com (T) sailed at midnight in response with *Centaur*, *Carysfort* and three destroyers in order to reinforce the escort for the Dutch Beef Trip convoy but saw nothing of the enemy.

Then, four days later, an intercepted German signal indicated that the German 9th Flotilla was leaving Zeebrugge for the Bight at 1900 on 30 November, and would arrive at Terschelling about 0500 on 1 December. This intelligence was passed to Tyrwhitt at 1808, together with instructions to try and intercept them but not to go north of Texel, as no support would be available. The Battle Cruiser Force was ordered to raise steam and Captain Waistell was instructed to send six submarines from Harwich to form a patrol line.

The Harwich Force was away by 2030 with *Centaur* leading *Carysfort*, *Canterbury*, *Cleopatra*, *Undaunted*, *Lightfoot* and sixteen destroyers. Tyrwhitt detached *Lightfoot* with seven destroyers to watch the area off Brown Ridge and the remainder of the ships went on towards Terschelling. At 2222, the Admiralty informed the Battle Cruiser Force that they were not required to sail but should remain at one hour's notice. Meanwhile, the submarine patrol left Harwich at 2100, comprising *E-29*, *E-37*, *E-54* and *E-56* plus two boats from Great Yarmouth.

At daybreak, Tyrwhitt was on station as instructed but at 0530 another intercepted German signal indicated that the 9th Flotilla had already passed beyond the Harwich ships and were out of reach. Tyrwhitt continued his rounds until 0737 and then returned to harbour. Another wasted sally, but one with tragic consequences; for the submarines stayed out until 2 December and on their return discovered that *E-37* was missing. The vessel had only been commissioned in March. Thirty-two-year-old Lieutenant Commander Robert Fellowes Chisholm and twenty-nine officers and men were never seen again.

Lieutenant Commander Robert Raikes of *E-54* reported that he had felt a violent shock on the night of the 30th as the submarines sortied out; he thought he had struck wreckage or a War Channel buoy. In fact, it was *E-37* hitting a newly-laid mine. German U-boat minelayers had been active off Orford Ness and around the Sunk; and their mines found a victim.

Peace?

On 3 December, de Robeck moved on, taking charge of the 2nd Battle Squadron at Scapa. That lost the commodore a supporter of his plans for Zeebrugge and CMBs; 'I have always looked forward to downing Zeebrugge under your orders. I don't think it will be done with the present regime,' Tyrwhitt regretfully wrote to the departing admiral.[22]

December saw another shift in the resources allocated to the Force. Com (T) was ordered to send *Nimrod* and eight destroyers from 10 DF to Bacon for Dunkirk. These were replaced by *Grenville* (1916) and eight other destroyers from 15 DF which were sent south from Scapa to assist in a large minelaying operation, after which Tyrwhitt was told to keep them under his command; these replacements arrived at Harwich on 19 December. They were much needed for aside from the loans to various other commands, five of his destroyers were under repair.

Grenville was a *Parker*-class flotilla leader, armed with four 4in guns mounted on the ship's centreline, with the forward two guns superfiring (one firing over the other), with one gun between the second and third funnel and one aft. Two 2pdr pom-pom anti-aircraft guns were also fitted and she bore two sets of twin 21in torpedo tubes. From June *Grenville* had carried two D-type depth charges, as with the other flotilla leaders.

The end of the year also saw significant changes in government and at the Admiralty. In general, the war had not gone well for Britain in 1916. The slaughter on the Somme, in which the British and French between them suffered 620,000 casualties, rocked the nation with grief and frustration. The failure of the navy to win a decisive victory at Jutland grated on a country which had paid a great deal of tax to build their ships, and German predation of British merchant shipping was once more on the rise. Sinkings rose from 43,345 gross tons in August to 176,248 tons in September and 168,809 tons in November.[23]

Secretary of State for War David Lloyd George wrote a memorandum for the Joint Allied Conference at Chantilly, held on 25 November, in which he stated that 'at sea the British, Allied and neutral shipping on which depends the life of the English people, its food, its munitions and those of its allies, is being destroyed at an alarmingly increasing rate'.[24]

By the end of November, total British war casualties had already topped a million men and the conflict was costing Britain £5 million per day, half of which was being raised in the USA. Additionally, Britain was forced to financially support its allies, especially Russia and France. And its precious coal mines maintained France, Italy and the Scandinavian neutrals (the latter at least part of the time). On the 13th of the month, the Conservative leader in the Lords and Minister without Portfolio in the government, Henry Petty-FitzMaurice, 5th Marquess of Lansdowne, circulated a paper which asked the Cabinet to consider a negotiated peace. He suggested that Britain's manpower and industrial resources might not be able stand the strain of the war. It was rejected. Nonetheless, Germany announced that it was willing to negotiate a peace on 12 December.

David Lloyd George, who became prime minister of the UK on 7 December 1916. (US Library of Congress LC-USZ62-8054)

Tyrwhitt was appalled at such talk. In December he wrote to de Robeck 'there is much peace talk at present but please God it will end in talk. There is only one sort of peace for us.'[25] Winning was what mattered.[*]

New Regimes in London

For much of the year, Prime Minister Asquith had increasingly been at loggerheads with several key members of his Cabinet and was being criticised in the press, where he was generally seen as not having sufficient 'grip' to prosecute the war successfully.

Led by Lloyd George, a cabal began to conspire for Asquith's removal, a putsch which was completed on 7 December when Lloyd George kissed hands as the new prime minister. Asquith left 10 Downing Street on the 9th and Foreign Secretary Sir Edward Grey followed him out of office the next day. The latter's replacement was the languid First Lord of the Admiralty, Arthur Balfour. Balfour and Jackson's reign at the Admiralty had not disturbed the navy's reputation for caution and was widely viewed as lacklustre.

Moving Balfour, and terminating Jackson's appointment, opened the way for a new top team, with the Ulsterman Sir Edward Carson taking the post of First Lord on 12 December and Admiral Sir John Jellicoe, who had been in command of the Grand Fleet since the beginning of the war, becoming First Sea Lord on the 4th. Vice Admiral Sir David Beatty took command of the Grand Fleet and Rear Admiral William Christopher Pakenham replaced him in charge of the Battle Cruiser Force.

An essentially pessimistic character, Jellicoe was not sanguine about his new appointment. On the night of 27 November, he entertained a group of staff and other officers. Jellicoe allegedly stated that the submarine war was

Vice Admiral Sir David Beatty who became CinC Grand Fleet in December 1916. He held a high opinion of Tyrwhitt and had known him since they served together in *Alexandra* in 1886 and the Royal Yacht *Victoria and Albert* in 1892.
(US Library of Congress LC-B2- 4084-13)

---

[*] The offer was largely for American consumption; on 15 and 19 December the British government declared itself unwilling unless Germany declared its war aims first. Through Lloyd George, Britain also insisted on restoration of pre-war conditions, reparations and guarantees of future German behaviour.

going to get so bad in 1917 that he would be blamed and would not last as First Sea Lord for more than six months.

One result of all these changes was that, given his close friendship with the new First Sea Lord, Bacon's position was again secured. This greatly displeased Tyrwhitt. Jackson had told the commodore that Bacon would be reassigned; but now 'the streaky one is in high favour and has completely restored himself to his pinnacle. It is wonderful how he does it.'[26]

✳　✳　✳

During the course of the year, Zeppelin raids had much exercised Britain and the Harwich Force had made many attempts to stop them, either by attacks on their bases or shooting at them from the sea. But in reality, their impact was more psychological than physical. In the whole of 1916, Zeppelins had made just twenty-two raids, dropping 125 tons of bombs, killing 293 people and wounding another 69.[27] By more modern standards it seems a pinprick but the impact on a citizenry which believed that their island status offered a measure of protection from enemy assault, and who had never experienced (but had been conditioned by war fiction to expect[*]) death from the skies, cannot be underestimated.

German Zeppelin raids on civilian targets were meant to break British Home Front morale and cause a withdrawal of resources from the battlefront. This recruiting poster plays on the psychological fear of the bombing. (Author's collection)

IT IS FAR BETTER
TO FACE THE BULLETS
THAN TO BE KILLED
AT HOME BY A BOMB

JOIN THE ARMY AT ONCE
& HELP TO STOP AN AIR RAID

GOD SAVE THE KING

---

[*] By such as, *inter alia*, H G Wells who wrote *The War in the Air*, a novel in which Germany dispatched 'a huge herd of airships', some as big as 2,000ft long, in a surprise bombing raid against New York City.

12

Under Pressure, January–April 1917

The Royal Navy of the late nineteenth and early twentieth century was an organisation which discouraged initiative. Orders were as per scripture and the senior officer present always knew best. As David Beatty put it, 'the whole system of training junior officers in the *Britannia* and later at Osborne and Dartmouth colleges was based on unquestioning discipline and absolute subordination to authority. More gold braid, we were taught, necessarily meant more wisdom; and any signs of originality were frowned on if not actively suppressed.'[1]

Admirals in charge of fleets were particularly considered to be figures of complete authority. Admiral Percy Scott noted that

> the rule was that the senior officer made out a fixed routine which all ships had to follow, irrespective of the time they had been in commission. What exercises the ships are to perform; what clothes the officers and men are to wear; what boats the ships are to use; what awnings the ships are to spread; when the men are to wash their clothes; when and how the washed clothes are to be hung up, and when they are to be taken down. All these are matters over which captains of ships have no jurisdiction; they are settled by the senior admiral present.[2]

This style of thinking continued into the war. In the Grand Fleet under Jellicoe every possible activity or response to incident was covered by the voluminous Grand Fleet Battle Orders. Captains who diverged from these instructions were likely to be subject of some form of disciplinary action. Personal initiative was discouraged.

This form of management was not practised everywhere, however. Beatty, when in command of the battlecruisers, allowed his captains a much greater freedom of decision making (a policy he tried to introduce to the Grand Fleet when he became CinC). Tyrwhitt too, held that his commanding officers should be capable of independent thought and action under the general framework that he laid down. He believed in inculcating some of his own aggressive spirit in his officers and an understanding of his general tactical beliefs and then left them, indeed expected them, to act on their own interpretation of these tenets when required.

But when officers who had spent the war under one sort of direction transferred to another culture, it could lead to problems, as January was to prove.

The Great Escape

On 22 January 1917, Room 40 made the Admiralty aware of planned German ship movements. The German 2nd and 6th Destroyer Flotillas had been ordered to Zeebrugge to reinforce vessels already there with a view to operations in the Dover Strait. They would leave in the afternoon. Tyrwhitt was instructed to intercept them between Schouwen Bank and the Maas and Bacon at Dover was directed to send six Harwich destroyers back to him.

At 1730 the commodore put to sea with six light cruisers, one flotilla leader and the ten destroyers that were ready, while *Nimrod* with the Dover contingent were on their way round. He divided his forces into three sections about 20 miles apart. The light cruisers were to patrol between the Hinder and the Maas; *Grenville* and her six destroyers off the Maas close to the Dutch

Three German torpedo boats at New York after the war. The first ship on the left is *V-43* which took part in the action of 23 January 1917; next to her is *G-102*, then *S-132*. (US Library of Congress LC-DIG-ggbain-31137)

coast; and *Nimrod* and her ten destroyers to the southward off Schouwen Bank. This latter patrol was split into two sections; *Nimrod* with *Moorsom*, *Morris*, *Matchless* and *Phoebe* (later joined by *Manly* and *Mansfield*) was to patrol between Schouwen Light Vessel and a position five miles southeast of it. *Simoom* with *Starfish*, *Surprise* and *Milne* was to patrol between Schouwen and a position five miles northwest of it. Patrolling would be at 20 knots.

The light cruisers were also divided into two detachments, *Centaur*, *Aurora* and *Conquest* would operate about 25 miles east of the North Hinder, while *Penelope*, *Cleopatra* and *Undaunted* were ordered further to the west. Two parallel lines were thus formed running northeast–southwest. It was bitterly cold; the ships arrived on station before midnight but their decks were soon coated with a film of ice.

The German flotilla comprised eleven ships, *V-69*, the leader under Korvettenkapitän Max Schultz, *S-50*, *G-87*, *G-86*, *V-44*, *S-49*, *G-41*, *V-43*, *V-46*, *V-45* and *G-37*. All were Großes Torpedoboot, armed with three 88mm/3.5in or 105mm/4.1in guns, six torpedo tubes, between twenty-five and fifty mines and capable of 33.5 knots. The prefix letters indicated the yard at which they were constructed.[*]

They had chosen a route passing about midway between North Hinder and the Maas and at 0245 in the morning of the 23rd ran slap-bang into *Centaur*'s division. *Aurora* saw them first, on the starboard beam, their funnels revealing themselves by the occasional glare, 2,000 yards away. The light cruisers went to full speed and *Aurora* opened fire. *Centaur* too commenced firing but only got six rounds away as she was unable to reload; the rammers were iced into their tubs. The leading German vessel fired a torpedo which *Centaur* turned to avoid and then tried to cut off the flotilla's escape to the northeast, but the Germans made smoke and escaped in the dark. But they did not escape with impunity. Three shots hit *V-69* causing heavy damage. Her rudder jammed and as she turned helplessly round she was rammed by *G-41* at 0250. The latter was also crippled by the smash and limped away from the area, heading for the coast at 8 knots. She reached the Deurloo at 1000, from where she was later collected by the 6th Flotilla and brought safely into Zeebrugge.

The other parts of Tyrwhitt's force had seen and heard the firing and he issued two signals, one giving the enemy's position and course and another that they had scattered. But neither contained an order. Commander Harold Victor Dundas in *Grenville* (until recently based with the Grand Fleet at Scapa)

---

[*] They were all *V-25* class (also known as the Type 1913). It was numerically the largest class ever built for the High Seas Fleet, consisting of seventy-one ships. The shipyard prefixes were V = AG Vulcan, G = Germaniawerft, and S = Schichau.

The damage sustained to her bows by *G-41* in the action of 23 January 1917 can be seen in this photograph of her after her return to safety. The handwritten text states 'sea battle in the Hoofden'; Hoofden is a name for the southernmost part of the North Sea. (Author's collection)

assumed that in the absence of orders he should remain the patrol line, and he signalled to his destroyers to do so. Two did. Two others made off for the Bight to try to cut off the retreat of the German ships. *Nimrod*, whose destroyers were patrolling in two lines, took one line off for the same purpose. Meanwhile, Captain Hubert Lynes in *Penelope* took his detachment east towards the sound of the guns. But the result was that Tyrwhitt's carefully chosen dispositions were broken up. The German destroyers were able to slip through undetected; all except the damaged leader, *V-69*.

Penelope sighted *V-69* at 0340, challenged and turned four points towards her. There was no reply to the challenge and so the three cruisers switched on their searchlights and opened fire. *Penelope*'s third shot hit home. *Undaunted* followed with a salvo which wrecked the after funnel. A 6in Lyddite shell from *Cleopatra* burst near the waterline. Her after funnel and her after control position were shot down; surely the German must now sink, and the sound of men in the water could be heard on the cruisers.

In fact, *V-69* was still afloat. Schultz and two officers had been killed but she manged to limp into IJmuiden, 50 miles away on the Dutch coast. As the British representatives were unable to convince the Dutch that she put in to escape the pursuit, the Netherlands Government refused to intern her. On 11

February, with an escort of nine Netherlands navy torpedo boats and a cruiser, she passed up the coast to home.

SMS *S-50* had become separated from her sisters and was on her own when she stumbled into the destroyer HMS *Simoom*; the German fired a torpedo which hit and blew up *Simoom*'s magazine. The explosion lit up the night sky for miles in all directions. Her captain, Commander Edward Inman, and forty-six other members of her crew died in the blast and the whole of the front half of the ship was blown off. Inman had already been torpedoed in *Mentor*, in roughly the same location. *Morris* came in to take the survivors off but the wreck continued to float until Tyrwhitt ordered it sunk by gunfire. The desert wind would blow no more.

Eventually, and with the threat of U-boats all around, Tyrwhitt wound up the operation. But that was not the end of the dying. On the way back to harbour, *Undaunted* burst a gun as the bore was iced up. Petty Officer Herbert Stretch and Able Seaman Alfred Tappenden were killed by the blast.

Given their overwhelming superiority in numbers, this was a disappointment for the Harwich Force. The enemy escaped, and no German ship was actually sunk. Tyrwhitt must bear some of the blame, for he did not issue any orders after the enemy had fled. This left senior officers without guidance as whether to act independently or maintain their patrol lines. In this was the inherent problem of expecting commanding officers to use their initiative in a non-homogenous force. Initiative meant different things to different folk on the night. As the Official History put it,

> in operations of this kind it is always possible that individual commanders may, at some moment, be out of touch with each other or with their commodore, or both, and so find themselves under the necessity of acting on their own initiative. A great deal will then depend upon the uniformity of their principles, whether derived from their previous training or from the nature of their orders for the occasion. Ideally all contingencies should be foreseen and provided for in orders; when this is difficult, or perhaps impossible of attainment, general training will be the only guarantee of unanimity. Here, when the critical moment arrived, each destroyer captain had necessarily to decide for himself; and as the senior officers had been trained partly in the Grand Fleet destroyers and partly in the Harwich Force, their professional judgments differed.[3]

Additionally, the difficulty of night fighting was again highlighted. Switching on searchlights made ships a beacon for U-boats; but firing in the dark was almost impossible. Tyrwhitt wrote to the Admiralty suggesting that a better star shell would help. It was a conversation that Tyrwhitt took up with Admiral Sir Percy Scott* when the latter visited him in late January. As Scott put it, 'the commodore mentioned to me how hopelessly his squadrons were handicapped in any night action, as they were not supplied with any star shells which would illuminate the enemy, and their searchlights could not be effectively used'.[4]

Tyrwhitt might just as well have blamed searchlights for

> it was a strange thing that although we had used searchlights in the Navy for so many years, we had continued a system which was so unscientific that the operator at the searchlight could not get his light on to the target because the glare made it invisible. It was a method ... which necessitated the employment of another man as an observer who, with his eyes on the object, would shout out 'go right' or 'left' or 'up' or 'down'.[5]

It was one reason why Jellicoe had not pursued a night action at Jutland for, according to Scott, 'we were inferior to the Germans in the power of our searchlights, and the control of them, and that our guns forming the secondary armament were not fitted for director firing, whereas the Germans had a good system'.[6]

The commodore's new political master, Sir Edward Carson, came to visit Harwich in January and Tyrwhitt found him 'very pleasant and told me that he knew nothing about his job and wanted to know more',[7] this despite him having 'a brogue you could cut with a knife'.[8] Hands-off was Carson's approach for all of his time in post. He didn't interfere with his senior officers, nor did he let anyone bother them. It was not, however, an approach guaranteed to light a fire under the Admiralty. When Jellicoe came under pressure regarding losses to submarines, Carson's response was to back him to the hilt. 'This was not the most prudent attitude to take for flexibility was essential if the challenge was to be met and intransigence only made Lloyd George more determined to have his way.'[9] It had cost Carson his job by July.

Tyrwhitt also visited Beatty in Rosyth, where he found the new CinC more receptive to his aggressive proposals for Zeebrugge. Beatty encouraged Tyrwhitt to continue to bring forward plans; 'any ideas are welcome, the wilder the better. One can always tame them down. What we lack is imagination'.[10]

---

* Scott, a gunnery expert, had retired in 1913 but was recalled to the Admiralty on the outbreak of war where he consulted on gunnery issues and in 1915 was put in charge of creating London's anti-aircraft gun defence system.

Total War

So far in the war, America had remained neutral. Indeed, US President Woodrow Wilson, who had gained the Democratic nomination unopposed on 2 September 1916, campaigned with the slogan 'he kept us out of the war'. On 9 November he was elected president for a second term.

Before and after his nomination, Wilson continued to display his aggravation with the British blockade, and especially the seizure of mail from neutral ships and the blacklisting of US firms trading with Britain's enemies; and most particularly with the British negativity around his proposal for a post-war League of Nations. He saw acceptance of such a body by all combatants as a means of ending the war. But he was also angry at German sinking of passenger liners and the loss of American life thus sustained. Wilson thought that 'the Kaiser's U-boats were an outrage. But British navalism was no lesser evil and possessed a far greater strategic challenge for the United States ... the war was, believed Wilson ... a quarrel to settle economic rivalries between Germany and England ... Wilson spoke of "England having the earth and Germany wanting it".'[11] The big question for both the Allies and Germany was whether the USA would enter the war. Britain and France, drained of men and money, desperately needed the reinforcement of American arms.

Then, on 1 February 1917, Germany declared unrestricted submarine warfare. In doing so the Imperial government knew that there was a very strong risk that America would be tipped into the war by such an action. Why did they do it? Firstly, the German command group had been convinced by some clever calculations from Department B-1(the Economic Warfare Plans group) that within five months Britain could be brought to her knees through lack of food, primarily wheat, as a result of such a campaign. Additionally, the morale of the German nation on the home front was at rock bottom. The harsh 'Turnip Winter' of 1916/17 had devastated Germany's food crops and the blockade of her trade was reducing supplies still further. Everything was in short supply and food rationing was severe, leading to public unrest and rioting. The Royal Navy had brought hunger and misery to the home front and many in Germany cried out to inflict similar pain on Britain and her allies.[*] Finally, Germany believed (correctly) that it would take America some time to place herself on a war footing and get men into the front line in meaningful numbers. If the Allies could be brought to their knees before then, America might be persuaded to stay her hand.

On 31 January, the German Ambassador to the United States of America, Count von Bernstorff, had written an exculpatory letter to US Secretary of

---

[*] Germany had introduced food rationing in January 1915. Imports fell by 55 per cent over the course of 1915–16 and food shortages were widespread. By 1917 the official ration gave just 1,000 calories.

State Lansing in justification of the new unrestricted warfare, in which he blamed Germany's decision on the British and called their blockade illegal under international law.

Wilson felt betrayed, especially after the assurances given post the sinking of the *Lusitania* and the '*Sussex* Pledge'. Then came the revelation of the Zimmermann Telegram, in which Germany attempted to enlist Mexico as an ally, promising that if Germany was victorious, she would support her in winning back the states of Texas, New Mexico and Arizona from the USA. The plot had been uncovered by the British through decrypts in the Admiralty's Room 40 and was revealed to the American government on 20 February 1917.

But still Wilson was unmoved. His reaction after consulting the Cabinet and Congress was minimal – only that diplomatic relations with the Germans should be paused. The president said, 'we are the sincere friends of the German people and earnestly desire to remain at peace with them. We shall not believe they are hostile to us unless or until we are obliged to believe it.'[12]

Merchant ship sinkings were already causing great concern in Britain. In 1916, 1.2 million gross tons of British shipping, or 2.3 million tons including other Allied and neutral nations, had been lost to enemy action. U-boats accounted for some 73 per cent of this total. In January 1917, the totals were 153,666 tons and 368,521 tons respectively.[13] Apart from the obvious loss of cargos, the shipyards could not replace the tonnage fast enough and hence the available shipping lift was decreasing every month.

There was no food rationing in Britain* at this time but the government was concerned that this might be necessary and hence kept the facts of the number of merchant ships sunk out of the public eye to avoid panic. At the War Cabinet (a new body introduced by Lloyd George to manage the war) of 13 February, it was decided that 'the Admiralty should stop at once the publication of losses of Allied and neutral merchant ships'. With regard to U-boats, 'a statement might be made in the sense that the Admiralty are not dissatisfied with the number of enemy submarines they have reason to believe never returned home'.[14] This was sophistry of the highest order.

The Harwich Force, already contending with destroyer raids on the Beef Trip and minefields appearing overnight, now had to defend their charges from unrestrained submarine attack. And the food that they were escorting took on an even greater priority. It was on such a mission, escorting the eastbound merchant ships, that HMS *Skate* (1917), the brand new 'R'-class destroyer only launched in January, was torpedoed at 1530 on 12 March by *UC-69*, near the Maas Light Vessel. Only one sailor, Chief Petty Officer James

---

* Rationing of sugar would be introduced on 31 December 1917.

Henry Adolphus Tremayne Bolton, was killed, and the ship itself suffered no critical damage. After managing to move under her own steam for a time, *Skate* was eventually taken in tow by *Nimrod* which, with two divisions, had been escorting the westbound convoy. *Skate* made the safety of Harwich at 0600 the following day. But it was another, albeit temporary, loss of resources for the Force, and the death of men such as 40-year-old Bolton was doubly difficult for the Harwich ships, for the ranks of the ratings were being increasingly filled by conscripted men, with no experience of the sea and not hardened to life and duty on a destroyer. Additionally, seasoned seamen were constantly being drafted away to fill other posts and induct recruits on new construction. This put an even greater strain on the Harwich Force's leading rates and warrant officers, who bore the burden of the training up required.

The Loss of the *Laforey*

The 9 DF, the 'L'-class destroyer HMS *Laforey* (1913) with her sisters *Lark* and *Laertes*, was on 'loan' from the Harwich Force to the Dover Patrol. On 23 March, all three were engaged in escort duty, taking several cargo vessels to Boulogne. This was a regular trip, sailing from Dover early in the morning, picking up transports at Folkestone and escorting them to Boulogne. On the return leg they would frequently sail up the coast to Calais to accompany hospital or escort vessels back to Dover. Then they would make another Folkestone-Boulogne crossing, before the ships returned to Dover in the early evening to take up night patrol positions.

On this occasion, the destroyers safely delivered their charges and had started their return to Folkestone, *Laertes* leading with *Laforey* on her port quarter, both steaming at 21 knots. Off Gris Nez at 1630, *Laforey* was suddenly rocked by a loud explosion which broke her back; she had run over a mine. Sub Lieutenant Q D Graham had been in the wardroom and, rushing on deck, 'saw nothing beyond the middle funnel. He had just time to clear away a couple of lifebelts and go over the side when he saw the stern rise in the air and go down.'[15]

The bow remained tantalisingly afloat, almost vertically with the stem about 20ft in the air, before it too sank beneath the waves. *Laertes* had attempted to take off survivors and she and *Lark* lowered her boats but there was a heavy sea running and only four officers and fourteen ratings were saved. Lieutenant Arthur Edwin Durham, her commanding officer, aged 28 and another clergyman's son, and sixty-three of his men perished.

At the subsequent board of enquiry, it was alleged that the ships were not following the swept channel and were on a direct route for home. It was also suggested that *Laforey* had possibly struck a mine which had been swept up and dumped; but the more likely explanation was that it was one of six laid by *UC-16* earlier in the month.

On board the destroyer *Laforey* (1913) of the 9th Destroyer Flotilla while at moorings in Harwich harbour in mid-1916. The *Ganges* shore establishment at Shotley is in the background. The photograph is looking forward from abreast the mainmast on the port side of the upper deck and shows some of the crew in the process of repainting the ship from black to grey. Note the gunnery range board abaft number two funnel, the range clock and repeater on the bridge, searchlight, torpedo davit and the Carley raft and torpedo sight on the aft bank of torpedo tubes. She was sunk by a mine on 23 January 1917. (Author's collection)

The destroyers were under great pressure and such a loss was not welcome. Neither was the further depletion of experienced men, such as 37-year-old Chief Stoker William Bristow. Son of a Crimean War veteran and husband to Annie, he held the Long Service and Good Conduct Medals, together with the Naval General Service Medal (Persian Gulf). Bristow had served at the Battle of Heligoland Bight and in the Dardanelles. But now he was lost to his family in Rochester, and to the navy.

Difficult Times

'1917 was a busy year,' wrote Domvile afterwards.[16] The Harwich Force continued to have more contact with the enemy than any other command in the navy bar the Dover Patrol. It had to escort the Beef Trip convoys, capture merchant ships suspected of contraband, intercept enemy light forces, attack enemy minesweepers and support British minelayers. Harwich provided the ships to attack returning Zeppelins and was constantly called upon to reinforce the Dover resources.

To carry out these multiple tasks, Tyrwhitt could call on 5 LCS, which by April boasted eight light cruisers (*Centaur*, *Carysfort*, *Cleopatra*, *Conquest*, *Concord*, *Aurora*, *Canterbury* and *Penelope*) and a seaplane carrier (*Vindex*) plus one destroyer flotilla, 10 DF*, of twenty-seven M- and 'R'-class ships (nine 'Ms' and eighteen 'Rs'), *Undaunted*, *Lightfoot* and *Nimrod*. Additionally, the 8th and 9th Submarine Flotillas were at Harwich and under his influence if not absolute control.

The 'R' class were the latest destroyers to be built, sixty-two of which were launched in 1916 and 1917. They were a development of the preceding 'M' class, especially with regard to fuel economy and hence range. They had two shafts and geared turbines, compared with the three shafts and direct turbines of their predecessors, and could be externally distinguished by the aft 4in gun, which was mounted in a bandstand. By the end of the year, twenty-four of these vessels would be serving with the Force.

These new ships were needed, for merchant ship losses to U-boats continued to rise. Total British, French and neutral gross tonnage sunk was 540,000 in February, 593,841 in March, and 881,027 in April;[17] the German unrestricted submarine campaign was clearly having a huge impact.

Food shortages began to bite. The Food Controller, Lord Davenport, officially declared that all premises serving food should observe one meatless day a week and serve potatoes only on two days of the week (they were in short

An example of a 'R'-class destroyer, HMS *Sceptre* (1917), in a painting by W J Sutton. (Author's collection)

---

* 9 DF had been disbanded at the end of March.

supply owing to the bad winter). The *Daily Telegraph* reported on 5 April that the impending Easter celebrations would be hit by 'scarce and dear food'. A leader on page four called for the use of German POWs in agriculture.

Panic set in at the Admiralty and in government. By 21 March the position was already considered so serious that Foreign Secretary Arthur Balfour informed the Dutch government that Britain was considering requisitioning their shipping.[18] Then, on 2 April, the War Cabinet noted that the outlook was 'most serious'.[19] At the same meeting, it was also mooted that compulsory mercantile service might be required due to the potential collapse of crew morale. And this chaos was being caused by no more than fifty U-boats.

The situation seemed so dire that on 27 April First Sea Lord Sir John Jellicoe was moved to tell the War Cabinet, via the First Lord, that

> the real fact of the matter is this. We are carrying on the war at the present time as if we had the absolute command of the sea, whereas we have not such command or anything approaching it. It is quite true that we are masters of the situation so far as surface ships are concerned, but it must be realised – and realised at once – that this will be quite useless if the enemy's submarines paralyse, as they do now, our lines of communication.
>
> Without some such relief as I have indicated [*inter alia* 'the import of everything that is not essential to the life of the country is ruthlessly and immediately stopped'.] – and that given immediately – the navy will fail in its responsibilities to the country and the country itself will suffer starvation.[20]

Maurice Hankey, secretary to the War Cabinet, noted Jellicoe's particular problems with regard to the English Channel and East Coast. In summary, he adumbrated them as;

1. Controlling the channel in the face of German Flanders bases [i.e. Zeebrugge and Ostend].
2. Number and size of U-boats small, but a major irritant, not least as covert minelayers.
3. German destroyers are a bigger danger, constantly posing a threat of a mass attack on British cross-Channel traffic.
4. The need to convoy ships to Holland to counter these threats.
5. The prospect of diverting scarce naval resources to provide Channel cover if the bases were not eliminated.
6. Jellicoe's pessimism about continuing the war without a decisive Flanders success.[21]

These threats were largely the ones which the Harwich Force were engaged in countering.

Lloyd George pressed hard for the adoption of universal convoying of merchant ships, as had been utilised at Harwich since mid-1916 in the French cross-Channel coal trade and latterly on the Scandinavian convoys.* The Admiralty resisted, as described in Chapter 10. But with the discovery that the number of movements to be covered was nowhere near the previous – erroneous – estimates, the prime minister eventually got his way and losses of British shipping fell dramatically from May onwards.

At Harwich, the convoying operations were now being supported from the air as well as the sea. During the spring of 1917, Felixstowe-based flying boats commenced air support for the Beef Trip. From 1 May, Curtiss H-12 'Large America' planes would overfly the route on the day prior to sailing and relays of flying boats would provide a distant escort, 19 to 15 miles ahead of the convoy. The object of both activities was to spot for mines on the surface or submarines. When, in October, daylight sailings resumed, the aircraft offered direct escort with the 11-hour voyage requiring two or three flying boats sorties per convoy. They flew at 500 to 600ft in order to observe periscopes or minefields ahead of the formation. Both Curtiss and (from late 1917) Felixstowe-type aircraft were used, magnificent machines both (see Chapter 19), recognised by the Admiralty as superior to all other available craft because of their 'reliability, speed and the facilities for accurate bomb dropping'.[22] Tyrwhitt called them all 'Portes' after the talented designer, engineer, pilot and station commander at Felixstowe, John Porte.

'This work called for extreme nicety in navigation', wrote one of the pilots, 'in order that the [flying] boats should make contact with the moving ships at the correct time and position. At first the results were rather ragged, but eventually it became an evolution.' Tyrwhitt was pleased to have the support. 'The pilots were later informed, in a letter of appreciation, that before they took a hand in the game the crews of the destroyers and light cruisers were kept at action stations throughout the entire trip, but that, now the flying-boats accompanied them, half of the men were allowed to stand off.'[23]

Tyrwhitt himself often sailed with the escort. The Germans had laid a large minefield across the route which required regular sweeping and which frequently slowed down the speed of the advance, increasing the risk of U-boat attack. But such was the success of the combined air and sea escort the during 1917 that '520 eastbound and 511 westbound merchant vessels were conveyed between England and Holland with the loss of six ships, four to submarine attack'.[24]

---

* For more detail on the Scandinavian convoys see Steve R Dunn, *Southern Thunder* (Barnsley: Seaforth Publishing 2019).

Given such efforts by the Harwich Force to ensure the safe arrival of the Beef Trip vessels, it was galling that the best endeavours were not always made to look after the goods themselves. The *Spectato*r magazine reported on

> the arrival at the port of Harwich of thirteen thousand bags of decayed potatoes accompanied by cases of margarine. Although these potatoes were so rotten when they reached Harwich that they were in a state of putrefaction and the heat from them had melted the margarine, they were brought up to London by rail, a hundred and twenty railway trucks being used for carrying them.[25]

America Enters the War

The United States of America finally declared war on Germany on 6 April. But it would take until the 1918 before their massive financial and industrial strength could begin to make itself felt on the battle front. There were, however, two immediate benefits to the Royal Navy. Rear Admiral William Sims, the US Navy head in Europe, strongly emphasised before the official declaration of hostilities that Britain must adopt convoy and needed more destroyers to provide anti-submarine escort. His request was heard and

> the morning of May 4, 1917, witnessed an important event in the history of Queenstown.* The news had been printed in no British or American paper, yet in some mysterious way it had reached nearly everybody in the city. A squadron of American destroyers, which had left Boston on the evening of April 24th, had already been reported to the westward of Ireland and was due to reach Queenstown that morning. At almost the appointed hour a little smudge of smoke appeared in the distance, visible to the crowds assembled on the hills; then presently another black spot appeared, and then another; and finally these flecks upon the horizon assumed the form of six rapidly approaching warships. The Stars and Stripes were broken out on public buildings, on private houses, and on nearly all the water craft in the harbour; the populace, armed with American flags, began to gather on the shore; and the local dignitaries donned their official robes to welcome the new friends from overseas. One of the greatest days in Anglo-American history had dawned, for the first contingent of the American navy was about to arrive in British waters and join hands with the Allies in the battle against the forces of darkness and savagery.[26]

---

* The main harbour and headquarters for the Coast of Ireland Command.

US Navy destroyers had come to join the fight. The second benefit was that the US made the supply of goods to Germany and her partners illegal. Given that much of the contraband supplies to Germany, which the Royal Navy had laboured for three years to stop, originated in the USA this was a major 'result'. The Northern Patrol, specifically intended to intercept such goods, could be wound down and men and ships deployed elsewhere, while the noose around the neck of the German supply chain tightened further.

13

Action and Awards, May–July 1917

Everyone was keen to deal with the menace posed by the German-occupied ports of Zeebrugge and Ostend and their attendant destroyer and submarine bases. Plans for landing and occupations had been discussed and rejected and Admiral Bacon had assured the Admiralty that he could accomplish the task of putting the bases out of action by bombardment from the sea (see Chapter 11). In May and June 1917, this proposal was put into operation. On each occasion, the Harwich Force provided considerable support.

The Bombardment of Zeebrugge, 12 May 1917

Zeebrugge translates as the 'Harbour of Bruges'. In Bruges itself the Germans had constructed a heavily fortified base for their submarines. It comprised a massive concrete shelter with a 6ft-thick roof and which gave protection from bombs and shellfire alike. Here was the opportunity that Bacon had seized upon, for the U-boats could only transit from Bruges by means of a canal and locks at Zeebrugge. With his engineer's mind, Bacon theorised that the heavy guns of his big monitors could, if they scored a direct hit, wreck the lock gates and prevent German entry or exit.

Whilst this seemed an excellent plan on paper, there were some difficulties which were underestimated. The defences of the Flanders coastline were

The German U-boat shelters at Bruges, from where U-boats would transit via the Zeebrugge locks, the target of Bacon's May 1917 bombardment.
(Photo courtesy of the National Museum of the Royal Navy)

exceptionally strong. A heavy battery (the *Kaiser Wilhelm II*) had been erected at Knocke to the eastward of the Bruges canal; one and a half miles to the west of Ostend was the *Tirpitz* battery; and two more were under construction. They were formidable barriers to Allied success. The *Kaiser Wilhelm II* mounted four 12in guns, range 41,000 yards; the *Tirpitz* mounted four 11in guns, range 35,000 yards. And between these batteries the coast was defended by a large number of mobile and semi-mobile guns, trenches and machine-gun nests.

Owing to the strong defences on shore, fire would be indirect, using aiming marks and with spotting from aircraft of the RNAS. The problem, simply defined, was to hit an invisible target 90ft long and 30ft wide from a distance of about 13 miles. But Bacon mathematically calculated that with a gun laid accurately for range and direction, one round in every sixty-three should hit a lock gate. Statistically therefore at least 126 rounds would be required to make a hit probable on each of the two gates. Making allowances for the fact that the laying would not be as exact as with a shore-mounted gun, Bacon determined that at least twice this number, or 252 rounds, should be allowed for. Whilst possibly algebraically correct, this required conditions of wind and weather which were rarely found on that coastline.

Bacon allotted forty-one ships and launches of the Dover Patrol to the operation. The three 15in monitors *Terror* (flag), *Marshal Soult* and *Erebus* would be the striking force assisted by the 12in monitor *Sir John Moore* and the *M-15* class vessels *M-24* and *M-26*. Destroyer leaders *Botha* and *Faulknor*, with destroyers *Lochinvar*, *Landrail*, *Lydiard*, *Mentor*, *Moorsom*, *Morris*, *Mermaid* and *Racehorse*, would defend the monitors. Paddle minesweepers and motor launches for smoke laying completed the flotilla. From the Harwich Force came *Lightfoot* with a group of destroyers who would provide distant cover, cruising near Thornton Banks in case German destroyers tried to interfere. And *Nimrod* took four destroyers to zig-zag around the bombardment force as an anti-submarine screen.

Three times the force assembled in the Downs and three times it was stood down owing to adverse weather conditions. On the evening of 11 May, the vessels again formed up and the ships began to leave between 2300 and midnight. A buoy was laid by the destroyer *Lochinvar* 15 miles to the northwest of the mole as a guide and a second buoy was placed in the position selected for the bombardment. A bearing was taken from the buoy to the base of the mole at Zeebrugge by *Lochinvar*, under Commander John Fraser, sailing from the buoy to the mole despite a mist which reduced visibility to a mile and meant that the ship advanced dangerously close to German shore batteries. The ship returned to the buoy by 0445, with the bearing and distance.

At this point things started to go wrong. The monitor *Marshal Soult*, capable of only 6 knots on a good day, had to be towed into position. This meant that bombardment opened late and the two RNAS artillery observation aircraft from Dunkirk, which had taken off at 0200, had to wait over Zeebrugge for almost two hours. One of the spotting aircraft had engine trouble and force-landed in the Netherlands and the other was running short of petrol. As a result, spotting the fall of shot, upon which successful targeting depended, was carried out by one machine with a failing supply of fuel.

The monitors opened fire around 0500 and at first fell short, with many of the shells failing to explode owing to the quality of the ammunition, and which made it impossible for the spotting aircraft to signal the fall of shot. But they eventually got the range and *Marshal Soult* hit the target with its twelfth shell and *Erebus* with its twenty-sixth. *Terror* was most hampered by the loss of the second spotting aircraft and dud shells; only forty-five of the 250 shells fired were reported upon and eventually the single spotter had to return because of lack of fuel at 0530, leaving the last half-hour of the bombardment reliant on estimated corrections. Two relieving aircraft had engine trouble and failed to arrive at all. At 0600 Vice Admiral Bacon judged that his mission was complete and ordered a withdrawal, just as the *Kaiser Wilhelm II* battery finally opened fire.

Bacon believed that, as he had fired the requisite number of rounds, the bombardment must have been successful, and at first it was thought that some success had been achieved. It was only later that aerial photographs demonstrated that about fifteen shells had landed within a few yards of the lock gates on the western side and on the eastern side four shells had done the same. The basin north of the locks had been hit and some damage caused to the docks. However, the mission had failed.

The Bombardment of Ostend, 5 June 1917

Bacon then turned his attention to how best to attempt to degrade the port of Ostend by a bombardment of the dockyard.

There were two advantages to this project which had been absent at Zeebrugge. Though the chance of doing some serious damage was perhaps less, the target was bigger. And Ostend was visible from the sea, unlike the Zeebrugge lock gates, giving more chance of making accurate shooting. Bad weather delayed the implementation of the plan but on 4 June conditions were deemed favourable and a bombarding squadron of two monitors (the 15in-gunned *Erebus* and *Terror*), two flotilla leaders (*Botha*, *Faulknor*), six destroyers, two P-boats and twelve smoke laying motor launches left Dover at 2200.

Tyrwhitt took out his whole available command to protect Bacon's flank for this action. At 2100 on 4 June he departed Harwich with four light cruisers (*Centaur*, *Concord*, *Canterbury* and *Conquest*) together with *Lightfoot* and

The 'C'-class cruiser HMS *Canterbury* (1915), part of the 5th Light Cruiser Squadron from May 1916 until November 1918, when she was despatched to the Aegean. (US Naval History and Heritage Command NH 61304)

eight destroyers. Thirty minutes later, *Undaunted, Cleopatra, Aurora, Penelope* and another eight destroyers sailed, with orders to prevent enemy interference from the Schouwen Bank area.

Around 0100 on the 5th, the Dover vessel HMS *Lochinvar* reported a group of German destroyers to her eastward. Bacon, at sea with his forces, decided not to reinforce the ship as doing so would deprive the bombarding squadron of its protecting vessels. But the presence of the German vessels prevented *Lochinvar* carrying out its task of deploying a sighting buoy; the bombardment position would have to be found by dead reckoning.

Meanwhile, after reaching his station near the Thornton Bank at 0215, Tyrwhitt started his patrol on a southwesterly course. When he was about halfway between the Bligh and Thornton Banks, he sighted two destroyers ahead. They were steering to the westward, and he took them at first to be part of Bacon's bombardment group, but was disabused of the notion when they commenced firing. Tyrwhitt opened his course to bring his full broadside to bear and returned fire from the whole squadron. For a few minutes the Germans, *S-15* and *S-20* of the VII Torpedo Boat Flotilla, hung on to a westerly course. But the weight of shellfire was too much for them and they turned and headed for Zeebrugge and safety.

SMS *S-20* had been hit in the boiler room and badly damaged, causing her to lag behind. Tyrwhitt now ordered a division of four destroyers (*Taurus, Sharpshooter, Satyr* and *Torrent*) to pursue the injured ship and its fleeing sister. The Germans made smoke but *Satyr* soon sank the crippled German vessel and remained to pick up survivors. *Taurus* and the rest of the destroyers chased the other fugitive until the range was down to 5,000 yards but then came under concentrated fire from the shore batteries and had to haul off;

Tyrwhitt recalled the division to its protective duties. A few minutes later Bacon opened his bombardment of Ostend, beginning at 0320 and finishing 40 minutes later.

There was a spirited reply from the shore and *Erebus* and *Terror* received a consistent and accurate fire which fortunately did no damage. One hundred and fifteen shells were fired by the monitors, of which about twenty exploded in or near the dockyard. Later reports from intelligence officers averred that the harbour workshops had not suffered much damage but that a lighter and a UC-type boat had been sunk and three destroyers of the flotilla, which were lying alongside the quays, were damaged. This latter point may have been true but there is no record of a U-boat being sunk on the day. These reports also stated that the bombardment had made an impression on the German High Command and caused them to doubt whether Ostend was suitable as a destroyer base at all. This could have been the case for later in the year the Germans abandoned their use of Ostend for such vessels.

Commander Hubert Henry de Burgh, captain of the Harwich Force destroyer *Satyr*, was awarded the DSO for his part in the action, in which he succeeded in saving seven men of *S-20*'s crew while 'under heavy fire from the shore batteries and with three German seaplanes hovering overhead'.[1] Irish-born, de Burgh represented Ireland at cricket and played a first-class match in India for the Europeans team against the Hindus club in February 1906. A right-handed batsman, he survived the war to play for Ireland in a first-class match against Oxford University 20 years later. Lieutenant Commander Edye Kington Boddam-Whetham, CO of *Sharpshooter*, also received a DSO; 'he handled his ship well in the face of superior forces and under the fire of the shore batteries' according to the official despatch.[2]

The Harwich Force had taken its part in supporting Bacon's bombardment plans, which had achieved little. Commodore Tyrwhitt could have been forgiven if he felt just a little pleased

*   *   *

Meanwhile, in between these two sorties against the Belgian coast, an enemy even more pernicious than the Germans claimed another victim. HMS *Setter* was an 'R'-class destroyer launched in August 1916. Under her captain, Lieutenant Commander Edward Sidney Graham she was out on a sweep on 17 May, in company with *Recruit* (leader)* and *Sylph*. The weather was poor with patches of drifting fog when they briefly sighted German destroyers before they disappeared into the murk. The British destroyers formed into

---

* Launched in December 1916, she was the second ship in the war to be so named.

line abreast and set off into the fog to try to gain contact with the enemy. *Setter* had *Recruit* to the north on her port side and *Sylph* to her south.

Darkness fell and, still surrounded by fog, it was difficult to maintain visual contact. At 2300, *Setter* suddenly saw *Recruit* looming out of the mist to port and had to make an emergency alteration to starboard to avoid a collision. This brought her right into the path of *Sylph*, which struck her on the starboard quarter at an angle of 60 degrees, pushing the propeller shafts into the hull and almost cutting *Setter* in two.

Fortunately, the stricken destroyer remained afloat for just over an hour before sinking and all of her crew were safely taken off. Even more remarkably, there were no fatalities. *Setter* sank by the stern, 21 miles northwest of the North Hinder Light, another loss of a valuable ship to the sailors' oldest enemy, weather and the seemingly ever-present fog.

At the subsequent court of enquiry, the CO of *Recruit*, British Columbian-born Lieutenant Commander Hugh Rose Troup,* who was acting as leader, was criticised for 'failing to communicate his movements'.[3] Edward Graham remained with the Harwich Force and was appointed to command *Teazer* on 11 June. One of two Thornycroft-built 'R' class, HMS *Teazer*, launched in April, was considered to be the fastest destroyer afloat at the time, exceeding 40 knots in trials.

Recognition

On 21 May, Tyrwhitt was made Naval Aide de Camp (ADC) to King George V. A largely ceremonial role, it demanded little of the holder. However, the appointment was nonetheless recognition for the commodore and for the Harwich Force. In all there were eleven ADCs at any one time, one of whom was usually an admiral and was styled First and Principal Naval Aide-de-Camp while the other ten were post-captains. Aiguillettes were worn on the right shoulder when in attendance on the sovereign. Then on 15 July, Tyrwhitt was advanced to Knight Commander of the Order of the Bath, entitling him to use the pre-nominal title 'Sir'. This was a signal honour, for it was only the second time in history to that date that a post-captain had been given such entitlement, the last being 78 years previously.

To explain, 'commodore' was not a rank but a position; it was used to describe an officer commanding a flotilla of ships. Tyrwhitt's substantive rank remained captain. So making him a knight for his naval service was indeed a tribute to his and to the Harwich Force's work and the esteem in which they were held. Jacky Fisher wrote a note of congratulation in his usual scrawl from the Duchess of Hamilton's house in Swanage; 'I really did rejoice – but you

---

* Described in 1917 as an officer of 'quick and nervous temperament, has a quick temper' (ADM 196/50/233, NA).

should have been made an admiral and given that wide scope of attack which I think you know all about.'[4] Close behind, a further accolade came from Italy. Sir Reginald was made an Officer of the Military Order of Savoy on 11 August. His fame was growing, as was the reputation of the Force.

The advancement to knighthood brought with it what was to Tyrwhitt some unwelcome publicity. Commander Carlyon Bellairs was the maverick, monocle-wearing Conservative MP for Maidstone and a self-appointed expert on naval matters, who had retired from the navy in 1902. He was opposed to the 'buggins turn' method of promotion to flag rank in the navy, stating the general point with regard to experienced captains that 'men of such attainments, who could be employed, have to wait their turn'.[5] In particular, he had several times expressed the view in the House of Commons that Tyrwhitt should be advanced in rank to rear admiral ahead of those senior to him in the navy list because he had the necessary warlike qualities of courage and drive, and in an article in *Truth* magazine during July Bellairs warmed to his theme.

Tyrwhitt was furious; 'advertising', as self-promotion was known in the navy, was a social crime of considerable proportions. He promptly wrote to Bellairs asking him to cease and desist and to refrain from taking an interest in his career. This 'stinging rebuke to a too intrusive an advocate'[6] eventually persuaded Bellairs to read out an apology in the House of Commons.

Teaching a Lesson

The British blockade of German and neutral shipping had caused the German merchant fleet to remain in port for fear of capture and persuaded many neutral ship owners to withhold sailings which involved cargos the British authorities might construe as contraband destined for Germany. But at the height of the unrestricted U-boat campaign, when the Germans were sinking over circa 15,000 gross tons of shipping every day, the Admiralty received news that German mercantile shipping was showing signs of life after three years of near-complete inactivity. A small coasting trade had begun between the Bight and Rotterdam. If this trade proceeded unhindered, ship owners' confidence in their ability to sail unmolested would increase.

> It was a matter of importance to cut down this growing confidence. If the feeling spread to the merchantmen which had lain at anchor in neutral harbours since the war began, the Admiralty would be faced with a general movement of enemy shipping in every ocean of the world, at a time when our cruiser forces were being rapidly absorbed into the convoy organisation.[7]

Tyrwhitt was given the task of stopping this nascent trade. Thinking that it would be dangerous to keep a large intercepting force off the Dutch coast, he first decided to use the Harwich submarines. Four 'E'-class boats were stationed along the coast of Holland and a number of destroyers were held in support, out of sight of land. The submarine commanders were to stop all suspicious vessels and divert them to the destroyers, where they would be detained and taken captive.

The first attempt was made on 21 June; it didn't work. Just one Dutch steamer, the *Boetan*, was stopped by *E-47* and then released. Nothing else was sighted and the Harwich Force returned to harbour. Almost immediately, the Admiralty received news that four German steamers had left Rotterdam on the 23rd, under the escort of a torpedo boat, and that others would follow. Tyrwhitt ordered out four submarines and two divisions of destroyers. They reached their stations at 0400 on the 25th, too late to intercept the vessels, which had sailed from Rotterdam two days beforehand. The Harwich ships gave chase but failed to find anything.

On 15 July, Tyrwhitt was informed that German ships were leaving Rotterdam that night. He sailed at 2015 with all of 5 LCS (eight ships), two flotilla leaders and fifteen destroyers and at dawn the following day was 15 miles to the westward of Texel. The commodore held this position until 0415, then turned to the south; as he did so he ordered *Undaunted* and seven destroyers to take station three miles on his port beam to prevent the enemy merchantmen from passing between his force and the shore. Just a quarter of an hour later, six merchantmen were sighted ahead. They were steaming together, in formation. *Undaunted* and her destroyers were at once ordered to chase and seize them and soon caught up with their prey. *Thruster* and *Springbok* 'made a particularly smart evolution'[8] in capturing two of them and put prize crews aboard. The remaining four made for the shore and British ships opened fire to cause the steamers to heave to, which inadvertently resulted in some shells landing in a Dutch internment camp for Germans. Two steamers ran themselves ashore but were disabled by gunfire. The other two were taken by *Sylph* and *Surprise*.

In the case of *Sylph*, her captain, Commander James Vandeleur Creagh,* was undeterred by the fact that his quarry had run herself aground and been abandoned by her crew. He not only succeeded in towing her off despite heavy swell but anchored the vessel and raised steam for sailing. For his tenacity and ability, the 'Appreciation of the Board [of Admiralty was] expressed for services on occasion of captured German merchant vessels'.[9]

From 0600, the action was observed by two Dutch torpedo boats and a Dutch cruiser, but they did not interfere and by 0700 all the prizes were on their way to Harwich under escort. Tyrwhitt took the cruisers northwards to

---

* Son of Charles Vandeleur Creagh, quondam governor of North Borneo and a noted botanist.

guard against any attempted interference from surface vessels; and the journey home for the cargo vessels and escorts was a slow one due to some engine problems and three unsuccessful U-boat attacks between the North Hinder and Shipwash lights. But the German *Pellworm* (1,370 tons), *Brietzig* (1,495 tons), *Marie Horn* (1,068 tons) and *Heinz Blumberg* (1,226 tons) all reached harbour on the 17th.

As the navy's *Official History* put it,

> this rapid blow was just what was needed. The German merchants who lost their ships and cargoes could not know that in order to make his stroke as impressive as possible Commodore Tyrwhitt had deliberately collected a force which was many times more numerous and powerful than the military objects of the operation demanded. All they could tell was that a powerful light squadron had appeared off the Texel with apparently no duty but that of intercepting coasting vessels, when it had been suggested to them by their own people that every available British destroyer was being sucked into the maelstrom of submarine warfare. The effect was decisive: two German vessels left Rotterdam during the week following the operation; after that movements practically ceased and the trade disappeared.[10]

Gotha Raids over the East Coast

Towards the end of 1916, the Zeppelin raiders began to suffer disproportionate losses. Better fighter interception and a ring of anti-aircraft guns around key targets had made life precarious for these slow-moving monsters. This caused the Germans to increase the ceiling of their airships, which was achieved by lightening the existing craft through removing one of the engines. The resulting weight saving gave them a ceiling of over 16,000ft.

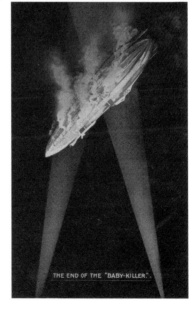

By the end of 1916, Zeppelins were suffering increased casualties. The picture shows a British propaganda postcard 'The End of the "Baby-Killer"', showcasing the demise of Schütte-Lanz *SL-11* over Cuffley when it was shot down by Lieutenant Leefe-Robinson on 3 September 1916. *SL-11* was one of a series of rigid airships designed and built by the Luftschiffbau Schütte-Lanz company from 1909 until 1917. (Author's collection)

THE END OF THE "BABY-KILLER".

At the same time, the German planners developed a daylight bombing offensive against London designed to cow the population and enhance their feelings of vulnerability. This campaign was codenamed Operation 'Türkenkreuz' ('Turk's Cross').

To execute the plan, a new formation – Kampfgeschwader der Obersten Heeresleitung 3 (Kagohl 3), nicknamed the England Geschwader – was formed, consisting of six Kampfstaffel (Kastas) under the command of Hauptmann Ernst Brandenburg. Kagohl 3 initially operated from Sint-Denijs-Westrem and Gontrode in the eastern Flanders area of German-occupied Belgium, around Ghent.

The first raids in March 1917 were unproductive but in the same month the Zeppelin force was supplemented by the arrival of Gotha G.IV aircraft,

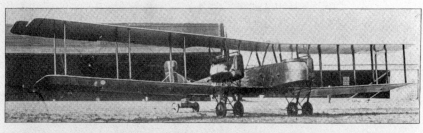

GOTHA BOMBER
TYPE G 5

A Gotha bomber, in this case the G-V, successor to the G-IV which took part in the raids on Harwich and Felixstowe in July 1917. (US Naval History and Heritage Command NH 112945)

large twin-engined biplane bombers. Armed with up to three machine guns, they could fly at 83mph, climb to over 16,000ft and carry 1,100lbs of bombs.

Subsequently, Kagohl 3 operated both airships and Gothas. Twenty-three of the latter set off to bomb London on 25 May but ended up attacking targets around Folkestone. They were intercepted by RNAS Sopwith Pups, losing one Gotha in the process.

Next it was the airships' turn. During the night of 16/17 June an attempted raid by six Zeppelins met with little success. Only two reached England and one was intercepted near Harwich and shot down by three British fighter planes, an FE 2b, a BE 12 and a DH 2. It eventually crashed just north of Felixstowe.

On 4 July, the Gothas came for Harwich and Felixstowe. At 0655 observers at Orford Ness heard the sound of aircraft. Five minutes later a formation of eighteen Gothas came into view flying at about 14,000ft. They were engaged by a single DH 4 without success and then split into two groups, one targeting Felixstowe and one heading for Harwich.

The Harwich-bound section dropped six bombs over Shotley, two of which exploded close to the RNAS Balloon Statio, killing two men and fatally injuring another. As they passed over Harwich harbour, thirteen bombs were unloaded at the ships below, all of which missed and exploded in the water. Three of the light cruisers, *Canterbury*, *Concord* and *Conquest*, returned fire. Several bombs aimed at Harwich and Dovercourt landed but failed to explode.

Reaching Felixstowe, the Gothas released two bombs on Trimley Marshes. This provided a fortunate increase in naval rations by killing twenty-one sheep. Seven other bombs fell on the marshes without damage. In Felixstowe town, two bombs exploded in Mill Lane killing five soldiers and injuring ten others. Three bombs exploded near the main railway station but caused only limited damage. Now over the docks, the Germans dropped another eleven weapons, which fell on waste ground, while four exploded near to the Beach Railway Station and two fell to the north of Felixstowe docks.

But now they were over the RNAS base and here more significant effects were felt. Two bombs destroyed a Curtiss H-12 'Large America' flying boat and badly damaged another. Three workmen and five RNAS balloon station personnel were killed. The matter was considered serious enough to be reported to the War Cabinet on 5 July, where it was stated that 'we had lost an America machine which was burnt and another America had been damaged by a shrapnel bomb'.[11] One bomb landed close to St Nicolas' church* and fortunately failed to explode; but in all the raid caused over £2,000 of damage and injured twenty-nine souls. Another seventeen were killed and one fatally injured.

---

* The bomb was preserved and is on display in the church.

A dud bomb dropped in the raid of 4 July 1917 and now on display in St Nicholas' church, Harwich. (Photo, David Whittle)

This latter casualty was Air Mechanic First Class James Edgar Stevens RNAS, who had been badly wounded in the bombing of the balloon station. The scion of a Thames boat-building family, he had volunteered in 1915, marrying Eveline Higgins a month later. He was taken to the Cliff Hospital, a requisitioned hotel, where he died 11 days later. His body was returned back home and James Stevens was buried in the Spring Road Cemetery in Abingdon, where his grave sported for many years a model stone aircraft with a (now broken) turning propeller. It also bears an inscription taken from Kipling's poem *The English Flag* (1891);

'Never the Lotus closes, never the wild-fowl wake,
But a soul goes out on the east wind that died for England's sake'.[12]

There was a further Gotha assault on Harwich and its surroundings on 22 July. Kagohl 3 was intending to attack London, but inclement weather meant that an easier raid against Felixstowe and Harwich was substituted instead. Sixteen bombers crossed the coast at 0805 and were engaged by the anti-aircraft guns ringed around the two ports two minutes later. Defensive aircraft were immediately put up as well. This time the defence was such that the Gothas turned for home after only 12 minutes over the target. At Felixstowe another RNAS kite balloon air mechanic was fatally injured and in Harwich harbour the minesweeping trawler *Touchstone*, once of Hull, was knocked about with two of her crew wounded. But in all the raid achieved little and was beaten off by a determined defence; nonetheless, thirteen people died and twenty-six were injured. The War Cabinet of the following day were told 'that an approximate estimate of the damage done was £3,000' and that 'one German aeroplane had been brought down over the sea'.[13]

Captain Domvile remembered that 'air raids were frequent and my poor wife had many bombs round our house. Every German with a bomb left seemed to drop it on Felixstowe on their way home.'[14] His wife might have felt it all the more, as she was of German ancestry. From June, all harbour anti-aircraft guns had been ordered to be manned from 0600. Harwich and Felixstowe suffered in the firing line.

14

Destroyer Losses, August–December 1917

The Admiralty Board of Invention and Research (BIR) had been established in 1915 by the then First Lord of the Admiralty, Arthur Balfour. Its mission was to develop and test new designs of weapons and equipment and get them to be mass produced quickly, without burdening the regular military command structure. Striving to keep ex-First Sea Lord 'Jacky' Fisher engaged in the war effort, Balfour asked him to chair the organisation.

Explaining the Board's purpose to Admiral Jellicoe, Balfour wrote that

> I feel that we ought not to rely simply upon repeating accepted models, but that both as regards anti-submarine devices and aircraft we ought to originate as well as copy. I have therefore got the Government to consent to the appointment of a small Inventions Commission under the First Lord of the Admiralty, but otherwise separate from the Department, housed elsewhere, and with no executive authority. It will in the main be largely composed of men of science, and I have asked Lord Fisher to be Chairman. I hope for some really good results. Even if nothing better happens, the Department [of War] will by this arrangement be relieved of the labour and responsibility of forming a judgement on the countless inventions which daily pour into it.[1]

Between 1915 and 1918, the BIR evaluated over 41,000 submissions from both members of the services and the general public.

Many eminent scientists were recruited to assist. The central committee of the BIR consisted of, under Fisher's leadership, three renowned scientists; J J Thomson, Cavendish Professor of Experimental Physics at Cambridge and discoverer of the electron, Sir Charles Parsons, inventor of the steam turbine, and Dr (later Sir) George Beilby, chairman of the Royal Technical College, Glasgow. The consulting panel consisted of twelve scientific experts with four chemists, four physicists (amongst them Sir Ernest Rutherford, Professor W H Bragg, and R J Strutt, later Lord Rayleigh, winner of the Nobel Prize for Physics in 1904), three engineers (William Duddell, inventor of the moving coil oscillograph, George Gerald Stoney, a pioneer of the steam turbine, and Professor Bertram Hopkinson, Professor of Mechanics at Cambridge), and one metallurgist.

Convening for the first time on 19 July, the BIR mainly concerned itself with naval warfare inventions, especially air power and, importantly, antisubmarine weapons, which was the focus of one if the BIR's six divisions. This body examined some rather *outré* suggestions, including training seagulls to obfuscate submarine periscopes with their excreta, arming cormorants with bombs and teaching sea lions to carry depth charges. Unsurprisingly these projects were not progressed. But the real focus of the work was on the key issue of detecting submarines when they were underwater and therefore, to all intents and purposes at that time, invisible.

This became the particular focus of Professor Sir William Henry Bragg who, together with his son William Lawrence, had been jointly awarded the 1915 Nobel Prize for Physics in connection with their work on crystal structure using X-ray spectrometry. Bragg's work for the BIR was directed at perfecting a hydrophone, a device for detecting underwater sound and thus pinpointing the location of a submarine. Sir Ernest Rutherford (a Nobel laureate for Chemistry in 1908 and the man who first postulated the existence of a charged nucleus in an atom) had originally produced a paper suggesting that underwater microphones offered the best potential for experimentation and Bragg, working for the BIR, became resident director of the navy's own Hawkcraig experimental research station at Aberdour (Fife), HMS *Tarlair*, which was under the control of Commander (later Captain) Cyril Ryan RN and a staff of RNVR officers.

By December 1916, it was obvious that premises larger than Hawkcraig were required and some naval officers and thirty-six civilian scientific staff relocated to start a new base in Harwich, at Parkeston Quay. By 26 December, the new organisation was in place and known as Admiralty Experimental Station (AES), Parkeston. A number of hotel rooms were used as offices. Other buildings for laboratories and workshops were provided on the wooden-planked

Sir William Henry Bragg pictured in 1915 when he and his son jointly won the Nobel Prize. His work with the Board of Invention and Research was – eventually – highly regarded. (Author's collection)

quayside. (In June 1918, when ready access to deeper water became a requirement for research into submarine detection, an annexe to Parkeston Quay was created by the Admiralty when they took over the Royal Hotel overlooking the mouth of the River Dart in Kingswear, Devon.)

And so, in addition to the Harwich Force, the Auxiliary Patrol and minesweepers, the Harwich submarines, the Harwich and Felixstowe kite balloon stations and the RNAS base at Felixstowe, Harwich could now boast a large number of boffins and technical naval officers, all of whom put even more strain on the town's limited facilities and accommodation.

Not everyone was enamoured of the BIR and Balfour's successor, Sir Edward Carson, was forced to defend it in the House of Commons.

> We have . . . the Board of Inventions and Research. It is presided over by Admiral Lord Fisher, and associated with him are the greatest scientists the country possesses. He is there to tell them the wants of the Admiralty, and they are there to work out the methods by which those wants can be met – men like Sir J Thomson, Sir Charles Parsons, Sir G Beilby, and many of equal distinction associated with them; and I am sorry that my right hon Friend opposite described a body of that kind the other night as a 'chemist's shop.' These are some of the greatest men we have. They give us of their best freely, and, as far as I am concerned, I cannot for a moment imagine that a great and distinguished public servant, who has done so much in the past as Lord Fisher has done, is not also giving to the Admiralty ungrudgingly the whole of his abilities and the whole of his services in trying to solve a problem of this kind, which threatens the very existence of this country.[2]

Be that as it may, it will come as no surprise that the forward-thinking Tyrwhitt was interested in the activities of the AES. Writing to de Robeck from his flagship *Centaur* on 3 August, Tyrwhitt alluded to a hidden reason for the shift of the AES to Harwich, to wit a falling-out between Bragg and Ryan, the latter of whom had remained in Fife to continue his own experiments. The two men had multiple disagreements, including over a Bragg invention called a 'photophone' and the control and use of vessels at Hawkcraig, such as the submarine *B-3* (1905), which had been allocated to the research station. In any case, Tyrwhitt asked de Robeck, 'please do tell me if the hydrophones are a success'.[3]

At Harwich, he suggested that Professor Bragg's work had not yet born fruit; 'any way he did not make a success of them here. It seems the great trouble is the noise of the . . . engines. We had a TBD [a destroyer] fitted up but no results. I quite see the desirability of knowing which way the submarine is travelling. I should very much like to know if Ryan succeeds.'[4]

In fact, both Hawkcraig and Harwich produced viable and eventually successful devices. After the war, Jellicoe credited Harwich with the development of the Mark I directional hydrophone in 1917 'and other exceedingly valuable work was carried out there connected with the detection of submarines'.[5]

But this success was not without tears. Divided reporting structures and dual control, parallel work, overlap and unclear lines of administration had been a feature of the research side of anti-submarine work in the BIR since its establishment. This led the Director of the Anti-Submarine Division (DASD) to demand that more be done to improve the effectiveness of the research facilities. In October 1917 the DASD, Captain William Fisher, wrote to Deputy Chief of the Naval Staff Admiral Henry Oliver suggesting that the BIR establishment at Parkeston Quay be brought fully under the control of the Naval Staff at the Admiralty. He stated that 'at present matters are unsatisfactory owing to the sort of dual control exercised by BIR and DASD'.[6] By the beginning of 1918 this wish had been granted and the experimental stations came fully under the remit of the Anti-Submarine Department, 'Apparatus Section'.

The Loss of HMS *Recruit*

Meanwhile, everyday duties had to be undertaken, never without danger in a North Sea congested with mines and infested with U-boats. HMS *Recruit* and Lieutenant Commander Hugh Troup have already been noted in regard to their role in the sinking of *Setter* in May. On 9 August, *Recruit* was one of a division of four destroyers escorting the outbound Beef Trip to the Netherlands. At 2150, about three miles north of the North Hinder Light, the division commenced a 16-point turn. *Recruit* was the last ship in the line, slightly outside of the wake of the ship in front of her. As she settled on her new course, there was a large explosion on the starboard side, aft of the engine room. Shortly afterwards there was a second explosion, probably a depth charge going off, which completely wrecked the after part of the ship. *Recruit* took a list to starboard and quickly settled by the stern; in three minutes her bows rose out of the water and she sank. At the time, it was thought she had hit a mine; but later it was understood to be a torpedo attack by *UB-16* (Kapitänleutnant Wilhelm Rhein). Troup survived, but fifty-three other crewmen died.

Amongst the dead was her Engineer Lieutenant Commander, 35-year-old Maurice James Rogers Sharp. He had been awarded the DSO for his 'services in vessels of the Harwich Force during the war'.[7] It was Gazetted on 14 September; by then he was dead. Sharp had followed his father William, who had risen to the relatively rarefied heights of Engineer Rear Admiral, into the navy. Another who died was Surgeon Probationer Arthur Mather Horsey RNVR, a part-trained doctor reading medicine at Cambridge University, who had joined up in October 1916. His parents caused a plaque to be erected at their local church, St John the Baptist, Widford. It reads

> In loving memory of/Arthur Mather Horsey Surgeon PROBR, RNVR/of Caius College Cambridge/only son of/ George Mather Horsey and Sarah Jane his wife./ He went down in HMS *Recruit* in the North Sea/ on August 9th 1917 aged 23./ 'Oh true brave heart, God bless thee, where so'er/ in God's side universe thou art today'.

Their grief at the death of their clever son can only be imagined. And the Harwich Force mourned not just its loss of colleagues but also of a much-needed ship, the second of that name to have been sunk in the war, the sinking of the first *Recruit* in 1915 having led to the Battle of North Hinder Bank (see Chapter 5).

*   *   *

Captain Arthur Waistell, known to be a relatively easy-going man, had served as Captain (S) at Harwich since the start of the war. On 14 August he was relieved by Captain (Albert) Percy Addison who took command of the depot ship *Maidstone* and became Captain (S) of the Harwich submarines, formally reporting to the Admiralty but under the direct influence of Tyrwhitt. Waistell went on leave and then took command of the battleship HMS *Benbow* (1913). Addison, a rather more hard-driving type of leader, would retain this post until the end of the war. He had previously been in command of the light cruiser *Dartmouth* (1910) in the Mediterranean.

All through 1917, the weather was poor. In August, it was especially unsettled with frequents bouts of rain and unseasonably cloudy skies. It was also very cool with a maximum temperature in London of only 13.9 degrees centigrade and heavy rain at the beginning of the month. The commodore was moved to write to de Robeck that 'the weather is very bad'.[8] And October was an extremely changeable month with strong winds and fast-moving frontal systems crossing the country. Generally, it had been a wet summer with 12.4in of rain recorded at Kew, twice the long-term average. The weather played havoc with operations all year. A typical example came on 24 October, when Tyrwhitt was informed that a flotilla of German destroyers was about to make a night-time dash from Zeebrugge to Germany. He immediately left Harwich in *Centaur*, with *Concord*, *Carysfort* and *Canterbury*, accompanied by four destroyers and a flotilla leader.

HMS *Concord* became Tyrwhitt's flagship after *Centaur* was badly damaged in October 1917. She is painted here in December 1918 by Cecil King in Copenhagen, moored alongside the *Langelinie*, with her sister ship *Cardiff* outside of her. (Author's collection)

In the dark, with a range of vision around one mile, the search was difficult and they found nothing. But an old enemy was waiting for them as they started the return journey. Turning for Harwich put them into the teeth of a southwest gale which soon rose to hurricane force. *Centaur* was reduced to just 3 knots in heavy seas; and then, at about noon, a wave broke over her stern and washed the armed depth charges there into the water. They exploded with such force that all aboard thought she had hit a mine.

Captain Domvile remembered that

there was a terrific explosion and the ship quivered and shook as if in her death agony. I must admit that for a brief moment I thought we were for it, as there would have been no chance of saving anyone in the weather prevailing . . . fortunately the rudder still worked and two of our four propellers were functioning . . . we had an anxious twelve hours . . . eventually made harbour about midnight.[9]

Tyrwhitt had yet another flagship broken under him. He shifted his broad pennant to *Concord*.

The 'V'-class leader *Valkyrie*, mined on the Beef Trip in 1918 and seen here leading the 13th Destroyer Flotilla in the Baltic Sea in 1919. (US Navy History and Heritage Command NH 50150)

An Avoidable Tragedy?

December 1917; the shortest days and the longest nights of the year. It was Saturday 22nd and another Beef Trip, ill-omened from the start. A seaman named Symonds in *Torrent* remembered that the destroyer in front of them 'had a dog on board which barked and being a very still night you could hear it'. His mate said to him 'have you ever heard a dog bark at sea before? That's a very unlucky sign. Something bad is bound to happen.'[10]

Eight destroyers had been detailed to provide the escort; one of them, the new 'V'-class destroyer leader *Valkyrie*,* struck a mine at 2215, near the Maas

---

* She was designed to lead the new 'R'-class destroyers and mounted four 4in guns in four single centre-line mounts. These were positioned as two forward and two aft in superimposed firing positions. *Valkyrie* also had a single 3in QF anti-aircraft gun aft of the second funnel. Aft of the 3in weapon, she carried four 21in torpedo tubes mounted in pairs.

light on the eastward journey. In drifting fog and in the dark, confusion reigned but *Valkyrie* stayed afloat and was towed back to Harwich by Commander Creagh's destroyer *Sylph*. Once again, Creagh showed his mettle in saving the badly-damaged *Valkyrie*. He got her back to Harwich, a feat which caused Tyrwhitt to write that '[her] condition was such that few officers could have even made the attempt and fewer still would have succeeded'.[11] Most of *Valkyrie*'s men were taken off or picked up by other destroyers but twelve of her crew were dead and the following day another five, all stokers, died of wounds received in the explosion. Unfortunately, worse was to come.

The routine followed by the escort was to deliver their charges to the Dutch coast and then loiter around the Maas light buoy awaiting the ships they were to usher back to Harwich. But the Germans knew this too and frequently mined the area. Unbeknown to the Admiralty or the waiting destroyers, a new minefield had been laid there overnight on 10/11 December; it was this field which had so nearly claimed *Valkyrie*.

At 0315 on the 23rd, another of the escort, HMS *Torrent*, thought that she saw men in the water and manoeuvred to pick them up. There was a massive explosion; when the smoke and debris cleared it could be seen that she had broken in two and *Torrent* sank rapidly, stern first.

The first impulse of any sailor is to save his fellow mariners if they are in trouble. It is an unwritten law of the sea. Commander Wilfred Arthur Thompson didn't hesitate and took his ship, *Surprise*, to pick up the men struggling in the water. At 0321 there was a second detonation; *Surprise* had hit another mine; abandon ship was ordered but as men rushed to obey, there was a further explosion as she again detonated a mine. *Surprise* broke up and sank within three minutes.

Three ships had been mined and two sunk; but Lieutenant Commander Ralph Michael Mack and *Tornado* attempted to pick up the survivors. There was still fog, drifting smoke and the sea was full of drowning men. At 0330 *Tornado* blew up and added to the carnage. She too broke in two and quickly sank.

Lieutenant Commander Geoffrey Stewart Fleetwood Nash in *Radiant* had a decision to make. Should he too risk his ship to pick up the crews floundering in the freezing waters of the North Sea? Men that his own ship knew as friends, colleagues whom he had shared a drink with, shared confidences and ambitions with. He gently nursed his destroyer into the area; some of the survivors had been in the water for too long and had no strength left to grab a rope so members of *Radiant*'s crew went over the side to pluck men from the sea. Edward Knight thought that 'most gallant was the conduct of the sub lieutenant and the men who went into the ice-cold water among the struggling and drowning men at great risk to themselves . . . Exceptional coolness too was displayed by the engine room and stokehole branch of the *Radiant* while rescue work was being performed in the dangerous area.'[12]

Nash and *Radiant** saved seventy-four souls. Only seven of *Torrent*'s crew survived; amongst the dead were Chief Stoker Stephen Pritchard, whose bravery had been recognised in 1914 at the Battle of Heligoland Bight, and her CO, Lieutenant Commander Frederick Archibald Warner. Forty-nine of *Surprise* and eighteen of *Tornado* were rescued. Two hundred and forty men from the three destroyers died.[13]

There was more than a slight similarity in this disaster to that of three years earlier when *Aboukir*, *Cressy* and *Hogue* were all torpedoed in the Broad Fourteens, each trying to rescue its sisters. The manpower and *matériel* loss in both cases was severe; incidents when human compassion trumped cooler reason.

After this, Tyrwhitt made a point of going personally with the escort. Perhaps he felt that he would have taken different decisions; or that he should have realised that the Germans would mine a regular meeting point? Certainly, he felt the loss deeply; writing to Jellicoe he admitted that 'I feel the loss of those three destroyers more than I can say. Poor fellows never had a chance and it is hard to be put down without hitting back.' And he seemed to imply that he would have acted differently, adding that 'it was case of brave but not good leading'.[14]

*   *   *

The Harwich Force's notional strength in December was 5 LCS, nine light cruisers, plus *Vindex* together with 10 DF. The cruiser squadron comprised the 'C'-class vessels *Concord*, *Carysfort*, *Cleopatra*, *Conquest*, *Centaur*, *Aurora*, *Canterbury*, *Curlew* and *Penelope*. With regard to destroyers, 10 DF had twenty-four 'R'-class destroyers and *Undaunted* with four flotilla leaders, of which *Valkyrie* had been one. But with her in the dockyard and three destroyers lost on 23 December, together with loans to Dover and elsewhere, Tyrwhitt remained constrained in terms of destroyer numbers.

A Man of Push and Go

Sir Edward Carson did not last long at the Admiralty, a victim of Lloyd George's desire to see more action and pace from that organisation and of his

---

* *Radiant* survived the war. She was sold back to Thornycroft on 21 June 1920, who then sold her on to the Royal Thai Navy in September 1920 where she was renamed *Phra Ruang*. A Royal Prince, Admiral Abhakara Kiartivongse, was sent to England to negotiate the purchase personally and commanded the ship during its subsequent voyage from England to Thailand. She served the Thai Navy until 1957, making her the last survivor of the Royal Navy's First World War destroyers.

siding with his admirals rather than challenging them. His replacement from July was Eric Campbell Geddes, neither a politician or a sailor but a hard-headed businessman and previously deputy general manager of the North Eastern Railway, one of several 'men of push and go' who the prime minster drafted into government to get things done.*

He and First Sea Lord Jellicoe had difficulty seeing eye to eye. The workaholic Jellicoe, a poor delegator who tried to involve himself in all decisions, was gumming up the works and making it difficult for the Admiralty to get things done. Geddes saw one of his roles as ungumming things.

Matters came to a head over two Scandinavian convoys, in October and December, when the whole of the convoys and nearly all the escort were lost to superior German forces, despite the Admiralty knowing that something offensive was being planned by the Germans. After the second incident, Geddes, thoroughly frustrated by what he saw as the quite unsatisfactory handling of the events, had usurped both Jellicoe's and Beatty's prerogatives and authority by personally ordering a court of enquiry into the affair and nominating the members himself. Jellicoe was ill in bed at the time and tried to prevent Geddes behaving as he did but, inexcusably, Geddes 'altered the text of a telegram from Jellicoe to Beatty and despatched it with an additional offensive message from himself'.[15] Beatty was incandescent with rage at this presumption and when Jellicoe next visited him, he had to spend a long time pacifying the Grand Fleet's CinC.

Then on Christmas Eve 1917, Admiral Sir John Jellicoe received a letter from Geddes asking for his resignation. Jellicoe himself believed that it was his determination not to 'acquiesce in his [Geddes] high handed treatment of senior flag officers' coupled with the issues around convoys. Writing on Christmas Day to his friend Vice Admiral Reginald Bacon, he noted that 'I have had many disputes of late with the First Lord on this subject. The latest was the convoy enquiry.'[16] As for

Eric Campbell Geddes, businessman turned First Lord of the Admiralty, pictured in 1917. (Author's collection)

* Geddes was also a keen singer; 'The prime minister and I came to the conclusion he is prouder of his singing than of his professional attainments' (Hankey, *Supreme Command*, Vol 2, p 787).

Tyrwhitt, he wrote to Jellicoe that 'your departure from the Admiralty comes as a great shock to me and all at Harwich. I can only say once more how dreadfully sorry I am.'[17]

Jellicoe was replaced by Admiral Rosslyn Erskine Wemyss, 'Rosy' to his friends, an emollient monocle-wearing scion of minor aristocracy, good friends with King George V, and well connected in society. He would also do Geddes' bidding rather more willingly than his predecessor.* Roger Keyes had been at the Admiralty since October, now a rear admiral and serving as director of plans. He and Wemyss had Bacon in their sights.

At issue was the Dover Barrage, Bacon's pride and joy, which turned out to be no obstacle to the transit of German U-boats at all. As Wemyss later put it 'the intelligence department satisfactorily proved to me that the enemy submarines did pass the Strait successfully and without challenge. Sir R Bacon on the other hand maintained that they did not, that his system of nets was satisfactory.'[18]

Amongst Keyes's new responsibilities, as defined by Geddes and Wemyss, was to establish and chair an Admiralty committee to oversee the design, construction and use of another new mine barrage at Dover. Keyes had been rumoured to be after Bacon's job since the beginning of 1917; nobody knew where the gossip had started – but everybody knew it, including Admiral Bacon himself.

Keyes reasoned that the immediate tasks were to stop the transit of submarines through the Strait of Dover and, importantly, to nullify the problem at source by denying the Germans the use of the Belgian ports. Bacon put forward a half-hearted proposal for a landing at Zeebrugge but refused Keyes's idea of permanent nighttime illumination of the Barrage, as he feared it would put the ships manning it at risk. This was all the ammunition Wemyss needed. Shorn of the protection of Jellicoe, on 1 January 1918 Bacon was dismissed from his post and replaced with Keyes who, to avoid the embarrassment of having a second in command senior in the service to himself, was appointed an acting vice admiral. Tyrwhitt was pleased. As he had told de Robeck at the end of 1916, 'I fear the streaky one bluffed them all and is [illegible] more than ever; but he will be found out one of these days in spite all it all'.[19]

---

* Writing to Rear Admiral de Chair on 29 December, Jellicoe stated that 'I fear Wemyss will not stick up to him. I have often told Wemyss that he must realise that he is a colleague and not the First Lord's servant' (de Chair, *The Sea is Strong*, p 236).

15

A Royal Visitor and the Everyday War,
January–June 1918

On 8 January 1918 Tyrwhitt was made an acting rear admiral, jumping ahead of forty-eight captains in front of him in the Navy List. Whether or not this had anything to do with Commander Bellair's promotion of his cause is unknown but, although this was something of an honour, it was also a little like a kiss from one's sister; for Tyrwhitt's substantive rank remained that of captain. It meant he could no longer sport the sobriquet Com (T), of which he was rather proud, and should also have meant that he would have to give up the position of ADC to King George V. But the king demurred, insisting that he retain the post. Somewhat amazingly, his admiralcy was not made permanent until 2 December 1919,[1] roughly when it would have occurred based on seniority, which suggests that the publicity his case received had some impact in a dark corner of the Admiralty.

To go with his titular elevation, Tyrwhitt also gained a new flagship. HMS *Curacoa* was a *Ceres* sub-class 'C'-class light cruiser. Launched on 5 May 1917 at Pembroke, she was a slightly larger and technically improved *Centaur*, especially with regard to gunnery layout. *Curacoa* mounted five 6in guns along the centreline and two 3in anti-aircraft weapons. The gun formerly between the bridge and fore funnel was moved to a superfiring position over the forward gun with a wider firing arc than in its old position (which would have pleased Domvile who had regretted not having two forward-firing guns on *Centaur*). The other weapons were also moved, one aft of the rear funnel with the remaining two at the stern, with one gun superfiring over the other. The two anti-aircraft guns were positioned abreast the fore funnel. Additionally, there were four twin mounts of torpedo tubes; the designed top speed was 29 knots. *Curacoa* reached at Harwich in February and Tyrwhitt and Domvile immediately transferred to her. To his sister, Tyrwhitt wrote '*Curacoa* arrived last week and is quite nice. She is a great improvement even on *Centaur*.'[2]

But the newly anointed rear admiral was not feeling at his best. Tyrwhitt was a fit man and of robust physical make up. But irregular hours, poor diet, lack of sleep and stress during the exigencies of war will destroy any man's constitution and at the beginning of 1918, Tyrwhitt began to feel somewhat under the weather. In May 1917, suspecting appendicitis, he had consulted Sir Alfred Fripp (surgeon to both King Edward VII and King George V), who

HMS *Curacoa*, Tyrwhitt's flagship in 1918. (Author's collection)

found nothing wrong with him. Fripp became a friend and occasionally visited the Tyrwhitt family in Harwich, often giving him a check-up. Maybe his influence caused First Sea Lord Rosy Wemyss to send for Tyrwhitt on 4 March and tell him to take three weeks' leave. Tyrwhitt handed over to Captain St John on the 13th and with Lady Angela went to stay with friends in Kelso where he went fishing on the Tweed every day, returning on 3 April. 'I was <u>sent</u> on leave in mid-April,' he wrote, 'with orders to forget the war and keep as far away as possible from any ship. It was very nice of the First Lord but rather a bother as I had to go away at short notice.'[3] Tyrwhitt's emphasis on the word 'sent' perhaps indicates his reluctance to go. For it was an anxious time in the progress of the war. The Germans launched a major offensive on the Western Front, starting with Operation 'Michael' on 21 March. They overran the Allied forces and succeeded in making a deep advance and inflicting large losses. However, the second phase, Operation 'Mars', at Arras on 28 March, was held.

In the midst of this crisis, the Allies decided to appoint French General Ferdinand Foch as co-ordinator, and soon after as Generalissimo, of Allied armies. Germany then launched Operation 'George' on 9 April; it was during this crisis that Field Marshal Douglas Haig issued on 11 April his famous order of the day;

> There is no other course open to us but to fight it out. Every position must be held to the last man: there must be no retirement. With our backs to the wall and believing in the justice of our cause each one of us must fight on to the end. The safety of our homes and the freedom of mankind alike depend upon the conduct of each one of us at this critical moment.

But the German offensive failed to gain the key railway junction of Amiens and eventually petered out. One of the side effects of the battles was that German soldiers captured Allied food stores and were amazed at the amount and range of comestibles available compared to the starvation rations in Germany. This was one of the morale-breaking impacts of the British naval blockade.

The King Comes to Harwich

Captain Bryan Godfrey-Faussett RN was a naval officer who was first and foremost a courtier. In 1890, he had acted as an unofficial aide-de-camp to the then Prince George of Wales (later King George V), who was still on active service with the navy, during a visit to Canada. Godfrey-Faussett's naval career then encompassed briefly serving as an instructor at HMS *Britannia* and a posting to HMS *Osborne*, the number two royal yacht. He was advanced to commander on 13 July 1899 but was soon afterwards re-attached to Prince George's entourage.

Godfrey-Faussett once more served as aide-de-camp to the prince, now the Duke of Cornwall and York, during his tour of the British Empire from March – October 1901. Upon George becoming Prince of Wales in November that year, Godfrey-Faussett became his equerry-in-ordinary. He was advanced to captain, made an MVO* on 11 March 1906 and retired from active service on 31 October the same year to attend the Prince.

On the outbreak of war in 1914, Godfrey-Faussett offered his services to the Admiralty and with the king's approval was given command of the armed yacht HMS *Thistle* in the Auxiliary Patrol. However, the king's wartime duties required the service of a permanent naval equerry and in 1915 Godfrey-

---

* Lieutenant Member of the Royal Victorian Order.

Faussett returned to that role and accompanied the king on his visits to France and Flanders and to the fleet. In 1917 he served for a short time in the Admiralty's Paravane Department but otherwise his service as equerry was not interrupted. Captain Godfrey-Faussett was also a cuckold. His wife Eugénie, who was his junior by 24 years, had been Beatty's mistress since 1916 (and would continue to be so until 1926). But his royal relationships made him a powerful ally in certain circumstances.

Tyrwhitt had invited him to Harwich to watch a planned CMB operation in the Bight. It is not clear why Tyrwhitt made the invitation but it may well have been to do with the forthcoming visit to the port and town by the king himself. Godfrey-Faussett took the 0810 train down and was collected from Parkeston station by the admiral's barge, which ferried him to Shotley, where Tyrwhitt met him with a car. They motored to the family home where he was introduced to Angela and watched the three children play tennis. Tyrwhitt had to tell him that CMB operation was off due to weather in the Bight 'which was distinctly disappointing'.[4] After a pleasant time in the bosom of Tyrwhitt's family, they repaired to the flagship for dinner, joined by Domvile. 'I sat up yarning with Reggie until midnight,'[5] reported the courtier. But he had obviously become addicted to his creature comforts since leaving the navy. 'I slept indifferently in his bridge cabin,' he reported 'and bathed and dressed in his lower cabin next morning.'[6] After which Godfrey-Faussett decided that 'as

King George V taking the salute during his visit to Harwich. Tyrwhitt is standing to his left.
The overhead construction is a coal conveyor and chute for re-coaling the ships.
(Photo; David Whittle/Harwich Society)

there was still too much wind to permit the CMB operation taking place I decided to return to London otherwise it might have meant waiting there for days'.[7]

Less than a month later, Godfrey-Faussett's master, King George V, visited Harwich and Felixstowe between 5 and 8 March. He was accompanied by Commander Sir Charles Cust, yet another courtier and a known 'fixer'. Cust was one of George V's oldest and closest friends, having met him at Dartmouth Naval College when they were both about 14 and served with him in the navy. He had been appointed an equerry in 1892.

Greeted by Tyrwhitt and Captain William Mitchell Moir of the destroyer depot ship *Dido*, the king first received and shook hands with the Force's captains, Domvile being fourth up, and then watched a series of march pasts by naval detachments, all the while accompanied by a naval band. Sailors and then Royal Marines filed past before the king was taken to see a demonstration of 'shot hole stopping', a drill for plugging shell holes in ships; the hole was blocked off in 36 seconds.

On the 8th, the king travelled by admiral's barge with Tyrwhitt to *Curacao* where he again met Domvile and inspected the ship. On board the flagship, King George presented medals to a few selected recipients. Five chief petty officers and ratings received the DSM. Another award was to Alfred William Newman. He received the Gold Albert Medal for Saving Life at Sea for his bravery in 1917. Newman, who had served on HMS *Laurel* at the Battle of Heligoland Bight, had been appointed Acting Mate on *Tetrarch* in June 1917. On 10 October, there was a sudden fire alarm from the aft magazine of the destroyer. Twenty-eight-year-old Newman, who was on the upper deck, proceeded to the magazine as soon as he heard the alert and

> seeing smoke issuing from a box of cordite, opened the lid and passed the cartridges on to the upper deck, where they were thrown into the sea. One cartridge in the middle of the box was very hot and smoke was issuing from its end. It is considered that by his prompt and gallant action, Newman saved the magazine from being blown up and the loss of many lives.[8]

Additionally, Captain Robert Arthur Hornell* was presented with the DSO in regard to 'Honours for Services in Destroyer and Torpedo Boat Flotillas',[9] and Lieutenant A E Thompson the DSC.

Tyrwhitt's barge next took the king around some of the ships in harbour before he made a further set of presentations to RNAS and RFC officers and

---

* Captain of *Nimrod* until February 1918.

King George V viewing the march past of naval personnel during his visit to Harwich.
(Photo; David Whittle/Harwich Society)

men, and then congratulated with a handshake some deserving American pilots as well. A final engagement saw a parade by the combined RNAS and RFC crews and mechanics and an inspection of the Harwich Auxiliary Force minesweeping crews before a return to London on the royal train. Tyrwhitt's command and their associated Harwich and Felixstowe colleagues had received much-merited royal recognition. It was a morale boost at a difficult time and well received.

The Everyday

Meanwhile, the everyday escort, sweep and reactive duties of the Harwich Force continued undiminished. On 14 January, four German destroyers suddenly appeared off Great Yarmouth and at 2255, in gale force winds and rain lashed seas, opened fire on the town. The bombardment lasted for only five minutes, but fifty shells were fired and much damage caused. Two civilians, 53-year-old Mary Ann Sparks and her husband Arthur, were in bed when a shell hit the roof of their house and bricks and rafters crashed down on them. Mary was killed outright and Arthur died later in hospital. Two sailors on a ship from Hull, which was in the harbour, were also killed.

There was no response to the bombardment from the military bases in the town. The bad weather prevented any aircraft from the air station from taking off and none of the submarines based in the port were sent out because the attacking force was considered to be too far away. The monitor HMS *Roberts* (1915) had been stationed in the harbour to defend against just such eventuality but did not open fire with her two 14in guns.

It was not until 90 minutes after the first shells had fallen on the town that the Harwich Force was called out by the Admiralty. By then, the Germans had long retired and although Tyrwhitt's ships manfully battled into the gale, they saw nothing and returned to Harwich at noon on the 15th.

It was the fifth time that Yarmouth had come under attack, twice from the air and three times from the sea. The perceived lack of action in defence of the town produced a tetchy exchange in the House of Commons. On 23 January, Sir Robert Houston, MP for Liverpool West Toxteth, asked Dr Macnamara, Parliamentary Secretary for the Admiralty and proxy for Geddes, 'seeing the repeated attacks on the east coast and northeast coast by enemy raiders, who invariably escape, will he say, who is in command of the east and northeast coast, and who is responsible?' The reply was cutting; 'if the suggestion that I should give the name of the responsible officer implies a dereliction of duty on his part, I think that is particularly ungracious and ungrateful of the hon member'.[10] But public anger was clear.

The next few weeks were exceptionally busy. The new flagship went out on two Beef Trips in three days followed by a voyage to the Bight escorting minelayers. Fog came down and made the return trip a little hairy. On the 18th, *Canterbury* arrived back from Chatham where she had been undergoing maintenance, followed the next day by *Centaur*, which four days later went up to Scapa Flow, to return on 17 February.

Then the Admiralty rushed the Force out on a rumour that the Germans were at sea, but fog came down and they had to anchor in the channel opposite Felixstowe in a line stretching back to the quayside; but it was a false alarm anyway. It was 'the dickens of a life, frequently sending them out to look for or intercept German destroyers which never materialised'.[11]

Their Lordships then made the less-than-helpful proposal to remove the North Hinder light on the grounds that it was useful to U-boats looking to lay mines off Harwich, ignoring the fact that it was also of assistance to British vessels returning at night in poor weather to check their position and work out their course through the swept channel to home. Tyrwhitt fought off the suggestion.

February and March brought with them changes to the composition of the Harwich Force. In February, *Undaunted*, bloody but unbowed and which had been with the Force since the start of the war, moved from leading 10 DF onto the books of 5 LCS, only to depart completely in March, together with *Aurora* and *Carysfort*, where they combined with *Penelope* to form the new 7th Light Cruiser Squadron under Commodore George Holmes Borrett, part of the Grand Fleet.

A paravane being deployed, in this instance from a USN ship in 1917. (Author's collection)

Also in February, the Harwich Force gained its very own minesweepers when *Eglinton*, *Gatwick*, *Melton* and *Pontefract* joined from the 6th Destroyer Flotilla at Dover. These were 'Racecourse'-class vessels, all completed between April and October 1916, to a design by the Ailsa Shipbuilding Company of Ayrshire. They were paddle-wheel driven and of shallow draught (only 6–7ft), thus allowing them to sweep in limited depths and coastal waters. Each carried two 12pdr guns and *Melton* had been built to carry two seaplanes but never did so. All were reasonable sea-boats but lost speed badly in a seaway when the paddle boxes tended to become choked with water. Their attachment to the Harwich Force can be seen as a recognition of the mine-infested waters in which the Force habitually operated and its need to have permanent attendance from minesweeping vessels which, unlike the auxiliary converted trawlers which formed the main minesweeping force, were capable of a higher speed. The 'Racecourses' could manage 15 knots as opposed to a trawler's 9 knots.

The light cruisers' log books[*] show that they now routinely trained their paravanes out when they went out to sea, and exercised regularly with them too, another example of the need to counter the pervasive threat from mines (both German and British). A paravane was a torpedo-shaped device, strung

---

[*] For example, HMS *Canterbury*, 26 January 1918, 0855: Sunk Light Vessel abeam. Course and speed as requisite for paravane trials up to 24 knots. 3 February, at sea, 0648: Slipped paravanes. 1000: Divisions Prayers. 2031: Hoisted in paravanes (ADM 53-36986, NA).

out and streamed alongside a towing ship, normally from the bow. The wings of the paravane would tend to force the body away from the vessel, placing a lateral tension on the towing wire. If the tow cable snagged the chain anchoring a mine, then it would be cut by the jaws of a 'knife' on the sweep, allowing the mine to float to the surface where it could be destroyed by gunfire. If the anchor cable would not part, the mine and the paravane would be brought together and the mine would explode harmlessly against the paravane. The cable could then be retrieved and a replacement paravane fitted. They worked best at a speeds of 13 knots or more and the lifetime of the invention lasted into the Second World War, when they were still in general use.

The Bight was now a heavily mined area, with both German defensive fields and British offensive ones, such that the Admiralty had ordered Tyrwhitt not to go into an area less than 100 miles out from the enemy shore. This swung the attacking or reconnaissance emphasis back to sea-air operations. As a result, March brought the introduction of a scheme first mooted by Churchill in 1914. Large barges were designed with a cut-away aft and sunk until half awash so as to carry and slip off a seaplane. Their structure combined a fast-planing hull shape with a semi-submersible docking bay. The hull was made of galvanised steel plates riveted or welded together and was designed such that at high speed the bow wave broke sideways, keeping aircraft wings dry. They were of monohull construction with a pointed bow and a single timber deck and were fitted with Kingston valves which opened to flood the buoyancy chambers in order to embark and disembark the aircraft. The water was then pumped out using onboard compressed air bottles. Later (see Chapter 16) they were modified to carry land aircraft by fitting an elevated inclined wooden deck from which the aircraft took off. The barges had no motive power and were intended to be towed into position by destroyers.

Lieutenant Theodore Hallam RNAS described how the aircraft were loaded into the lighter.

> Motor-boats seized the flying-boats as they touched the water and towed them to the sterns of their appointed lighters, which were lying at buoys at the ends of the slipways. The five men in the crew of each lighter had flooded the water-tanks in the sterns, and the boats were quickly floated into their cradles, hauled up by a winch into position and secured. With a hiss the compressed air was turned into the tanks, the water was blown out, and the lighters rose into towing trim.[12]

Five fitters and machine handlers stayed aboard each lighter as it was towed out to the launch site, sheltering in a cramped forecastle which was equipped

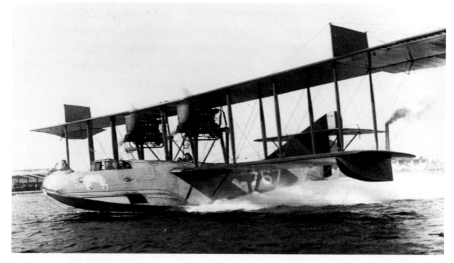

A Curtiss H-12 flying boat, the same model as the one which successfully took off from a lighter in March 1918, pictured in November that year when taxiing for take-off. Armed with four Lewis guns, they could carry around 400–450lbs of bombs.
(US Navy History and Heritage Command NH 91603)

with two bunks and an electric heater tapped off the main cable (which was connected to the towing vessel and provided power for the aircraft engine heaters).

The first such operation was conducted on 19 March, during Tyrwhitt's absence on leave. Three seaplanes, a Curtiss H-12 and two Felixstowe F2As, were towed out to the Haaks Light Vessel, near Texel, at dawn but it proved tricky to get the seaplane engines to start after a cold and wet night trip out there. However, perseverance paid off and a reconnaissance flight proved possible. The destroyers slowed to 3 knots and then made a right-hand turn away while the seaplanes slid off the lighters. Destroyers formed a protective anti-submarine circle around the three aircraft, and they eventually took off and flew over the British minefields surrounding the Heligoland Bight, noting where German minesweepers were clearing channels.

There was a brief skirmish with two German seaplanes and an F2A shot down one of them while the second was driven off. However, during the exchange of fire the starboard engine of one F2A, flown by Flight Lieutenant Norman Magor, was damaged and had to be shut down. While Magor kept the F2A in the air on one engine, Leading Mechanic Sydney Anderson stripped off his leather flying coat and climbed onto the starboard wing to work on the damaged engine in the 90mph slipstream. After one-and-three-quarter hours, he succeeded in repairing and restarting it. Unsurprisingly, this act of bravery was considered worthy of the award of a DSM.

A further lighter-borne flight took place on 21 March, when three RNAS flying boats were fired on by German minesweepers and retaliated by strafing them. And on 18 May, despite the attentions of a Zeppelin, a further patrol of 470 miles in seven and a half hours by one aircraft was carried out. Yet again, the Harwich Force was in the forefront of naval aviation.

Operation 'ZO'

On St George's Day the much-anticipated assault against Zeebrugge, codenamed Operation 'ZO', finally took place. First Lewis Bayly, then Tyrwhitt had suggested landings in force to destroy the U-boats' route to the sea. Tyrwhitt's final proposition, dated 7 May 1917,[13] proposed to use four 'Insect'-class (aka Large China) river gunboats as landing vessels and was, as we have seen, ignored. But now, with Roger Keyes in command at Dover and fame in his sights, the scheme was finally on. It was an all-volunteer, unmarried men only, all-navy effort to a plan which bore all of Keyes's hallmarks – bravery and valour for sure but unrealistic and lacking detailed analysis.

The attack was compromised from the beginning. The intended date for the raid was 11 April, but it was postponed after sailing owing to the weather, not before the Germans had captured the secret instructions and charts from a stranded CMB. They therefore knew to expect some sort of demonstration at Zeebrugge. No-one bothered to think that the tides would be different on 23 April to those considered in the original plan so that when the assault ships reached the mole, the water was 4ft lower than expected and the men could not get off until improvised ladders had been made. Brave men died in droves. And the operation failed, although it was bruited around as a success for propaganda purposes. A similar attack on Ostend on 9 May, also failed with significant loss of life. Fisher's opinion of the raids was damming. He later wrote that 'no such folly was ever devised by fools as such an operation as that of Zeebrugge . . . it's murder and it's criminal'.[14] But Britain needed a victory and Keyes provided one, albeit under false pretences. As the historian Richard Hough noted, 'Zeebrugge was a courageous and thrilling exploit deserving its place in history, not for its tangible results . . . but for its inspiration'.[15] Frankly, that's a generous assessment.[*]

The Harwich Force had almost no role in the proceedings, acting as flank guard, patrolling the approaches to the Flanders Bight with seven light cruisers, two flotilla leaders and fourteen destroyers; they were untroubled by any German intervention. German U-boats and destroyers continued to issue from the Belgian coast. Perhaps it is just as well that Tyrwhitt did not get to execute his original plans.

---

[*] For a more detailed description of the raids see Steve R Dunn, *Securing the Narrow Sea* (Barnsley: Seaforth Publishing, 2017)

The Last Hurrah of the High Seas Fleet

On 23 April 1918, the German High Seas Fleet made its final sortie into the North Sea. The Harwich Force played but a tangential part in the subsequent actions but one of its submarines made a name for its commander.

The German naval strategy had always been to try to destroy elements of the Grand Fleet in detail, avoiding a full fleet-on-fleet encounter until the numerical advantage in battleships held by the Royal Navy had been eroded. Flushed with the success of his two surface attacks on the Scandinavian convoys in 1917, Sheer began to formulate a strategy which would encompass both the war on trade and the long-held 'erosion and reduction' strategy that had been pursued since the start of the war. He planned a full-scale attack on a large Scandinavian convoy.

He was encouraged in this regard by intelligence supplied that the 3rd Battle Squadron had been disbanded to provide crews for the anti-submarine war in the North Sea. He believed that this meant that the Grand Fleet was depleted, having failed to appreciate that the squadron had been moved to Sheerness on 29 April 1916.

Admiral Scheer assembled his ships in the Heligoland Bight on the 22nd, keeping radio silence as far as humanly possible. Because of this, Room 40 picked up nothing untoward and Beatty was informed that the Bight was quiet.

At 1345 that same day, a homebound convoy of thirty-four ships left Selbjorns Fjord in Norway under the escort of the *Duke of Cornwall*, an armed boarding steamer, and the destroyers HMS *Lark* and *Llewellyn*. They were covered by the 2nd Battlecruiser Squadron and the 7th Light Cruiser Squadron, which met them outside and steamed across the North Sea to the south of them. At daylight on the 23rd the convoy was about 140 miles to the east of the Orkneys; and Admiral Scheer, with his movements still unknown to the British, was beginning to take his squadrons northwards through the swept channels out of the Bight.

Almost immediately a fog descended but Scheer continued to the edge of the British minefields where he anchored to let his minesweepers get to work. At 2030 Beatty was again told by the Admiralty that the Bight was quiet. Once more the Germans resumed their progress, entering an area being watched by four RN submarines. One, HMS *J6*, spotted ships and identified them provisionally as a group of destroyers and light cruisers. Lieutenant Commander J Geoffrey Warburton, captain of the submarine, had been ordered to be aware that British ships might be operating in his area. He therefore took the vessels now observed to be friendly and no report was passed back to Rosyth. Scheer slipped into the North Sea, free and unknown.

But German intelligence failings began to show. Their agents and consuls in Norway could easily have supplied the information that convoy sailings operated all week and to a regular schedule. But Scheer relied on information provided by his U-boat commanders and had been misinformed that movements took place in the middle of the week. Thus, he planned to intercept the convoy on Wednesday 24th. If he had sailed 24 hours later or earlier, he would have fallen in with a large convoy. As it was, by darkness on the 23rd, the westbound convoy and its covering force had reached the latitude of Buchan Ness, off the extreme northeastern coast of Scotland. No other convoy was due to leave until the 24th. Scheer and his battle squadrons were steaming into an empty sea, devoid of warships and merchantmen alike.

His progress was further hindered when the *Moltke* suffered an engine failure.* She had been steaming ahead in a scouting role. Now she was ordered to retire on the main fleet; and for this order to be transmitted, radio silence, so assiduously kept thus far, was broken. And Room 40 heard it.

Confusion now reigned. Scheer reluctantly turned for Horns Reef and home. Beatty, alerted by the Admiralty, ordered his ships out to sea. He was able to send out thirty-one battleships, four battlecruisers, two cruisers, twenty-four light cruisers and eighty-five destroyers. He wrote to Eugenie that 'thanks to the capabilities and fine qualities of my flag officers and captains we got out 193 ships in the shortest time on record without an accident'.[16]

Tyrwhitt was told to sail and at 0004 on the 24th he left Harwich, heading east-northeast. But for both Beatty and the Harwich Force it was already too late. By 2000, Tyrwhitt was told to return home and at 1340 on the 25th, the Admiralty ordered Beatty back to Rosyth.

But Harwich was able to chalk up a minor success. The submarine *E-42* of the 9th Flotilla was out on patrol when her captain, Lieutenant Charles Henry Allen, spotted a number of heavy units crossing his path. One of them was the injured *Moltke*. Allen fired four torpedoes, one of which hit the battlecruiser, causing damage† but not sinking her. For this action, Allen was awarded the DSO, the citation for which read 'in recognition of his services as commanding officer of HM Submarine *E-42*, which carried out a successful attack on the German battlecruiser *Moltke*, on the 25th April, 1918'.[17]

---

* The starboard propeller fell off the shaft, and before the turbine could be stopped, a gear wheel was destroyed. The broken wheel flung pieces of steel into an auxiliary condenser, which flooded the engine room and stopped the operation of the centre and starboard engines.

† The ship took in 1,800 tons of water but was able to reach harbour under her own steam. She was put out of the war while repairs were carried out in Wilhelmshaven in the Imperial Dockyard, between 30 April and 9 September.

Two Submarines and One Survivor

The German submarine *UB-16* had been commissioned in May 1915 and served with the Flanders flotillas all her service career. She had sunk twenty-six ships by May 1918, twelve of them fishing smacks in 1915, and had seen a variety of captains. Converted to a minelayer in 1917, on 6 May 1918 she departed Zeebrugge for minelaying operations off the Harwich coast, under Oberleutnant zur See Vicco von der Lühe, who had only assumed command on 22 April.

At 1850 on 10 May, *UB-16* was spotted on the surface by the Harwich-based 9th Submarine Flotilla's HMS *E-34*, commanded by Lieutenant Richard Ivor Pulleyne. Pulleyne initially thought that she must be British, given the proximity to Harwich, but then realised his error and submerged to attack. Von der Lühe, a petty officer and two seamen were on the bridge of *UB-16*, with the conning tower hatch open. They sighted a column of smoke on the horizon and decided to investigate. 'Suddenly, a look out called "there is a submarine" and at the same time [von der Lühe] perceived the conning tower of *E-34* and the wake of two torpedoes.'[18] Pulleyne had fired his two tin-fish from a distance of 400 yards at 1915. One hit the bows and failed to explode; but the second detonated below the conning tower, sinking the German U-boat in less than five minutes. After waiting a short while, Pulleyne surfaced to find one survivor swimming in the oily waters. It was her 28-year-old captain, von der Lühe. He had been blown into the air by the explosion. The other fifteen crewmen were lost.

Von der Lühe was escorted to London for interrogation by Lieutenant Stephen King-Hall, once of HMS *Southampton*, and now attached to the depot ship *Maidstone* on the mining and torpedo staff. They discovered that they had been close to each other during the Battle of Jutland, Von der Lühe then serving in destroyers. King-Hall reported that 'the prisoner repeatedly let slip in general conversation that a great many submarine officers had nervous breakdowns. Trouble with crews as well. A certain number of officers suffered from eye-trouble . . . the mines in the Bight were a continual anxiety.'[19]

Lieutenant Pulleyne, who had already earned a DSC, was awarded the DSO[20] for his actions. But it turned out to be hollow and posthumous recognition. *E-34* was mined near the Eijerlandse Gronden, the sands between the Frisian islands Texel and Vlieland, on 20 July 1918. There were no survivors. Pulleyne's body washed ashore at Vlieland on 30 July and was buried at Noordwijk General Cemetery with full military honours. On his grave is inscribed 'we will fall into the hands of God not into the hands of men'.

Nor did von der Lühe live to enjoy his escape from a watery grave; he died of the Spanish Influenza epidemic on 1 March 1919 while still a prisoner of war in England.

*   *   *

The weather was poor in May and frustrated three efforts in as many weeks to get seaplanes into the air from the sea. On the anniversary of Jutland, a rather quixotic attempt was made to tempt out the High Seas Fleet, when Tyrwhitt took the Force into the minefields of the Heligoland Bight to act as bait. The Grand Fleet cruised in support some distance away, clear of the mines. The destroyers penetrated as far as positions off Heligoland and Borkum while the light cruisers patrolled just inside the mine barrier. Nothing was seen but the inevitable happened when the flotilla leader *Shakespeare* (1917) was mined with one officer, 40-year-old Engineer Commander Charles Main, killed. *Centaur* took her in tow and they regained England safely and without interference. *Shakespeare* was under repair at Chatham until 21 October, when she returned to Harwich and 10 DF.

To Crack a Code

As has been noted, Room 40 could read German codes and thus provide excellent intelligence as to the High Seas Fleet's intentions. But occasionally, the Germans would issue a new codebook, such as happened in March and again in June 1918. Naval Intelligence asked the Operations Division to see if they could acquire one.

The job was given to the Harwich Force and Tyrwhitt decided to make nightly sweeps through the minefields and into the Bight in an attempt to intercept some hapless German patrol boat. This did not attract much approbation from Domvile; 'we had one or two mad expeditions into the Heligoland Bight,' he wrote, 'in which we were very thankful for our paravanes as we were constantly cutting mines, mainly our own. I cursed the genius at the Admiralty who first mined the Bight and then sent us into our own minefields.'[21]

The risk of mining from such effrontery was high, and on 13 June the predictable did happen when *Centaur* was mined in the Bight, still searching for codebooks. Her log book records the lead-up to the event. At 1615, she 'passed capsized boat in 53°10' N, 3°20' E and pieces of wreckage for 2½ miles. Altered course N55E.' This was surely a warning. Then later, '1800: Passed old German drifting mine, horns. 1911: In Lat 54° 5' N, Long 4° 1' E, altered course East. 2025: Port paravane cut a mine, five horns, green in colour, probably British, position 54°10½' N, 4°39'E. 2125: Struck mine, explosion right forward under chain lockers, position 54°16' N, 5°12½ ' E. Stopped, turned ship slowly to south, shored up decks and bulkhead.'[22] *Centaur* seemed surrounded by mines, her log recording cutting a German mine at 2155 and sighted two drifting and three moored ones awash close to her.

The 'C'-class light cruiser HMS *Centaur*, one of Tyrwhitt's flagships,
displaying damage sustained when she hit a North Sea mine in June 1918.
(US Naval History and Heritage Command NH 530)

Canterbury took her in tow but later *Centaur* rediscovered the ability to
steam at 6 knots and *Canterbury* cast her off whilst remaining in close
attendance as escort. Tyrwhitt put out from Harwich too with reinforcements
and after a nervous 24 hours *Centaur* made it to the Humber and safety.

That same day, *Conquest* was mined just off the Sunk Light Vessel, outside
Harwich. *Curcaoa* was able to tow her round to Sheerness for repairs which
lasted for the rest of the war. Seven men were killed, all of them in the
boiler/engine room. Two light cruisers lost to the force in one day was a sizable
price to pay for what transpired to be something of a wild goose chase.

16

Not With A Bang But A Whimper,
July–November 1918

'C'-class submarines were the last hurrah for petrol-engined boats in the Royal Navy and represented the end of the development of the *Holland* class. Thirty-eight were constructed between 1905 and 1910. They possessed limited endurance and only a 10 per cent reserve of buoyancy over their surface displacement, which made them poor performers when on the surface. However, their spindle-shaped hull made for good underwater performance compared to their contemporaries. But by 1918, they were obsolete; slow, unpleasant to sail in, armed with only two torpedo tubes and no reloads and no deck gun. They should not have been deployed in a war zone. But they were; in July 1918, Harwich's 9th Submarine Flotilla still operated three of them. One was *C-25*. Launched in March 1909, on 6 July 1918 she was under the command of 23-year-old Lieutenant David Courtenay Bell and on patrol in the North Sea off Harwich. The only other officer on board was Sub Lieutenant Roland Cobb; the crew numbered fourteen.

At around noon, *C-25* was running on the surface when Courtenay spotted five aircraft coming from the west; he paid them little heed thinking they were British heading for Flanders. In fact, they were German seaplanes, returning from a raid on Lowestoft and Walmer. The aircraft held their course until they were clear of the boat and then turned and swooped on their unobservant victim from out of the sun.

Realising his mistake, Courtenay called for the Lewis gun to be mounted. But it was already too late. The enemy seaplanes opened a heavy fire on the conning tower, killing the captain and two of the three men there before they could even man the gun to return fire. The little submarine was raked with fire from repeated passes and the thin hull was penetrated in many places; with no internal bulkheads, bullets ricocheted around inside.

Alerted by the lack of orders coming down from the bridge, Cobb scrambled up the conning tower ladder to investigate the situation. There he found only Leading Seaman William Barge still alive, though seriously wounded. 'Dive sir,' said Barge, 'don't worry about me, I'm done for anyway.'[1] However, Cobb refused to abandon his crewman and manhandled the injured sailor to safety down the narrow, cramped conning tower. Barge died as soon as he was deposited on the deck.

Cobb ordered the petrol engine shut down, batteries engaged and prepared to dive. But he couldn't close the lower conning tower hatch. One of the bodies from the bridge had fallen down the tower and lodged in the hatchway. The man was wedged tightly in the hatch-ring, one leg dangling into the command position, the other jammed in the tower above. Try as they might there was no moving the corpse and two more men were mortally wounded during their attempts to clear the hatchway.

Unaware of this crisis, the ten surviving crewmen, some of whom were wounded, went about their duties. While some rigged the boat for diving, others plugged the bullet holes as best they could with rags and clothing, jammed into place with bolts and bits of wood, anything to allow the boat to submerge and escape the deadly fire. Chief Engine Room Artificer C J Crawford, having secured the petrol engine and wondering why they were not diving, came forward to find out what was going on. He saw Leading Seaman Barge huddled where he had fallen and the tightly-wedged body that stood was preventing escape. Another man, who had been hit in the neck, was trying to stop his own blood from pumping out with his bare hands. Two or three others were standing on the rungs of the conning tower ladder trying to force the body out of the hatchway in order to close the hatch. Crawford realised that desperate times called for desperate measures. He returned aft, found a hacksaw and a large knife, cleared the men away from the hatchway and amputated the dead man's jammed leg at the thigh. Smothered in blood from his surgery, he cleared away the obstruction and slammed the hatch shut.

Now *C-25* could dive. But then it was discovered that the motor was no longer working. Sea water, leaking into the boat through the poorly-plugged bullet holes, had seeped into the battery tank and mixed with the sulphuric acid in the cells below, creating chlorine gas. As the interior of the boat began to fill with the poisonous fumes, Crawford wrapped a towel around his face and led the work of plugging-up newly-discovered leaks.

Moreover, the steering gear was jammed both from the control room and the bridge steering positions. Both compasses were out of order and there was no sun to steer by and no land in sight. The radio was not working, the Aldis Lamp was broken and the grenade rifle was damaged.

With no propulsion and now no air, Cobb decided they could not continue the dive. He blew tanks and surfaced where, to his delight, he found that *E-51*, commanded by Lieutenant Commander Hugh Marrack, was close by and was firing on the enemy seaplanes for all she was worth with her 12pdr and Lewis gun. *E-51* signalled for help and tried to establish a tow; but more German aircraft appeared overhead and the attempt had to be abandoned.

Finally, *Lurcher* arrived to drive off the enemy for good and towed *C-25* back to harbour. When the battered submarine reached Harwich, 'the interior of the boat looked like nothing so much as a slaughterhouse. Blood was splattered everywhere.'[2]

Six men were dead; Bell and Barge were both buried at Shotley (St Mary) Churchyard in the Submarine Enclosure. Lieutenant Commander Marrack received 'Their Lordship's commendation for conduct when SM *C-25* was attacked by hostile seaplanes'.[3] And unbelievably, *C-25* was repaired and put back into service.

Coastal Motor Boats in Action

The Harwich Force, having 'invented' the coastal motor boats, finally got them back under its control and a base was established at Osea Island, on the River Blackwater, under the command of Captain Wilfred Frankland 'Froggie' French. Here the boats were maintained and fitted out and some 2,000 men, mechanics, sailors, officers and ratings were billeted in prefabricated huts. 'The idea was that this should eventually become the permanent peace base and so the most complete workshops of every description were erected.'[4]

Tactical doctrine for CMBs at the time, according to Lieutenant William Bremner, stated that 'their proper function is to attack a definite known objective or to perform a set piece of work. They are, as well, quite suited to an offensive patrol by night in enemy waters, and in close vicinity to enemy ports. They should not be used for this work in daylight, as they are very vulnerable to machine gun attack from the air.'[5] But owing to the heavy mining in the Bight, and the prohibition of Tyrwhitt's forces going to within 100 miles of it, using CMBs against the German ships near their harbours was impossible.

Tyrwhitt decided that instead they could be used against German minesweepers while they attempted to cut a passage through the British minefields off Heligoland. These fields had been laid originally to prevent U-boat egress and were now maintained, mainly by Harwich Force minelaying submarines, to delay the exit of the High Seas Fleet into the North Sea. By now the obstruction had worked back a long way from Wilhelmshaven as a result of repeated minelaying by British vessels, who had laid 15,686 mines in the North Sea in 1917, as opposed to 1,679 the year before,[6] together with mines laid by Scheer's forces to block the approach of Royal Navy's minelayers and other light craft. German minesweepers had to come some 150 miles out into the North Sea before they could start sweeping.

The plan called for the skimmers to be carried out to the minefield border on the davits of the light cruisers with the intention of finding the sweepers at the break of dawn and be back with the cruisers soon after daylight. They carried one torpedo and one or two Lewis guns apiece. Seaplanes were to operate in concert with the motor boats to provide air cover and to help them find their way back to the waiting 'mother ships'.

The first such operation was conducted on 29 June. The Harwich Force cruisers, each carrying two CMBs, dropped them just outside the British minefields around the Heligoland Bight. The usual problem was encountered – weather conditions. On this occasion only one flying boat of three on lighters, a Felixstowe F2A, succeeded in getting airborne. One of the others was so badly damaged while attempting to take off that it sank and the third had to abandon its attempt to fly as in the process it had come to grief. However, the single F2A did complete a reconnaissance flight before it suffered engine failure and had to ditch. The crew was rescued by a Dutch trawler and later transferred to a Harwich destroyer. No minesweepers were found.

Several more such operations were essayed, all bedevilled by seaplane problems and no minesweepers were encountered. Consequently, it was suggested, by the CMB crews themselves, that a daylight operation might bear more fruit.

On 10 August, the operation began. *Curacoa, Coventry, Concord* and *Danae*[*] set sail from Harwich at 2100 together with thirteen destroyers. Of these, *Retriever, Thisbe* and *Teazer* each towed a lighter with a seaplane on it while *Redoubt* and *Starfish* jointly took out lighter H-5 fitted with a wooden take-off platform carrying a Sopwith Camel.[†]

At 0600 on the 11th the flotilla had reached a point about 25 miles northwest of Vlieland (one of the West Friesian Islands) and the skimmers were dropped to start a run which was to take them past Ameland (another West Friesian Island). Once again, the seaplanes could not get off, this time because it was too calm – there was not a breath of wind. The CMBs therefore headed eastward with no aerial escort. Tyrwhitt did not recall the boats as he had arranged for a flight of aircraft from Yarmouth to rendezvous with him. These arrived at 0700 but the admiral's frantic signals to them did not get through and they acted independently all morning.

---

[*] HMS *Danae* was the lead ship of the new 'D'-class light cruisers. She was commissioned on 22 July 1918 and immediately joined the Harwich Force. The 'D' class were based on the design of the preceding 'C' class, but were lengthened by 20ft to allow for six 6in guns to be fitted. Additionally, the twin torpedo tubes of the 'C' class were replaced by triples, giving the *Danae*s a total of twelve tubes, the heaviest torpedo armament for a cruiser at that time.

[†] The first attempt at flight from a lighter in a fighter was by Charles Rumney Samson (the first British pilot to take off from a moving ship) who was CO of the aircraft base at Great Yarmouth. He used a Camel fitted with skids to run in slots on the lighter which was towed behind a destroyer at high speed. As soon as aircraft started to lift off, it went out of control and plunged into the water ahead of the lighter which ran over it. Remarkably, Samson survived and, as he was hauled from the sea, remarked 'That was no damn good, we must do it better next time' (Smith, *Voices in Flight*, p 48).

Meanwhile the six coastal motor boats had reached Terschelling and were moving at high speed close to the shore. They were cruising in pairs arranged in a rough echelon, for the water through which the boats moved was so churned by the enormous bow wave that no boat could follow in another's wake. As they swept past the low sand dunes of Terschelling in bright, clear sunlight, six aeroplanes were sighted: three were ahead and three astern.

The CMB flotilla was under Lieutenant Commander Anthony Lancelot Henry Dean Coke. He at first thought the aircraft were his lost escort; but then he discerned the large black crosses under their wings. Coke ordered the flotilla to close up so as to concentrate the fire of their Lewis guns; and the aeroplanes, by now eight in number, opened fire with their machine guns. Undismayed, Coke decided to continue with his reconnaissance.

'I was bound to be attacked by other machines whatever I did,'[7] he wrote later, and so a running fight developed which continued for some 30 minutes. The aeroplanes swept up towards the motor boats from astern, firing through their propellers; when they reached the motor boats they rose sharply, and flew back to a position well in the wake of the flotilla. Given that the CMBs were travelling at well over 30 knots and the German seaplanes at around 70 knots, it was surely the fastest action of the war to date. From time to time the German aeroplanes also dropped bombs but none scored a hit.

Around 0800, Coke turned westward with Ameland lighthouse abeam. 'Up to now the flotilla had held its own,' states the *Official History*. 'It had suffered no serious damage and one of the enemy's planes had been seen to come down sharply.'[8] But now the Germans had the sun behind them and four land-based fighter planes, each armed with two guns, had joined the fray. These machines, according to Lieutenant Commander Coke, 'caused more trouble and did more damage than the eight that had appeared previously'.[9] During the next quarter of an hour the coastal motor boats suffered badly, and by 0815 they had practically ceased to fire. In some the guns had jammed; in others the ammunition had been exhausted. The Germans now flew over the boats almost at point blank range. But there was still some devil in the skimmers; with virtually their last rounds *CMB-40* and *CMB-44* peppered one of the German planes so heavily it crashed into the sea.

However, the flotilla was finished. Bullet-riddled, out of ammunition, *CMB-47* on fire, several with engines failing and holed hulls sinking under them, they were out of the fight. The Dutch coast was three or four miles away and *CMB-41* reached the shore where the Dutch authorities impounded her. Royal Netherlands Navy torpedo boats came out and took the disabled *CMB-44* and *48* in tow and interned them. The other three (*CMB-40, 42* and *47*) were set on fire and abandoned by their crews; not one craft made it back to the supporting force. Nor did they ever sight a British aeroplane.

A Sopwith Camel on a lighter being towed behind a destroyer 'at 14 knots'.
(photo; private collection)

Meanwhile, the main body of the Force, stationed off Terschelling, was bothered by the attention of Zeppelin *L-53*, which had almost certainly first alerted the German air crews to the presence of the CMBs. This was the opportunity that 22-year-old Lieutenant Stuart Douglas Culley* RAF and his Sopwith Camel (number N6812) had been waiting for. At 0841, *Redoubt* went to 30 knots and towed the lighter at the end of 600 fathoms of line, with Culley's plane on its 30ft-long wooden platform. He was able to get airborne and begin the long climb up to the airship's high altitude, rising rapidly and by 0930 he was out of sight in the clouds. The Zeppelin remained on station.

At 19,000ft Culley was still below the airship. One gun had frozen up, as had his hands, but ten minutes after he had disappeared into the clouds, those below heard a short rattle of machine-gun fire from the celestial realms. At the maximum height his craft could obtain and with the controls mushy in

---

* Born in Nebraska of an English father and Canadian mother, he had been educated in California and Vermont.

his hands, Culley had stood the Camel on its tail and opened fire. According to the *Official History*, the seabound watchers 'then saw a sheet of flame sweep across the white cloud bank and a shower of splintered metal fall from it. Lieutenant Culley had destroyed his enemy in those upper regions of the air from which neither sea nor land is visible.'[10] Culley had flown unseen to within 300ft of the underside of the Zeppelin and the fire of the Camel's remaining machine gun, using incendiary bullets, had ignited the hydrogen in the gasbag. It crashed into the sea, killing all but one of the nineteen-man crew.

It was on this occasion that Tyrwhitt made a signal which combined his sense of humour with his religious upbringing. As Lieutenant Schofield related it,

A hit by a fighter plane set [the Zeppelin] on fire, whereupon [Tyrwhitt] made a general signal to the force. 'See hymn number 224, last verse'. A scramble to find each ship's navy hymn book revealed the text;

'O happy band of pilgrims,
Look upward to the skies,
Where such a light affliction
Shall win so great a prize!'[11]

Meanwhile, the Camel had stalled and fallen into a spin; by the time Lieutenant Culley recovered it he was faced with the problem of locating the Harwich Force ships. He had no idea where he or they were, so headed for the Dutch coast to get his bearings. His main pressure petrol tank ran dry and he switched to the emergency gravity feed. Below him he saw a Dutch fishing boat and decided to land next to it. As he dived down to the sea, providence came to his rescue and he spotted two destroyers. Culley ditched in the sea next to HMS *Redoubt* and its empty lighter; both he and his aircraft were recovered by noon.

Tyrwhitt was mightily impressed by the young pilot. When Culley boarded the destroyer he was told by its captain, Commander Reginald Vesey Holt, that

he would have to stand on the aft gun platform alone as the whole fleet was going to pass by *Redoubt* in line astern led by *Curacoa* . . . and so it happened, notwithstanding of the danger from submarines, *Redoubt* remained stationary and all the ships of the Harwich Force with decks lined by ship's companies, passed in review, cheering the pilot of the new service who had given them such a display.[12]

Coke and Culley were both honoured with award of the DSO. Coke's citation noted that

Lieutenant Commander Coke, who was Senior Officer of the flotilla, showed great determination, gallantry and courage in continuing his reconnaissance in spite of the presence of the enemy. The Coastal Motor Boats led by Lieutenant Commander Coke fought a very gallant action against superior odds, and continued to do so until all their ammunition was expended or their Lewis guns rendered useless by jambing [sic]' [13]

Tyrwhitt had recommended Culley for the VC and presented him with a cigarette case engraved 'Hymn 224, v7'. But in fact the pilot was given a DSO. His medal citation stated that 'the highest praise is due to Lieutenant Culley for the gallantry and skill which he displayed'. [14]

The Price of Beef

On 15 August, a group of Harwich Force destroyers led by the Thornycroft-built flotilla leader HMS *Spenser* were at the Hook of Holland, tasked with escorting another Beef Trip convoy, this time consisting of two tugs towing lighters. *Retriever* and *Ulleswater* were ordered to be the close escort and at 1130, *Ulleswater* passed between the tugs to take up position to their starboard. As she did so, there was a sudden explosion on her port side, next to the after end of the engine room. She immediately took a list to port. One of the tugs, *Torfrida*, cast off its tow to try to offer aid while the flotilla leader *Scott*, commanded by Captain the Hon William Spencer Leveson-Gower,* closed to assist and was manoeuvring into position when she too was rocked by an explosion aft, which triggered off the after magazine, followed a few seconds later by another detonation amidships. Several observers claimed to have seen torpedo tracks in the water and the remaining destroyers launched a hunt for a U-boat, firing off numerous depth charges without effect.

Ulleswater broke in two in about 15 minutes and both parts then slipped below the waves. *Scott* also sank within 15 minutes of being hit. She had been preparing a tow and Gunner Richard Stephen Charnock was aft supervising; he was injured in the explosions 'but showed a great example of coolness under trying conditions to the rest of the men who with him were cut off from the rest of the ship by flames and steam'. For this he was Mentioned in Despatches. [15]

Five men were killed in *Ulleswater* and twenty-two in *Scott*. The bodies of four of those from *Scott* were later washed up on the Dutch coast and Able Seamen Thomas Morgan and Jesse Mitchell, Chief Stoker Edwin Goodman

---

* Later, William Spencer Leveson-Gower, 4th Earl Granville, Lieutenant Governor of the Isle of Man and Governor of Northern Ireland.

HMS *Ulleswater* sinking, 15 August 1918, by Charles Pears. She was mined amidships. The
destroyer is shown port side on and has been almost cut in half by the explosion. In the
foreground survivors are sitting in a rubber life-ring and other sailors are in the water.
(© Imperial War Museum, Art.IWM ART 1351)

and Ordinary Seaman William Edward Parker were all buried in the cemetery
at Noordwijk.

There was some dispute as to how the ships were actually sunk. The Court
of Enquiry was undecided whether it was mine or torpedo and thought that
a submarine would have to arrive at a firing solution very quickly to have sunk
Ulleswater.[16] After the war, the confusion continued. Dittmar and Colledge
(*British Warships 1914–1919*) recorded them as torpedoed by *U-17*; *British
Warships Lost at Sea* states they were sunk by a submarine. But more recent
scholarship suggests that both were mined in a field laid by *U-71*. Whatever
the cause, twenty-seven sailors died and two valuable ships were sunk, another
sacrifice by the Harwich Force to ensure that food continued to flow to Britain.

End Game

Following the loss of the two destroyers came a quiet period when the Force
did not go to sea as a whole for six weeks. But in September, the Allied armies
on the Western Front stormed the Hindenburg Line and the whole of the
German front line was shaken. A sequence of Allied offensives began with
attacks by American and French armies on 26 September from Rheims to the
Meuse, two British armies at Cambrai a day later, and British, Belgian and
French armies in Flanders on 28 September. Then on 29 September the British
Fourth Army (including the US II Corps) attacked the Hindenburg Line from

Holnon north to Vendhuille while the French First Army assaulted the area from St Quentin to the south. The British Third Army attacked further north and crossed the Canal du Nord at Masnières. In nine days, British, French and US forces crossed the Canal du Nord, broke through the Hindenburg Line and took 36,000 prisoners and 380 guns. German morale was shattered and in combination with the collapse of the Bulgarian front,[*] it seemed to many in the German hierarchy that the end was nigh.

Admiral Scheer determined to bring his destroyers home from their Flanders bases, a plan which was expected at the Admiralty. Tyrwhitt had his ships on standby, in readiness to intercept the enemy destroyers on their route north. Just before 0400 on 30 September, he was ordered out. Two light cruisers and five destroyers were detailed to go to the northern end of the Flanders Bight and sweep towards the Dogger Bank Light Vessel. Two hours later, Tyrwhitt himself sailed with the rest of the Force.

The weather was atrocious with a great gale blowing all day and heavy seas pounding the ships. No enemy vessels were sighted and the Harwich ships had all returned to harbour at 2030. They were no sooner in port than they were ordered out again. *Montrose, Radiant, Thruster, Swallow, Tempest* and *Teazer* all sailed at 1415 on 1 October for the Schouwen Bank and *Canterbury, Dragon* and five destroyers departed at 2100 for Texel on another mission to find the fleeing enemy.

But these dispositions, and those of subsequent days, were in vain. Twenty-eight destroyers escaped between 29 September and the next few days, the majority making their way along the coast of Holland within territorial waters. Five were blown up as they could not sail in time or were under repair. The submarines had left earlier by detachments.[17]

Tyrwhitt blamed the Admiralty for the failure, writing to Keyes that 'we started five hours too late. Their Lordships also made the stupid mistake of not letting the cruisers go alone. We were hampered by the destroyers . . . and they could not keep up. I left them behind but, in any case, I doubt if we should have been within two hours of the Huns.'[18]

On 3 October, the new submarine HMS *L-10*, commissioned in June into the 9th Flotilla and under the command of Lieutenant Alfred Edward Whitehouse, was on patrol in the Heligoland Bight. Why such patrols were still considered necessary by the Admiralty was a moot point, as most of the German destroyers had been withdrawn; but not all. The destroyers SMS *S-34, S-33, V-28* and *V-79* had been sent out on patrol but *S-34* had hit a mine and was stopped, protectively surrounded by her sisters, when the group was spotted by Lieutenant Whitehouse. At periscope depth, he was able to fire one

---

[*] Bulgaria signed an armistice on 29 September.

torpedo, hitting *S-33*, which immediately began to sink. But in firing, *L-10* lost buoyancy control and shot to the surface. Rather than dive again, Whitehouse turned away on the surface and was pursued by the enraged Germans. Repeatedly hit by gunfire, *L-10* sank with all hands, just after 1100. Another submarine and crew were lost.*

The following day, the Force again put out on the intelligence that German U-boats returning from sea were going to be met by minesweepers to take them into the Heligoland Bight. The destroyers were sent to intercept them, with the light cruisers 10 miles away as backup, but nothing was found except a German armed trawler, SMS *Johs Thode*, which was disposed of.

The final Harwich Force lighter operation took place on 24 October. Four flying boats and four Sopwith Camels on lighters were towed out to Terschelling with the intention of luring German seaplanes from Nordeney and Borkum into a trap. But, as so often, the operation had to be abandoned when neither the heavily-laden flying boats nor the Camels were able to take off due the weather and the sea conditions. Three of the Camels broke up on their lighters and some German aircraft appeared, only to be driven off by gunfire from the British ships. This was the last occasion on which the Harwich Force fired its guns in anger.

This operation also marked the end of the experiment. The practical difficulties of conducting lighter operations in the North Sea were now clearly understood, and the frequent abandonment of missions due to a failure to get airborne were wasteful of resources and time. There were also more effective tools available for conducting longer-range bombing, such as the Handley Page O/100 and O/400 'Bloody Paralysers'; or the new aircraft carriers such as HMS *Furious* and *Argus*. But once more, the Harwich Force and its admiral had been at the forefront of a combined arms innovation.

Germany had begun to seek an armistice under its new government of Prince Max of Baden on 5 October and had asked President Woodrow Wilson of the USA to mediate between all parties. One of Wilson's preconditions for so doing was that Germany should end its submarine war. Overriding the objections of Admiral Scheer, now Chief of the Imperial Navy Staff, the German Government made this concession on 20 October. The following day all U-boats at sea were recalled home. The seas became largely free of submarine predators for the first time in over four years.

An enraged Scheer ordered Admiral Hipper, commanding the German High Seas Fleet, to prepare for an attack on the British fleet, utilising the main battlefleet, reinforced by the newly available U-boats released from Flanders. According to orders cut on 24 October this was to include an attack against

---

* Her wreck was only discovered in 2020, off Terschelling.

the Flanders coast by the 2nd Torpedo Boat Flotilla, supported by three light cruisers, and against the Thames Estuary by the 2nd Scouting Group with four light cruisers and the 2nd Torpedo Boat Half-Flotilla. The raid on the Thames and the Flanders coast were scheduled for dawn on 31 October. It was expected that these raids would draw out the British Grand Fleet from Scapa and the encounter between that force and the High Seas Fleet was planned for the afternoon and evening of the same day.

The Harwich Force would have undoubtedly been part of this battle, one that would be fought only for the honour and pride of the Kaiserliche Marine when the war was effectively over, and indeed the Force stood by each day in late October for just such an eventuality. U-boat concentrations and wireless traffic all alerted the Admiralty to the possibility of a major fleet action. Tyrwhitt may well have welcomed the fight, and Keyes certainly would have. But many lives would undoubtedly have been lost.

Fortunately, Scheer's plan did not come to pass. Revolution was in the air within the German fleet. Years of inactivity and poor officer-men relationships had allowed the disease of Bolshevism to infect the crews. The evening of 29 October was marked by unrest and serious acts of indiscipline aboard the German ships, with the men convinced their commanders were intent on sacrificing them in a deliberate attempt to sabotage the Armistice negotiations. Open revolt broke out in many of the battleships and the men refused to follow orders. Hipper saw no alternative to cancelling the operation, which he did on 30 October and ordered the fleet dispersed in the hope of quelling the insurrection. It was a narrow escape for all concerned from what would have been a needless and bloody fight.

On 7 November, a rumour circulated that an Armistice had been signed. This was swiftly denied and the Force was ordered to sea that evening. *Concord* and *Curlew* with eight destroyers slipped at 2300 and spent a day and a half on patrol trying to catch some German steamers, expected to make a dash for home. But they evaded capture by creeping along the Dutch littoral. This was the last patrol undertaken by the Harwich Force off the Dutch coast.

Then on 9 November, when many officers and crews were ashore enjoying some R&R, when the wail of the sirens once more called them back to their ships. Two German cruisers had sortied but turned back at Terschelling; and the Force did not leave harbour. It was a rather feeble denouement.

17

Life in the Harwich Force

What was it like to serve in the Harwich Force?

At Sea

The North Sea weather played a significant part in the Force's success or failure, fog and wind in particular. And it made life at sea very unpleasant.

> We detested the gales and the horrible, short, steep seas which wetted us through and through and made our destroyers uncomfortably skittish. We disliked the snow and the sleet and the ice with which our decks were sometimes covered . . . But above all we hated the fog, cold clammy fogs which dripped from our eyebrows . . . and came down at a few minutes notice to reduce the range of visibility to a few yards.[1]

Destroyers were small, wet ships. The bridge was reached by steep iron ladders, leading to a high perched, circular, canvas-screened structure in which were crowded several ratings, a gun, a chart table, wheel, helmsman and navigating officer. In any sort of sea, the ship rocked giddily to and fro such that descending the bridge ladders became fraught with danger. Progress along the decks was risky and hanging on to the lifelines essential. Spray and waves regularly soaked everybody on deck, including the occupants of the bridge. Commander Dorling wrote that 'going along the upper deck, which was constantly swept by the seas, was an undertaking of no little danger'.[2]

Darkness brought its own kind of misery; 'a queer kind of cold, that wet cold. It made you feel as if the marrow inside your bones was freezing and swelling, swelling until it would burst . . . you have just got to grope along eyes and ears alert, waiting, seeing things'.[3]

It was not a job for those who liked their creature comforts. As a contemporary wrote, 'the commanding officer, who came aboard in immaculate gold lace and spick and span uniform climbs the bridge, sea-booted and with a thick muffler round his throat, wearing a cap and jacket in which he would in no circumstances be seen ashore'. All the rest of the crew followed their skipper's example, both to protect their expensive naval uniforms but also because 'destroyer work tells heavily upon clothes as well as upon the men who wear them'.[4]

In any sort of weather 'the green seas came over everywhere while the ship lurched and tumbled pitched and rolled, wallowed and buried herself without ceasing. The water found its way through our oilskins and down into our sea-boots within a quarter of an hour of leaving harbour. One remained wet . . . for four or five days on end.'[5]

Conditions were spartan. Sheffield-born William H Campbell had attended *Ganges* aged 15 and then joined the light cruiser HMS *Conquest* as a Boy First Class. He vividly recalled his first sea trip in her. 'I spent most of it clinging to the whaler's davits and gazing miserably at the huge white horses and for the most part wondering if I had any insides left.' He also recalled that 'we ate and slept on the mess decks. There was no heating at all and moisture used to roll down the inside of the ship's walls.' However, he didn't find it boring. 'There was always a housey-housey school, cards, reading, writing and swapping family news.'[6]

Whilst on patrol, the destroyer crews remained at action stations. They slept in their duffle coats alongside the guns or torpedo tubes. 'The only consolation was that they received their "Grub and Grog" with reasonable regularity.'[7] And of course, there was the ever-present danger of mines, submarines or enemy destroyers appearing out of the murk, with death and destruction coming from sea or air.

For seamen's food, cooking was done by messes. Two men from each mess were deputed to prepare the food each day, none of whom had any training. When 'cooks to the galley' was piped just before meal time, the sailors whose turn it was for the duty would also go there to draw bread. On board, the cook was aptly named the 'hash slinger'. 'It will be readily understood,' wrote William Spencer, 'what dishes were contrived by amateur cooks, it took some of us all our time to make a fanny full of tea'.[8] Some dishes became favourites because they were simple to prepare. 'Schooner on the Rocks' was a joint of meat in batter which was taken to the galley to cook off. It could only be made, however, if it was the mess's turn for a joint from the butcher. For others, boiled kippers were the best that they could manage. When at action stations, men waited impatiently (and often hungrily) for the arrival of boiling hot thick greasy cocoa for which, since 1832, the navy had a peculiar addiction.

The submariners endured very poor conditions. Because of the limitations of the range of their electric batteries, they left port on the surface, often in the early morning or at night and only submerged when spotted by the enemy or after conducting an attack. The vessels might stay out on patrol for four or five days, with no contact from anyone. There was a complete inability to fulfil basic hygiene requirements so both the submarine crews and the vessels stank. Officers would douse themselves in cologne to mask their own body odour and that of their men. Once ashore, crews were accommodated on the flotilla depot ships, a slightly more convivial existence.

Submerged, the electric batteries could pose a real threat to the crew. The storage battery cells, located under the living spaces, generated gas and a ventilation failure risked explosion, a catastrophic event which would sink the boat. If sea water got into the battery cells, poisonous chlorine gas was generated which choked, incapacitated and sometimes killed the crew.

The often shallow seas in which the submarines had to work also caused discomfort. As Roger Keyes expressed it, 'the short steep seas which accompany westerly gales in the Heligoland Bight made it difficult to keep the conning tower hatches open. There was no rest to be obtained, and even when cruising at a depth of sixty feet, the Submarines were rolling considerably and pumping – i.e. vertically moving – about twenty feet.'[9]

Lieutenant Blacklock, who took command of *E-31* in November 1916, thought that 'it was a lonely and dull job . . . the submarine losses from Harwich were greater in proportion than in any other branch of the service'.[10] When an officer was lost, 'after a certain interval . . . an officer specially detailed for the job would disappear into the cabins of our lost mates and pack up all their belongings. The cabins would be repainted and then another boat would arrive'.[11] But there were compensations. After every second sea patrol, four days leave was awarded.

Ashore
Abstinence
King George V, under pressure from Lloyd George, then Chancellor of the Exchequer, decided to give up alcoholic drink in March 1915 for the duration of the war. He asked his subjects to follow his example and Tyrwhitt, an ardent royalist, decided that not only would he do so but his officers would too.

On 9 April, they all took a last glass of hot grog* and subsequently everybody felt 'pretty fed up'. The gesture was rendered all the harder to bear by Churchill, who never followed his monarch's request for sobriety. When he came aboard Tyrwhitt's flagship two days after this dismal renunciation, the First Lord drank port, wine and brandy and said he saw no reason why not. Churchill rarely rose before noon. He would work late into the night in his office until one in the morning, or lying in bed with his boxes following a decent dinner, and drank a bottle of brandy and an imperial of champagne† every day and wine with his meals to boot; he would have found this alcoholic proscription too much to bear. As for Tyrwhitt, he found abstinence 'a total bore'.[12]

---

* Diluted rum.
† His favourite brand was Pol Roger; an imperial was an obsolete measure of around half a litre.

Nor was the king a paragon of virtue in keeping his pledge. Cider 'was deemed non-alcoholic' and the Prince of Wales reported that 'his father would withdraw after dinner to attend to a small matter of business. This was assumed to be a glass of port'.[13]

The general public suffered too, less than their king or Tyrwhitt and his officers, but they faced limitations. Licencing hours were controlled and in February 1916 new legislation passed under the Defence of the Realm Act restricted opening hours for public houses to noon to 1430 and 1830 to 2130.

Wives

Tyrwhitt had forbidden the presence of his officers' wives and families in Harwich and did not move Angela and their three children to Essex either. He felt their presence, and that of his officers' spouses, would distract all of them from their martial, as opposed to marital, purpose.

His own visits home were brief and rare, and while Angela occasionally came to stay with Commodore Cayley of *Ganges* and his family, Tyrwhitt saw little of her or his offspring. During Christmas 1914 for example, when he returned from the Cuxhaven Raid, he found that 'the whole of my enormous family [was] at Shotley . . . the Cayleys put them up for five nights but I did not see much of them'.[14] This was at Mrs Cayley's insistence for the commodore had instructed his wife not to come to Harwich as 'I expect to be at sea on Christmas Day'. Mrs Cayley had however firmly insisted that 'you [Angela] are to come <u>whether I like it or not</u>'.[15]

In this policy, which followed accepted navy thinking, he took the opposite view to that of his near neighbour, Vice Admiral Reginald Bacon, commanding the Dover Patrol. Bacon thought 'the work of the Patrol was so dangerous, so hard and so incessant that I sincerely desired that whenever the officers and men had a day or two off, those days should be as pleasant as possible, and therefore the more wives and families accumulated at Dover the better I was pleased'.[16]

Late in 1915, Angela Tyrwhitt put her foot down. The family would move to Harwich, they would let their home in Hampshire, and the commodore would have to deal with it. He surrendered on the grounds that they did not live in Dovercourt, a residential suburb of Harwich, which for some reason he had taken a dislike to. 'I do not want to live in Dovercourt for hundreds of reasons,' he averred, 'so please don't think of it.'[17]

In the end they took the lease on an old farmhouse called Nether Hall in Shotley, opposite *Ganges*. Amongst its attractions, it had a tennis court and room for Tyrwhitt to indulge his hobby of woodwork, making hen coops, huts, miniature furniture and the like. He never stayed there overnight though. Whenever he was in harbour, he would come ashore at 1500 and go home, but leave at night to sleep in his ship.

Nether Hall in a modern photograph. (Photo; David Whittle/Harwich Society)

Tyrwhitt did use the tennis court, but preferred singles; he was too competitive to play with a partner. He also birds-nested with Captain Hubert Lynes of *Penelope*, a noted ornithologist and afterwards a gold medal winner at the Royal Ornithological Society, and walked long and vigorously with Barry Domvile.

The commodore's yielding to domesticity meant that the prohibition on wives in Harwich had to be abandoned; but in fact it had been widely obeyed only in the breach. Submariner Ronald Blacklock recalled that 'a good many of the wives lived in Dovercourt nearby and they often came on board [the depot ship] for dinner and to watch the cinema. A few of the officers' wives lived in the Parkeston Hotel.'[18] And Nether Hall 'was always at home for tea on Sundays to all who cared to drop in and were free to do so'.[19]

Entertainment

The sailors at Harwich made a lot of their own entertainment. The submarine depot ships *Maidstone* and *Dido* staged concerts and amateur dramatic productions; the destroyer depot ship *Woolwich* was also prominent in the thespian arts. Lieutenant Blacklock thought that 'life in the harbour at Parkeston Quay was very cheerful. We were allowed on shore in the afternoon for games and exercise but all leave ended at 1900.'[20]

Of course, this sort of self-made entertainment was often subject to the exigencies of war. On St Patrick's Day 1916, Harold Hewitt in HMS *Meteor*

The Alexandra Hotel, a favourite haunt for dancing and socialising.
(Photo; David Whittle/Harwich Society)

recorded in his dairy that 'we were organising a ship's concert but instead we are ordered to sea. We joined up with the minesweepers and cruised around all night. Dark as the inside of a cow . . . I'd like to meet the bloke who said "join the navy and see life".'[21]

On occasion, professional companies would visit to perform. Sometime in 1915, Tyrwhitt 'dined with Waistell and then went to see some private theatricals given on Parkston Quay. Very good they were too. Quite a good piece and pretty near the knuckle at times, with unlimited means of being funny.'[22]

The Alexandra Hotel at Dovercourt, opened in 1904 and once patronised by King Edward VII, overlooked the quay from just above the Marine Parade and was a favourite haunt for officers ashore. Dances were held there every Saturday afternoon between 1400 and 1700. Concerts in the hotel's spacious ballroom were also popular. And the Quay Pavilion, previously a Swiss chalet style wooden dining room annexe to the adjacent Great Eastern Hotel, became a canteen with entertainment facilities and a bar for naval personnel.

For those of a more rugged bent, there were outdoor sports; cricket, rugby, football, hockey (Domvile played centre-forward for the Harwich Force XI), tennis and nine-hole golf. Matches were played inter-ship or against the various army units in the area. For those who liked it there was also croquet and boxing. Some officers purchased yachts or other small vessels and sailed them on the rivers.

Lieutenant Stephen King-Hall 'bought a horse, and I found stables in the establishment. In fact, it would be difficult to say what we could not find in

Parkeston. I could continue for pages describing the piggeries, the duckeries, the heneries, the Petty Officers' Club, the periscope room, the wet canteen, the dry canteen, the barber's shop, etc.'[23]

In some ways it was a strange sort of existence, for immediately over the harbour wall, next to where they took their pleasures, was the naval 'front line', a place where enemy warships or aircraft might emerge from the horizon at any moment. Captain Domvile reported one such experience when, one day at 1600, returning to Felixstowe where he and his wife lived, he found a great flap on at the seaplane base. 'I was informed that there were six German seaplanes sitting on the water waiting for a fight and that our Porte flying boats were off to take up the challenge . . . three hours later our machines were just back from a regular dog fight with the Germans.'[24]

Parliament had passed the Cinematography Act in 1909 which specified structural fire precautions for cinemas and caused a spurt of new

The Electric Palace in Harwich, photographed in 2021 after restoration. (Author's collection)

establishments intended to satisfy the new regulations. One such was Harwich's 'Electric Palace', one of the earliest to be designed (by H R Hooper of Ipswich), and built for Charles Thurston, a well-known East Anglian showman. This new attraction was opened by the mayor in November 1911, and transformed King's Quay Street into the centre for Harwich nightlife. It was immediately successful and the introduction of the Harwich Force ensured its continued success as the cinema, and the area around it, became a haunt for sailors on day leave.

There was a great camaraderie in the Force. Lieutenant Schofield of the destroyer *Manly* thought that

> we were all immensely proud of being members of the Harwich Force and the only note of discord curiously enough arose between the destroyer chaps and the submariners. I never knew quite why but there was a lot of feeling between us and we had really little to do [with them]. They kept much to themselves and we kept to ourselves. The cruisers of course were much lower down the harbour and anchored off Harwich so we didn't naturally see so much of them . . . but we knew each other very well and we used to foregather in each other's ships and that sort of thing in harbour.[25]

The submariners probably felt that they were a slightly underappreciated minority. Ronald Blacklock believed that 'the senior officers . . . thought that the submarine was a completely caddish way of behaving in warfare and disapproved of it altogether and most of them there disapproved of the officers in the submarine and thought that they were an ill disciplined and lousy lot'.[26] And both factions saw themselves as a slightly maverick elite. Author and Harwich submariner Lieutenant William Guy Carr RNR felt that 'the big ships' crews looked down on them with contempt . . . and nicknamed the officers and men serving in them "The Trade"'.[27]

But submariners were appreciated by at least one famous visitor. The author and poet Rudyard Kipling visited Harwich several times during 1915 and 1916 and 'his closest contacts with fighting men were made in ships of the Royal Navy'.[28] In particular he befriended the ship's company of *Maidstone*, depot ship for the 8th Submarine Flotilla. Indeed, he was even induced to go down in a submarine at Harwich which 'must have been one of the things he did for England, since he suffered from claustrophobia, but that would no doubt have heightened his admiration for the submariners'.[29]

Submarines, the second section of his collection of naval poems *The Fringes of the Fleet*, was largely derived from visits to Harwich, where Kipling had 'a close liaison with the 8th Submarine Flotilla and their depot ship, HMS

Maidstone.[30] Moreover, he wrote several pieces for *Maidstone*'s in-house magazine, initially called the *Maidstone Muckrag* and then the *Maidstone Magazine*. One of them, *L'Envoi*,* appeared nowhere else during the course of the war. It runs;

> Even the *Maidstone Magazine*
> For whom my ribald rhymes are made,
> Strikes out far more than it sticks in.
> That is the custom of 'The Trade.'

The fourth and fifth lines of the fourth verse of the poem, also, as originally conceived were;

> No journal prints the yarns they spin
> Above the bitters and the gin.

Which was afterwards altered to;

> 'No journal prints the yarns they spin
> (The Censor would not let it in).'[31]

A second poem, *Farewell and Adieu to you, Harwich Ladies*, was also first prepared for *Maidstone*'s enjoyment and was preceded in the magazine by the statement 'lines written by our recent visitor, Mr Rudyard Kipling, on a half-sheet of notepaper, after hearing of the experience of a British submarine in a German minefield. Mr Kipling has most kindly promised us an article for this magazine at an early date.'[32] As eventually widely published, the poem ends with the line 'From here to Cuxhaven it's go as you please'.

Sports Days
The Harwich Force had an annual sports day. In 1917, for example, the flagship HMS *Centaur*'s relay race team were the champions that year. Tyrwhitt took a close personal interest in these events. At the end of August 1916, he wrote to Rear Admiral de Robeck, commanding the 3rd Battle Squadron, asking for one of his destroyers back; 'we are holding an athletic sports [*sic*] on Tuesday and Thursday and I particularly want *Melpomene* as she has a wonderful tug of war team.'[33] Tyrwhitt even went as far as to participate himself, entering and winning (after careful training) a veterans' race.

Felixstowe RNAS station also had regular sports days. On Saturday 28 July

---

* A title he had also used in 1886.

Harwich Force Sports Day in 1916. (© National Maritime Museum N22666)

1917, a 'Station Sports' was held, with their prized Pipe Band in attendance, to commence at 1315 with Wing Commander J C Porte, the station commander, presenting the prizes. The programme (price one pence) promised that the next issue of *The Wing*, the station in-house magazine, would feature reportage and photographs of the event for the bargain price of threepence.

Pets and Comforts

Just about every warship in the Royal Navy had an animal mascot and a number of pets aboard. Not only did they provide undemanding companionship, cats and dogs at least could earn their keep by hunting the mice and rats which were rife on most warships.

Reginald Tyrwhitt loved cats. So it was no surprise that, in the period of uncertainty before the war actually started, he found himself the inadvertent owner of a small black female kitten. This stayed with him and produced several progenies which he distributed amongst his friends including, it has been suggested, Winston Churchill.[34] After her first litter, he wrote to his children that the kittens 'have been in their box close to my fire ever since'.[35] And a little later, he confided that 'one of my little moggies has just climbed up my leg and is walking about on my writing'.[36] Such was his love of the creatures that, on 11 February 1916 when he was the last man to leave the stricken *Arethusa*, Tyrwhitt returned to his flagship to look for his cat, but failed to find her. One of the offspring succeeded his mother as 'Admiral's Cat'. It is understandable that the driven and quick-tempered Tyrwhitt should appreciate feline company. Cats are never anxious, in the absence of any direct threat. Their default option is happiness, living in the present, contentedly purring. It would be balm to his soul.

Amongst the other ships, *Laforey* had a wire-haired terrier, *Conquest* had a black and white terrier and *Aurora* had a tame magpie. *Liberty*'s pet nearly caused the loss of the ship; on 19 June 1915 she stopped to rescue the destroyer's dog, which had fallen overboard, and was bombed by a German seaplane resulting in a near miss. Quite how her captain, Lieutenant Commander Reginald Becher Caldwell Hutchinson, explained this to Tyrwhitt is lost to history.

Another, non-animal, form of succour for Tyrwhitt was the community of nuns to which his sister Kitty belonged. They were intensely patriotic and prayed for Tyrwhitt and his ships daily, sent him frequent votive offerings to pass on to the likes of Jellicoe, and knitted many small comforts such as socks and scarves for the men.

Hospitals at Harwich

As noted in Chapter 1, the Great Eastern Hotel and several other large buildings in Harwich were taken over for medical use. The former Great Eastern was known as the Garrison Military Hospital and provided beds for six officers and 121 other ranks. These may not have come from Harwich itself, for patients were referred in from other part of Essex too. All the furniture in the hotel was replaced with hospital beds.

The Dovercourt Military Hospital was a so-called 'section' establishment and was able to take patients directly from disembarkment, but only five officers and 115 other ranks. A large house, Cliff Hall, became a convalescent home for servicemen and the Harwich Borough Isolation Hospital was used to care for soldiers and sailors with infectious diseases. Finally, a beautiful house called 'The Grange', built only in 1911 and in possession of a lodge, formal gardens, large ponds, an orchard and kitchen garden, was commandeered by the government from the two Skinner* family sisters who owned it and also used for the convalescence of the injured.

The medical facilities in HMS *Ganges* at Shotley had been extended in 1913 and wounded sailors were often first placed there. There was also a cemetery at St Mary's Church, which filled during the war with the graves of 201 British

---

* The family wealth came from the footwear industry.

The Great Eastern Hotel in use as a hospital with the nursing staff posing at the entrance.
(Photo; David Whittle/Harwich Society)

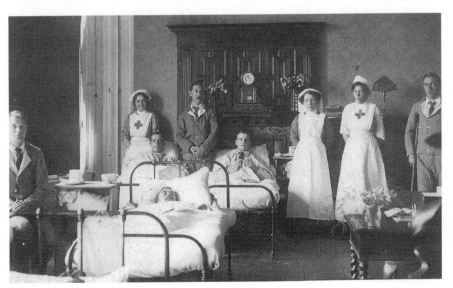

Patients and nurses in the Great Eastern Hotel when it was in use as a Harwich hospital.
(Photo; David Whittle/Harwich Society)

and Commonwealth sailors (including eight unidentified) from the Harwich patrols, who have their last memorial there. There are also thirteen German burials (one unidentified), lying side by side with their quondam enemies.

A special memorial and enclosure were set aside for the Harwich submariners, where the graves include those of men from *C-16*, *E-4* and *E-14*. The funeral processions up the hill from *Ganges*, via Frog Alley, to the roughcast Church with views out over the estuarial waters was a regular and surely deeply moving sight.

And, of course, death could be unexpected and not as a result of war at all. Lieutenant Commander Henry Raymond Clifton-Mogg was captain of HMS *Milne*. He died of double pneumonia in Shotley Sick Quarters on 2 November, 1915, aged 32. Born in Weston super Mare, educated at Haileybury College, he married in Kent in 1911, died in Essex four years later and was buried there. His wife Gladys was with him at the end.

The Submariners war memorial at St Mary's Church, Shotley. The inscription reads; 'There is but one task for all, one life for each to give; Who stands if freedoms fall? Who dies if England lives?' (photo: Author's collection)

Internment

Apart from the obvious risks of death or injury, for which the Harwich hospitals were increasingly equipped and experienced to deal with, for the submariners there was the added disagreeable possibility of internment. According to international law, soldiers and sailors of the warring nations who entered a neutral country were liable to be interned for the duration of the war. Denmark and the Netherlands were neutral and both the Dutch and (to a lesser extent) Danish coasts were a regular part of the Harwich Force's patrol area.

Destroyers or cruisers had ships' boats or life rafts and often sailed in company. But the Harwich submarines were lone hunters, and carried no means of self-salvation. If a boat was crippled or sunk on a foreign shore, then imprisonment or internment would surely follow. On the Dutch coast, the Netherlands government was intent on playing its neutrality strictly by the rules and the Danes behaved in a similar fashion. Neither wished to give Germany any reason to invade them across their common border.

On 17 August 1915, one of three submarines sent from the 8th Submarine Flotilla at Harwich to reinforce the British effort in the Baltic, *E-13* (Lieutenant Commander Geoffrey Layton), ran aground at Saltholm in Danish waters. Given their concern to remain strictly neutral, the Danes played by the letter of international law. The Danish gunboat *Narhvalen* arrived on the scene at 0500 and gave Layton the statutory 24 hours to exit their territory or suffer internment. Despite pumping out the tanks and trying to work their way free, the submarine remained grounded in only 10ft of water. There was no chance of getting her off before the deadline.

Next, the German navy took a hand when the torpedo boat *G-132* hove into view, soon to be joined by *G-134*. Three more Danish warships, *Støren*, *Sbaekhuggeren* and *Tumleren*, also arrived. The submarine's crew had by now given up on trying to re-float her off and were resting on the deck casing. Receiving their orders directly from Berlin, the German vessels raised the flag signal 'Abandon ship immediately' and launched a torpedo, machine-gun and shellfire attack on the helpless submarine. Desperate to remain neutral, and despite this taking place in their national waters, the Danish warships did not engage the German vessels. Layton ordered his men to abandon ship as *E-13* was turned into an inferno of exploding ammunition and escaping chlorine gas (from the batteries) but still the Germans fired at the men in the water. This was finally too much for the Danish ships and two of them placed themselves in the line of fire causing the Germans to turn away, chased out of Danish waters by a third. Fifteen British sailors died in the assault; in neutral waters, watched by a neutral navy. Another fifteen survived and were interned.

The incident caused outrage in Britain and Denmark as an overt and serious breach of international law. Danish newspapers published indignant articles protesting at the Germans' violation of Danish neutrality and in London, *The Times* of 21 August stated that 'the unjustifiable slaughter of the men of the *E-13* is one more notch in the long score we have to settle with the homicidal brood of Prussia'. The Germans eventually offered a grudging apology to Denmark.

Lieutenant Commander Layton initially gave his word that no one would escape from Danish internment so that all fifteen survivors had, in the circumstances, a relatively free life in the few first weeks. This parole could be terminated by either party with three days' notice. The men could move within a radius of 10 miles from Copenhagen, and there were a few other minor restrictions. As a result, the internees could accept social invitations, as long as they were in the Copenhagen area. But after 24 days Layton did not renew his parole and on 29 October he escaped to Norway, along with his first officer, returning to England to continue the war.

This led to harsher conditions for the remaining sailors and eventually the interned crewmen were sent to a camp at Aarhus on 22 February 1916, where they remained pent up until the armistice. They were latterly kept company by three Sopwith Camel pilots, who had attempted to attack a Zeppelin base at Tondern in a raid on 19 July 1918. Seven Camels from the aircraft carrier HMS *Furious* bombed the base, hitting two of the three airship hangars.

In the case of the Netherlands, many of the initial British detainees were RNVR men from the 1st Royal Naval Brigade, egregiously sent by Churchill to Antwerp in 1914. It was a disaster. The Naval Brigade went into action in the outskirts of the city in the small hours of 6 October. By the early evening of the 8th, orders were given for them to retire from the city. In the confusion of the withdrawal most of the 1st Brigade, the Hawke, Benbow and Collingwood Battalions – 1,500 men in total – crossed the Dutch frontier and were interned at Groningen for the rest of the war; a further 1,000 men were captured by the Germans. Only the Drake Battalion got away, having left Antwerp early. On 10 October the city surrendered.

The regime at Groningen was quite mild and allowed for trips into the city, provided that the internee had given his parole not to escape. But if parole was not given, harsher terms were applied. All the Royal Navy internees were put in a community of wooden barracks called the Engelse Kamp – 'English Camp' – and the British sailors quickly came up with their own name for their accommodation; they called it HMS *Timbertown*.

The crew of the Harwich 8th Submarine Flotilla's *E-17* passed into internment at the hands of the Dutch at the beginning of 1916. Lieutenant Commander J R Guy Moncreiffe[*] and his men departed Harwich for patrol

---

[*] From 1931, Commander (rtd) Sir John Robert Guy Moncreiffe of That Ilk, 9th Baronet.

duty on 5 January. The following morning, at 0100 the officer of the watch, Lieutenant Peploe, suddenly observed a white streak directly ahead. He ordered the helm over but the boat struck hard and grounded twice on a hidden shoal. Huge rollers from astern lifted up the submarine and flung it down again with a crash; one large wave washed Moncreiffe over the side and he was lucky to struggle back on board. Eventually, they manged to free the submarine but heading seawards immediately ran onto another part of the shoal, where the vessel turned broadside on and was repeatedly thrown against the rocks. For two hours the crew tried to get free while water filled the boat and started an electrical fire. The rudder was torn off, the propeller shafts were bent, the hull was leaking and the ballast tanks holed. As dawn broke, Moncreiffe could make out that they were north of the island of Texel. He was also able to see a cruiser and it seemed to be training its guns on them, an act which he took to be that of an enemy. Despite the condition of the boat, he ordered a dive; she went right to the bottom and then bounced up again, whilst waves of water rolled inside the boat and washed men from their stations. As there was no alternative but to re-surface, Moncreiffe directed the torpedo tubes to be loaded, determined to go out in a blaze of glory. But their persecutor turned out to be a Dutch training ship, *Noord Brabant*; the guns he had seen moving had been part of a training exercise.

The Dutch captain took them off and *E-17* sank later that morning. But now what would happen to them? Moncreiffe and his officers were interviewed and then told that they would be interned under the terms of the Tenth Hague Convention of 1907. Moncreiffe protested vigorously, emphasising that he could have saved his vessel if the Dutch cruiser had not appeared and behaved in what appeared to be a hostile manner. On 8 January, the *Portsmouth Evening News* reported that

a message in the *Nieuws van den Dag* from Nieuwdier explains how the British submarine was lost. When off the North Hinder the vessel got out of her course, and running aground on the Haaksgrond Bank, sprang a leak. According to the *Handelsblad*, the submarine was not sighted by the cruiser *Noord Brabant* until she had been ten hours in trouble. The crew are at present in the naval barracks at Willemsoord awaiting the decision of the Dutch government as to whether they shall be interned or not.

And then the newspapers announced that

the Dutch Government has decided to intern the crew of the *E-17*, the submarine accidentally sunk off Northern Holland last week. The thirty-two men of the crew have been conveyed to Groningen, where they have joined their 1,600 comrades of the Royal Naval Division, who gave them a rousing reception. The submarine's officers were taken to the fortress of Wierieckeschans, as they are not on parole.[37]

Moncreiffe continued to protest. In September 1917, he even gave his parole and took special leave in London to talk to both the Foreign Office and the Admiralty about the injustice of the situation. Eventually, the Dutch convened a commission to reinvestigate the decision to intern. It was to commence sitting on 18 November 1918; but the Armistice of the 11th meant that the whole matter was dropped. Internment was just another risk of 'The Trade'.

18

The Auxiliary Force

Harwich was not only home to the Harwich Striking Force and the submarines; it also hosted a section of the Auxiliary Force. This was a heterogeneous collection of civilian vessels; private yachts, fishing vessels – trawlers, drifters, even whalers – paddle steamer ferries and packet boats, motor boats and launches. Basically, anything that could float and carry a weapon. They were acquired by the Admiralty – through hire arrangements, requisition or voluntary loan – and used for a range of purposes which included anti-submarine patrols, minesweeping, boom defence and net management.

The vast majority of the force was comprised of fishing vessels, ordinary trawlers and drifters of which some 1,500 of each type served in the Royal Naval Auxiliary during the course of the war. Trawlers and drifters taken up by the Admiralty in time of need usually came complete with their pre-existing crews. Skippers were given warrant officer rank. Crewmen signed on under a T-124 agreement whereby they consented to serve under Admiralty rules (specifically it bound them to the Naval Discipline Act) in any commissioned vessel but retained certain aspects of their civilian pay and benefits. The ship's complement was supplemented by the addition of a signals rating and/or W/T operator and sometimes a regular navy sub lieutenant or other officer. Petty officers from the Royal Fleet Reserve (RFR*) were also recruited for service in trawlers; they were intended to act as third in command and offer advice on 'proper' naval signalling, record-keeping and other procedures. Additionally, annual courses for officers on the retired and emergency lists, provisionally assigned to unit-command of minesweepers, were run in the immediate pre-war years.

Trawlers taken into the RN initially either joined what became known as the Auxiliary Patrol or the Minesweeping Service. At first all the requisitioned trawlers were sent to Lowestoft for conversion to naval vessels. Most also needed basic equipment such as stays and a general refit. Later more ports became capable of the work. Then they would sally forth looking for U-boats, or other enemy vessels, and mines

---

* Founded in 1905, initially to provide civilian-manned coaling ships for the fleet in home waters or abroad, it was a force drawn from former naval ratings and petty officers who, after completing their contractual service with the Royal Navy, were liable to recall in times of emergency. The liability lasted for a specified number of years after leaving active service in the navy.

At the outbreak of war, the defence of the coastline of Britain was the responsibility of the Admiral of Patrols. Under his aegis were twenty-seven patrol areas, each in the charge of a senior naval officer, often a 'dug out' (a retired senior officer recalled to duty) with a shore base. A Senior Naval Officer (SNO) in each port exercised local command. At Harwich, Commodore George Cayley became SNO on 3 September 1914. Cayley added this responsibility to his duties at HMS *Ganges*. He was further appointed Commodore-in-Charge, Harwich, as of 10 March 1915.[1] His brother Henry (another 'dug out' who had retired from the navy in 1904) commanded the minesweeping section under him. The Harwich patrol area (known as Harwich Local Area) was effectively a sub-section of Patrol Area X, as was the Nore Local Area. Area XI, the next south, was centred on Dover and The Downs.

At the outset of war, there were intended to be six minesweeping trawlers at Harwich. Tyrwhitt's orders dated 2 August 1914 directed his captains that 'six trawlers are allotted to the port of Harwich for minesweeping duties. On outbreak of war (if ready for service) these will commence sweeping at dawn daily.' The areas to be swept were defined as being from the entrance to the harbour to the Cork Light Vessel; from Ship Wash Light Vessel to Cork Light Vessel; and from the South Shipwash Buoy to the Cork Light Vessel. 'These are the channels to be used by HM ships entering Harwich.'[2]

By 1 January 1915, there were a total of twenty-three auxiliary vessels based at Harwich. And at the beginning of 1917, this had grown to sixty-nine and a year later seventy-three. Armed trawlers and drifters made up the majority of the resources (see also Appendix 2). Patrol trawlers were armed with a 6pdr gun, later upgraded to a 12pdr, and sent out to hunt submarines in patrol units of four to six boats under an RN or RNR officer in overall command. They were hampered by the fact that, generally, a U-boat was faster underwater than a trawler on the surface!

Those vessels intended for minesweeping duties on the eastern coast of Britain 'belonged' to the Minesweeping Division, headed from 4 September 1914 by Rear Admiral Edward Francis Benedict (Ned) Charlton, as Admiral of Minesweepers, with his flag in the hired yacht *Zarefah* (ex *Maretanza V*). By 1915, command of the patrol forces passed to the local admiral; in the case of Harwich that meant The Nore, under Admiral Sir George Callaghan. The minesweepers were locally organised under a SNO, known as the Port Minesweeping Officer (PMSO). The Admiralty believed that 'trawlers have shown themselves to be peculiarly suitable for minesweeping by reason of the powerful steam winches they carry and their seaworthy qualities, and the fact that they are available in large quantities'.[3] They used the standard British sweeping system, the A-sweep, in which a single steel wire was towed between two parallel vessels. In trawlers, the sweeps were run through gallows mounted aft, originally intended for dragging fishing nets.

By 1916, the minelaying activities of the Germans, particularly by their *UC*-type submarines, led to a change of role for the Harwich auxiliaries. 'In 1916 it became apparent that the minesweeping force was not strong enough to cope with the large number of enemy mines laid in the area. Consequently, the patrol trawlers were converted into minesweeping trawlers.'[4] For Commander Taprell Dorlin, 'one felt compelled to give the enemy full marks for his submarine minelaying. The *UC* boats from Zeebrugge used to plant their detestable eggs in the very approaches to Harwich harbour with uncanny prescience.'[5] He believed that mines had become a particular bugbear by 1916; 'the whole area between Orford Ness and the North Foreland soon became an ocean graveyard. Our chart became spotted with the little red ink symbols denoting sunken ships.'[6] And submariner William Guy Carr felt that the mines 'were thicker than peas in pea soup'.[7]

By 1917, Admiral Jellicoe thought that

> by far the greater proportion of mines swept up were laid in Area X, i.e. the Nore, Harwich and Lowestoft area. This part of the coast was nearest to the German submarine base at Zeebrugge, and as the greater part of the east coast traffic passed through the area it naturally came in for a great deal of minelaying attention. Out of some 2,400 mines swept up in the first half of 1917, over 800 came from Area X alone. The largest number of casualties to merchant ships from mines during this same period also occurred in Area X.[8]

It is no surprise that the Harwich Force itself gained purpose-built minesweepers in early 1918 (see Chapter 15).

At Harwich, in the first five months of 1917 the Germans made a major attempt to close the access to the port by mining, as well as using mines to disrupt the passage of mercantile traffic through the adjacent War Channel. Harwich auxiliary minesweepers destroyed 'a staggering total of 188 mines in the area; eighty-four of these alone were eliminated in the month of March'. In April the number cleared was even higher at 108, 'many of which were found in five separate fields distributed along the War Channel'.[9] At least two minesweepers were lost in this burst of activity and the sweepers were so stretched that drifters were called in and equipped with a newly-designed lighter serrated wire sweep which was more suited to their limited capabilities.

German records revealed that during 1916 and 1917 they had laid some 2,450 mines off the coastline of Harwich and Lowestoft, of which 2,084 were cleared up by the local minesweepers. Off Harwich alone, in the section of the

War Channel that became the exclusive responsibility of the Harwich sweepers from March 1917, 680 mines were laid in a 19-mile fairway. Of these, 468 were sown within two miles of Shipwash Shoal.[10]

Perhaps unsurprisingly, ships were mined and wrecked off Harwich with monotonous regularity, despite the attentions of the sweepers. This meant that the auxiliaries were also involved in rescuing passengers from sinking vessels. From August 1914 to December 1917, a remarkable '1,065 men, women and children had been plucked from the seas by the port's minesweepers'.[11]

During 1918 there was no respite for the Harwich sweeping forces. Twenty mines were destroyed in January and the following month fifty-four were discovered near the Shipwash Light Vessel. Three steamers (the British *Coalgas* and *Estrella* and the Norwegian *Tusnastabb*) were sunk on 5 March alone, all within 10 minutes of each other. In April fifty-one mines were swept up and two more minesweepers lost, the requisitioned British-built Belgian trawler *Numitor* (mined by *UC-4* with five dead) on the 20th, and on the 25th the railway steamer *St Seiriol* (in the same field as *Numitor*, twelve men lost) – the latter of which had destroyed more mines than any other British vessel at the port. In May and June, another twenty-nine mines were dealt with but then the German attentions turned elsewhere and the capture of Ostend and Zeebrugge in mid-October, meant that the minelaying submarines lost their base, reducing their activity at Harwich to almost nothing.

British North Sea mining was even more intense than German. By the end of the war, whereas the Germans had laid 22,067 mines in the North Sea and a total of 43,646 in all areas, the British laid 112,354 and 128,652 respectively.[12]

Minesweeping at Harwich was particularly dangerous because of the high tidal range which meant it was dangerous to sweep at low tide. However, sweeping was best undertaken in daylight, so the risks had to be accepted. Later in the war, motor launches (MLs) were used in such shallow waters when the weather was calm. The MLs were 'admirably suited for exploring suspected minefields and the sinking of mines both above and below water. They were also employed for patrol work and sometimes for light mine sweeping operations.'[13] They were invariably crewed by RNVR officers, men from all walks of life who before the war had an interest in the sea.

Originally driven by petrol engines, the MLs had an alarming tendency to catch fire, and *ML-19* was destroyed in such fashion at Harwich on 31 January 1916. By the middle of the year, they had been converted to use one part petrol to two parts paraffin to try to mitigate this risk.

Apart from mining, the Royal Navy had a peculiar obsession with nets to catch or obstruct submarines. Indicator nets carried flares which would ignite if a U-boat snared them and indicate its presence to potential attackers on the

Two depictions of the versatile motor launch type, *ML-22*, and another ML being hoisted into the water (drawn by Lieutenant Geoffrey Stephen Allfree RNVR). MLs were the brainchild of the American Elco Company of Bayonne New Jersey. They were twin engined, much faster than a trawler (at ~19 knots), just about seaworthy (they were wet ships and rolled a lot), armed with one 3pdr gun (and Type D depth charges when available) plus machine guns and carrying a crew of nine or ten, two officers, two engineers and five or six deckhands. Allfree died in September 1918 when *ML-247* grounded in a gale and blew up. (Author's collection)

surface. Mined nets became common during 1916, whereby a U-boat entangled in one would detonate small bombs which would be drawn onto its body. The nets at Harwich were used to protect harbour entrances or bays where U-boats might lurk and the job of laying and maintaining them was the role of the drifters. Harbours were also protected by booms and the opening and closing of these was often assigned to trawlers converted for boom management.

A Dangerous Occupation

Minesweeping and patrol work in the war was inherently dangerous and difficult. In particular, hunting mines with only the mark one eyeball as search technology, of necessity operating in mined waters, and using craft not specifically designed for the purpose, all made for a heady brew of risk. Many ships and men paid the ultimate price and Harwich-based vessels were not excluded.

On 6 July 1915, the *Portsmouth Evening News* reported a Lloyd's Harwich message: 'the Norwegian steamer *Peik*, from Cherbourg for Warkworth, in ballast, when abreast of the Sunk Light Vessel, at 1000, was torpedoed, and the vessel foundered in five minutes. The crew left in one of the boats, and were afterwards picked up and landed at Harwich.'

Two weeks later, the armed patrol yacht *Rhiannon*, Harwich-based but sent to patrol in the Thames Estuary, was in company with the trawler *Strathspey*. *Rhiannon* had been the private steam yacht of Thomas Evelyn Scott-Ellis, 8th Baron Howard de Walden, 4th Baron Seaford, landowner, writer, patron of the arts and power boat racer in the 1908 Olympics. After succeeding to his family titles in 1899, Lord Howard de Walden received his inherited estates when he came of age in 1901. These included a large part of Marylebone and earned him the title of 'Britain's wealthiest bachelor'.

Taken up by the navy in 1914, *Rhiannon* was fitted with two 3pdr guns and became part of the Harwich auxiliary patrol. On 20 July 1915, she was sailing towards the wreck of the *Peik* when at 1040 there was a large explosion under her bows. She had hit a mine. The forepart was blown away but the aft section floated for some time before sinking. Five men died, including her captain Lieutenant Commander George William Wellburn RNR.

The area had been swept for mines after the loss of the Norwegian ship and the Admiralty became concerned that the *Peik* might have been a German decoy which was now releasing mines on a time delay. Equally, her insurers, Bowring's Insurance Agency and Lloyd's of London, seemed to think that she may have been deliberately scuttled.[14]

The following day, the Harwich armed patrol trawler *Briton*, once of Aberdeen, was mined in the same place whilst acting as outer guard for a group of minesweepers. Skipper Peter Christie and ten men died with only three survivors. All three vessels had in fact been mined in a field laid on *UC-3* on 5 July, which had not been detected in the subsequent clearance operation. Christie and Seaman Albert Ward RNR were interred at Shotley St Mary's, as were 50-year-old Cook Alexander Wilson MMR and Leading Seaman Richard Harvey RNR from *Rhiannon*.

Paddle steamers were used for minesweeping because they had a shallow draught, usually around 8–9ft, compared to 13–14ft for a trawler. But this did not always protect them from harm. The *Duchess of Hamilton* was a paddler built in 1890 for the Caledonian Steam Packet Co Ltd of Glasgow. She had been designed to ferry holidaymakers to the Isle of Arran, but in November 1915 was working as a minesweeper, number 933, out of Harwich. On the 29th she hit a mine laid by *UC-3* and sank near the Galloper Lightship. Nine men lost their lives.

Oberleutnant zur See Erwin Wassner and *UC-3* claimed another paddle steamer victim just a month later. On 21 December, *Lady Ismay* was one of seven paddle minesweepers which departed Harwich that morning to sweep to the southwest of the harbour. Visibility was poor and at noon the group was ordered back to port; but only three boats received the signal. *Lady Ismay* continued until slipping sweeps at 1500. The four remaining ships headed for the Longsand Light Vessel as a navigation mark. Three passed to starboard, but *Lady Ismay* was forced by the tide to pass on the port side, where she hit one of *UC-3*'s mines and sank like a stone. Nineteen sailors were killed, including 29-year-old Seaman Leonard Bennett of the Newfoundland RNR, who had come a long way to die in the North Sea.

A third Harwich paddler was lost on 20 July 1917. Built in 1895, the *Queen of the North* was operated by the Blackpool Passenger Steamboat Company as an excursion steamer until 29 March 1916, when the Admiralty requisitioned her as a minesweeper. She was sunk by a mine set by *UC-4* off Orford Ness; twenty-nine men were lost, including another Newfoundlander, William Freake, aged just 19.

But the bulk of the minesweeping work was done by the fishing vessels. During the course of the conflict, a total of 246 hired and eighteen Admiralty-built trawlers were destroyed, together with 130 hired drifters, representing a total of 71,828 gross tons.[15] Additionally two whalers were sunk. The worst year for sinkings was 1917, the year of the greatest German U-boat and mining efforts, when ninety-one Admiralty and hired trawlers together with forty-two hired drifters were lost. Harwich suffered its share of loss, amongst which the following four examples might be taken to speak for the whole.

Japan was a steam trawler built in 1904 by Cochrane's which in peacetime fished out of Grimsby. In the afternoon of 16 August 1915, she was at sea with

Touchstone, sweeping at the southern end of the Shipwash Shoal, off Felixstowe. Suddenly, a mine was observed on the surface, fouled in the sweep. *Japan* was the winching boat, heaving the cable in. By the time they had stopped the winch, the mine was only three yards away from the boat. Desperate attempts were made to let the cable out but the result was that the mine instead passed under the trawler and exploded. Five men died. The bodies of two deck hands, Charles Wing and Harold Moisey, were taken from the sea by *Touchstone* and another trawler *Lord Roberts*, and landed at Shotley for burial. The Admiralty blamed Skipper A Barber and the RNR officer commanding, Lieutenant Richard Harcourt, for the loss, indicating that they were guilty of not keeping way on the vessel when the mine was sighted.[16]

It was not just mines that tried to kill the fishermen turned navy men (known affectionately as 'fisherjacks'). Their oldest enemy, the weather, was always ready to ambush them. *De La Pole* was an ex-Hull trawler, now working out of Harwich as a sweeper. On 4 February 1916, a strong gale blew her onshore at Trinity Bay in the Goodwin Sands. The North Deal lifeboat responded to her distress flares and found that the *De La Pole* was full of water and of her twelve-man crew, eight were lashed to the rigging with the vessel breaking up rapidly. By means of a lifeline the crew were taken aboard the lifeboat although one man, Engineman James Batty, was drowned. William Adams, coxswain of the lifeboat, was awarded the RNLI silver medal for his part in the rescue.

Lord Roberts (1907), originally from Hull and noted above, had been taken up by the Admiralty in November 1914 and had been based at Harwich for all of her war service. On 26 October 1916, she had been detailed to find and mark the wreck of SS *Framfield*, mined and lost two days previously between the Sunk and Shipwash Light Vessels. At 1445 the crew identified the mast of the wrecked ship and buoyed it. That done, they set off back towards the Sunk, but had barely got underway when there was large explosion amidships which broke her in two; *Lord Roberts* rapidly sank. The mine had been laid by *UC-11* some days earlier. Nine crewmen died, including Skipper Henry Walker; there were just two survivors. The trawler had been such a familiar and welcome sight that a Trinity House pilot, missing her from the usual haunts, 'wrote a letter to the authorities asking what had become of "our old friend the *Lord Roberts*"'.[17]

A final example of the sacrifices made by the fisherjacks came on 2 February 1917. *Holdene* was a new (1915) trawler intended to fish at Fleetwood but instead commandeered by the Admiralty and based at Harwich. In company with *Drummer Boy*, she was preparing to carry out a sweep to the east of Orford Ness. As the two vessels were connecting the cable, there was a large explosion on the starboard quarter and *Holdene* sank immediately. The

The Dovercourt Minesweepers' Memorial, seen in 2021. (Author's collection)

mines had again been laid by *UC-11*. Seven men lost their lives, including Boy Cook John L Brown from Parkeston, aged just 17. But in this instance, Harwich eventually had the last word; *UC-11* hit a mine off the town whilst submerged, blew up, and sank with eighteen dead and only one survivor.

Overall, it has been estimated that twenty-four Harwich Auxiliaries were sunk or badly damaged with many more injured but gaining shelter and safety. Another fifteen were accounted for next door at The Nore.[18]

The Harwich minesweepers have their own memorial in the town. The Dovercourt Minesweepers Memorial, designed by Frederick Brook Hitch,[*] was unveiled at the junction of Fronks Road and Marine Parade on 20 December

---

[*] Hitch also designed, *inter alia*, the National Submarine War Memorial on Victoria Embankment, London.

Order of service for the dedication of the Minesweepers' Memorial in 1919.
(Photo; David Whittle/Harwich Society)

Harwich Minesweepers and Auxiliary Patrol Memorial

DOVERCOURT.

Tuesday, December 16th, 1919, at 2.45 p.m.

The form of

Memorial Service

Dedication and Unveiling of Cenotaph

in memory of

OFFICERS AND MEN OF THE
HARWICH MINESWEEPERS
. AND AUXILIARY PATROL .
FORCE, who gave their lives for
their Country during the Great War,
August, 1914 — November, 1918.

The Unveiling will be performed by Rear-Admiral Cecil
S. Hickley, M.V.O.

The Dedication by The Right Rev. The Lord Bishop of London

1919 by Rear Admiral Cecil Spencer Hickley,[*] who released the large flags which covered the memorial.

Despite rain and wind, there was a considerable turnout to watch the procession consisting of local clergy, the mayor and corporation, boys from HMS *Ganges* and other representatives of the Armed Forces. The memorial itself was made of Portland stone with tablets in cast bronze and four bronze dolphins, one at each corner. The dedication reads:

> To the Glory of God and in proud memory of the officers and men of the Royal Naval Reserve & Royal Naval Volunteer Reserve serving in the Auxiliary Patrol & Minesweepers at Harwich who died in the performance of their duties that the sea might be made free. Twilight and evening bell, and after that the dark and may there be no sadness of farewell when I embark; for tho' from out our bourne of time and place the flood may bear me far. I hope to see my Pilot face to face, when I have crossed the bar.

Clearing Up the Mess

The war ended on 11 November 1918 but the work of the Auxiliaries didn't, especially the minesweepers. Amongst the first priorities was the clearance of the many minefields that surrounded the British coastline and elsewhere. Britain was one of twenty-six countries represented on an International Mine Clearance Committee dedicated to clearing 40,000 square miles of sea of leftover mines. Each power was allotted an area to clear. Around Britain, according to First Lord of the Admiralty Walter Long, 'during the war no less than 1,360 minefields or groups of mines were laid by the Germans in proximity to our coast, ... in waters abroad to be cleared by the British about

---

[*] Hickley, who had played first class cricket for Somerset and Western Province in his younger days, was appointed Senior Naval Officer, Harwich, on 1 April 1918, superseding Cayley. He also took charge of Shotley Training Establishment and Naval Barracks.

USS *Aphrodite* anchored off Harwich, while serving as station ship there, around the end of 1918. Launched in 1898 she was an armed yacht, armed with four 3in guns, two machine guns and a depth charge thrower, originally built for Colonel Oliver H Payne of New York City, at the time one of America's wealthiest men. The navy took her over in May 1917 and she came to Harwich from France just after the Armistice to serve as station ship. (US Naval History and Heritage Command NH 104493)

sixty fields or groups, totalling some 1,200 mines, . . . while British mines, which had also to be swept up, numbered about 65,000 in home waters and 8,000 in the Mediterranean'.[19]

Experienced minesweeping sailors were asked to volunteer for another 12 months' service with the promise that they would only be engaged in peaceful mine clearance, not martial activities. A special 'Mine Clearance Service' was formed to this end with its own badge, which was presented to each volunteer – the 'His Majesty the King's Mine Clearance Badge' – and an increased weekly pay supplement was awarded. This was particularly necessary for the fishermen as they would otherwise have returned to fishing where, for the moment, they could earn four times as much as a rating in the RNR(T). Some 600 officers and 15,000 men served in this fashion, with service to expire automatically on 30 November 1919.

This service is reflected in the fact that 1919 actually saw the highest number of recorded Auxiliary ships at Harwich, 131, especially minesweeping vessels (see also Appendix 3). The Harwich paddler minesweepers were under the command of Lieutenant D McClymont DSC, RNVR in the paddler *Eagle III* (1910), requisitioned from Buchanan Steamers who had purchased her for the Glasgow–Rothsay route; the trawlers came under Lieutenant Geoffrey Wright RNVR. There was also one yacht, *Aphrodite*, actually American and acting as station ship overseeing the American interests at the port, especially the U-boat surrender (see Chapter 20).

A Lone Survivor

Destroyers had dash and glamour, minesweepers had determination and danger; but there were many necessary and quotidian jobs that had to be undertaken for the Force at Harwich and auxiliary craft were necessary to perform them.

One such was *Pinmill*,* probably the only twenty-first century survivor of the many auxiliary vessels that operated from Harwich in the Great War. She was built in 1910 by the Whitstable Barge Company, and was fitted out by Dan Marine Motor and Shipbuilding Company of Ipswich as an open passenger launch. Her working life was based on Harwich. In 1911, *Pinmill* was used by Sir Thomas Lipton's company to deliver supplies to Royal Navy vessels in harbour. A year later, she was sold to the Great Eastern Railway to open the Harwich–Felixstowe–Shotley ferry. Then, like so much of the Great Eastern's fleet, *Pinmill* was requisitioned by the Admiralty for service with the Harwich Force. She was always a welcome sight bringing supplies, mail and passengers to the ships of the Force. After the war she reverted to ferry work and then became a workboat at Harwich and Parkeston Quay. The Second World War saw her back in Admiralty service; at its end, she returned to workboat usage before in 1987 the launch was laid up after sinking. In 1988 *Pinmill* was purchased by the Ipswich Maritime Trust and was used to operate pleasure trips from Ipswich.

Finally, in 2005 *Pinmill* was purchased for restoration at the Iron Wharf yard in Faversham, Kent, with the intention of sailing as a passenger boat on the Gloucester and Sharpness Canal. Sadly, on 14 October 2017 she was destroyed by an arson attack at the boatyard. Even survivors eventually have to die.

---

* Probably named for a village on the south bank of the Orwell in the Shotley peninsula.

19

Felixstowe and the Air War

The Harwich Force worked closely with the seaplane base across the water at Felixstowe. The Royal Navy was initially a reluctant adopter of the concept of aircraft.* But the idea developed that airborne observation would extend the range at which an enemy could be sighted, be useful in spotting the fall of shot and provide a faster way of conveying messages. Bombing of ships from the air might also be possible. Additionally, aircraft which could land and take off from water would be a tremendous advance on the basic idea of flight from land.

In 1912, a Naval Air Station was established at Eastchurch on the Isle of Sheppey. Pilot training was carried out here and the station was designated the air HQ. In 1913, further air stations were opened on the Isle of Grain (at the mouth of the River Medway), Calshot (on the Solent), Great Yarmouth and Felixstowe. Grain and Felixstowe were designated experimental units (the former initially specialising in balloons and blimps).

The Felixstowe Naval Air Station, known as Seaplanes Felixstowe in 1913, was run on true naval lines, firstly by two Royal Marines, Captain C E Risk (1913–14), and then Lieutenant C E H Rathbone (1914–15). Despite being entirely ashore, the base pretended to be a ship. Going out through the main gate was 'taking the liberty boat'; in doing so one 'went ashore'; and it proudly boasted its own pipe band. There were three huge (300ft long, 200ft wide) seaplane sheds/hangars, built by Boulton and Paul of Norwich, with a concrete hardstanding in front of them, onto which the aircraft and/or their trollies could be wheeled, and which sloped down to the water for floating the boats off. The sheds looked out onto the estuary, across to Harwich or Shotley.

An early visitor to the station was First Lord of the Admiralty Winston Churchill. On 24 April 1914, he was flown from the Isle of Grain to Felixstowe by Lieutenant R T Seddon in a Short Type 74. Unfortunately, the Gnome

---

* Following an enquiry held in 1908 under Lord Esher's leadership, the scepticism of the heads of the Navy and Army regarding the usefulness of heavier-than-air craft meant little progress was initially made. The committee recommended the construction of one rigid airship (the *Mayfly*) in 1909 as well as some kites and balloons but that the development of winged craft should be left to private enterprise. Near the end of 1911, the only aircraft in the Navy were gifts from private donors. It was not until 1911–12 that aviation was taken seriously at the highest levels of the services and in 1912 the Committee of Imperial Defence recommended that military aviation be formalised. This led to the founding of the RFC with a naval and a military wing. The naval wing became the RNAS in July 1914.

100HP engine failed and they had to make a forced landing on the other side of the river; rather ignominiously, the First Lord was towed into the base.

Developing an aircraft which could take off from water was a more difficult proposition than a land-based one. The frictional resistance on water is greater than that of wheels on grass or roads, as floats or boat hulls give a craft increased aerodynamic drag. Given the low power outputs of the primitive engines of the time, this was a problem.

Early designs added floats to existing airframes but float structures were inherently fragile and it soon became clear that hulled craft would be more seaworthy and efficient. How to develop a successful hull-based craft became the mission of the Felixstowe station and of one man in particular, John Cyril Porte.

More than anyone, perhaps, Porte brought the large long-range naval flying boat to life and perfection. As Canadian-born Flight Lieutenant Theodore Douglas Hallam, who became the leader of the War Flight at the station, noted after the war 'there would probably not have been any big British flying boats but for the vision, persistence and energy of Colonel J C Porte, CMG, who designed and built at Felixstowe Air Station the experimental machine of each type of British flying boat successfully used in the services'.[1]

The Man Who Made Flying Boats

John Cyril Porte was born on 26 February 1884 to the Reverend John Robert Porte and Henrietta (née Scott) in Bandon, County Cork. Porte senior was Rector of St Peter's, Ballymodan, Bandon, before moving to England with his family as Vicar of St Matthew's church, Denmark Hill, London, in 1890. But he was also a most accomplished man, a civil engineer, member of the Royal Irish Academy, Fellow of the Royal Geological Society of Ireland and founder member of the Dublin Microscopical Club. His son would inherit his technical abilities, and more.

John Cyril Porte in 1914. (Author's collection)

Porte joined the Royal Navy in 1898, aged 14, passing through HMS *Britannia* and eventually transferring to the submarine service. His first command was HMS *B-3* (1905), a petrol-engined boat, in 1906. Here he met Murray Sueter, a pioneer of naval aviation, who became Director of the Air Department of the Royal Navy in 1912. Sueter encouraged his interest in flying, but before this could take full shape, in 1911 Porte was invalided out of the navy in the rank of lieutenant RN with pulmonary tuberculosis.

Porte had learnt to fly by the end of 1910 using a Santos-Dumont Demoiselle that he built himself. He took a flying course sponsored by the Admiralty in England and gained his flying certificate with the Aero Club de France at Reims flying a Deperdussin monoplane. A natural aviator, despite his illness in summer 1912 he applied to be a pilot for the year's Army manoeuvres. In September Porte was surveyed as to his fitness for service in the RFC. Although he was not judged fit for entry, he was permitted to join the Naval Wing of the Royal Naval Reserve.

Out of the navy, Porte became test pilot for the British arm of the Deperdussin company but this went bankrupt, taking Porte's savings with it. He then joined White and Thompson, who had the rights for the American-made Curtiss aircraft in the UK, as test pilot. This brought Porte into contact with Glen Curtiss, the owner and designer of Curtiss, and Porte left the UK in April 1914 to join him to work on a transatlantic flying boat, known as the Model-H 'America'; this craft was intended to compete for a £10,000 prize offered by the *Daily Mail*.

A photograph of John Cyril Porte with the Curtiss Model H flying boat 'America' which was launched on 22 June 1914. (US Library of Congress LC-DIG-ggbain-16394)

However, the outbreak of war supervened, Curtiss' 'America' transatlantic project was postponed and Porte left the USA to return to England. Despite his poor health, he was commissioned into the RNAS on 13 August 1914, with the rank of squadron commander. After a spell at Hendon, Porte transferred to Felixstowe, where he took command of the station in August 1915.[2]

Flying Boat Development

On his return from the USA, Porte advised Sueter to buy Curtiss flying boats. An initial order for two was placed, both Model H-4s. These boats were evaluated at Felixstowe and a further sixty-two then obtained, eight of which were built in Britain. This type retrospectively acquired the designation 'Small America' and came into service during 1915.

The H-4 was deficient in several areas, most of all in its power plant and poor seaworthiness. According to Theodore Hallam 'these were comic machines weighing well over two tons with two comic engines giving, when they functioned, 180 HP; and comic control, being nose heavy with engines on and tail heavy in a glide'.[3] The engines were twin 90HP Curtiss, 100HP Anzani or 110HP Clerget.

These were followed by the larger and more powerful H-12 'Large America' but even here the twin 160HP Curtiss engines were inadequate and were replaced by Porte with 275HP Rolls-Royce power plants. This did not, however, solve their overriding problem which was that the design of the hull planing bottom meant that take-off was dangerous in all but the calmest seas. Like the CMBs, flying boats had to hydroplane and hull 'step' design was critical to enabling this. Nonetheless seventy-one were eventually acquired by the RNAS.

At Felixstowe, Porte was officially posted as Commander of the Experimental Flying Wing (and advanced in rank to wing commander ten months later). Here, Porte and his chief engineer J D Rennie began to develop new planing hulls which performed much better, and to examine alternative power solutions. This led to a series of designs conceived by Porte and his team at Felixstowe which resulted in the Felixstowe F-series of flying boats, producing quite the best aircraft of their type in the war. The F-1 was an experimental craft which combined the Curtiss wings and tail from an H-4 with a newly conceived 'Porte Hull'. It proved very successful and led to the F2A, which used the tail and wing assembly of an H-12, again married to a Porte-designed boat hull. Two Rolls-Royce Eagle VIII engines produced 345HP each, and the craft bristled with up to seven machine guns, together with two 230lb bombs carried in racks under the wings. According to air historian Owen Thetford, 'the F2A earned a reputation comparable with that of the Sunderland in the Second World War'.[4]

Certainly, the F2A was a formidable fighting machine, as demonstrated by an incident on 4 June 1918 when four Felixstowe F2As and a Curtiss H-12 from both Felixstowe and Great Yarmouth went searching for enemy seaplanes. One F2A was lost due to broken petrol pipe feed, its crew being interned in Holland, while the H-12 set off in pursuit of some aircraft which had attacked the downed flying boat. The three remaining F2As encountered fourteen enemy floatplanes near Terschelling and shot down at least three German Hansa-Brandenburg machines (a two-seat, low-wing, single-engined seaplane, armed with two forward-firing machine guns and another mounted in the rear). All three aircraft survived and returned to Felixstowe after a patrol of some six hours.

The Porte hulls gave much better seaworthiness than their American equivalents and were designed in such a way as to enable them to be constructed by firms with no previous experience of boats or aircraft, a great boon in a time of massive demand on production resources. Contracts for Felixstowe flying boats could therefore be awarded not only to experienced seaplane builders like Short Brothers and S E Saunders, but also to companies like Dick, Kerr and Company and the Phoenix Dynamo Company, which were building marine aircraft for the first time. By March 1918, 160 had been ordered and 100 had been delivered by the time of the Armistice. Various derivative such as an F2C and F3 were also produced, but it was the F2A which was the triumph of Porte's art.

A Felixstowe F3 in flight, displaying the colourful paint schemes they often wore. This dazzle camouflage aided identification during air combat and on the water in the event of being forced down. At Felixstowe, a standard pattern of coloured squares and stripes was adopted and copies of the design of each individual craft were held at all East Coast stations for recognition purposes. (Author's collection)

The giant Super Porte Baby, the largest flying boat in existence at the time. It was fitted with five Rolls-Royce Eagle engines arranged in tandem sets and one single pusher. Total wing span was 123ft and length 60ft. It is shown here in an official RAF photograph of 1918 reproduced in the *Illustrated London News* of 25 January 1919. (Author's collection)

Curtiss developed the H-16, based on the learnings from Porte's work and also again known as 'Large Americas', which were used by the US Navy and by the RNAS, the latter of whom had ordered 125 in total, although fifty were cancelled at the end of the war. They used American Liberty or Rolls-Royce Eagle VIII power plants.

Felixstowe and Porte produced other designs, such as the Felixstowe Porte Baby. The prototype Baby had three 250HP Rolls-Royce engines, two tractors and a centrally-mounted pusher. Ten production machines followed with 325 or 360HP engines. Various armaments were tried including torpedoes carried under the wings and a 6pdr recoilless Davis gun.[*] To overcome the inability of the big flying boats to attack Zeppelins at maximum height, one Baby was configured to carry a parasite Bristol Scout single-seat fighter on its upper wing. This combo successfully flew on 17 May 1916, but the experiment does not seem to have been pursued. Another innovative craft was the Super-Baby, a triplane flying boat, officially known as the Felixstowe Fury, with five engines

---

[*] An American design which connected two guns back-to-back, with the backwards-facing gun loaded with lead balls and grease of the same weight as the shell in the other gun, thus acting as a counter to the recoil.

and 15 tons in weight. Hallam flew the prototype and carried twenty-four passengers aloft.

Porte was in poor health anyway and the stress of the job no doubt aggravated his weakness. Between 19 April and 24 May 1917, he was 'found unfit' and was relieved of his duties for a rest. He then left England in June on the SS *Mongolia* for Malta where he was to advise on the establishment of flying boat operations in the Mediterranean.[5] He was back in Felixstowe by late July. The contribution of John Cyril Porte to the success of British and American flying boats design was huge. But he never received a service decoration for it in Britain. Why not?

Nolle Prosequi

Whilst in the USA before the war, Porte had arranged with the Curtiss company's sales manager that he would receive a 25 per cent commission on any aircraft sold in Britain subsequent to the projected transatlantic prize flight. This arrangement was never dissolved and Porte received monies through a commission agent for all the Curtiss aircraft purchased by the Admiralty, which by July 1917 had amounted to a total payment of £48,000 (perhaps £3 million in today's money).

When this came to light as a result of questions in the House of Commons in early 1917, the then First Lord Sir Edward Carson ordered a committee of enquiry and this was followed by a case brought against Porte and two others accusing them of profiteering under the Prevention of Corruption Act of 1906. It was heard at Bow Street Court in July. The case was dropped only in the November, when the money was returned and the Attorney General entered a plea of *nolle prosequi** in the case, in view of Porte's failing health and important war service.

With his physical condition severely damaged by the stress of the trial, Porte returned to Felixstowe where he had to be nursed back to some sort of wellbeing by his wife. But the knock-on effect of the accusations against him meant that he was denied recognition by the service he loved.

After an attack on a U-boat in July 1917 (see below) Porte had been recommended for the award of a DSO. This was denied him by the Admiralty. A note in his personal file recorded that 'in view of the special circumstances of this officer's case, the First Sea Lord is not prepared to consider any decoration for paid services'.[6]

John Porte was elected a Fellow of the Royal Aeronautical Society in July

---

* Literally, 'to be unwilling to pursue', a legal term used for prosecutors' declarations that they are voluntarily ending a criminal case before trial or before a verdict is rendered. In English law only the Attorney General can so act.

1918 for his design work and eventually received the CMG* in 1918 'in recognition of distinguished services rendered in connection with the War'.[7] But even this is a mystery, for this award is given for service overseas.

Anti-Submarine Patrol

At the beginning of 1917, the patrol work of the station was rather at a low ebb. When flying boats had been available, patrols had been frequent; but the first five big twin-engine boats to be erected and tested at Felixstowe, together with many good pilots and engineers, had just been ordered to the Scilly Isles to help protect the Western Approaches. The weather was poor for flying and there was no tactical doctrine for carrying out anti-submarine patrols. As a result, the energy levels of the station were low. Which is not to say they were idle. A great deal of the endeavour of the station was taken up in experimental work and the erection of flying boats, of which forty in all had been assembled, fitted out, and tested during 1916. But 'there was a feeling among the majority of the pilots that there was little use in patrols from Felixstowe, as from the beginning of the war only two enemy submarines had been sighted by pilots on patrol from the station'.[8]

As leader of the War Flight, Lieutenant Hallam decided on a new strategy. In his own words,

> in sketching out the campaign from Felixstowe against the U-boats, it was decided that the only sure method of protecting shipping was to damage or destroy submarines, and that all other methods were merely palliative. It was considered that ships proceeding in the shipping lane, which was close to the coast of England and protected by shallow mine-fields and surface patrol craft, were well looked after, and that enemy submarines, if operating in these busy waters, would be so on the alert and keep such a good look-out that the flying-boats would not be given a chance; for submarines cannot be seen from the air when once below the surface of the North Sea. It was therefore decided to expend all available flying time where submarines were to be found on the surface, and that the efficiency of the patrols would not be decided by the number of flying hours put in, but by the number of submarines sighted and bombed.[9]

U-boats had limited endurance under water and therefore cruised on the surface whenever possible. The distance they could travel submerged was only about 75 miles and they could only run below surface at 8 to 10 knots for

---

* Companion of the Order of St Michael and St George.

around two hours before exhausting the batteries which drove the electric motors. Moreover, their approximate position could be known by this time, through direction finding wireless stations on the east coast.* These fixes showed that the U-boats often passed in the vicinity of the North Hinder Light Vessel. And so a method of planned search was devised which used this navigational point as a fulcrum from which air patrols could be flown; it became known as the Spider Web.

The Web was 60 miles in diameter and allowed for the searching of 4,000 square miles of sea, right across the path of the transiting U-boats. The Spider Web Patrol was centred on the North Hinder light.

It was an octagonal figure with eight radial arms thirty sea-miles in length, and with three sets of circumferential lines joining the arms ten, twenty, and thirty miles out from the centre. Eight sectors were thus provided for patrol, and all kinds of combinations could be worked out. As the circumferential lines were ten miles apart, each section of a sector was searched twice on any patrol when there was good visibility.[10]

The patrols were carried out at the height of 1,000ft, because at that altitude silhouettes of the submarines and surface craft could best be seen and the run of the wind on the water could be spotted and its direction and force determined. It was also easy to drop down to 800 or 600ft to bomb the target. Hallam was given the resounding title of 'Commander War Flight' and just two aircraft to prosecute the new plan. But it was a start.

Resources grew, however. Soon Felixstowe was able to put eight flying boats into the air each month. Tyrwhitt was moved to write that 'the big seaplanes are playing havoc with them [U-boats] and are forever bombing them, sometimes with success'.[11] Certainly, the aviators claimed U-boat sinkings. In his book *The Spider Web*, written in 1919, Hallam states that Felixstowe flying boats sank (*inter alia*) *UC-1*, *UB-20* and *UC-6*. In the case of *UC-1*, on 24 July 1917 Porte – who was back on station after a brief absence helping to establish flying boat operations in the Mediterranean – had decided to attempt a mass patrol by five flying boats. The station had never put so many in the air at one time but five machines were eventually manhandled down the slipway, with Porte himself in the brand-new Felixstowe F2C (number 8689). This was his latest experimental craft with 'Queenie' Cooper, Porte's regular test pilot, at the controls.

---

* Such an arrangement was also used for Zeppelins. On 26 April 1917 the Admiralty put a new tracking system in place to detect them. As Zeppelins patrolled, their courses were methodically plotted by the British wireless interception stations and, if they approached within 150 miles of the English coast, their position, course, and speed were communicated direct to one or more of the East Coast flying-boat bases. Local commanders then had discretion to send out aircraft – keeping them up to date with the airship's position by wireless.

When all five had been floated off and jockeyed into position Porte signalled for them to open up their engines and they must have made a fine sight as five white trails of roiled water marked their passage down the harbour and into the air. The formation passed the Shipwash and North Hinder Light Vessels and 1055 sighted *UC-1*, a minelaying U-boat, on the surface. The submarine began to dive, but three flying boats, including Porte's, dropped a total of five bombs on the target and oil and bubbles came to the surface. According to Lieutenant Hallam, 'the career of *UC-1* was ended'.[12] Except it wasn't.

For, regrettably, later scholarship disproved all of these assertions. *UC-1* actually succumbed to mines off Nieuwpoort on 18 July 1917; *UB-20* hit a mine and sank whilst conducting diving trails off Zeebrugge on 28 July 1917; and *UC-6* was destroyed by a mined net off the North Foreland.

But this is not to say that the patrols were of no value. The key achievement of all such overflights by aircraft was to force the submarines to make their transit of the North Sea under water; this was much slower, ate into their on-station time for hunting merchant ships, and forced them to surface frequently when they might not have wanted to in order to replenish the air in the boat.

Additionally, air observation was more effective than searching from the surface. At the time the crow's nest on a battleship, perhaps 75ft above the sea, might provide visibility out to 10 nautical miles in clear weather. From a destroyer the equivalent range might be five miles. But from an aircraft at, say, 3,000ft the range of vision was some 60 miles. Furthermore, wireless-equipped flying boats could direct warships to a sighted submarine or fly over it to keep it below the surface where its slow speed and extremely limited visibility made it difficult for the U-boat to attack shipping.

And they certainly put the work in. For the period from 13 April 1917 to 12 April 1918, Lieutenant Hallam calculated that they averaged eight flying boats on patrol each month, 190 flying days, 605 patrols of 105,397 miles covered, forty-seven submarines sighted and twenty-five bombed.[13]

The Destruction of *L-43*

On 14 June 1917, Canadian-born Flight Lieutenant Basil Deacon Hobbs (known to his friends as Billiken) and second pilot Flight Sub Lieutenant Robert Frederick Lea Dickey were on patrol off the Dutch coast in Curtiss H-12 'Large America' flying boat, number 8677. With them were wireless operator H M Davies and engineer A W Goody. If it came to a fight, the latter two crewmen would man the waist/rear guns whilst Dickey would occupy the nose gun position.

---

* Rear Admiral, Harwich (Cayley), commended Porte for this operation and suggested him for a DSO.

They had left Felixstowe for patrol duty some two and a quarter hours ago, sometimes dropping down to 200ft to pass under banks of heavy mist. At 0730 they were off the coast of Ameland and, sweeping in a 20-mile circle, headed back down the coast homeward bound. The mist was patchy and visibility intermittent.

At 0840, Dickey suddenly saw a Zeppelin. Although they did not yet know it, the pilots had sighted *L-43* (Zeppelin LZ-92) under the command of Käpitanleutnant Hermann Kraushaar. Commissioned on 15 March 1917, *L-43* was the first naval airship capable of operating at over 18,000ft. This was intended to put it beyond the reach of enemy fighters and anti-aircraft guns. The big Curtiss could never have reached her at that height. But Kraushaar was stooging along, five miles on the starboard beam, at a height of only 1,500ft. Hobbs swung the bow of the H-12 towards the airship. Opening up his two engines to full power, he climbed straight towards the enemy airship, intending to get above it.

Dickey scrambled behind the bow gun and Davies took the midships weapon. The Zeppelin appeared almost stationery, her propellers just ticking over. Hobbs had now achieved tactical advantage; he was at 2,000ft and 1,000 yards away from the airship. At last, the German lookout saw them. The engines speeded up, the Zeppelin changed course, and two men ran respectively to her tail gun and the midships gun on the top of the envelope.

Hobbs put his craft into a dive, plummeting down on his intended prey at 140 mph. As the H-12 passed diagonally across the airship from starboard to port, Davies fired tracer from his position behind the pilots; but Dickey got off two bursts from his machine gun, using the deadly Brock and Pomeroy bullets (see Chapter 8).

Hobbs now made a sharp right-hand turn, placing his aircraft slightly below, and heading straight for, the enemy. He was able to read her tactical number, *L-43*. And he could see that she was on fire. Little spurts of flame stabbed out where the incendiary and explosive bullets had torn into the fabric and set alight the escaping hydrogen. Pulling back the controls, Hobbs lifted the aircraft over the airship just in time, for a huge burst of flame, hot enough to be felt by all the flying boat crew, blew from the Zeppelin. It broke in half, with each burning section falling towards the water.

The top gunner tumbled into the flames and vanished. Three men fell out of the gondolas. Turning over and over they struck the water before the wreckage. Bits of the destroyed Zeppelin rained into the sea and a thick pillar of black smoke marked its last resting place. The flying boat crew were ecstatic; it was Felixstowe's first Zeppelin victim. They headed for home, landing at 1100 after a flight of nearly 400 miles, but not before they had circled their air station, Dickey firing off Very flares of jubilation and the handkerchiefs of the crew bravely fluttering from the barrels of their machine guns. There was a very considerable Mess celebration that evening, which apparently involved the downing of many cocktails.

Dickey received the DSC for his part in the action. Hobbs, who already held the DSC, received the DSO.[14] Both men would subsequently win Bars to their DSCs.

Pigeons

One of the more unusual jobs at RNAS Felixstowe would seem to be that of pigeoneer. But that would be to underestimate the importance of the pigeon. In a world where airborne radio was unreliable and of short range, a homing pigeon could be the difference between life and death. In a short instruction manual for the men of the Felixstowe flying boat, crews preparing to crash or ditch were exhorted to 'save anything, four things should take precedence – pigeons, emergency rations, Very's lights, and the Red Cross outfit'.[15] Much of this equipment was the responsibility of the aircraft's wireless operator.

> He coded and de-coded all signals. The code-book had weighted covers, so that if the boat were captured by the enemy, it would sink immediately when thrown overboard. He had an Aldis signalling-lamp for communicating with ships and other flying boats. He also looked after the Red Cross box, which contained a tourniquet, first aid kit, the sandwiches for immediate needs, the emergency rations for five days, and the carrier pigeons.[16]

Before take-off, the pigeoneer* brought out the birds to the aircraft from the military loft in Felixstowe town. While on the station the birds were watered but not fed. Two of them were placed in a basket with two compartments and put on board, well up from the bottom, as petrol fumes gathered there and made them confused and dopey. Each pigeon had a tiny aluminium receptacle clipped to its leg to hold a message, and a ring with its number, so that it could be identified if it came back without a signal.

When released, they would fly home, land on a ledge outside the loft, and walk through some swinging wires which rang a bell. The pigeoneer, warned by the bell, went into the loft, removed the flimsy paper from the carrier and sent it down to the station. More than once lives were saved by these little birds; and the ones which failed to perform satisfactorily were generally eaten.

When word came that an aircraft was down, crews were quick to volunteer for the rescue mission. One man who gained a reputation for such altruism

---

* From 1915, experienced pigeon fanciers and racers were invited to join the RNVR to handle the birds.

at Felixstowe was yet another Canadian-born pilot, James Lindsay Gordon.[8] Born in Montreal, he had learned to fly at the Wright School of Aviation in Dayton, Ohio. Gordon joined the RNAS in 1916, aged 23, and was awarded the DFC in 1918; the citation read, 'a pilot of great experience, initiative and skill. Has led formations over the seas and attacked with success enemy aircraft in their own area. Captain Gordon has been instrumental in saving life in disabled seaplanes on several occasions, and whenever any arduous duty has to be done, he is always to the fore to carry it out.'[17] By then he had already been recognised for a specific rescue mission by the presentation in May 1917 of the Board of Trade Medal for Saving Life at Sea (also known as the Sea Gallantry Medal) for carrying out, despite heavy seas, a dangerous rescue of two RNAS seaplane crew who had been afloat in the North Sea for five days. And it had been their pigeon that saved them.

The End of the Service

On 1 April 1918 the RNAS ceased to exist;[†] the service was merged with the RFC to produce the Royal Air Force (RAF). Such amalgamation and loss of identity was not welcomed by the Royal Navy; many officers thought the choice of date prophetic. For Theodore Hallam 'the service we belonged to and loved came to an end and although the War Flight carried on until the armistice, and did great work under the Royal Air Force, the rose by another name did not smell as sweet'. And worse 'the bitterest pill of all, the navy, our natural parent, was willing that we should be put under the guardianship of an unknown and alien stepmother'.[18] Under the RAF, Felixstowe became 'Seaplane Experimental Station, Felixstowe'.

Roger Keyes, at Dover, was another who was less than pleased. On taking over the Dover Patrol he had under his orders 5 Group of the RNAS, comprising five squadrons and approximately ninety aeroplanes, mainly based on airfields to the west of Dunkirk. These were all lost to him at the formation of the combined force and he subsequently received 'only a fraction of what he wanted and the British air attacks were neither sufficiently heavy nor sustained long enough for really effective results'.[19] Keyes believed that 'golden opportunities were lost for inflicting heavy losses on the enemy on the Flanders coast'.[20]

There is no doubt that the general neglect of naval aviation which followed this amalgamation was to Britain's detriment throughout the post-war period and left the Fleet Air Arm badly under equipped in 1939. But at Felixstowe, the RNAS and its flying boats had for four years ensured their moment in the sun.

---

* Later, Gordon became the first Director of the Royal Canadian Airforce, a post he held between 1922 and 1924.

† By this date the RNAS had grown to a force of 67,000 officers and men with 126 air stations in the UK and abroad with 2,949 aircraft and 103 airships on its books. (Data from Thetford, *British Naval Aircraft*, p 12.)

20

'The Harwich Force has made its name'

At 1100 on 11 November 1918, all hell broke out in Harwich harbour. There was a cacophony of sirens, whistles and hooters as every ship in the port, warship, auxiliary, passenger, tender or fishing boat, celebrated the coming into force of the Armistice. Signal rockets and flares soared up into the sky, and did so again at night to colourful effect. Ships' and town bands played, crews cheered, and the noise continued for many hours, all over Harwich, Felixstowe, Shotley and everywhere else in Britain. The 'War To End All Wars' was finally over.

On the submarine depot ships, at 1115, the lower decks were cleared and assembled in number three shed on the quayside. Captain Addison stood up and said;

> My lads, I can't make a speech, I'm too excited, but I have a signal here to read to you. 'Admiralty to all ships. Armistice is signed; hostilities are to be suspended forthwith. All anti-submarine measures in force till further notice. Submarines on surface not to be attacked unless hostile intentions are obvious. Armistice to be announced at 1100. All general methods of demonstrations to be permitted and encouraged, including bands'.[1]

Addison then called for three cheers for the king and one more for the submarine service. According to Lieutenant King-Hall 'The whole building shook'.[2]

Next, a piano and a makeshift band played the National Anthem, which was sung 'with a fervour I've never heard equalled before'.[3] And then this *sui generis* orchestra, accompanied by hundreds of sailors, emerged from the shed and the piano was put on a rail trolley, on top of which was placed Lieutenant King-Hall. From there he conducted the players as the contraption was pulled along the railway lines of the quay, surrounded by a cheering, surging mob.

Tyrwhitt made a general signal to his ships from *Curacoa*. 'On this day of rejoicing I wish to thank the captains, officers and ships' companies of the Harwich Force for the unbounded gallantry, zeal and endurance they have invariably displayed during the war. The Harwich Force has made its name and will not be forgotten during the future annals of history.'[4]

First Lord of the Admiralty Eric Geddes sent a personal message of congratulations to Tyrwhitt in which he noted that

> you have been continually in touch with the enemy, and harried his light forces on every occasion when he has ventured outside his defences, and you have inflicted heavy losses upon him. It is in a large measure to this that our present victory is due. The arduous work of escorting the Dutch convoy traffic has been of immense value in maintaining connection with and bringing succour to a neutral country which has suffered cruelly on account of the method of warfare adopted by Germany.[5]

Lieutenant Ronald Blacklock had been in command of the minelaying submarine* E-45 since the August and thought that 'to command a minelayer was a prestigious job'. As the Armistice came into effect, he was at sea. When he and his crew returned to harbour 'we found Harwich in a state of jubilation, into which we gladly joined, and on reporting to Percy Addison he informed me "this is your lucky day my boy, I never expected to see you alive again"'.[6]

That evening, the admiral and Lady Angela entertained the captains and commanders of the Force to dinner at the Alexandra Hotel. Domvile was responsible for the menu. Freed at last from their collegiate vow of abstinence, he archly described one of the wines as 'Kaiser, 1918 (bottled in Holland)'.†

But what Captain Domvile enjoyed most was 'the cheerful light flooding out through the open portholes in the ships' sides – portholes that had been closed for four and a half years . . . it brought it home to me that the war had ended'.[7] For the first time since the start of the conflict, ships were at eight hours' notice for steam and officers and men were allowed late or night leave. It all seemed slightly surreal to men who had endured years of unending action. But there was still one more job for Rear Admiral Tyrwhitt and the Harwich Force to undertake.

The Surrender of the U-boats

The Armistice had been negotiated from the Allied side by Maréchal Ferdinand Foch and Admiral Rosslyn Wemyss. Foch was supreme Allied commander of the armies; he was therefore an obvious choice. His goal was to reduce Germany and its army to a state whereby not only could they not re-start the war but that they could never again threaten France's national

---

* British 'E'-class minelaying submarines were not purpose-built like the German UC class; the mines 'were laid by being launched through a kind of trap-hatch in the stern' (King-Hall, *My Naval Life*, p 156).

† Kaiser Wilhelm II had fled to Holland, where he remained for the rest of his life.

Admiral Rosslyn Wemyss, First Sea Lord in 1918 and the British plenipotentiary at the Armistice negotiations. (US Library of Congress LC-DIG-ggbain-23138)

integrity, as they had done in 1870 and 1914. The choice of Wemyss as Britain's representative also reflected her priorities. Britain wanted to remove the German navy from the maritime chessboard, especially her submarines which had come so close to destroying the country's ability to fight on.

The terms which the Allies presented to the German delegation were very tough and there were some politicians, in Britain, France and the USA, who thought they should be relaxed a little. The French considered that any easing should be in the naval terms of surrender. As Wemyss put it, 'naval terms are stiff – but not more than we deserve. Military terms are also stiff so that the politicians want a softening somewhere. I really don't think that we can afford to ease down. Haig* agrees and thinks the military terms should be softened. The French and Foch of course would like the naval terms eased.'[8]

He also wanted to avoid a position whereby Germany was allowed to keep a proportion of her U-boats. He therefore decided that the terms should call for the surrender of 160 such vessels, believing this to be more than Germany possessed. The Germans indeed denied that they had so many, 'so this gave me the chance of getting what I had always wanted, *viz* all the submarines'.[9]

The Armistice was finally signed at 0545, to come into effect at 1100. With regard to the surrender of the German submarines, it specified in section E clause XXII, that the German navy would

> surrender at the ports specified by the Allies and the United States all submarines at present in existence (including all submarine cruisers and minelayers), with armament and equipment complete. Those that cannot put to sea shall be deprived of armament and equipment and shall remain under the supervision of the Allies and the United States. Submarines ready to put to sea shall be prepared to leave German ports immediately on receipt of a wireless order to sail to the port of surrender, the remainder to follow as early as possible. The conditions

---

* Field Marshal Sir Douglas Haig, commanding the British armies on the Western Front.

of this article shall be completed within fourteen days of the signing of the armistice.

It remained to decide where the surrendered vessels would go.

*   *   *

At around 1900 on 15 November, Rear Admiral Hugo Meurer of the Kaiserliche Marine crossed from his light cruiser SMS *Königsberg* (1915) to HMS *Queen Elizabeth*, Admiral Beatty's flagship, where he and his staff of four were received by Beatty, Admiral Sir Charles Madden and three others from Beatty's entourage.

His mission was to ascertain the requirements for the delivery of the German surface and submarine vessels in accord with the provisions of the Armistice. At the first conference, held at 1940, he was handed a paper printed in two parallel columns. On the left were brief summaries of the Armistice conditions, on the right the information which Meurer was requested to give, or the orders with which he was to comply. At the conclusion of the meeting, he made an emotional plea, noting that 'the old institutions had everywhere been overthrown and replaced by democratic committees, or by soldiers' and workmen's councils. He begged earnestly that the confusion in Germany might be kept in mind throughout the next critical weeks during which the terms of the naval armistice were to be carried out.' Beatty responded that 'if he were satisfied that a ship which was mentioned by name in Article XXIII [see Appendix 3] could not be made ready for delivery owing to the disorganisation of the German dockyards, he would agree that another should be substituted'.[10]

Harwich had been chosen as the destination for the surrendered U-boats. Its wide estuarial haven was the only natural deep-water harbour between the Thames and the Humber, ideal for receiving the enemy vessels. Accordingly, Tyrwhitt had left his flagship on the 14th and travelled to Rosyth by train and road. He attended

Rear Admiral Hugo Meurer, who was tasked with agreeing the logistics of the surrender of the German fleet.
(Helsinki City Museum N32545)

two of the four meetings held between the German and British representatives where submarines were specifically discussed. The discussions were on technical issues only; the submarines that were to be assembled, the points at which they were to be met by the British forces, the supplies of fuel and water they were to carry, the crews that were to be allowed in them for the voyage, and how transport was to be supplied for carrying away the surplus seamen when the ships were interned and left in charge of care and maintenance parties.

When Beatty was satisfied that all the elements had been addressed, Meurer departed the flagship at 2200 on 16 November, and sailed soon afterwards. Beatty's staff prepared the orders for the forces detailed to escort the German surface ships to the Firth of Forth and the German submarines to Harwich. 'In order to make the proceedings as impressive as possible, it was arranged that all the available ships and squadrons of the Grand Fleet should perform the first duty and the entire Harwich Force the second.'[11]

Tyrwhitt returned to Harwich and issued his own orders on the 17th. In them he insisted that there would be no triumphal demonstrations from his ships and that they maintain a strict silence when passing or being passed by a German vessel.

A print from an original by the Australian artist Percy F S Spence showing the Grand Fleet escorting the High Seas Fleet towards Scapa Flow to be interned after the First World War. It bears a likeness of Beatty and his facsimile signature.
(US Library of Congress LC-DIG-ppmsca-58715)

My orders re the disposal of the German crews not actually attending to the working of the engines are to be strictly adhered to, i.e. they are to be fallen in on the forecastle and no communication whatsoever is to take place between them and our crews . . . It must be remembered that we are still at war, so that friendly advances, such as an offer to shake hands etc are quite out of the question. There must be an absolute absence of any form of fraternisation.

Moreover, he insisted that 'all ships of the Harwich Force are to maintain a strict silence when passing or being passed by German submarines. There is to be no manifestation of any sort whatsoever.'[12] He also specified that all gun crews were to be closed up and hands at action stations; the admiral was taking no chances of either foul play or provoking a response.

A day later, Tyrwhitt was informed that the first batch of U-boats was leaving Wilhelmshaven. The Harwich Force began to prepare to receive them. There was some disappointment that they were not also to receive the surrender of the destroyers which they had battled for so long, but orders were orders.

On the 19th *Centaur* received a kite balloon from the Shotley base; it was to help spot the incoming flotillas. Then she and the rest of the Force prepared for sea and during the afternoon moved to new moorings outside of the harbour, off 'Shingle Street'.[13] At 0430 next day, *Curacoa* weighed anchor with Tyrwhitt's flag flying proudly at the masthead, and with all the cruisers and destroyers available headed out to meet the vanquished foe at the agreed rendezvous off Lowestoft. Mines were still very much a present danger and the cruisers deployed their paravanes at 0550. Having fought so long for it, Captain Domvile was to miss the whole thing. He was confined to his bunk with the Spanish Influenza.

Rear Admiral Tyrwhitt on board his flagship, HMS *Curacoa*, at Harwich from where he took the surrender of the German U-Boats in November 1918, at the conclusion of the war.
(US Naval History and Heritage Command NH 42495)

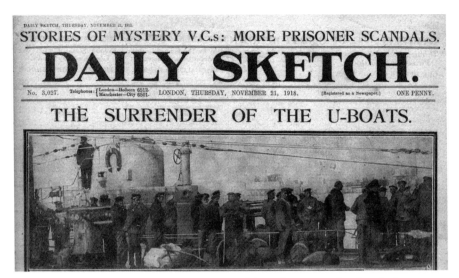

DAILY SKETCH, THURSDAY, NOVEMBER 21, 1918.

STORIES OF MYSTERY V.C.s: MORE PRISONER SCANDALS.

DAILY SKETCH.

No. 3,027.   Telephones: {London—Holborn 6512. {Manchester—City 6501.   LONDON, THURSDAY, NOVEMBER 21, 1918.   [Registered as a Newspaper.]   ONE PENNY.

THE SURRENDER OF THE U-BOATS.

All the major British newspapers covered the U-boat surrender. Here is the
Daily Sketch's headline and picture lead for 21 November. (Author's collection)

At 0715, two German transports, the hospital ships tasked to take the crews
back home – *Sierra Ventana* and *Titania* – were sighted, followed soon by a
single line of the latest mark of U-boat, twenty of them, arranged in four
divisions of five boats.

The Force steamed past them at 10 knots and then turned through 16
points, while four destroyers – flying blue ensigns at their foremast heads –
came alongside each submarine division to shepherd them to their initial
moorings northeast of South Cutler Buoy. Waiting there were *Firedrake*,
Lurcher and *Melampus*, carrying British prize crews. Above them hovered the
airships *R-26* and *SR-1*.[*][14]

For Lieutenant Gordon Maxwell in *ML-314*,

the actual surrender was an . . . impressive sight. A flotilla of some
twenty U-boats . . . were the first to arrive; these were met a few miles
out to sea by our ships. Here British crews were put aboard and the
surrender taken. Every U-boat entered Harwich harbour flying the
white ensign above the German flag. They came into harbour to their
moorings in dead silence. Not a cheer was raised from the crowds that
watched to break the grim stillness that witnessed this piece of history
– these sea monsters that were to have defeated the British navy now

---

* An earlier airship of the same 23-class, *23r*, was also present at some stage. She was being used as a test
bed for flying off 'parasite' Sopwith Camel fighters.

throwing in the sponge without striking a last blow and passing, for ever dishonoured, to their eternal shame.[15]

And for *The Scotsman*, 'those who were fortunate enough to have the first view of the approaching fleet were much impressed . . . No sirens, whistles, or hooters were permitted . . . It was a silent entry into captivity.'[16]

More came the following day, another nineteen in company with the battleship *Helgoland* (1909), which was to return with the crews. Again, the Force turned out to meet them, sighting the battleship at 0854. By 1400, *Centaur* was moored back in harbour again; she returned the kite balloon that evening.[17]

When the U-boats had anchored, they were boarded by a Royal Navy officer. He required the German CO to sign a paper which stated that the submarine was fit to be navigated, disarmed and not booby-trapped ('no infernal machine', see also Appendix 4). The White Ensign was then hoisted above the German flag and when all the submarines were ready, they were sailed into harbour, with the Germans fallen in on the forecastle, and were made fast to a submarine trot off Parkeston Quay. The German crews were taken to their transports.

A British naval officer boards a surrendered U-boat at Harwich to examine her papers.
(Author's collection)

'U-boat avenue'. Surrendered German submarines at Harwich at the end of the First World War. (US Naval History and Heritage Command NH 2421)

This process did not always go to plan. Lieutenant Blacklock recalled that

> *U-64* hauled down his ensign as I approached him. Stepping on board I ordered the captain to hand it over, so that I could re-hoist it beneath the White Ensign. This he refused to do, until I threatened him in no uncertain term as to what his fate would be if he disobeyed my command. After a few moments thought he replied 'very well sir, you have the power' and complied.[18]

By 1 December, when the sixth batch arrived, 122 boats had been surrendered at Harwich. And in 1919, after a hiatus, more arrived, continuing until May. Soon the line of submarines stretching up the River Stour became known as 'U-boat Avenue'.*

Gordon Maxwell thought that

> the sight of the long double line of surrendered U-boats which stretched for about half a mile in the River Stour at Harwich was one of the most impressive I have ever seen. Over a hundred boats were there at one time, moored in trots of four at a buoy, which gave them the appearance of a street, especially at night, when each boat carried a riding light, and lines diverging into what seemed almost the far distance made this impression doubly real.[19]

---

* Eventually, 176 submarines were surrendered to the Royal Navy, seven foundered en route to Harwich, eight were recovered from neutral ports and one was scuttled by its crew at Ferrol in March 1919. Any found in German shipyards were destroyed on the stocks.

A 'trot' of U-boats at Harwich. (Photo; David Whittle/Harwich Society)

British naval officers looking at some of the surrendered German U-boats as they were
handed over at Harwich. (US Naval History and Heritage Command NH 2900)

The arrival of the first few batches triggered off an epidemic of souvenir
hunting as the surrendered U-boats were stripped by the Royal Navy officers
and men of watches, chronometers and anything moveable. It was 'an orgy of
looting' thought Lieutenant Stephen King-Hall. 'In vain we tried to guard them
from the assaults of the officers and men of the Harwich Force who swarmed
up the river at night in a fleet of small boats and even duck punts.'[20] Senior
officers were not immune from the disease. The infection had spread to
London and 'one of the Lords of the Admiralty sent a peremptory message to
my captain that he was to be got a German chronometer'.[21]

UC-100 was a Type UC III minelaying submarine, surrendered at Harwich. She was commissioned into the German Imperial Navy on 30 September 1918 but conducted no war patrols and sank no ships. (Photo; David Whittle/Harwich Society)

And there the U-boats lay, until the Admiralty began to dispose of some for scrap. They were sold for 'breaking up only, under bond and inspection',[22] a process which began on 3 March when fifty-four boats were sold to be scrapped on behalf of the Allies in general and with the proceeds shared between them. The engines were offered separately from the hulls.

U-9, which had sunk the three cruisers in the Broad Fourteens in September 1914, had survived the war and was one of the U-boats sold in the first batch. But she foundered at Dover on 13 March and had to be salved and returned to Harwich; she was eventually scrapped at Morecambe in May. And *U-60* and *UB-60*, both sold to George Cohen Sons and Company, sank whilst under tow to Swansea. Several others were lost while being towed but by and large the initial disposals went well. The U-boat threat was over. For now, anyway.

Amongst the equipment surrendered to Tyrwhitt at Harwich was a giant floating U-boat dock. These two photographs give a good impression of its size and structure. (David Whittle/Harwich Society)

Winding Down

On 30 November, the commanding officers of all the destroyers gave a dinner in Tyrwhitt's honour. By then *Concord* had already departed Harwich, sailing for Danzig with the marvellous concert pianist turned politician, Ignacy Jan Paderewski, on board and *en route* for Poland. He had been appointed Prime Minister and Foreign Minister of the newly independent state of Poland and would represent the country at the Versailles Conference. Possibly against his better judgement, Paderewski entertained the officers on the battered and abused wardroom piano during the voyage. *Concord* would then join the Baltic squadron, fighting to defend the fledgling states of Latvia and Estonia.[*]

On 6 December, Tyrwhitt slept on shore at his house for the first time in the war and on the 11th departed for five days' leave, with another 12 days taken in January when he went shooting in Wales. More shooting followed at the end of January, when he was invited to Sandringham to shoot with the king, an avid killer of all types of birds. It was a great honour for both the rear admiral and by association, the Force.

In early February, Tyrwhitt spent three days in Oxford, his birth town. On the 3rd he received the Freedom of the City of Oxford,[†] an honour that would also be bestowed on Beatty and Haig in June. Two days later, he visited his old school and gave a little talk to the boys, before receiving from Oxford University the honorary degree of Doctor of Civil Law, resplendent in academic robes.

At the invitation of the French, who wished to pay tribute to the work of the Royal Navy during the war, Beatty – now an Admiral of the Fleet – took four battleships over to France on 21 April; Tyrwhitt was also invited and crossed the Channel with four of the Harwich light cruisers and a flotilla of destroyers. Beatty and Tyrwhitt then processed to Paris, together with 450 officers and men, taking in the 'Tranchée des Baionnettes' at Verdun, before a review and march past by Royal Navy and French forces in the Court of Honour of the Hotel des

Rear Admiral Reginald Tyrwhitt on the occasion of the presentation of an honorary degree of Doctor of Civil Law (DCL) by Oxford University in 1919. (Author's collection)

---

[*] For details of this little-known campaign, see Steve R Dunn, *Battle in the Baltic* (Barnsley: Seaforth Publishing, 2020).
[†] Tyrwhitt was also awarded the Freedom of Ipswich. He dreaded both; 'I am horrified at the idea of the Freedom of Oxford ... I don't hanker after these sort of things' (Letter to sister Polly, 5 December 1918, PC).

Six captains from the Harwich Force row Rear Admiral Tyrwhitt ashore in his admiral's galley, his personal standard fluttering above them, after he hauled down his flag in May 1919. (Author's collection)

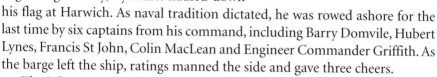

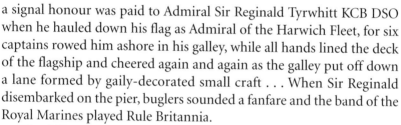

Invalides, conducted by the Governor of Paris, and with Beatty and Tyrwhitt present along with their staffs.

But it was time for farewells. At the beginning of May, Tyrwhitt hauled down his flag at Harwich. As naval tradition dictated, he was rowed ashore for the last time by six captains from his command, including Barry Domvile, Hubert Lynes, Francis St John, Colin MacLean and Engineer Commander Griffith. As the barge left the ship, ratings manned the side and gave three cheers.

The Sphere reported that

> a signal honour was paid to Admiral Sir Reginald Tyrwhitt KCB DSO when he hauled down his flag as Admiral of the Harwich Fleet, for six captains rowed him ashore in his galley, while all hands lined the deck of the flagship and cheered again and again as the galley put off down a lane formed by gaily-decorated small craft . . . When Sir Reginald disembarked on the pier, buglers sounded a fanfare and the band of the Royal Marines played Rule Britannia.
>
> The following farewell message from Sir Reginald was signalled to the Fleet: 'On hauling down my flag as Rear-Admiral in command of the Harwich Force, I wish to express to captains, officers, and ships' companies my deep appreciation of their services rendered during the war. I am deeply sensible of the arduous work they have performed, and am grateful for their loyalty and assistance on every occasion.' Sir Reginald is now due six weeks well-deserved leave before setting off for his new appointment as the Senior Naval Officer at Gibraltar.[23]

Once on dry land, there was a further farewell ceremony at Shotley RN barracks, before 'Com (T) and Lady Tyrwhitt got into a car and drove home'.[24] It was over.

Tyrwhitt's command may have been over, but the honours were not yet finished. On 5 August, the House of Commons voted in favour of giving him a monetary grant of £10,000* (say £520,000 today). And finally, on 13

---

* Keyes also received £10,000; Jellicoe was given £50,000 and a viscountcy, Beatty £100,000 and an earldom.

December 1919, Tyrwhitt was created a baronet; he took the title 'of Terschelling and the City of Oxford', stating that he chose the former because he had spent so much time off its coast during the war.

As for the Force itself, it was quickly wound down after the war and became the 'Harwich Detachment' of a few light cruisers and destroyers.

Repatriation

The port and town of Harwich had one last role to play during the closure of the war. At end of the conflict, Britain had 24,500 enemy aliens held in internment camps. After the Armistice, about 80 per cent of them indicated that they wanted to leave the country.

As shipping became available, from the end of December 1918 to April 1919, repatriations took place at around 600 persons per week, rising to a peak of 2,000–3,000. Most of the repatriates travelled from Harwich to Rotterdam.

> Each was allowed to take a maximum of 100 lb luggage, excluding light hand baggage, and a maximum of £100 in the currency of his own country (earlier the limit had been £10, then £50). They could take no British currency. Voluntary repatriates who could afford it were charged £2 towards the cost of their journeys. All aliens were carefully searched by the police before they left British custody and their baggage was placed under guard until embarkation. This was to prevent repatriates taking with them goods which were scarce in their own countries.[25]

21

Endings

By what criteria should we assess the success or otherwise of the Harwich Striking Force? It was established to act as the southern arm of the Grand Fleet; but in fact the Force never made this conjunction, joining only with Beatty's battlecruisers at Heligoland Bight and Dogger Bank and missing a rendezvous with the Grand Fleet in August 1916.

The occasion when the Harwich Force could and should have come out, and when Tyrwhitt strained every sinew to be allowed to sail, was Jutland. But an overcautious Admiralty refused permission and when they eventually relented, it was far too late. If Tyrwhitt had been able to get behind the High Seas Fleet's line of retreat, who knows how the battle would have played out. Alternatively, as historian Andrew Gordon has written, the Harwich Force was 'the only substantial British destroyer force whose war training had comprised offensive, independent operations, as opposed to the protective chivvying of capital ships . . . His presence at a full fleet encounter – especially in poor visibility when pockets of action might take place on a haphazard basis – might have been of critical value.'[1] Whatever the case, it was clearly a missed opportunity and a negation of the role for which the Force had been established.

But the Force could point to a number of successes. The development of naval aviation in 1914 and 1915, with aircraft carried on firstly cruisers, then converted passenger ferries and latterly lighters, was one in which it was to the fore. And although results were strictly limited, the work of Tyrwhitt and his crews laid the groundwork for further and better usages at a later date. And through both attacks on the landing places and patrols to intercept by anti-air gunnery, the Force played a part between 1915 and 1917 in the attempt to see off the Zeppelin threat to Britain's towns and cities. The Harwich Force also pioneered the CMBs and their novel hydroplaning system. This laid the basis for all manner of fast attack craft and achieved its crowning moment during the Baltic naval intervention of 1918–20.

Perversely, the greatest success for the Force, and one not envisaged when it was established, was the Beef Trip. This would no doubt stick in the craw of the aggressive and daring destroyer commanders who saw convoy escort as the very negation of their *raison d'etre*. But there can be no doubt that the protection they afforded to the Dutch convoys was both successful and an excellent piece of naval strategy – exercising sovereignty of the seas and maintaining British naval control for the passage of goods.

As Admiral Jellicoe wrote

> the extraordinarily small losses in the convoys were a very great tribute
> to the handling of the protecting force and to the organisation in
> Holland for arranging sailings, when it is borne in mind that it was
> almost impossible to prevent leakage of information to German agents
> once the time of sailing was given out, and that the convoys were open
> to attack from destroyers and submarines operating either from
> Zeebrugge or from the Ems or other German ports.[2]

The development of air cover, using the Felixstowe and Curtiss aircraft from
the Felixstowe RNAS air base, was also of significant benefit from late 1917
onwards. In 1917 alone, '520 eastbound and 511 westbound vessels were
convoyed between Dutch and British ports with the loss of only four ships by
submarine attack, one by destroyer attack, and one by mine'.[3] Indeed, from its
inception in July 1916, 1,861 vessels were escorted on the Beef Trip and only
seven ships were lost over that period, one before the declaration of
unrestricted submarine war in February 1917 and six afterwards.[4]

Moreover, command of the sea meant that German attempts at coastal
trade were much disrupted. 'Forces from Harwich also succeeded in capturing
or sinking twenty-four merchant ships trading between Antwerp and Dutch
ports and Germany during the year [of 1917], but the main result of the
operations of this force was shown in the refusal of the enemy to risk his vessels
except under cover of darkness in the area in which the Harwich Force
worked.'[5] The Force also disrupted the German fishing trawler fleet and
captured some such vessels to add to the British war effort.

The strain on the men and ships of the Harwich Force involved in this duty
was considerable. As Jellicoe recognised, there were 'frequent collisions . . . due
to the conditions under which the traffic was carried out at night without lights,
and to the prevalence of fogs. The procedure adopted by the force was
frequently changed as it necessarily became known to the Germans.'[6] Of course,
such dangerous work involved losses. Two light cruisers and eleven destroyers
were sunk (see also Appendix 5). Losses were particularly heavy amongst the
submarines. According to Eric Knight, twenty 'E'-class, two 'D'-class and one
'L'-class vessel from Harwich's 8th and 9th Submarine Flotillas were sunk.[7]
Stephen King-Hall, who was with the 9th Submarine Flotilla from 1917 in HMS
Maidstone, shared this view of submarine casualties. The 9th were 'E'-class boats
and 'operated on reconnaissance and minelaying in the Heligoland Bight off
the front doorstep of the High Seas Fleet. The casualties in this flotilla – and
they were by the nature of things almost always fatal – rose to the fearful figure

of thirty-three per cent.'[8] Tyrwhitt felt that some had been sacrificed on suicide missions, for the Admiralty persisted on ordering them into the Bight, even when it was so heavily mined, to look out for any German sally.

The Harwich Striking Force was in the front line of the naval war for the entire duration, as was its leader too – a unique distinction in a position of high sea command in the Royal Navy of 1914–18. And the Force took some of its character and work ethic from its commander. Rear Admiral Dudley de Chair, who had commanded the Northern Patrol between 1914 and 1916, thought that 'Jellicoe, de Robeck, Beatty and Tyrwhitt had the flair *par excellence* of great commanders and fortunate were those who were lucky enough to be with them in war; their line was action, action, not words'.[9] And the maverick naval thinker (and clearly no believer in the naval education system) Captain Herbert Richmond believed that 'Beatty, Keyes and Tyrwhitt, the three outstanding naval commanders of the war. They muster one first class [exam pass] between them.'[10]

Lieutenant Brian Schofield was a huge admirer; 'if by the Nelson touch one means the capacity to inspire in his subordinates a passionate loyalty and devotion, then Com (T) had it in full measure'.[11] And from the lower deck, Petty Officer Joe Leach put it simply; 'Commodore Tyrwhitt is the finest sailor Britain has produced since Nelson.'[12] Tyrwhitt would have been more than satisfied with that encomium, whilst at the same time deprecating it.

Memory

The camaraderie of the Harwich Force and the memory of service under Tyrwhitt lived on in the years following the war. Ad hoc dinners and reunions took place at regular intervals after the war. One such was on 10 December 1936, the night of King Edward VIII's abdication. Brian Schofield, now a commander, remembered that after the loyal toast had been drunk, Tyrwhitt announced that 'there is a broadcast about to take place which some of you might want to hear'.[13] People went out into the lobby to listen to the radio but Tyrwhitt, a monarchist through and through, merely sat at the table with his head bowed.

These get-togethers were put on a more structured basis when, in 1938, The Harwich Naval Force Association (HNFA) was founded, under the presidency of Tyrwhitt himself. Membership was open to anyone who had served in the Force and an annual formal dinner was held in London for 'we happy few, we band of brothers' despite many having 'scattered to the four corners of the earth'.[14]

The first of what was intended to be an annual dinner of the Association*

---

* It had been preceded four months earlier by a dinner for 110 to launch the new organisation.

was held on 5 November in the Temple Bar Restaurant, 227–228 The Strand, London, with Tyrwhitt presiding and speeches from the floor including a toast proposed by Vice Admiral William Douglas Paton, who as a captain had commanded *Concord* at Harwich. And after the second global conflict at a HNFA dinner of 10 May 1950, a presentation was made to Tyrwhitt of a painting of *Arethusa*, signed on the back by all the extant captains of his ships in the Force.

In faraway New Zealand, the Harwich Force's legacy was also recognised. In 1924, Sir Frederick Chapman, a former Supreme Court judge and member of the Honorary Geographic Board of New Zealand, suggested new names for two features on Lake Wanaka, on the country's South Island. In the main lake, there was an island, Pigeon Island, with another lake within it. He proposed that this body of water should be named Arethusa Pool and that the island's highest point should be entitled Tyrwhitt Peak. Permission was sought for these changes from the then Governor General, Admiral Sir John Jellicoe, and perhaps unsurprisingly, he authorised the new nomenclature. Indeed, Jellicoe gilded this particular lily by suggesting that Pigeon Island itself be renamed, as 'Harwich Island'.

But the name Harwich Island did not gain common local acceptance. In both 1972 and 1988, the New Zealand Geographic Board (NZGB) received submissions asking for a return to the original 'Pigeon Island'. In the light of new legislative requirements to favour Māori names, and wishing to avoid

A wicker U-boat on the beach at Harwich, created in 2018 to commemorate the 100th anniversary of the German U-boats' surrender. (Photo: Iain Ballantyne)

confusion with Pigeon Island on Lake Wakatipu, the NZGB put forward 'Manuka Island' as an alternative. But this did not meet with approval either.

Finally, evidence was discovered dating to the 1920s that that the name Pigeon Island had actually been pre-dated by 'Mou Waho', or 'Outer Iisland'. This was accepted by the NZGB in 1988. However, a connection with Harwich was retained. In 2011, the area was officially titled Mou Waho Island (Harwich) Scenic Reserve.

And 100 years after the surrender of the German U-boats, and in remembrance of the last berth of the German submarine threat, a 15ft sculpture of a U-boat, made of willow, was placed on Dovercourt beach in November 2018. It was so positioned and designed that it would eventually collapse into the sea. In the end, the sea washes all memory away. The waters of Lethe lie all around us.

Scattered to the Four Corners of the Earth

Rear Admiral Reginald Tyrwhitt became Senior Naval Officer, Gibraltar, in July 1919, commander of the 3rd Light Cruiser Squadron in the Mediterranean Fleet, wearing his flag in the light cruiser *Cardiff*, in 1921 and Commander-in-Chief, Coast of Scotland, in June 1923. Advanced to vice admiral on 18 January 1925, in November of the following year he next took up the post of Commander-in-Chief, China, with his flag in *Hawkins*. It was a difficult period of disturbances and tension with the Nationalist Government and Tyrwhitt acquitted himself well. He was made an admiral on 27 February 1929, the same year as he was advanced to Knight Grand Cross of the Order of the Bath in the July, and subsequently took over the position of Commander-in-Chief, The Nore, in May 1930.

In 1932, Tyrwhitt was appointed First and Principal Naval Aide-de-Camp to King George V. But retirement was now beckoning. When he hauled down his flag for the final time, in May 1933, Tyrwhitt was the last British flag officer who had served in the First World War to do so. He was made an Admiral of the Fleet on 31 July 1934, briefly served in the Home Guard during the Second World War and died aged 81 on 30 May 1951, of a perforation of the duodenum which caused peritonitis. His ashes were consigned to the sea off Harwich.

Tyrwhitt and Angela had three children, two girls and a boy. His son St John also pursued a naval career, and was appointed CinC Mediterranean Fleet in 1958 and Second Sea Lord from 1959–61. St John was advanced in rank to admiral on 9 September 1961 and died a month later, aged only 56. Both daughters also saw military or war service. The elder, Mary, became a brigadier in the Women's Royal Army Corps (WRAC) during the Second World War. She was appointed an Officer of the Order of the British Empire in 1946 and was Senior Controller and Director, Auxiliary Territorial Service (ATS), between 1946 and 1949. That year Mary was made a Dame of the British Empire and held the office of ADC to King George VI between 1949 and 1950, during which years she was also Director of the WRAC. Mary Tyrwhitt died unmarried in 1997, aged 93. Younger daughter Patricia was a Senior Commander, Auxiliary Territorial Service, during the Second World War and married immediately it ended, raising a daughter and three sons, one of whom took holy orders, like his great grandfather. As a family, Reginald Tyrwhitt had clearly instilled in his children a dedication to the service of their country.

Tyrwhitt's one-time great friend Roger Keyes also became a Knight Grand Cross of the Order of the Bath, on 8 May 1930. After the war, he commanded the Battlecruiser Force and was advanced to vice admiral on 16 May 1921. He was appointed Deputy Chief of the Naval Staff in the November followed by Commander-in-Chief of the Mediterranean Fleet in June 1925, with elevation to admiral on 1 March 1926. Keyes very much wanted to be First Sea Lord after Beatty and Madden; but Madden believed (almost certainly rightly) that he would have been 'a political liability at a time of financial economy',[15] and Keyes ended his service as CinC Portsmouth in 1931.

On retirement from the navy, Keyes was elected MP for Portsmouth North in 1934. When the Second War broke out, he became liaison officer to King Leopold of the Belgians, with whom he had a personal relationship, and was then made the first Director of Combined Operations in June 1940 by Churchill, purely on the basis of Zeebrugge. In this post Keyes was not a success and his plans did not meet with the favour of the Chiefs of Staff, leading to his removal from the position 16 months later. His son Geoffrey won a posthumous VC in 1941 and Roger Keyes died in December 1945.

For much of the war, Barry Domvile was Tyrwhitt's flag captain. It was not an easy post but Domvile was astute and committed and they worked together well. After the war, his career prospered. In May 1920 he became Director of Plans at the Admiralty. Two years later he took command of the battleship *Royal Sovereign* (1915) and in August 1927 Domvile was appointed Director of Naval Intelligence, a post he held for three years. Elevation to rear admiral also came in 1927 and vice admiral in 1931, in the middle of his stint commanding the 3rd Cruiser Squadron (where he flew his flag in *Curacoa*). On 1 August 1932 he became President of Royal Naval College, Greenwich. Four years later he was advanced to the rank of admiral, on 1 January 1936, and placed on the Retired List the following day. So far, so conventional.

On retirement, Domvile founded a magazine called *The Link*. Its declared mission was to 'promote good relations between the British and German peoples'. In summer 1935, Domvile had visited Germany, toured Dachau concentration camp and spent three days with Heinrich Himmler, and in the process had been impressed with the new Nazi regime. In 1936, and again in 1937, at Hitler's invitation, Domvile had attended the Nazi Party rallies at Nuremberg and in 1938 Domvile acted as a go-between for Himmler when the latter wished to influence Prime Minister Neville Chamberlain to allow a German mountaineering expedition passage through India to Tibet without being treated as spies by the authorities. Domvile had also become fanatically anti-Jewish. Increasingly, *The Link*, and its associated branches, came to be seen as a secretive pro-Nazi organisation and, after war broke out, one which believed that Britain would be better off if Hitler invaded and took over the country.

In July 1940, Domvile and his German wife (and eldest son) were arrested and detained without trial under Defence Regulations 18B, as the government was fearful that Domvile and other fascists could be potential collaborators in the event of a Nazi invasion. He was not released until July 1943. Whilst imprisoned, he wrote a book called *From Admiral To Cabin Boy*, the cabin being the cell he was confined in.

After the war, Domvile re-emerged as a leading conspiracy theorist, claiming that a Judeao-Masonic combination had been behind most of the wars and revolutionary movements in Europe for centuries past. He contributed articles to the right-wing journal *The Patriot* and also wrote for *The Britons' Publishing Society*, a notoriously anti-Semitic organisation. Domvile died in 1972, aged 93.

Had he but known, Domvile would have found common cause with Lieutenant (later Commander) William Guy Carr, a reservist who served at Harwich throughout the war as a navigator in submarines. Carr, born in Formby but domiciled in Canada, became a major conspiracy theorist and anti-Semite. He believed in a great collusion of the Illuminati, International Bankers, the Freemasons, the Communists and the United Nations to produce a world revolutionary movement. Carr's book *Pawns in the Game* (1955) claimed that the First World War had been fought to enable the Illuminati and International Bankers to overthrow the powers of the Russian tsar and to turn Russia into the stronghold of atheistic communism. The disagreements created by the agents of the Illuminati between the Britain and Germany were used to cause the war. After the war, communism was bolstered to destroy other governments and weaken religions. Carr died in 1959 but allegedly his writings influenced a range of other conspiracist authors.

Domvile was not the only member of the Harwich Force to fall foul of political incarceration. Another was Cecil John L'Estrange Malone, quondam captain of *Engadine*. An ardent supporter of communism after the war, Malone gave a provocative speech in the Albert Hall on 7 November 1920, after which he was charged with sedition under Regulation 42 of the Defence of the Realm Act and was sentenced to six months in prison. Later, in 1928 Malone became Britain's first Communist MP and Personal Private Secretary to Frederick Roberts, Minister for Pensions, in Ramsey MacDonald's second ministry.

Barry Domvile's near namesake, Sir James Domville, who had distinguished himself in the action of 1 May 1915, met with a different fate. In September 1919, he shot himself in his evening clothes at the United Services Club, dying at Charing Cross Hospital around 2200. He had left a note reading, 'I much regret this should have taken place in the club. Glad if you will convey this sentiment to your Committee.' *The Times* revealed that 29-year-old Domville was facing bankruptcy and in April had been sued by his wife, Lady Kathleen Agatha née Charlesworth, for 'restitution of conjugal rights'.* In return, he had sent 'her a letter in November detailing suicidal thoughts and a readiness for the insane asylum'.[16] Had war service tipped the balance of his mind?

After being demobilised from the RAF, John Cyril Porte joined the Gosport Aircraft Company in August 1919 as chief designer. Here he hoped to use his patents, especially one relating to hydrofoils, and develop the Felixstowe F-boats for commercial use. But wartime overwork and worry had taken a heavy toll of his already weakened body. On 22 October 1919, he died at his Brighton home, 8 Norfolk Terrace, of pulmonary tuberculosis, aged just 35. Just weeks before his death, America had recognised his contribution to the war effort on 19 September, by the award of the US Navy Distinguished Service Medal.

Porte was buried in Brighton but then re-interred in June 1920 at West Norwood Cemetery alongside his mother and three of his brothers who had pre-deceased him. His monument is a cross and anchor with the epitaphs 'Colonel Porte was the inventor of the British flying boats' and 'erected by a sorrowing widow'. Today, the weathered headstone stands untended, crowded around by other memorials and under the shade of an old yew tree, barely noticeable. In 1922 Porte was recognised by the Royal Commission on Awards to Inventors and his widow received a payment of £1,500 (perhaps £85,000 in today's money). What he could have produced in the field of flying boat development had he lived is now beyond speculation; but what he did produce during the war is his legacy, even if it probably killed him.

And Ronald Blacklock and William Bremner gained no rest after the Armistice for both were sent to the Baltic to serve in the naval force under the

---

* Under the Matrimonial Causes Act 1884, failure to comply with an order for restitution of conjugal rights served to establish 'statutory desertion' which gave the other spouse the right to an immediate decree of judicial separation and, if coupled with the husband's adultery, allowed the wife to obtain an immediate divorce.

command of Rear Admiral Walter Cowan, which was fighting the Bolsheviks to protect the fragile independence of Latvia and Estonia. Blacklock witnessed the death of his friend, and fellow 8th Submarine Flotilla Harwich veteran, Lieutenant Commander Charles Chapman, who died when *L-55* blew up in a minefield under Russian attack. He also took the surrender of a Bolshevik naval patrol boat. Ronald Blacklock survived the campaign and served with the Royal Navy until 1938, when as Deputy Director of Plans he was placed on the retired list for medical reasons, with the rank of captain.

William Bremner, cast as a CMB expert, took part in the famous raid on Kronstadt harbour when, on 18 August 1919, eight CMBs attacked the Red Fleet in a daring raid in which three boats were sunk, another two damaged, and two Victoria Crosses were won. One of the CMBs sunk was that commanded by Bremner and he was presumed dead. His navy personnel file was marked 'Killed in Action, Baltic Sea 18 August 1919',[17] and Rear Admiral Cowan wrote to his father expressing his condolences, stating that 'I cannot tell you what grief it is to me, but him I envy, it was such a glorious death'.[18]

But in fact, Bremner survived to be taken prisoner and endured months of vicious Bolshevik captivity before his release in February 1920. In 1920 he was awarded the DSO for his exploits at Kronstadt[19] to go with his DSC, won in 1918. On 6 December 1937, William Bremner was also placed on the retired list as medically unfit, in the rank of commander.

*　*　*

Tyrwhitt thought that 'the Harwich Force will not be forgotten during the future annals of history'. And Prime Minister Lloyd George, speaking to the House of Commons on 6 August 1919, spoke warmly in praise of Tyrwhitt and the Force; 'Admiral Tyrwhitt, who commanded the torpedo flotillas on the east coast is the outstanding representative of that special branch of naval service which embodies that ceaseless vigilance ever watching, ever pursuing, ever chasing, ever striking, night and day, summer and winter, fair weather and foul, which ultimately ended in completely baffling the designs of the foe.'[20]

But Clio often plays false; today the exploits of the Force are at best half remembered, whereas Jutland and Zeebrugge still have a hold in popular memory. The task of the Harwich Striking Force was a tough one, always in the front line of the naval battle for mastery of the waves. Ships and men died in the mine-choked, fog-ridden, windswept, unforgiving North Sea. They deserve to be better remembered; hopefully, this book will make it so.

Envoi

But we will go to Zion,
By choice and not through dread,
With these our present comrades
And those our present dead;
And, being free of Zion
In both her fellowships,
Sit down and sup in Zion—
Stand up and drink in Zion
Whatever cup in Zion
 Is offered to our lips!

ZION, RUDYARD KIPLING (FROM DESTROYERS AT JUTLAND, 1916)

Appendix 1

Grand Fleet Memorandum, 24 August 1916

1. In the event of the German Fleet being reported at sea and there being a probability of a Fleet action, the following steps will be taken as regards the Commodore (T)'s force.
2. In the first instance the Admiralty will order the Commodore (T)'s force to proceed to one of five general rendezvous in the southern part of the North Sea, until sufficient information of the intentions of the enemy is available.

   The rendezvous selected are areas of some extent in order to give the Commodore (T) sufficient freedom of movement in case of mines being laid or there being other reasons for avoiding fixed positions.
   No. of Rendezvous. Locality.

   – West of North Hinder. (Anywhere between North Hinder Light Vessel and Orfordness.)
   – East of North Hinder. (Anywhere between the North Hinder and Maas Light Vessels.)
   – The Brown Ridge. (Outside " K " Channel between long 3° E and 4° E.)
   – Off Texel. (From 15 to 40 miles North-westward from Texel Island.)
   – Outer Silver Pit. (Off the entrance to 'H' and 'G' Channels.)

4. When the situation has developed sufficiently to render it improbable that enemy forces are going to operate south of lat. 53° N, the Admiralty will order the Commodore (T)'s forces to co-operate with the Grand Fleet. If it is undesirable at the time for the Commander-in-Chief, Grand Fleet, to use W/T, the Admiralty will give the Commodore (T) the necessary directions to enable him to close the Commander-in-Chief on a safe course; these directions can be modified if necessary by the Commander-in-Chief later.
5 In the event of the enemy having stronger flotillas than the Dover Patrol can account for, based on the Belgian Ports, it may be necessary to retain some part of the Commodore (T)'s force in southern waters.

Iron Duke
August 24 1916.
(Source; Naval Monographs XVII, p. 273)

Appendix 2

Auxiliary Vessels in the 'Harwich Local Area'

At 1 January	1915	1916	1917	1918	1919
Yachts					1
Trawlers	17	21	26	30	30
Whalers					2
Drifters	2		24	30	30
Motor Launches		6	5	6	23
Motor Boats	4	2			
Boom Defence		5	9		21
Minesweepers			5	7	24
Total	23	34	69	73	131

(Source: Dittmar and Colledge, *British Warships 1914–1919*, p 147)
NB: the civilian paddle steamers also served in the Auxiliary Force but are not broken down by port in the sources

Appendix 3

Article XXIII of the Armistice

The following German surface warships, which shall be designated by the Allies and the United States of America, shall forthwith be disarmed and thereafter interned in neutral ports, or, failing them, allied ports, to be designated by the Allies and the United States of America, and placed under the surveillance of the Allies and the United States of America, only care and maintenance parties being left on board, namely:

  6 battlecruisers
  10 battleships.
  8 light cruisers (including 2 minelayers).
  50 destroyers of the most modern type.

All other surface warships (including river craft) are to be concentrated in German naval bases, to be designated by the Allies and the United States of America, completely disarmed and placed under the supervision of the Allies and the United States of America. All vessels of the auxiliary fleet are to be disarmed. All vessels specified for internment shall be ready to leave German ports seven days after the signing of the armistice. Directions for the voyage shall be given by wireless.

Appendix 4

Tyrwhitt's Orders for the Condition of the Surrendered U-boats

The commanding officer of each German submarine will, on the arrival of the British Officer, hand over a signed declaration that he has complied with the demands laid down as follows:

1. Batteries fully charged up
2. Full complement of torpedoes on board, launched back clear of torpedo tubes and without warheads
3. That no explosives of any sort are on board
4. That the submarine is in running condition, full blown
5. That all periscopes are in place and in working and efficient condition
6. That all sea valves are closed and watertight doors left in efficient condition
7. That no infernal machine or booby traps of any sort are on board

(Source: Tyrwhitt order number No 00116/1, *Curacoa* 17 November 1918, papers of the Harwich Society)

Appendix 5

Harwich Force Losses

Ship	Date Lost
Light Cruisers	
Amphion	6 August 1914
Arethusa	11 February 1916
Destroyers	
Medusa	25 March 1916
Lassoo	13 August 1916
Simoom	23 January 1917
Laforey	23 March 1917
Setter	17 May 1917
Recruit	9 August 1917
Surprise	23 December 1917
Torrent	23 December 1917
Tornado	23 December 1917
Ulleswater	15 August 1918
Scott	15 August 1918

In total, two light cruisers and eleven destroyers. Five hundred and forty-nine men were lost. *Tipperary* and *Turbulent* were sunk after transfer to the Grand Fleet

Some sources (for example Temple Patterson, *Tyrwhitt of the Harwich Force*, p 209) state that *Louis* was sunk with the Harwich Force, but this is untrue. She went down in the Gallipoli campaign on 30 October 1915, wrecked in Sulva Bay.

Author's Notes

Writing a book of naval history is a solitary occupation; but it could not be done without the help of many people and organisations. Julian Mannering of Seaforth Publishing commissioned this book, my eighth for that esteemed house, and as always was a helpful and supportive 'patron'. David Bremner, Bristol Scout restorer extraordinaire, provided photographs and documents concerning his great uncle. Dr Vaughan Michel and John Foreman, chairman and treasurer of the Britannia Naval Research Association, assisted me with, respectively, a photograph of a CMB and details from Abingdon cemetery. Prolific author and magazine editor Ian Ballantyne found time to let me have his picture of the wicker U-boat. Derek Nudd kindly tracked down a prisoner of war interrogation report for me. Local historian David Whittle of the Harwich Society was most helpful with information and illustrations and also gave me a guided tour of the town.* And finally, Sir Reginald and Lady Charlotte Tyrwhitt were kind enough to welcome me into their home, allow me access to their family papers and even feed a starveling author.

The first draft of this book was written through lockdowns when some of our biggest archives closed their doors and in one instance refused to provide any research to historians at all. Fortunately, others took a more responsive view. Alan Packwood and his team at the Churchill Archives, Churchill College, Cambridge, provided top class support from a distance, as did the Special Collection Unit of the Library of Leeds University. I am grateful to both these organisations for their help. And as usual, the National Archives at Kew proved a fertile hunting ground.

American picture archives are both extensive and more generous than British ones; many images are provided free of charge, a boon not granted by any British picture repository and more's the pity. I offer heartfelt thanks to the Library of Congress in Washington DC and the US Naval History and Heritage Command at the Washington Navy Yard for their munificence in this respect. Their imagery adds much to the comprehensiveness of this book.

Peter Wilkinson produced his usual excellent map and Janet Andrew devised the index.

Finally, my thanks go to Vivienne, without whom the task of writing any book would be so much harder, if not impossible.

Most books contain errors of commission or omission. If there are errors or solecisms in this volume the fault is mine and I should like to hear of them; to err is human.

Steve R Dunn
Worcestershire, 2022

---

* At the time of my visit, David was also the driving force behind the town's new Harwich Museum, largely his creation.

Notes

'The following abbreviations will be used for brevity.

Collections

BL	British Library, London.
CAC	Churchill Archive, Churchill College, Cambridge.
HFNA	Harwich Force Naval Association.
IWM	Imperial War Museum, London.
LC	Liddell Collection, Liddle Collection, Brotherton Library, University of Leeds.
NA	National Archives, Kew.
NMM	National Maritime Museum, Greenwich.
NMRN	National Museum of the Royal Navy, Portsmouth.
PC	Tyrwhitt MSS Held in Private Collection. (Note: Admiral Tyrwhitt frequently failed to date his letters.)
PC2	Bremner MSS Held in Private Collection.
PC3	Bacon MSS Held in Private Collection.

Books

FTDTSF	Marder, *From the Dreadnought to Scapa Flow*, Vols I–V.
NO	*Naval Operations, The History of the Great War based on Official Documents*, Vols I–V.
SK-H	Stephen King-Hall.

It is the convention that page numbers be given for citations. This is not always possible in the modern world. Some digitised documents lack page numbering and some archives hold unnumbered single or multiple sheets in bundles under one reference or none at all. Thus, page numbers will be given where possible but the reader will understand that they are not always available or, indeed, necessary.

Preface

1. Schofield, *With the Royal Navy in War and Peace*, p 29.

Chapter 1

1. Wilson, *Empire of the Deep*, p 300.
2. 26 Feb 1904 memo to Cabinet, quoted in Burk, *The Lion and The Eagle*, p 363.
3. Lambert, *Admirals*, p 312.
4. Conrad, *Notes on Life and Letters*, p 150.
5. Defoe, *A tour thro' the Whole Island of Great Britain*.
6. Quoted in Rouse, *Harwich and Dovercourt*, p 12.
7. Bayly, *Pull Together*, p 121.
8. CHAR 13/12/61-62, CAC.
9. Liddle/WW1/RNMN 029.

Chapter 2

1. Patterson, *Tyrwhitt*, p 39.
2. Jameson, *The Fleet that Jack Built*, p 255.
3. Ibid, p 245.
4. Patterson, *Tyrwhitt*, p 6.
5. ADM 196/89/41, NA.
6. Marder, FDTSF, Vol II, p 8.
7. Ibid, p 15.
8. Jameson, *The Fleet that Jack Built*, p 254.
9. Marder, FDTSF, Vol I, p 408.
10. Hough, *The Great War at Sea*, p 156.
11. Marder, FDTSF, Vol V, pp 39–40.
12. Liddle/WW1/RNMN 029.
13. Carr, *Brass Hats and Bell Bottomed Trousers*, p 28.
14. Letter to sister Kitty, 3 August 1914, PC.
15. Letter to Angela, 4 August 1914, PC.
16. Letter to brother Beauchamp Tyrwhitt, 5 August 1914, PC.
17. Patterson, *Tyrwhitt*, p 45.
18. Lichnowsky, *My Mission to London*, p 38.

19. *Birmingham Mail*, 6 August 1914.
20. NO, Vol 1, p 39.
21. Patterson, *Tyrwhitt*, p 48.
22. Ibid, p 51.
23. CHAR 13/36/76, CAC.

Chapter 3

1. SK-H diary, 28 August 1914.
2. Letter to brother Beauchamp, 26 August 1914, PC.
3. NO, Vol 1, p 104.
4. Letter to sister Kitty, 2 September 1914, PC.
5. Knight, *The Harwich Naval Forces*, p 20.
6. Ibid.
7. SK-H diary, 28 August 1914.
8. King Hall, *My Naval Life*, pp 103–04.
9. *Spectator*, 31 October 1914.
10. Ibid.
11. *London Gazette* 28948, 20 October 1914, Tyrwhitt's despatch.
12. SK-H diary, 28 August 1914.
13. King Hall, *My Naval Life*, p 104.
14. Marder, FTDTSF, Vol II, p 52.
15. *London Gazette* 28948, 20 October 1914.
16. King-Hall, *My Naval Life*, p 105.
17. Patterson, *Tyrwhitt*, p 61.
18. *London Gazette*, 28948, 20 October 1914, Tyrwhitt's despatch.
19. Letter to Angela, undated 1914, PC.
20. Ibid.
21. Letter to sister Kitty, 2 September 1914, PC.
22. King-Hall, *My Naval Life*, p 105.
23. Hough, *The Great War at Sea*, p 67.
24. *Daily News and Leader*, 29 August 1914.
25. Knight, *The Harwich Naval Forces*, p 23.
26. Patterson, *Tyrwhitt*, p 64.
27. Roskill, *Earl Beatty*, p 84.
28. Patterson, *Tyrwhitt*, p 65.
29. *London Gazette*, 28948, 20 October 1914.
30. ADM 137/995, NA.
31. Letter to sister Kitty, 2 October 1914, PC.
32. Letter to sister Kitty, 30 September 1914, PC.
33. Ibid.
34. CHAR 13/40/2, CAC.
35. Patterson, *Tyrwhitt*, p 77.
36. *Daily Mirror*, 19 October 1914.
37. Patterson, *Tyrwhitt*, p 79.
38. CHAR 13/40/40, CAC.

Chapter 4

1. *Spectator*, 7 November 1914.
2. Telegram of 3 December, CHAR 13/37/2, CAC.
3. RMSY 2/2, 7 January 1915, CAC.
4. Marder, FTDTSF, Vol II, p 149.
5. Ibid.
6. SK-H diary, 16 December 1914.
7. Patterson, *Tyrwhitt*, pp 93–4.
8. RMSY 2/2, 7 January 1915, CAC.
9. Churchill, *The World Crisis* Vol 1, p 339.
10. Patterson, *Tyrwhitt*, p 82.
11. Letter to Angela, 24 October 1914, PC.
12. Marder, FTDTSF, Vol II, p 15.
13. Letter to Angela, 18 November 1914, PC.
14. Patterson, *Tyrwhitt*, p 95.
15. RMSY 2/2 7 January 1915, CAC.
16. Letter to sister Polly, undated 1915, PC.
17. Carr, *Brass Hats and Bell Bottomed Trousers*, p 99.
18. RMSY 2/2, 7 January 1915, CAC.
19. Patterson, *Tyrwhitt*, p 98.
20. *Flight*, January 1915.
21. *Warrnambool Standard*, 30 December 1914.
22. CHAR 13/60/22, CAC.
23. RMSY 2/2, 7 January 1915, CAC.
24. Ibid.
25. Letter to Angela, 30 December 1914, PC.

Chapter 5

1. *London Gazette* 29088, 2 March 1915.
2. Ibid.
3. Letter, unknown addressee, 25 January 1915, PC.
4. Ibid.
5. Ibid.
6. Marder, FTDTSF, Vol II, p 166.
7. Roskill, *Earl Beatty*, pp 113–14.
8. Letter to brother Beauchamp, 27 January 1915, PC.
9. Letter to Angela, 18 February 1915, PC.
10. Marder, FTDTSF, Vol II, p 165.
11. Naval Monographs VIII part IV, p 3.
12. Striner, *Woodrow Wilson*, p 26.
13. Patterson, *Tyrwhitt*, p 113.
14. Domvile, *By and Large*, p 72.
15. Taffrail, *Endless Story*, p 89.
16. Ibid, p 90.
17. Detail from ADM 53/34495, NA.
18. ADM 196/43/90, NA.

19. Hurd, *The Merchant Navy*, Vol 1, p 440.
20. Patterson, *Tyrwhitt*, p 122.
21. *Cambrian Daily Leader*, 5 May 1915.
22. Hurd, *The Merchant Navy*, Vol 1, p 442.
23. Ibid, p 441.
24. *London Gazette* 29211, 29 June 1915.
25. ADM 196/125/167, NA.
26. CHAR 13/64/8, CAC.
27. Patterson, *Tyrwhitt*, p 123.
28. Letter to Angela, 26 June 1915, PC.
29. Carr, *By Guess and By God*, p 259.
30. ADM 196/49/213, NA.

Chapter 6
1. Patterson, *Tyrwhitt*, p 127.
2. Letter to Angela, undated, PC.
3. White, *Zeppelin Nights*, p 124.
4. Domvile, *By and Large*, p 73.
5. Naval Monologues XIV, p 150.
6. Taffrail, *Endless Story*, p 94.
7. ADM 196/44/462, NA.
8. Taffrail, *Endless Story*, p 94.
9. Naval Monographs XIV, p 152.
10. Ibid, p 154.
11. HFNA circular 1969, PC.
12. Letter to Angela, 5 October 1915, PC.
13. ADM 196/141/483, NA.
14. Letter to Angela, 23 November 1915, PC.
15. Taffrail, *Endless Story*, p 102.
16. Letter to Angela, 31 December 1915, PC.
17. Liddle/WW1/RNMN 029.
18. Naval Monologues XV, p 38.
19. Fayle, *Seaborne Trade*, Vol 3, pp 465–6.
20. Corbett Paper no 18.

Chapter 7
1. Weather Consultancy Services Ltd.
2. Patterson, *Tyrwhitt*, p 137.
3. Domvile, *By and Large*, p 75.
4. Naval Monologues XV, p 58.
5. Knight, *The Harwich Naval Forces*, p 23.
6. HFNA circular 1967, appendix, PC.
7. Naval Monologues XV, p 77.

Chapter 8
1. Naval Monologues XV, p 94.
2. Patterson, *Tyrwhitt*, p 151.
3. Hansard HC Deb 07 March 1916 Vol 80 cc1401-46.
4. Ibid.

5. Naval Monologues XV, p 163.
6. Taffrail, *Endless Story*, p 194.
7. Naval Monologues XV, p 165.
8. Taffrail, *Endless Story*, p 198.
9. NO, Vol III, p 277.
10. Naval Monologues XV, p 182.
11. Weather Consultancy Services.
12. Ibid.
13. Liddle/WW1/RNMN/REC012.
14. *London Gazette* 29573, 9 May 1916.

Chapter 9
1. Taffrail, *Endless Story*, p 118.
2. *The Times*, 25 and 26 April 1916.
3. NO Vol 3, pp 303–04.
4. Fisher, *Memories*, p 38.
5. LIDDLE/WW1/RNMN/REC/012.
6. Ibid.
7. *London Gazette* 29635, 20 June 1916.
8. ADM 188/715/34318, NA.
9. Schofield, *With the Royal Navy in War and Peace*, p 29.
10. Ibid, p 30.
11. ADM 188/463/288420, NA.
12. *London Gazette* 29635, 20 June 1916.
13. Schofield, *With the Royal Navy in War and Peace*, p 30.
14. Knight, *The Harwich Naval Force*, p 25.
15. *Aberdeen Daily Journal*, 27 April 1916.
16. Marder, FTDSTSF, Vol II, p 427.
17. ADM 12/1567A, NA.
18. Letter 3 May 1916 in PC.
19. Roskill, *Earl Beatty*, p 145.
20. Patterson, *Tyrwhitt*, p 159.
21. Beatty memo 26 May 1916, copy in PC.
22. Agar, *Footprints in the Sea*, p 46.
23. Fayle, *Seaborne Trade*, Vol III, p 465.
24. Patterson, *Tyrwhitt*, p 163.
25. Naval Staff Appreciation, p 43.
26. Ibid, p 24.
27. Letter to Angela, 3 June 1916, PC.
28. Quoted in Marder, FTDTSF, Vol III, p 51.

Chapter 10
1. *London Gazette* 29608, 2 June 1916.
2. Naval Monographs XVII, p 79.
3. 5 August 1916, DRBK 5-10, CAC.
4. Hough, *The Great War at Sea*, p 55.
5. Hansard HC Deb 13 July 1916 Vol 84 c511511.

6. Taffrail, *Endless Story*, p 104.
7. Patterson, *Tyrwhitt*, p 168.
8. Hallam, *Spider Web*, p 79.
9. Knight, *The Harwich Naval Forces*, p 28.
10. 15 August, DRBK 5-10, CAC.
11. Patterson, *Tyrwhitt*, p 169, Naval Monologues XVII, p 80.
12. 22 August 1916, DRBK 5-10, CAC.
13. 19 September 1916, DRBK 5-10, CAC.
14. Naval Monographs XVII, p 80.
15. 15 August 1916, DRBK 5-10, CAC.
16. 22 August 1916, DRBK 5-10, CAC.
17. Quoted in Marder, FTDTSF, Vol III, pp 295–6.
18. Add MS 49032, BL.
19. Churchill, *Thoughts and Adventures*, p 102.
20. Marder, FDTSF, Vol II, p 353.
21. Cunningham, *A Sailor's Odyssey*, p 97.
22. 23 November 1916, DRBK 5-10, CAC.
23. 19 September 1916, DRBK 5-10, CAC.

Chapter 11
1. FROB2/1, CAC.
2. Bremner, RNSC Lecture, PC2.
3. Ibid.
4. Ibid.
5. Ibid
6. Evans, *Keeping the Seas*, p 187.
7. 23 November 1916, DRBK 5-10, CAC.
8. 17 August 1916, DRBK 5-10, CAC.
9. 31 August 1916, DRBK 5-10, CAC.
10. 19 September 1916, DRBK 5-10, CAC.
11. 26 October 1916, DRBK 5-10, CAC.
12. Bremner, RNSC Lecture, PC2.
13. 21 July 1916, DRBK 5-10, CAC.
14. 30 December 1916, DRBK 5-10, CAC.
15. Halpern, *The Keyes Papers*, Vol 1, p 376.
16. 19 September 1916, DRBK 5-10, CAC.
17. Naval Monographs XVII, p 164.
18. *London Gazette* 29886, 29 December 1916.
19. Mowthorpe, *Battlebags*, p 45.
20. 3 August 1917, DRBK 5-10, CAC.
21. Roskill, *Naval Air Service*, pp 630–2.
22. 2 December 1916, DRBK 5-10, CAC
23. Fayle, *Seaborne Trade*, Vol 3, p 465.
24. Cameron, *1916*, p 163.
25. 30 December 1916, DRBK 5-10, CAC
26. Ibid.

27. Naval Monographs XVII, p 221.

Chapter 12
1. Roskill, *Earl Beatty*, p 186.
2. Scott, *50 Years in the Royal Navy*, p 198.
3. NO, Vol IV, p 79.
4. Scott, *50 Years in the Royal Navy*, p 323.
5. Ibid, p 324.
6. Ibid.
7. Letter to sister Polly, 27 January 1917, PC.
8. Letter to Angela, 27 January 1917, PC.
9. Stewart, *Edward Carson*, p 110.
10. Patterson, *Tyrwhitt*, p 181.
11. Tooze, *The Deluge*, p 45.
12. Heckscher, *Woodrow Wilson*, pp 428–9.
13. Fayle, *Seaborne Trade*, Vol III, p 465.
14. CAB 23/1/64, NA.
15. Naval Monographs XVIII, p 345.
16. Domvile, *By and Large*, p 87.
17. Fayle, *Seaborne Trade*, Vol III, p 465.
18. 21 March 1917, CAB 23/2/18, NA.
19. 2 April 1917, CAB 23/2/28, NA.
20. NO, Vol V, pp 21–4.
21. Summarised from Hankey, *Supreme Command*, Vol 2, p 679.
22. AIR 1/71/15/9/124, NA.
23. Hallam, *The Spider Web*, p 81.
24. Taffrail, *Endless Story*, p 103.
25. *Spectator*, 4 August 1917.
26. Sims, *The Victory at Sea*, p 40.

Chapter 13
1. *London Gazette* 30285, 14 September 1917.
2. Ibid.
3. ADM 137/3250, NA.
4. Letter Fisher to Tyrwhitt, 14 August 1917, PC.
5. Hansard HC Deb 21 February 1917 Vol 90 cc1359-98.
6. *Morning Post*, 1 November 1917.
7. NO, Vol V, p 59.
8. Tyrwhitt's report 17 July 1917, copy in PC.
9. ADM 196/126/115, NA.
10. NO, Vol V, pp 60–1.
11. CAB 23/3/24, NA.
12. Information on Stevens from John Foreman, BNRA.
13. CAB 23/3/41, NA.
14. Domvile, *By and Large*, p 87.

Chapter 14

1. Letter of 4 July 1915, Jellicoe Papers, Add. MSS. 48990 f 202.
2. Hansard HC Deb 21 February 1917 Vol 90 cc1359-98.
3. 3 August 1917, DRBK 5-10, CAC.
4. Ibid.
5. Jellicoe, *Crisis of the Naval War*, pp 66–7.
6. Fisher to Oliver, 11 October 1917, ADM 137/2715, NA.
7. *London Gazette* 30285, 14 September 1917.
8. 3 August 1917, DRBK 5-10, CAC.
9. Domvile, *By and Large*, pp 88–9.
10. HFNA circular 1969 appendix 2, PC.
11. ADM 196/126/115, NA.
12. Knight, *The Harwich Naval Forces*, p 30.
13. ADM 137/3738, NA.
14. Add MSS 49036, f227, BL.
15. Winton, *Jellicoe*, p 256.
16. Letter of 25 December 1917, Jellicoe to Bacon, PC3.
17. Ad MSS 49036, f34, BL.
18. WMYS 6/4/19 p16, CAC.
19. 23 November 1916, DRBK 5-10, CAC.

Chapter 15

1. ADM 196/43/134, NA.
2. Letter to sister Kitty, 5 February 1918, PC.
3. Letter to sister Polly, 16 April 1918, PC.
4. Diary 8/9 February 1918, BGGF 1-70, CAC.
5. Ibid.
6. Ibid.
7. Ibid
8. *London Gazette* 30557, 5 March 1918.
9. *London Gazette* 30564, 5 March 1918.
10. HC Deb 23 January 1918 Vol 101 cc963-4963.
11. Patterson, *Tyrwhitt*, p 197.
12. Hallam, *The Spider Web*, p 221.
13. Add MS 82499 f1, BL.
14. Fisher, *Memories*, pp 50–1.
15. Hough, *The Great War at Sea*, p 316.
16. Roskill, *Earl Beatty*, p 259.
17. *London Gazette* 31303, 18 April 1919.
18. ADM 137/3899, NA.
19. Ibid.
20. *London Gazette* 30833, 6 August 1918.
21. Domvile, *By and Large*, p 89.

22. ADM 53/37431, NA.

Chapter 16

1. Carr, *By Guess and By God*, p 218.
2. Ibid, p 219.
3. 14 August 1918, ADM 196/51/236, NA.
4. Bremner, RNSC lecture, PC2.
5. Ibid.
6. Friedman, *Fighting the Great War at Sea*, p 176.
7. NO Vol V, p 345.
8. Ibid, p 346.
9. Ibid.
10. Ibid, p 347.
11. Schofield, *With the Royal Navy in War and Peace*, p 31.
12. Smith, *Voices in Flight*, p 69.
13. *London Gazette* 31038, 26 November 1918.
14. Supplement to the *London Gazette*, 2 November 1918.
15. Supplement to the *London Gazette*, 5 October 1918.
16. ADM 1/8534/228, NA.
17. NO, Vol V, p 363.
18. Patterson, *Tyrwhitt*, p 205.

Chapter 17

1. Taffrail, *Endless Story*, p 86.
2. Ibid, p 263.
3. Carr, *Brass Hats and Bell Bottomed Trousers*, p 91.
4. Jackstaff, *The Dover Patrol*, p 180.
5. Taffrail, *Endless Story*, p 12.
6. LIDDLE/WW1/RNMN/REC012.
7. Carr, *Brass Hats and Bell Bottomed Trousers*, p 32.
8. LIDDLE/WW1/RNMN/REC012.
9. Supplement to the *London Gazette*, 17 October 1914.
10. Liddle/WW1/RNMN 029.
11. King-Hall, *My Naval Life*, p 152.
12. Patterson, *Tyrwhitt*, pp 120–1.
13. Rose, *King George V*, p 179.
14. RMSY 2/2, 7 January 1915, CAC.
15. Underlining in original, letter to Angela, undated 1914, PC.
16. Bacon, *The Dover Patrol*, Vol 2, p 591.
17. Letter to Angela, 27 January 1916, PC.
18. Liddle/WW1/RNMN 029.

19. Patterson, *Tyrwhitt*, p 143.
20. Liddle/WW1/RNMN 029.
21. Carr, *Brass Hats and Bell Bottomed Trousers*, p 213.
22. Letter to Angela, undated 1915, PC.
23. SK-H, *North Sea Diary*, p 210.
24. Domvile, *By and Large*, p 82.
25. LIDDLE/WW1/RNMN/259.
26. LIDDLE/WW1/RNMN 029.
27. Carr, *Brass Hats and Bell Bottomed Trousers*, p 45.
28. *Kipling Journal*, June 2000, Vol 74, no 279, pp 56–7.
29. Ibid, March 1963, Vol XXX, no 145, p 28.
30. Ibid.
31. Ibid, July 1928, no 6, pp 12–13.
32. Ibid.
33. 31 August 1916, DRBK 5-10, CAC.
34. Patterson, *Tyrwhitt*, p 45.
35. Letter to Angela, undated 1915, PC.
36. Letter to his children, undated 1915, PC.
37. *Hull Daily Mail*, 10 January 1916.

Chapter 18
1. ADM 196/42/482, NA.
2. Copy memo 2 August 1914 in PC.
3. ADM 186/382, NA.
4. Knight, *The Harwich Naval Forces*, p 74.
5. Taffrail, *Endless Story*, p 105.
6. Ibid.
7. Carr, *Brass Hats and Bell Bottomed Trousers*, p 128.
8. Jellicoe, *Crisis of the Naval War*, p 195.
9. Robinson, *Fishermen*, p 59.
10. Ibid, p 62.
11. Ibid, p 63.
12. Taffrail, *Swept Channels*, p 337.
13. Carr, *Brass Hats and Bell Bottomed Trousers*, p 162.
14. ADM 1/8427/194, ADM 1/8427/206, NA.
15. *British Vessels Lost at Sea*, Section 1, p 28.
16. ADM 137/3135, NA.
17. Knight, *The Harwich Naval Forces*, p 87.
18. Taffrail, *Swept Channels*, p 355.
19. Statement of the First Lord of the Admiralty, Explanatory of the Navy Estimates, 1919–1920.

Chapter 19
1. Hallam, *The Spider Web*, p 4.
2. ADM 273/2/17, NA.
3. Hallam, *The Spider Web*, pp 21–2.
4. Thetford, *British Naval Aircraft*, p 191.
5. ADM 273/2/17, NA.
6. Ibid.
7. *London Gazette*, 12 December 1918.
8. Hallam, *The Spider Web*, p 29.
9. Ibid, pp 30–1.
10. Ibid, pp 33–4.
11. 3 August 1917, DRBK 5-10, CAC.
12. Hallam, *The Spider Web*, p 137.
13. Ibid, p 242.
14. *London Gazette* 30194, 20 July 1917.
15. Hallam, *The Spider Web*, p 44.
16. Ibid, p 45.
17. *London Gazette* 30913, 20 September 1918.
18. Hallam, *The Spider Web*, pp 242 and 244.
19. Halpern, *A Naval History of World War One*, p 415.
20. Keyes, *Naval Memoirs*, Vol 2, p 341.

Chapter 20
1. King-Hall, *A North Sea Diary*, pp 226–7.
2. Ibid, p 227.
3. Ibid.
4. Patterson, *Tyrwhitt*, p 207.
5. *The Colonist*, Volume LXI, Issue 15032, 28 March 1919.
6. Liddle/WW1/RNMN 029.
7. Domvile, *By and Large*, pp 91–2.
8. Wemyss, *Life and Letters*, p 388.
9. Ibid, p 394.
10. NO Vol V, p 379.
11. Ibid, p 380.
12. Tyrwhitt order No 00116/1, papers of Harwich Society.
13. ADM 53/37436, NA.
14. Mowthorpe, *Battlebags*, p 130.
15. Maxwell, *The Motor Launch Patrol*, p 280.
16. *The Scotsman*, 21 November 1918.
17. ADM 53/37436, NA.
18. Liddle/WW1/RNMN 029.
19. Maxwell, *The Motor Launch Patrol*, p 278.
20. King-Hall, *My Naval Life*, p 161.
21. Ibid, p 162.
22. Dobson, Cant, *Spoils of War*, p 21.
23. *The Sphere*, 10 May 1919.

24. *Daily Mirror*, 2 May 1919.
25. Bird, *Control of Enemy Alien Civilians*, pp 197–8.

Chapter 21
1. Gordon, *Rules of the Game*, p 419.
2. Jellicoe, *Crisis of the Naval War*, p 222.
3. Ibid, p 221.
4. AIR 1/2387/228/11/59, NA.
5. Jellicoe, *Crisis of the Naval War*, p 221.
6. Ibid, p 222.
7. Knight, *The Harwich Naval Forces*, p 51.
8. King-Hall, *My Naval Life*, p 151.
9. de Chair, *The Sea is Strong*, p 238.
10. Marder, *Portrait of an Admiral*, p 326.
11. Schofield, *With the Royal Navy in War and Peace*, p 24.
12. Carr, *Brass Hats and Bell Bottomed Trousers*, p 132.
13. Schofield, *With the Royal Navy in War and Peace*, p 105.
14. Ibid, p 34.
15. Callo and Wilson, *Who's Who in Naval History*, p 176.
16. *The Times*, 16 September 1919.
17. ADM 196/145/642, NA.
18. Cowan letter 18 August 1919, PC2.
19. *London Gazette*, 8 March 1920.
20. Hansard HC Deb 06 August 1919 Vol 119 cc415-59.

Bibliography

Primary Sources
Various files in the ADM, AIR and CAB series, The National Archives, Kew.
Various files in the CHAR series, Churchill Archive Centre, Churchill College, Cambridge.
The Papers of Admiral Sir Bertram Home Ramsay, RMSY 2/2, Churchill Archive Centre.
The Papers of Admiral Sir John de Robeck, DRBK 5/10, Churchill Archive Centre.
The Papers of Sir Bryan Godfrey-Faussett, BGGF 1/70, Churchill Archive Centre.
The Papers of Air Commodore Francis Banks, FROB 2/1, Churchill Archive Centre.
The Papers of Admiral of the Fleet Lord Wester Wemyss, WYMS, Churchill Archive Centre.
Papers of Captain R W Blacklock, Liddle/WW1/RNMN 029, University of Leeds Library Special Collections, Leeds.
Papers of W H Campbell, Liddle/WW1/RNMN/REC012, University of Leeds Library Special Collections.
Papers of Admiral B B Schofield, LIDDLE/WW1/RNMN/259, University of Leeds Special Collections.
Memoirs of Admiral Sir Henry F Oliver, 2 vols, 1946 (unpublished), OLV/12, National Maritime Museum, Greenwich.
Lieutenant (later Commander) William Bremner, Lecture Notes for the Royal Naval Staff College, 1922-23 term, held in private collection.
Papers of the Harwich Society.
Jellicoe Papers, Add. MSS. 48990, Add MSS 49032, Add MSS 49036, British Library, London.
Keyes Papers, Add MS 82499, British Library.
Papers of Admiral Sir Reginald Y Tyrwhitt, held in private collection.

Secondary Sources
The following books and other publications have been cited in the text. The place of publication is London unless otherwise indicated.

Books
Abbatiello, J, *Anti-submarine Warfare in World War 1* (Routledge, 2011).
Agar, A, *Footprints in the Sea* (Evans Brothers Ltd, 1959).
Bacon, R, *The Dover Patrol*, 2 vols (New York: George Doran Company, 1919).
Bayly, L, *Pull Together* (G Harrap and Co, 1939).
Boyd, A, *British Naval Intelligence* (Barnsley: Seaforth Publishing, 2020).
Burk, K, *The Lion and The Eagle* (Bloomsbury, 2018).
Bywater, H and Ferraby, H, *Strange Intelligence* (Constable, 1931, republished Biteback, 2015).
Cameron, J, *1916, Year of Decision* (Oldbourne, 1962).
Carr, W, *By Guess and By God* (Hutchinson and Co, 1930).
_____, *Brass Hats And Bell-Bottomed Trousers: Unforgettable and Splendid Feats of the Harwich Patrol* (Hutchinson, 1939)
Callo, J and Wilson, A, *Who's Who in Naval History: From 1550 to the Present* (Abingdon: Routledge, 2004).
Churchill, W, *The World Crisis*, Vol 1 (Thornton Butterworth, 1923).
_____, *Thoughts and Adventures* (Thornton Butterworth, 1932).
Conrad, J, *Notes on Life and Letters* (1921, republished Floating Press, 2011).

Corbett, J and Newbolt, H, *Naval Operations, The History of the Great War based on Official Documents, vols I – V* (republished Naval and Military Press and Imperial War Museum, 2014).

Cunningham, A, *A Sailor's Odyssey* (Hutchinson, 1951).

De Chair, D, *The Sea is Strong* (George G Harrup and Co, 1961).

Defoe, D, *A tour thro' the whole island of Great Britain, divided into circuits or journies* (1724).

Dittmar, F and Colledge J, *British Warships 1914-1919* (Ian Allen, 1972).

Dobson, A and Can, S, *Spoils of War* (Barnsley: Seaforth Publishing, 2020).

Domvile, B, *By and Large* (Hutchinson, 1936).

Duckers, P, *British Gallantry Awards* (Botley: Shire Publications, 2001).

Evans, E, *Keeping the Seas* (Sampson, Low, Marston and Co, 1920).

Fayle, C, *Seaborne Trade*, Vol 3 (reprinted by Naval and Military Press, undated).

Fisher, J, *Memories* (Hodder and Stoughton, 1915).

Friedman, N, *Fighting the Great War at Sea* (Barnsley: Seaforth Publishing, 2014).

Gordon, A, *The Rules of the Game* (John Murray, 1996).

Hallam, T, *The Spider Web* (Edinburgh: William Blackwood and Sons, 1919).

Halpern, P, *The Keyes Papers*, Vol 1 (Navy Records Society, 1973).

_____, *A Naval History of World War 1* (UCL Press, 1994).

Hankey M, *Supreme Command*, Vol 2 (George Allen and Unwin, 1961).

Heckscher, A, *Woodrow Wilson* (Connecticut: Easton Press, 1997).

Hough, R, *The Great War at Sea* (Oxford: OUP, 1986).

Hurd, A, *The Merchant Navy*, Vol 1 (John Murray, 1921).

'Jackstaff', *The Dover Patrol* (Grant Richards, 1919).

Jameson, W, *The Fleet that Jack Built* (Rupert Hart-Davies, 1962).

Jellicoe, J, *The Crisis of the Naval War* (New York: George H Doran, 1920).

Keyes, R, *Naval Memoirs*, Vol 2 (Thornton Butterworth, 1935).

King-Hall, S, *A North Sea Diary* (Newnes, 1937).

_____, *My Naval Life* (Faber and Faber, 1951).

Knight, E, *The Harwich Naval Forces* (first published Hodder and Stoughton, 1919, republished Leonaur, 2011).

Lambert, A, *Admirals* (Faber and Faber Ltd, 2009).

Layman, R, *The Cuxhaven Raid* (Conway Maritime Press, 1985).

Lichnowsky, K, *My Mission to London* (New York: George H Doran, 1918).

Marder, A, *From the Dreadnought to Scapa Flow*, Vol II (Oxford: OUP, 1965), Vols III and V (Barnsley: Seaforth Publishing, 2014).

_____, *Portrait of an Admiral* (Cambridge, Mass: Harvard University Press, 1952).

Maxwell, G, *The Motor Launch Patrol* (J M Dent and Sons, 1920).

Mowthorpe, C, *Battlebags* (Stroud: Allan Sutton Publishing, 1995).

Patterson, A, *Tyrwhitt of the Harwich Force* (MacDonald and Jane's, 1973).

Robinson, R, *Fishermen, The Fishing Industry and the Great War at Sea* (Liverpool: Liverpool University Press, 2019).

Rose, K, *King George V* (Papermac, 1984).

Roskill, S (ed), *The Naval Air Service, volume 1, 1908-1918* (Navy Records Society, 1969).

_____, *Earl Beatty* (Collins, 1980).

Rouse, M, *Harwich and Dovercourt* (Amberley Publishing, 2013).

Schleihauf, W (ed), *Jutland, The Naval Staff Appreciation* (Barnsley: Seaforth Publishing 2016).

Schofield, B, *With the Royal Navy in War and Peace* (Barnsley: Pen and Sword Maritime, 2018).

Scott, P, *50 Years in the Royal Navy* (John Murray, 1919).

Sims, W, *The Victory at Sea* (John Murray, 1920).

Smith, M, *Voices in Flight: the Royal Naval Air Service During the Great War* (Barnsley: Pen and Sword Aviation, 2014).

Stewart, A, *Edward Carson* (Dublin: Gill and Macmillan, 1981).

Striner, R, *Woodrow Wilson and World War 1* (Lanham, Maryland: Rowman and Littlefield, 2016).

'Taffrail', *Endless Story* (Hodder and Stoughton, 1938).
_____, *Swept Channels* (Hodder and Stoughton, 1938).
Thetford, O, *British Naval Aircraft since 1912* (Putnam, 1977).
Tooze, A, *The Deluge; the Great War and the Remaking of the Global Order* (Penguin, 2015).
Wemyss, V, *The Life and Letters of Lord Wester Wemyss* (Eyre and Spottiswoode, 1935).
White, J, *Zeppelin Nights* (Vintage, 2015).
Wilson, B, *Empire of the Deep* (Weidenfeld and Nicolson, 2014).
Winton, J, *Jellicoe* (Michael Joseph, 1981).

Newspapers and Magazines
Aberdeen Daily Journal.
Birmingham Mail.
Cambrian Daily Leader.
Daily Mirror.
Daily News and Leader.
Daily Sketch.
Daily Telegraph.
Hull Daily Mail.
Kipling Journal (the magazine of the Kipling Society).
London Gazette.
Morning Post.
Portsmouth Evening News.
Spectator.
The Colonist (New Zealand).
The Scotsman.
The Sphere.
Truth.
Warrnambool Standard (Victoria, Australia).

Other
Hansard.
British Warships Lost at Sea 1914–19 and 1939–45 (Patrick Stephens Ltd, 1988).
Statement of the First Lord of the Admiralty, Explanatory of the Navy Estimates, 1919–1920 (HMSO, 1 December 1919).
Naval Monographs VIII, part IV, Admiralty Training Division.
Naval Monographs XIV, part V, Admiralty Training Division.
Naval Monographs XV, part VI, Admiralty Training Division.
Naval Monographs XVII, part VIII, Admiralty Training Division.
Naval Monographs XVIII, part VIII, Admiralty Training Division.
Diary of Stephen King-Hall; https://sites.google.com/site/kinghallconnections/7400-s-hms-southampton—1914
Weather Consultancy Services Ltd.
Corbett Paper no 18, King's College, London.
Bird, J, *Control of Enemy Alien Civilians in Great Britain 1914-1918*, PhD thesis, University of London, August 1981.

Index